# GRIPPING CHAPTERS

# GRIPPING CHAPTERS

## The Sound Movie Serial

## by Ron Backer

BearManor Media
2010

Gripping Chapters: The Sound Movie Serial
© 2010 Ron Backer

For information, address:

**BearManor Media**
P. O. Box 71426
Albany, GA   31708

bearmanormedia.com

Cover design by John Teehan and Emma Backer

Typesetting and layout by John Teehan

Published in the USA by BearManor Media


ISBN—1-59393-531-5

*To my Wife, Leslie,*
*for her love and support*

# Table of Contents

# Introduction

**At the end** of the Columbia serial chapters, the announcer usually hyped the next episode as an exciting chapter, a thrilling chapter, an excitement-laden chapter or something similar. I always liked it when the next chapter was called "gripping" (whatever that means). That is the genesis of the title of this book.

This book is not a history of the motion picture serial nor is it an encyclopedia of serial facts. Rather, it is a compilation of research and writing on topics that are not usually addressed in books on the sound movie serial. For example, there is an entire chapter devoted to all of the sources for the sound movie serials, including comic strips, comic books, the pulps, novels and radio shows. There are three chapters analyzing the cliffhanger endings to serial chapters, since the cliffhanger is the one element of the serial genre which distinguishes it from all other types of movies. Other topics addressed include serial sequels and series, the stars who appeared in serials, prolific contributors to serials and stock footage and bloopers. The book ends with appreciations of three serials that are special to me.

Early on, while researching sound movie serials, I realized that the best sources of information for the material in this book were the serials themselves. In addition to watching many serials over many years, I had to watch and re-watch portions of a number of serials to locate a particular cliffhanger, a piece of stock footage, a line of dialogue or the like. In the process, I gained renewed respect for the genre, which entertained millions for over 35 years on very limited budgets.

Secondary sources were also an important source of information for this project. While I looked at numerous books and magazine articles, I only included in the bibliography those written sources which provided information actually used in the book. The other printed materials that I consulted were often helpful but mainly were used to confirm information I already had.

The web is an important source of information in this computer age. I probably viewed hundreds of websites to check and cross-check information I had discovered on my own or had learned about from other sources. Obviously, I could not list all of those sources in the bibliography. Instead, I listed the sites that provided either substantial or very important information for this book.

Many of the photographs and all of the lobby cards used in this book are from my personal collection. With the use of web sources and attendance at conventions, it is amazing how quickly a significant collection of movie memorabilia can be assembled. In addition, several of the photographs are web captures. The sites that gave me permission to use their photographs were: The Old Corral, Greenbriar Picture Shows, and Bill & Sue-On Hillman's ERBzine. Their web addresses are listed in the bibliography. I recommend all of these sites, not just for their great photographs, but also for their interesting discussions of all aspects of film.

The other photographs are screen captures, taken from DVD's of serials. They were then digitally enhanced by my daughter, Emma Backer, who was then a photography major in college. In addition, Emma worked to improve the quality of all of the other photographs and lobby cards used in the book and helped to design the cover. Without Emma's help, this project would not have been possible.

I hope you enjoy this book. While I cannot promise that each chapter will be exciting or thrilling, I am sure that all of the chapters are gripping (whatever that means).

# Chapter 1:
# A Short History of the
# Sound Motion Picture Serial

**In 1926,** the movie, *Don Juan*, was released. It was the first feature film with synchronized music and sound effects. In 1927, the first talking and singing feature film, *The Jazz Singer*, was produced. Although known as the first talking picture, the film had long silent sections. In 1928, the first all talking film, *Lights of New York*, was released. From that point forward, silent films were on their way to extinction.

Serials went through a similar variation in the early use of sound. Some early sound serials were silent movies with synchronized music and sound effects. Examples of these are *Tarzan the Tiger* (Universal, 1929) and *The Lightning Express* (Universal, 1930). Other early serials also had some dialogue sequences, such as *The King of the Kongo* (Mascot, 1929) and *The Ace of Scotland Yard* (Universal, 1929). *The Lone Defender* (1930) was the first all talking, all sound serial produced by Mascot and *The Indians Are Coming* (1930) was the first one produced by Universal. Both were 12 chapter westerns, the first being about the fight for a hidden gold mine and the latter about Indians, a wagon train and a quest for gold.

The last serial produced for motion picture theaters was *Blazing the Overland Trail* (Columbia, 1956). It was a 15 chapter western about raids on settlers heading west on the Overland Trail and a villain planning to create a private army to take over the territory. Thus, serials came full circle, with the first and last all talking serials being westerns.

In all, there were 231 sound serials produced in Hollywood, of which 224 were all talking. Slightly less than one-third were westerns. The others were generally jungle adventures, science fiction films or contemporary spy or crime dramas.

The major studios, MGM, Warner Brothers, Fox and Paramount, did not release any sound motion picture serials. Another major studio,

3

RKO, released only one, which was the 1932 production of *The Last Frontier*. United Artists, considered a minor studio, also did not produce any serials. Indeed, in the early sound era, the serial tradition of the silent era was kept alive by the independent studios and by Universal Pictures.

## I. THE INDEPENDENTS AND MASCOT

Independent film companies which produced serials during the early 1930s included these forgotten names: Metropolitan Pictures, Syndicate Pictures, Victory Pictures, and Screen Attractions. In all, there were 14 sound serials produced by the small independent companies. Most of these serials were forgettable and many, such as Stage and Screen's releases of *Custer's Last Stand*, *The Clutching Hand* and *The Black Coin* (all 1936), are very difficult to watch today.

*Law of the Wild* (1934). While many famous stars performed in Mascot's serials, such as John Wayne, Tom Mix and Gene Autry, a horse named Rex and a dog named Rinty may have been Mascot's biggest stars. In this serial, Rinty was portrayed Rin-Tin-Tin, Jr. The human actors pictured in this lobby card are Ernie Adams and Lucile Browne.

Nevertheless, the independents provided a romantic lead and hero's role to Bela Lugosi in *The Return of Chandu* (Principal, 1934), which gave that serial a unique flavor and makes it watchable today. Edgar Rice Burroughs was able to do his own version of Tarzan in the 12 chapter serial entitled *The New Adventures of Tarzan* (Burroughs-Tarzan Enterprises, 1935). That serial gave viewers a chance to compare Burroughs' screen interpretation of his own creation with the more successful MGM feature films of the day.

Another independent studio, Mascot Pictures, produced 24 serials in the sound era, many of which were westerns or contained western elements. This was in addition to the studio's production of six serials during the silent era. Mascot was innovative in the early years of sound movies, releasing the first sound serial with spoken dialogue, *King of the Kongo* (1929) and one of the first all-talking serials, *The Lone Defender* (1930).

Mascot's serials are remembered for their convoluted plots, the outdoor action, and most importantly, the stars who appeared in them. Mascot provided John Wayne with three of his earliest screen appearances, in the 12 chapter serials, *The Shadow of the Eagle* (1932), *The Hurricane Express* (1932), and *The Three Musketeers* (1933). Tom Mix, one of the most popular cowboy stars of the silent cinema, gave his last screen performance in *The Miracle Rider* (1935). In that same year, Mascot introduced a new cowboy star to movie audiences, giving Gene Autry his first major film role, in *The Phantom Empire*. Indeed, *The Phantom Empire* is undoubtedly one of the best-remembered and best-loved serials of all time, with its crazy mixture of a western, a science fiction movie and a musical all rolled into one.

Mascot also brought "real" people to its chapter plays. Football legend Red Grange appeared as himself in *The Galloping Ghost* (1931). Clyde Beatty, the animal trainer, appeared as himself in *The Lost Jungle* (1934).

While the Mascot serials were not as sophisticated as the Republic serials to follow, the Republic serial formula began to develop at Mascot. In addition, actors, writers and directors went to Republic from Mascot when Mascot merged with other independents in the middle 1930s, thus giving Republic a substantial base with which to begin its production of serials.

## II. REPUBLIC SERIALS

Republic Pictures was formed in 1935, with the consolidation of several independent studios including Mascot Pictures. Mascot had its own studio facility in Studio City, the former Sennett lot. Thus, Republic immediately began operating with a studio and the expertise to make serials and other B-films.

Republic was famous for its B-westerns and its serials. In the mid-1940s and early 1950s, it also produced an occasional A-film, such as *The Sands of Iwo Jima* (1949) and *The Quiet Man* (1952). In all, Republic produced 66 serials.

Republic had a set formula for its serials. At first blush, however, the formula was not that much different from the plot outlines for the Universal and Columbia serials of the same era. There was a hero, a female assistant or ally, a master criminal or master spy or Nazi, henchmen willing to carry out their leader's directions without question and a significant McGuffin or quest by the villain, such as the Golden Tablets of Hippocrates, which contained the only known cure for cancer but also the whereabouts of a vast treasure (*Perils of Nyoka* (1942)) or the scepter of Genghis Kahn, which could help Fu Manchu conquer the world (*Drums of Fu Manchu* (1940)).

Often, either the hero or the villain was masked. Almost always, the villain's true identity or nefarious motive was unknown to the hero until the last chapter of the serial. Oftentimes there was a mole in the hero's camp, giving vital information to the villain to thwart the hero's efforts. In an early chapter, a significant but disposable character, such as the father or brother of the hero, was killed, thus fuelling the plot.

Of course, there were variations on this formula. *Zorro's Black Whip* (1944) and *Jungle Girl* (1941) had female leads, although they were ably assisted by male companions. Some serials had large sections of "comic" relief while others had none or very little. In serials such as *The Masked Marvel* (1943) and *The Lone Ranger* (1938), it was the identity of the hero which was the mystery and not the identity of the villain.

This Republic serial formula was used, to some extent, by both Universal and Columbia. What set Republic's serials apart were the simplicity of the Republic plots and the simplicity of each chapter. A chapter ended with a cliffhanger. In the next chapter, the cliffhanger was resolved in the first two minutes or so. Then the serial seemed to reload. Either the plot

*The Black Widow* (1947). Republic sometimes varied its serial formula by having a female lead, such as in *Zorro's Black Whip* and *Jungle Girl*, or by having a female lead villain, such as in *Perils of Nyoka* or *The Black Widow*. Pictured is Carol Forman playing the title character, Sombra, in *The Black Widow*.

turned back to the villain, who had a new idea to accomplish his nefarious schemes or the plot turned back to the hero, who had a new idea to trap the villain. Each chapter, along with two minutes of the next chapter, was a unit, with little transition between chapters. Thus, it was easy to pick up a Republic plot if one were starting the serial in the middle. In addition, if a chapter were missed, the viewer could quickly come up to speed on the story by watching just a few minutes of the next chapter.

*The Tiger Woman* (1944). Here is Linda Stirling playing the title character and lead female role. Also pictured from left to right are Allan Lane, sitting down and George J. Lewis with the gun.

The Republic formula made the writing of Republic serials less important than that of other studios. Republic therefore had to rely on its execution to distinguish its product from that of the other studios. In that regard, Republic excelled.

Republic had a number of excellent directors, the most famous of whom were William Witney and John English. Together, they directed 17 serials at Republic, and by themselves or with others, another nine serials at Republic. Their joint efforts are among the most widely admired serials of all time, including *Daredevils of the Red Circle* (1939), *Zorro's Fighting Legion* (1939), *Drums of Fu Manchu* (1940), and *Jungle Girl* (1941). Their serials are still noted for their slimmed-down plots, action-oriented stories and spectacular cliffhangers.

Republic was also famous for its choreographed fights. It seemed that in some serials, there was at least one fight per chapter. These were not, however, the unplanned fights of prior serials with wild punches thrown at random. Republic had carefully planned fisticuffs, with realistic punches, jumps off furniture or anything else in sight, swings on ropes, and fighting up and down steps. Furniture was smashed, often over the backs of the fighters. By the end of a fight, there was little furniture or other breakable property left undamaged in the room. When the audience members became involved in a Republic fight, they knew they had been in a fight.

Closely related to fights were the stunts that were accomplished by Republic's outstanding array of stunt men, including Yakima Canutt, Dave Sharpe, Tom Steele and Dale Van Sickel. Their stunts included jumps into moving trucks, runs up walls, dives through windows, jumps onto horses from great heights, falls from stagecoaches between the wheels and the like.

Republic serials were also famous for their special effects, usually developed by Howard and Theodore Lydecker. The brothers created outstanding miniature work, which resulted in awesome explosions, large avalanches and tremendous crashes. They also developed the greatest flying sequences of all time, in *King of the Rocket Men* (1949) and its progeny.

The effectiveness of the music in the Republic serials cannot be underestimated. Unlike the other studios, Republic invested in significant original scores, such as Mort Glickman's memorable music for *Spy*

*Trader Tom of the China Seas* (1954). This is one of the last Republic serials, featuring two of its 1950s stars, Harry Lauter (pictured) and Aline Towne.

*Smasher* (1942), *Perils of Nyoka* (1942), and *Secret Service in Darkest Africa* (1943), William Lava's exciting score for *King of the Royal Mounted* (1940) and others, and Albert Colombo's tension-filled music for *The Fighting Devil Dogs* (1938). Some of this music and other original scores then reappeared in other Republic cliffhangers.

After World War II, however, the quality of the Republic serials deteriorated. The formula became stale, the serials became shorter and the re-use of footage from prior serials, especially in the cliffhangers, grew substantially. By this time, Republic seemed to pay less attention to its serial product and so did the movie audience.

## III. UNIVERSAL SERIALS

Of all the different studios that produced either silent or sound serials, Universal produced the most serials over the longest period of time. Universal's first serials were released in 1914; its last serial, *The Mysterious Mr. M*, was released in 1946. In all, Universal produced over 140 serials, of which 69 were sound serials. Undoubtedly, Universal's most famous serial, in Universal's 30 years of serial production, was *Flash Gordon*, released in 1936.

*Flash Gordon* had the highest production budget of any serial up until that time, reputed to be approximately $350,000. To put this in perspective, *The Phantom Empire* and *Undersea Kingdom*, made around the same time and each with some science fiction elements, cost under $100,000 per serial. Few other serials cost more than $150,000.

The budget showed on the screen. Although the rocket ship sequences are often criticized today, they were state of the art special effects for their time and, frankly, sometimes seem more realistic than the computer-generated effects of modern day. Flash did battle with giant creatures, something unique to this serial. Ming's palace was lavish.

In story and performances, the serial holds up today. Although Republic Studios was often credited with ushering in the golden age of serials (a period from approximately 1937 through the end of World War II), it was *Flash Gordon* which resurrected viewer interest in the serial format. *Flash Gordon* was so popular that it played evening performances at first run movie theaters and not just matinees. The serial was Universal's second highest grossing film of the year, behind only *Three Smart Girls*, starring Deanna Durbin.

*Flash Gordon* (1936). Flash Gordon (Buster Crabbe) and Dale Arden (Jean Rogers) in a publicity photo. They are standing on the steps to Dr. Frankenstein's laboratory from *Bride of Frankenstein* (1935).

However, Universal's serials were not just the *Flash Gordon* trilogy and its other science fiction adventure, *Buck Rogers* (1939). Universal turned out a number of excellent serials, including many westerns such as *The Rustlers of Red Dog* (1935) and *Riders of Death Valley* (1941), crime stories, such as *Gang Busters* (1942) and *Mystery of the River Boat* (1944),

*Tailspin Tommy in the Great Air Mystery* (1935) Based on a comic strip, the three heroes of the story, Betty Lou Barnes, Tommy Tompkins and Skeeter Milligan, are all excellent aviators in the serial. Pictured from left to right are Jean Rogers, Clark Williams and Noah Berry, Jr.

and spy stories, such as *The Adventures of Smilin' Jack* (1943) and *Lost City of the Jungle* (1946). In addition, Universal emphasized aviator heroes in its serials, such as *Tailspin Tommy* (1934), *Ace Drummond* (1936) and *Sky Raiders* (1941). Even in serials which were not about aviators, flying scenes were abundant. Universal also based a number of its serials on comic strips, including *Tailspin Tommy* (1934), the first serial based on a comic strip, *Flash Gordon* (1936), *Buck Rogers* (1939), *Jungle Jim* (1937) and *Secret Agent X-9* (1937 and 1945).

Universal Studios often did not use much original music in its serials. *Les Preludes*, by Liszt, was a common background theme in many of its serials, such as *Flash Gordon Conquers the Universe* (1940) and *The Phantom Creeps* (1939). Other music was lifted from prior Universal films. For example, the music in the *Flash Gordon* trilogy was lifted from many sources, including early 1930s horror films such as *The Invisible Man* (1933), *The Black Cat* (1934) and *The Bride of Frankenstein* (1935). Once familiar with the *Flash Gordon* serials, it can be jarring to hear this music played in a movie, even though the movie was released before *Flash Gordon*, because the music has became so identified with *Flash Gordon*. Nevertheless, the music from all three *Flash Gordon* serials is always interesting. Other notable Universal scores include *Winners of the West* (1940), with its western theme music and *Riders of Death Valley* (1941), which incorporated the classical music of Mendelssohn.

As contrasted with Republic Pictures, Universal Studios emphasized plot and writing in its serials. Where the Republic serial seemed to reload after the cliffhanger resolution at the beginning of each chapter, the Universal chapter plays seemed to flow, with the cliffhanger ending and resolution just a part of the whole story, rather than an independent episode, with little relationship to the remainder of the serial. Thus, in *The Great Alaskan Mystery* (1944), at the end of the first chapter, a boat bringing the heroes to Alaska hit an iceberg. That cliffhanger was resolved at the beginning of the second chapter but it still took the heroes until the middle of Chapter Three to make it to their ultimate destination in Alaska.

*Riders of Death Valley* (1941). Universal's million dollar serial required a million dollar cast. In the top row, from left to right, are Buck Jones, Dick Foran and Leo Carrillo. In the bottom row, from left to right, are Noah Berry, Jr. and Guinn "Big Boy" Williams.

In *Rustlers of Red Dog* (1935), the first cliffhanger was related to a wagon train in trouble. Although that cliffhanger was resolved at the beginning of the next chapter, the people on the wagon train remained at risk for several more chapters, with each cliffhanger in some way related to the wagon train or the people traveling with it. That story arc then concluded and the serial moved to chasing after the gold shipment which arrived on the wagon train.

With this approach, Universal serials were not simply cliffhanger to resolution to cliffhanger to resolution but they could be something more. For example, *Secret Agent X-9* (1945) was more of a spy v. spy story, with moves and countermoves by the hero and villain to attempt to thwart each other's plans. These types of serials had interest more for the story lines than for each individual cliffhanger.

Universal ended its production of serials in 1946, long before Republic and Columbia ended their production. Apparently, Universal chose to end its production of cliffhangers and other "B" films because it wanted to focus on the production of "A" feature films. Prior to the end of that production, there was no perceptible drop in the quality of the cliffhangers that Universal produced. Thus, each viewing of a Universal serial today is an adventure, because the year of production is not a clue to the quality of the serial, as it can be with the Republic product.

## IV. COLUMBIA SERIALS

Columbia was the last studio to enter the serial market, with its release of *Jungle Menace* in 1937. It was a story about pirates, smugglers and wild animals, starring real life wild animal trainer, Frank Buck. Columbia was also the last studio to end movie serial production, with its 1956 release of *Blazing the Overland Trail*. In all, Columbia produced 57 serials.

Columbia's serials, in terms of plot and structure, were generally more like the serials of Republic than those produced by Universal. It was not unusual for a Columbia product to have a masked villain, such as The Gargoyle in *The Spider's Web* (1938), The Skull in *Deadwood Dick* (1940) (a rare masked cowboy villain) or The Wizard in *Batman and Robin* (1949). There were even masked heroes, such as the title characters in *Batman* (1943) and *The Phantom* (1943). Much like the Republics, there were seldom long story arcs but, rather, a chapter tended to stand on its own.

*Holt of the Secret Service* (1941). This is a publicity photo for the serial directed by James W. Horne, with Jack Holt playing his namesake, Jack Holt, in the serial, although he usually uses his alias Nick Farrell, and Evelyn Brent, as secret service agent, Kay Drew, who poses as Nick's wife throughout the serial.

However, it is nearly impossible to stereotype the Columbia serial product. In the early years, some of the Columbia serials were actually produced by the Weiss Brothers, who had previously produced their own independent serials, such as *Custer's Last Stand* (1936) and *The Clutching Hand* (1936). Thus, an early Columbia serial such as *The Secret of Treasure Island* (1938) had a rambling plot, with chapters that did not always end in cliffhangers. The early Weiss product produced for Columbia was not like the cliffhangers of either Republic or Universal.

Thereafter, Columbia went through a series of three producers, Jack Fier, Larry Darmour and Rudolph Flothow, who brought Columbia's serial product closer to that of Republic and, to a lesser degree, Universal. The most famous Columbia director during this era was James Horne who, from 1938 until his death in 1942, directed or co-directed 12 serials at Columbia. His solo efforts were known for their comedy elements, including double takes and over the top acting. His experience in comedy shorts, including work with Laurel and Hardy, came in handy in those serials.

In terms of comedy, the difference between the Horne product and that of the other studios was that in these Horne serials for Columbia, the comedy did not come from minor characters introduced solely for that reason, such as Smiley Burnette's character in *Dick Tracy* (1937). Rather, the humor came from the antics of the villain and his henchmen, in serials such as *The Green Archer* (1940), *Captain Midnight* (1942) and *The Spider Returns* (1941).While Horne's serials had more real humor

*Who's Guilty?* (1945). In this Columbia serial produced by Sam Katzman, policeman Bob Stewart, played by Robert Kent (on the right) is investigating a murder at the Calvert Mansion. He is "assisted" by newspaper reporter Duke Ellis, played by Tim Ryan (on the left). Also shown is one of the suspects, Ruth Allen, played by Amelita Ward.

than the serials of either Republic or Universal, Horne's humor also tended to undercut the effectiveness of the serial because it undercut the menace brought by the villain. Love them or hate them, however, Horne's novel approach to serials gave a unique flavor to the Columbia product of the Horne era.

In 1945, Columbia turned to Sam Katzman to produce its serials and he did so, through the last serial produced in Hollywood in 1956. Katzman's previous work had been at Monogram Studios, one of the Poverty Row production companies known for its low budgets. While Katzman did produce serials at Columbia on an efficient basis, with cartoons often employed in place of special effects, the use of the same music in serial after serial and the use of the same sets and locations over and over again, there was no immediate drop in the quality of the Columbia serials that he produced, until, of course, the 1950s, when even the quality of Republic serials fell.

Also, whatever justifiable criticism there may be of the serials produced by Sam Katzman at Columbia, at least, from time to time, Katzman did attempt to stretch the serial form by using different story material than the standard crime, spy or western melodrama. For example, *Son of the Guardsman* (1946) and *Adventures of Sir Galahad* (1949) were set in old England. *The Great Adventures of Captain Kidd* (1953) was a pirate adventure. *Brick Bradford* (1947) and *Captain Video* (1951) represented a return, in part, to the other world serials of the 1930s such as *Flash Gordon* and *Buck Rogers. Who's Guilty?* (1945) was an attempt to create a whodunit in serial form. While those were hardly the greatest serials of all time, there was at least a variety to the setting and the plot that was missing in the Republic serials of the same era.

Columbia based a number of its serials on comic strips, such as *Mandrake the Magician* (1939) *Terry and the Pirates* (1940), *The Phantom* (1943) and *Brenda Starr, Reporter* (1945). Others were based on comic books, such as the two *Batman* (1943, 1949) and two *Superman* (1948, 1950) serials, along with *Congo Bill* (1948), *Blackhawk* (1952) and others.

In terms of quality, most serial fans put the Columbia serials behind those of both Republic and Universal. There is a lot of truth to that. Even though Columbia was larger than Republic, it did not match the special effects, stunts or music from the Republic cliffhangers. Unlike Universal, Columbia did not replace those elements with strong writing and acting.

*Blazing the Overland Trail* (1956). This was the last movie serial produced in Hollywood. Even though this serial and other Columbias of the era were shorter and used more stock footage than the Columbia serials from the 1940s, Columbia promoted this serial as a "Super-Serial." Pictured on the right is hero Lee Roberts.

However, Columbia produced a number of excellent serials, such as *Holt of the Secret Service* (1941), *The Secret Code* (1943), *Batman* (1943) *The Phantom* (1943), and *Atom Man vs. Superman* (1950). Indeed, the two *Superman* serials, produced in 1948 and 1950, very late in the serial cycle, were major productions which were very popular. *Superman* (1948) is often mentioned as the highest grossing serial of all time. Much like *Flash Gordon*, it played first run theaters, not just neighborhood theaters.

## V. THE DEMISE OF THE SERIAL

Both internal and external reasons caused the demise of movie serials. On an internal basis, by 1950, after 20 years of sound motion picture serials, there was nothing new to be tried. There seemed to be no innovative plots, stunts, or cliffhangers left. Sometimes it seemed as if everything that could be done had already been done several times before. Even when Republic introduced the special flying effects in *King of the Rocket Men* (1949), there was nothing special about the serials that made use of those effects.

Also, budgets were going down and the Republic serials, at least, became substantially shorter. Both Republic and Columbia made more use of stock footage, thereby reinforcing the view that serials had nothing new to say.

The external force was television. As television became popular after 1949, the slimmed down serials could not compete. The television product, in weekly half hour episodes, albeit without cliffhangers, was at least as good as the serials then being produced. Many serial stars went into television, such as Clayton Moore (*Lone Ranger* (1949-1957, with a break)), Ralph Byrd (*Dick Tracy* (1950-1951)) and Duncan Renaldo (*The Cisco Kid* (1950-1956)). Indeed, certain serials were transformed into television shows, such as the aforesaid *Dick Tracy*, *Superman* (1952-1958 - *Adventures of Superman*), and *Terry and the Pirates* (series of the same name in 1952). The 15 chapter serial, *Captain Video* (Columbia, 1951), was even based on a television character.

*Radar Men from the Moon* (1952) The rocket man trilogy contained the most innovative flying effects all of the serials. Here is an actor in the rocket man suit along with Aline Towne.

*Undersea Kingdom* (1936). This was an inventive, science fiction serial made in the early days of Republic, involving a trip to another world, which in this case, was the lost city of Atlantis. Here Unga Kahn (Monte Blue) and an assistant, Ditmar (Boothe Howard) are using the new-fangled invention of television to spy on Crash Corrigan (Ray Corrigan) and an ally.

Television did not just affect serials; it affected all motion pictures. In 1946, the American film industry had gross revenues of 1.7 billion dollars. In 1958, just 12 years later, gross revenues had dropped below 1 billion dollars. By 1962, they had fallen to around 900 million dollars. To battle television, the studios had to concentrate on bigger productions, wider screens and color. Serials, along with newsreels, shorts and cartoons, became expendable.

As any avid serial fan knows, television was invented in the 1930s by nefarious villains (e.g., Zolok in *Lost City* (1935), Unga Khan in *Undersea Kingdom* (1936) and Tiger Shark in *The Fighting Marines* (1935)) who used the device to communicate with their henchmen, or to spy on the hero. Despite the use of this new technology by the villain, the hero somehow managed to survive, and then defeat the villain. However, by the 1950s, television triumphed where the villains could not. Television finally killed off all the serial heroes, along with the villains, henchmen, sidekicks and scientists that made serials so special.

# Chapter 2:
# Serial Sources

**Almost forty** (40%) of serials originated from other sources, such as comic strips, comic books, novels and even a poem. The following is a survey of the sources of the motion picture serials. A summary of the sources for serials is contained in Appendix A.

## I. DAILY AND SUNDAY COMIC STRIPS

Comic strips (or cartoon strips, as some of the credits read) from the daily and Sunday newspapers were a significant source of material for serials. Universal was most famous for basing serials on comic strips, using eleven different comic strip characters in its serials. With sequels, that meant that comic strips were the source material for sixteen different Universal serials. Columbia also found the comics to be a great source of material for its chapter plays, basing six serials on comic strip characters. Republic also relied on comic strips as source material, particularly with its longest serial series, *Dick Tracy*. Here is a look at serials based upon comic strips.

### Tailspin Tommy (Universal)

*Tailspin Tommy* (1934) was the first serial based upon a comic strip. It was followed a year later by *Tailspin Tommy in the Great Air Mystery*. According to the credits, these serials were based on Hal Forrest's cartoon strip, *Tailspin Tommy*. The strip debuted as a daily comic strip in 1928 and added a Sunday feature in 1929. Hal Forrest was the original cartoonist for the strip, but the stories were written by Glen Chaffin. In

1933, Forrest bought out Chaffin's interest in the strip and that is why Forrest had the only credit in the serials. Although there were eventually a number of comic strips about airplanes and aviators, *Tailspin Tommy* was the first.

The strip told the story of young Tommy Tomkins, who lived with his widowed mother in Littlefield, Colorado, a small town about a hundred miles from Denver. Tommy, who had an interest in airplanes from an early age, talked "airplane" so much that he even acquired the nickname, "Tailspin Tommy," before he ever rode in a plane. While an older Tommy worked on autos at the local garage, he took a correspondence school course in aviation in the hope of learning to fly a plane through the mail.

Tommy's life changed forever when one day, Tommy spotted a plane in trouble and ran to help out. The plane was flown by mail pilot Milt Howes, who made a successful emergency landing near Littlefield. Howes took Tommy under his wing, so to speak, and got him a job fixing airplanes at Three Points Airlines in Texas, which was owned by Paul Smith. There, Tommy met his girlfriend-to-be, Betty Lou Barnes, a waitress at the airport café.

Tommy eventually obtained his pilot's license, as did Betty Lou Barnes and Tommy's childhood friend, Skeeter Milligan, who followed Tommy from Colorado to Texas. The three then became involved in airplane adventures all over the world.

The strip was not long-lived, ending in 1942. Tommy also made appearances in pulp magazines, a radio series and four motion pictures for Monogram Studios in 1939 and 1940.

Although the main plot to the 1934 serial, *Tailspin Tommy*, was original to the serial, a number of incidents therein came from the comic strip, such as Tommy earning his flyer's license, a payroll robbery, an attempt to hijack valuable shipments being transported by air and the filming of a World War I movie, "The Midnight Patrol." The main characters from the strip, Tailspin Tommy, Skeeter Milligan and Betty Lou Barnes were present, as was Three Points Airlines.

The sequel, *Great Air Mystery*, took much less from the comic strip, but still included some plot ideas from the comics, such as a dirigible that catches fire and crashes and a civil war in a South American country. The sequel clearly maintained the spirit of the comic strip with an emphasis on aviation and the adventures of Tailspin, Skeeter and Betty Lou.

**Flash Gordon (Universal)**

*Flash Gordon* (1936) was the second serial to be based upon a comic strip, and it was the first Universal serial to be based on a comic strip distributed by King Features. The strip first appeared in the Sunday comics on January 7, 1934. Alex Raymond was the cartoonist and Don Moore the writer. It was not until 1940 that Flash Gordon also became a daily strip.

In the opening credits of the original *Flash Gordon* serial, the phrase "Alex Raymond's cartoon strip" appeared under the title. The credits went on to state that the serial was "based on the newspaper feature entitled "Flash Gordon" owned and copyrighted by King Features Syndicate." The two sequels also credited King Features but only the third serial mentioned Alex Raymond again.

The original *Flash Gordon* serial relied substantially on the original comic strip story, from the strip's opening with the impending destruction of the Earth, the meeting of Flash Gordon, Dale Arden and Dr. Zarkov, and the rocket ship trip to the Planet Mongo. There the three earthlings

*Flash Gordon's Trip to Mars* (1938). In this sequel to the original, the earthlings meet the Clay People and the Tree People. Here the heroes are out in the land of the Tree People, looking for Prince Barin's rocket ship. Pictured from left to right are Buster Crabbe, Jean Rogers and Donald Kerr.

*Flash Gordon's Trip to Mars* (1938) Pictured is the most merciless serial villain of them all, Emperor Ming (Charles Middleton) with his nemesis, Flash Gordon (Buster Crabbe).

met Ming the Merciless, Princess Aura, Prince Barin, Thun, Prince of the Lion Men, and Vultan, King of the Hawk Men. Anyone who has seen the serial will recognize these characters from the comic strip.

The second serial took place on Mars, thus the title *Flash Gordon's Trip to Mars* (1938). Although all of the main characters returned, except for Princess Aura, the story line did not come from the comic strip. However, the new villain, Queen Azura of Mars, was based upon a character from the original comic strip, Azura, the Witch Queen of the Blue Magic Men.

The third serial in the trilogy was *Flash Gordon Conquers the Universe* (1940). The setting returned to Mongo and the story line was based more on the comic strip by Alex Raymond than was *Trip to Mars*. Prince Barin and Princess Aura were now married. In order to thwart Ming's plans, Flash enlisted the aid of Queen Fria of Frigia, who was based on a character from the original strip.

Although Alex Raymond's involvement with the comic strip ended in 1946, *Flash Gordon* continued in the comic pages in different forms and styles with different writers until 2003, when it ended as a daily strip. It continued after that date as a Sunday feature. Flash Gordon also appeared in other media, including radio, television, books and pulp magazines, along with a full length movie in 1980. Interestingly, the radio show ended after 26 weeks, with Flash and his gang crashing into the jungle and being rescued by Jungle Jim. *Jungle Jim* then took *Flash Gordon's* place on the schedule and the jungle adventure became a long running radio series in its own right.

### Ace Drummond (Universal)

Eddie Rickenbacker was an ace fighter pilot during World War I, purportedly shooting down 26 enemy planes. For his war time actions, Rickenbacker was awarded the Congressional Medal of Honor in 1931. Rickenbacker used his wartime experience to write a comic strip known as *Ace Drummond*, which was illustrated by Clayton Knight. Knight was also an ex-pilot. The strip was distributed by King Features and ran in newspapers from 1935 to 1940, first as a daily strip and then in the Sunday papers starting in 1938. The comic strip featured aviator Ace Drummond and his adventures around the world. He was often accompanied by his co-pilot, Dinny Doyle, and a teenager named Bill. Drummond's first name was probably based on Rickenbacker's nickname, "Ace of Aces."

*Ace Drummond* (1936). Jean Rogers, in the center, plays the female lead, Peggy Trainor. On the left is Guy Bates Post, as the Grand Lama, and tied up is Chester Gun, as Kai-Chek.

Continuing its relationship with King Features, Universal made a serial of *Ace Drummond* in 1936. The credits clearly utilized Rickenbacker's reputation by stating that the serial was based on the newspaper feature created by Captain Eddie Rickenbacker. Also, at the beginning of each episode, a picture of Captain Eddie Rickenbacker was shown, with the caption "America's Beloved Ace of Aces, The Inspiration of Youthful Airmen the World Over." The plot was original to the serial, although there was a young boy named Billy in the serial.

### Jungle Jim (Universal)

In addition to *Flash Gordon*, Alex Raymond's drawings and Don Moore's writing were the source for another Universal serial based upon a comic strip. The serial was *Jungle Jim*, which was released in 1936. The strip of that same name debuted in the newspapers on the same date as *Flash Gordon,* i.e., January 7, 1934. Although not as well-known as *Flash Gordon, Jungle Jim* was popular enough to continue in the papers until 1954. It was just a Sunday feature and never a daily strip.

The comic strip was set in the jungle with a jungle hero named Jungle Jim Bradley. However, the hero was not a Tarzan-style hero but rather, was a westerner who lived in the jungle. The jungle was not in Africa but was in Malaya, Borneo and Sumatra in Southeast Asia. Jim was accompanied on his adventures by his faithful sidekick, Kolu, and he had a recurring female friend, Lil.

These general concepts were carried over into the serial, but without any of the characters from the comic strip, other than Jungle Jim. The story of the serial was also original. In the credits to the serial, the only reference to its source was the comic strip owned and copyrighted by King Features Syndicate. In the comic strip recap for each chapter beginning with Chapter Two, however, Alex Raymond received a credit in both the first frame and across the top of the strip, in the title line.

In terms of movies, *Jungle Jim* was most famous for the sixteen movies made by Columbia beginning in the late 1940s, starring Johnny Weissmuller. Weissmuller also appeared in a television version of the character which was syndicated for one season beginning in 1955. A radio version of *Jungle Jim* was on the air for almost 20 years, starting in 1935 and ending around the time the strip was cancelled in the newspapers.

## Dick Tracy (Republic)

Dick Tracy has been called the second most familiar fictional detective in the world, falling behind only Sherlock Holmes. The comic strip was first published in 1931, in both Sunday and daily versions, by the Chicago Tribune-New York Times Syndicate. It told the story of a police detective from a city resembling Chicago who pursued a set of vicious, but colorful characters, such as Pruneface (reflecting the distortion of his sun-damaged face), Flattop (reflecting the shape of his head), the Blank (a faceless killer after being shot in the face with a gun), the Brow (who had scars across his forehead), Mumbles (who was very hard to understand from the way he talked) and the Mole (who lived underground). Other early series regulars included Tess Trueheart (Tracy's girl-friend and eventual wife), Pat Patton (Tracy's sidekick), and Junior (an orphan adopted by Tracy, who eventually became a police artist).

The serials brought almost nothing from the comic strip, even though each had a credit for the cartoon strip by Chester Gould. Dick Tracy was turned from a city police detective into an FBI agent. In that capacity, he fought memorable villains, namely the Lame One, Pa Stark, the Ghost and Zarnoff. Junior was introduced in the first serial and the character was carried

*Dick Tracy's G-Men* (1939) Phyllis Isley (Jennifer Jones) has something to say to Ralph Byrd (seated) while Ted Pearson (in the middle) looks on.

*Dick Tracy vs. Crime, Inc.* (1941). When studios re-released their serials, they sometimes gave them new names, yet for some reason used both names in the advertising.
Here, Ralph Byrd, in the dark suit, portrays his signature character, Dick Tracy. Note
that the source material of the Gould comic strip is mentioned on the card.

over into the second serial. However, none of the other regulars appeared in
the serials and none of the memorable villains from the comic strip were
used. Some of the scientific methods of police work which were employed in
the serials were, at least, inspired by the comic strips. However, the movie
serials were all original works and if the name "Dick Tracy" were not in the
titles and if Chester Gould were not mentioned in the credits, no one would
have recognized any relationship between the serials and the comic strip.

The comic strip itself continues in the newspapers to this day. Dick
Tracy has also been the star of a long–running radio program, a short-
lived television show and several motion pictures.

### Secret Agent X-9 (Universal)

*Secret Agent X-9* (1937) was, according to the credits, based on the
newspaper feature owned and copyrighted by King Features Syndicate.
There were no other source credits, which was surprising since several

famous people were associated with the strip in its early days.

The original strips, which were first published in 1934, were a confusing mixture of a private eye and government spy tale. Dashiell Hammett, the original writer assigned to the strip, and probably the best-known hard-boiled detective writer of that era, left the strip early, contributing only four stories. He was replaced for a short time by Leslie Charteris, best known for writing the *Saint* mystery stories. Alex Raymond, one of the best-known cartoonists of the era, based on the comic strip, *Flash Gordon,* and to a lesser extent, *Jungle Jim,* was also involved with the strip in its beginnings. Raymond also left *X-9* after one year, being very busy on the Sunday strips for his other two comics. Charles Flanders took over the strip from Raymond, and it was then disclosed that X-9 actually worked for the FBI. The strip continued in the newspapers until 1996.

In the first serial, Agent X-9 also worked for the FBI. The plot, about a gang of thieves who stole the crown jewels of Belgravia, a fictional European country, was original to the movies. It took nothing from the comic strip.

*Secret Agent X-9* (1937). Scott Kolk plays the title character and Jean Rogers plays Shara in this first serial based upon the comic strip. In the 1945 version of this comic strip, Lloyd Bridges played the title character.

*Secret Agent X-9* (1945) was, according to the credits, based upon the newspaper feature entitled "Secret Agent X-9" owned and copyrighted by King Features Syndicate, Inc. No reference was made to Hammett, Raymond or Flanders. Mel Graff had taken over the strip in 1940 and thereafter, X-9 became a spy and was given a name, Phil Corrigan. Eventually, the strip was re-named *Secret Agent Corrigan.*

The 1945 serial version of *X-9* was based on the Graff version of the serial, with X-9 being a spy for the United States in a serial set in a foreign country. He even used his real name, Phil Corrigan. However, the plot was original to the serial.

## Radio Patrol (Universal)

The comic strip *Radio Patrol* began as a daily strip in 1933 and became a Sunday feature the following year. It continued as a daily strip through 1950. It was written by Eddie Sullivan and drawn by Charlie Schmidt, who both worked for the same Boston newspaper. The strip was a police detective story about Sgt. Pat (the strip's lead character), Pat's partner in patrol car 11, Stutterin' Sam, police woman Molly Day, a young boy, Pinky Pinkerton and Pinky's Irish setter, Irish. *Radio Patrol* was the first adventure strip to feature uniformed policemen. The strip was originally called *Pinkerton, Jr.* The revised title of the strip was inspired by the then new device of radio-dispatched police cars.

The serial was based generally on the comic strip, as it was also about a city police force. The police characters, Pat and Sam, were carried over to the movie. None of the other characters made the transition to film, although the serial character, Pinky Adams, had some similarity to the comics' character, Pinky Pinkerton. Pinky, who did have a dog named Irish in the serial, was actually more of a partner to Pat in the serial than his supposed police partner, Sam. There was also a character named Molly Selkirk, who used the pseudonym Molly Day for a part of the serial. She was not, however, a policewoman and therefore had no relationship to the Molly Day of the comic strip. The police did use radio-dispatched cars to chase the villains, a concept taken from the comic strip. The plot of the serial was not based on any particular comic strip story. The only credit in the serial was the usual one for King Features Syndicate.

## Tim Tyler's Luck (Universal)

Universal continued its relationship with King Features Syndicate by creating a serial based on *Tim Tyler's Luck,* a strip first published as a daily in 1928. A Sunday version of the strip was added in 1931. The strip was created by Lyman Young, who is now most famous as the older brother of Chic Young, the creator of the comic strip, *Blondie.* At one point, Alex Raymond drew the strip, making this the fourth serial based on his work. *Tim Tyler's Luck* continued in the papers until the 1990s but in a steadily decreasing number of publications.

*Tim Tyler's Luck* (1937). Lora Lacey, played by Frances Robinson, who is in the jungle trying to obtain information to clear her brother of a crime he did not commit, acquires a jungle admirer.

The strip was about an orphan, Tim, who traveled the world with his friend, Spud, seeking adventure. For a number of years, starting in 1932, the setting of the story was Africa, and that was incorporated into the 1937 serial, *Tim Tyler's Luck*. At the beginning of the serial, Tim was not an orphan; he was searching for his father, a professor, who had disappeared in Africa. Tim was assisted by the Ivory Patrol, which was a paramilitary outfit which policed parts of Africa at the time. In the comic strip, Tim and Spuds eventually became members of the Ivory Patrol. As was the practice with many of the serials produced by Universal, the only source credit was to the King Features Syndicate.

## Red Barry (Universal)

King Features' *Red Barry* provided another source for a Universal serial. The comic strip debuted in 1934 and only ran until 1939. It was created by Will Gould, who was no relation to Chester Gould, the creator of *Dick Tracy*. Interestingly, both were police dramas, with Red Barry being an undercover policeman, whose true identity was only known by his friend, Captain Scott. Other regulars were youngster Ouchy Mugouchy and a blond newspaper woman, Mississippi.

In the serial, the Captain Scott character reappeared, called Inspector Scott, as did newspaper crime reporter, Mississippi. However, the only aspects of the strip carried over into the serial were the urban setting and Red Barry's job of police detective.

## Buck Rogers (Universal)

*Buck Rogers* (1939) marked a return to a serial based on a comic strip where plot elements of the comic strip were incorporated into the serial. The initial story in the comic strip involved Buck Rogers, from the 20th century, who was overcome by fumes while being trapped in a mine cave-in. He awoke 500 years later, in the 25th Century, when fresh air finally entered the cavern. He immediately became involved on the resistance side of a war against Mongols who had conquered the Earth. Other important characters in the strip included Buck's love interest, Wilma Deering, her younger brother, Buddy and inventive scientist, Dr. Huer. Rocket ships, robots, ray guns, and other scientific devices were a major part of the story. Killer Kane was also an important villain in the strip, although not at the very beginning of the story.

During the war with the Mongols, Rogers was involved in several side adventures. After a few years of the story, the Mongols were over-

*Buck Rogers* (1939). Constance Moore, as Wilma Deering, is shown with some strange looking aliens known as Zugg Men, from the Planet Saturn, in this serial set in the 25th Century.

thrown. The strip then continued with the further space adventures of Buck Rogers.

The initial plot of the serial was substantially similar. Buck Rogers, with his young friend, Buddy Ward, were flying in a dirigible, when it crashed on an icy mountain. Luckily, the ship contained a new invention, Nirvano gas, which preserved them in a state of suspended animation for over 500 years. Buck and Buddy were brought back to consciousness by a team of scientists, working for the resistance in the 25th century, which was fighting Killer Kane and his gangsters, who had conquered the Earth. The resistance was led by Wilma Deering and Dr. Huer and now by Buck Rogers, who immediately adapted to all of the new technology created during the 500 years that he was sleeping.

Obviously, changes were made in the serial from the initial plot of the original strip, and the events in the serial, once Buck reawakened, were original to the movie. However, this was still a change from the most recent comic strip serials which essentially only used a name, a profession and sometimes a setting and not much else.

The credits to the serial indicated that the serial was adapted from the comic strip. The story itself was first published in the August, 1928 issue of *Amazing Stories* magazine, titled "Armageddon 2419 AD" and was written by Philip Frances Nowlan. The hero was named Anthony Rogers. A newspaper syndicator, John Dille, hired Nowlan to turn the story into a comic strip and change the name of the character to something more memorable. As a result, the name "Buck Rogers" was created. Dille hired Richard Calkins as the illustrator. Nowlan, Calkins and John F. Dille Co. were all referred to in the credits of the serial.

The comic strip debuted as a daily strip on January 7, 1929, which was the day *Tarzan* also debuted in the newspapers. Some people believe that the Golden Age of Comic Strips started on that day. A Sunday strip followed. Nowlan and Calkins left the strip in the 1940s. The strip was cancelled in 1967, although it returned for a short time after the television series debuted in the late 1970s. *Buck Rogers in the 25th Century* was also a long-running radio series which first aired in 1932.

**Mandrake the Magician (Columbia)**

*Mandrake the Magician* (1939) marked Columbia's first foray into a serial based upon a comic strip. The comic strip version of *Mandrake* was first published as a daily strip on June 11, 1934, as a part of the King Features Syndicate. A Sunday version was instituted on February 3 of the following year. The creator was Lee Falk, who later went on to create *The Phantom* comic strip. The strip was drawn by Phil Davis. Both Falk and Davis received credit in the serial. *Mandrake the Magician* was also a short-lived radio show which was on the air from 1940 to 1942.

Mandrake was a much more exotic figure in the comic strip than in the serial. In the strip, Mandrake used his incredible powers of hypnosis and illusion to combat crime. He had a valet and bodyguard, Lothar, who was one of the first black comic strip characters. Another regular was Narda, a princess from a small European company, who became Mandrake's love interest and eventual wife.

The serial began with Mandrake returning from Tibet on an ocean liner. As in the comic strip, Tibet was Mandrake's spiritual homeland. Mandrake was accompanied by Lothar, his servant and bodyguard. Narda was nowhere in sight. While Mandrake was still a magician, he did not have the special hypnotic powers of the comic strip hero. The plot and villain were original to the serial.

**King of the Royal Mounted (Republic)**

Zane Grey was a well-known author of over 90 books, many of them cowboy stories. The serial, *King of the Royal Mounted,* had an official title of *Zane Grey's King of the Royal Mounted.* Why then did the sequel, *King of the Mounties,* not have Zane Grey in the title? The probable reason was that neither serial was based upon any book by Zane Grey. Rather, they were based on a comic strip syndicated by King Features Syndicate.

Steven Slesinger, a comic strip promoter who also had input into *Red Ryder,* came up with the idea of having a comic strip hero who was a member of the Royal Canadian Mounted Police. He named his hero Dave King, thus the title of the strip. Slesinger promoted his new strip by tying it to the famous writer, Zane Grey, even though Grey probably had no input into the stories. However, Grey's son, Romer, did contribute to some of the stories. Some sources credit the serials to Zane Grey, Romer Grey and Steven Slesinger and that seems appropriate, given the true background of the comic strip.

The comic strip premiered in February of 1935 as a Sunday feature and the next year it debuted in the daily papers. Various artists were used during its run, including Allen Dean (the original artist), Charles Flanders (also involved with *Secret Agent X-9, The Lone Ranger,* and *Tim Tyler's Luck*) and Jim Gary (from 1939-1955). The strip continued in the newspapers through March, 1955. King also made extensive appearances in comic books.

The 1940 serial and its sequel detailed the exploits of Sergeant Dave King of the Royal Canadian Mounted Police. The serials were obviously inspired by the comic strip, although with an emphasis on fighting foreign agents during the war years.

**Adventures of Red Ryder (Republic)**

Before the credits, *Adventures of Red Ryder* (1940) showed frames from the comic strip from which the serial originated. The actual *Red Ryder* strip debuted on November 6, 1938, first as a Sunday comic and shortly thereafter as a daily strip. It was based upon a prior strip by Fred Harmon, which was modified by the advice of a comic strip promoter, Stephen Slesinger. Later, Harmon also became well known for his paintings of the Old West. The serial only gave official credit to the famous NEA newspaper feature, although Fred Harmon's name can be seen in the first frame of the comic strip which opened each chapter.

The serial retained many of the basic elements of the strip. In both media, Red was assisted by Little Beaver, a young Indian boy. (In the first episode of the strip, Chief Beaver was killed and Red adopted the little Navaho Indian.) Ace Hanlon was the villain in the serial and oftentimes in the comic strip. Another character from the strip, Red's Aunt, the Duchess, also appeared in the serial. While Red's girlfriend from the strip, Beth Wilder, did not appear in the serial, a character named Beth Andrews did. The serial had a traditional western plot, with Hanlon trying to take over all of the local ranchers' lands because he knew that a railroad was going through. Presumably, a similar plot was featured at some point in the comic strip's long history. The strip stopped publication in 1964.

*Red Ryder* was also the subject of a successful radio show which was on the air from 1942 to 1951, although mainly on the West Coast. Interestingly, for serial fans, during the early years of the radio show, Reed Hadley (Zorro in *Zorro's Fighting Legion* (1939)) played Red Ryder and Tommy Cook played Little Beaver, the same role Cook had in the serial.

## Terry and the Pirates (Columbia)

*Terry and the Pirates* first appeared as a daily comic strip on October 22, 1934, with the Sunday version starting later that year. The first strip involved young Terry, a "wide-awake American boy" who arrived in China, accompanied by his adult friend, Pat Ryan, a "two-fisted adventurer." They were searching for a mine that had once belonged to Terry's grandfather. They soon met George Webster Confucius, known as "Connie," who became their interpreter and guide. Once they solved that case, and as Terry grew to adulthood, they had more adventures in the Far East. Along the way, they met Terry's love interest, Normandie Drake, and his constant female opponent, The Dragon Lady.

The strip was created by Milton Caniff, who received the credit in the movie serial. Because the strip was owned by the Chicago Tribune Syndicate, Caniff left the strip in 1946 to create *Steve Canyon,* a strip in which he could have a financial interest. *Terry* was turned over to George Wunder who continued the high quality level of the strip established by Caniff. The strip was discontinued in 1973, although there was an attempt at a revival in the 1990s. *Terry and the Pirates* was also a long-running radio program, having its greatest success during the war years, when Tony and Pat battled Japanese, Nazis and other fascists.

The serial adopted some of the concepts of the strip, with Terry on a jungle adventure with his friend, Pat Ryan. Terry was trying to locate his missing father, Herbert Lee, an archaeologist, who had led an expedition into Asia to discover a lost civilization. The Dragon Lady was an important character. At first, she appeared to be a villain but quickly became an ally of Terry and Pat. Normandie Drake was in the movie but she was not a love interest for Terry, who was a teenager at the time of the serial. Connie was in the serial but in a small and ambiguous role. He was joined by another character from the strip named Big Stoop, who was mute in the strip but did talk in the film. Although the plot of the serial was original, it is presumed that parts of it were not unlike strips from the comic pages.

## Don Winslow of the Navy (Universal)

The comic strip, *Don Winslow, U.S.N.*, more popularly known as *Don Winslow of the Navy*, was the inspiration for two Universal serials, *Don Winslow of the Navy* (1942) and *Don Winslow of the Coast Guard* (1943). According to the credits, each was based on the newspaper feature, "Don Winslow of the Navy," owned and copyrighted by Frank V. Martinek.

Martinek was in Navy Intelligence during World War I. Martinek got the idea for the strip after an admiral complained to him about the difficulties of navy recruiting in the midwest. The strip was originally created to aid in that recruitment. Leon A. Beroth was the lead artist for the strip and Carl Hammond did the lay-outs and research. When the strip became a success, other artists were used. The strip debuted as a daily strip in 1934 and became a Sunday feature the following year. The strip continued in the newspapers into 1948, and then there were two subsequent revivals.

Don Winslow was a lieutenant commander in Navy intelligence, much like his creator. He was aided by his pudgy sidekick, Lieutenant Red Pennington, and his Navy girlfriend, Mercedes Colby, the daughter and niece of two Navy admirals. Together, they fought colorful enemies, such as the Scorpion, the bald-headed leader of an international gang of plotters, the Crocodile, who was killing American soldiers in the South Seas by dropping hollow ice cubes of poison gas on them, and Dr. Q, who desired to destroy the Panama Canal.

The two serials were wartime serials with Winslow fighting The Scorpion, one of his enemies from the comic pages. The Scorpion was allied with the Axis forces and was attacking the military in the Pacific.

Red Pennington and naval nurse Mercedes Colby were along for the action. The plots of the serials did not come from the comic strips but were clearly inspired by the comic strips. *Don Winslow of the Navy* was also a radio series, on the air for several years beginning in 1937.

**The Phantom (Columbia)**

Columbia turned again to a King Features Syndicate comic strip when it produced *The Phantom*, in 1943. *The Phantom* was the first comic strip or comic book hero who wore a distinctive costume and a mask. The strip made it to the daily comic pages in 1936. *Batman* did not make it to the comic books until 1939.

The modern Phantom was the 21st in the line of Phantoms which stretched back for over 400 years, with each Phantom turning over the costume, mask and job to his son. The Phantom's home was in Skull Cave in the "Deep Woods" in the country of Bangalla, an ill-defined mythical locale apparently in Africa. There, in later strips, the Phantom was the secret commander of the Jungle Patrol. Although without supernatural powers, the Phantom was a crime-fighter, with adventures all over the world but primarily in his jungle. The natives of the jungle where the strip was usually set did not realize that there had been many new Phantoms over the years. Thus, the Phantom had the nicknames, "The Ghost Who Walks" or "The Man Who Cannot Die."

*The Phantom* serial was clearly inspired by the comic strip. In fact, early on in the serial, a Phantom died and he was replaced with his son, the new Phantom, portrayed by Tom Tyler. The natives were unaware of the substitution and the masked figure was known as "The Ghost Who Walks" and "The Man Who Cannot Die," just as in the comic strip. In that role, the Phantom battled evildoers who were searching for the Lost City of Zoloz, which supposedly contained a large hidden treasure.

Characters from the strip who appeared in the serial included Diana Palmer, the Phantom's fiancée, whom he eventually married in the strip, but not until the 1980s. In the serial, the Phantom was saved several times by his dog, Devil, who also originated in the comic strips.

Leon (Lee) Falk was the creator of *The Phantom* and wrote the daily and Sunday strip from 1936 to his death in 1999. Falk drew the strip himself for the first few weeks, and then Ray Moore became the artist. Both received credit in the serial. This was the second comic strip of Falk

*The Phantom* (1943). Tom Tyler dons the tights as the modern day Phantom, the 21ˢᵗ in a line that stretched back over 400 years. In the serial, he fights evildoers who are searching for a large treasure that is supposed to be hidden in the Lost City of Zoloz.

which was eventually turned into a serial, the first being *Mandrake the Magician*, which was also a King Features strip. *The Phantom* was also turned into a full length motion picture in 1996.

### The Adventures of Smilin' Jack (Universal)

This comic strip was created by Zack Mosley who began work in the comics field by being an assistant on the *Buck Rogers* strip. Mosley, who was interested in aviation, developed the strip about a flyer when he learned that the editor of the Chicago Tribune was taking flying lessons.

*Adventures of Smilin' Jack* (1943). The boyish looking Tom Brown appeared nothing like the drawings of Smilin' Jack in the comic strip, but that did not stop the movie hero from defeating Fraulein Von Teufel in her quest to locate the secret Mandon passage. Here, Jack has captured Hito (Rico de Montez), a henchman of the Black Samurai.

Mosley also started taking flying lessons around the same time. In fact, during his lifetime, Mosley owned nine airplanes and logged over 3000 hours at the controls.

The strip debuted for the Chicago Tribune Syndicate as a Sunday strip on October 1, 1933. The original title was *On the Wing*. The strip became a daily feature in 1936 and continued in newspapers until Mosley's retirement in 1973. *Smilin' Jack* was also the subject of a short-lived radio show in the 1930s.

While the strip was an immediate success, the title was not. Given that Mosley's nickname around the newspaper office was "Smilin' Mack," it was easy to adjust the name of the strip to "Smilin' Jack," even though the main character's name was Mack Martin. It soon became Jack Martin. Jack, who was an airplane pilot, fought villains such as the Claw, Toemain the Terrible and the Head.

The serial gave credit to the newspaper feature "Smilin' Jack," by Zack Mosley. However, the serial took little from the comic strips. While the movie Smilin' Jack was a pilot, he did very little flying in the serial. The incredibly handsome Jack of the comics, with his pencil-thin mustache, was replaced by the clean-shaven and more boyish actor, Tom Brown. None of the other characters or plots of the comic strip were used. In making this serial, Universal was trading on the name of the strip only and not on any of its characteristics that kept it on the comic pages for 40 years.

## Brenda Starr, Reporter (Columbia)

The comic strip, *Brenda Starr*, was both soap opera and adventure story. It told the tales of red-headed newspaper woman, Brenda Starr, who, despite her profession, spent little time in the newsroom and more on globe-trotting adventures and romances.

The creator was Dale Messick, one of the few female cartoonists of her time. Indeed, she stopped using her real first name, Dalia, after initial rejections from comic strip syndicates. *Brenda Starr* was eventually picked up by the Chicago Tribune Syndicate in 1940, but the strip was relegated

*Brenda Starr, Reporter* (1945). This is the only serial based upon a comic strip or a comic book featuring a female lead. In this scene Frank Jaquet, editor of the newspaper, is berating his employees, Syd Saylor and Joan Woodbury, for interfering in police affairs.

to a comic book supplement. When *Brenda* was finally put into regular syndication, the strip had such little respect that it was not published by the flagship paper of the syndicate, the *Chicago Tribune*. That eventually changed. While *Brenda* started out as only a Sunday strip, a daily strip was added in 1945. Despite the slow start, *Brenda Starr* became very popular and is still being published today.

The 1945 serial gave credit to Dale Messick. The story itself involved newspaper reporter, Brenda Starr, fighting gangsters to recover a stolen payroll. Little of the tone and spirit of the comic strip was evident in the serial.

## Brick Bradford (Columbia)

*Brick Bradford* started out as an adventure strip when it first appeared in the daily comics on August 21, 1933. It was distributed by Central Press Association, which specialized in small town newspapers. A Sunday strip appeared in 1934 and the comic began to be circulated in larger newspapers. At that point, it became one of the most popular science fiction strips of its time with some story lines involving time travel to the future.

The strip was created by two newspapermen working in Ohio. The stories were written by William Ritt, from Cleveland, Ohio, and they were drawn by Clarence Gray, an editorial writer and sports cartoonist working in Toledo. Neither received credit in the serial, which only referred to the cartoon strip of King Features Syndicate, which was the national distributor of the comic. The strip continued in the newspapers until 1987.

The serial itself was clearly inspired by the comic strip. It was a science fiction serial and used an important device from the original, being the Time Top, which enabled Bradford to travel through time. Brick was also transported to the moon through a crystal door. Given the popularity of the *Flash Gordon* and *Buck Rogers* serials in the 1930s, it is amazing that it was not until 1947 that Brick Bradford made it to the movies.

## Bruce Gentry (Columbia)

*Bruce Gentry* came late to the comic strips and even later to serials, being the last serial based on a comic strip. The serial, sometimes titled *Bruce Gentry — Daredevil of the Skies*, was released in 1949. No credit was given to the creator of the strip and the only reference to its origin was to the newspaper feature.

In fact, the strip was created by Ray Bailey in 1945. Bailey had extensive experience in cartooning, having worked at the Fleischer studios on the animated *Betty Boop* and *Popeye* cartoons, as well as assisting Milton Caniff on the *Terry and the Pirates* strip. The title character, Bruce Gentry, was a former pilot in the U.S. Air Force, working for a small airline in South America. However, his adventures took place all over the world, as he tracked down smugglers, escaped killers and criminal masterminds.

In the serial, Gentry was a pilot and, apparently, a daredevil of the skies. The serial was a spy story at least inspired by the strips, although not based on any particular storyline. In fact, the strip itself barely outlasted the serial, with the strip's last publication on January 6, 1951.

## II. COMIC BOOK HEROES

Comic books were another important source of material for the serials. Here, Columbia led the way, with seven comic book characters used to only three for Republic. Counting sequels, there were nine different comic book serials for Columbia. Universal did not have any comic book serials, relying instead on the comic strips for its serial sources. Here is a look at serials based on comic books.

### Captain Marvel (Republic)

*Captain Marvel* first appeared in the comic book, *Whiz Comics*, in February, 1940. It told the story of an orphaned newsboy, Billy Batson, who followed a mysterious cloaked stranger into an abandoned subway tunnel. There, Billy met a 3,000 year old wizard named Shazam, who had chosen Billy to be his successor in fighting the forces of evil. Shazam then gave Billy all of his special powers. Thereafter, whenever Billy said the wizard's name (which was an acronym for Solomon, Hercules, Atlas, Zeus, Achilles, and Mercury), he was struck by a magic lightning bolt and  transformed into the World's Mightiest Mortal, Captain Marvel. Unfortunately, during the first transformation, the wizard died when a granite block fell on him. However, the wizard was still thereafter able to guide Billy and Captain Marvel when necessary, as a ghost.

The original story was created by Bill Parker and C.C. Beck, the artist and writer who later created *Spy Smasher*. Over the years, other characters

*Adventures of Captain Marvel* (1941). Tom Tyler, as Captain Marvel, and Louise Currie, as Betty Wallace, apparently see something unusual above them.

were added to the stories, including Captain Marvel, Jr. (no relation) and Billy's sister, Mary Marvel. Each acquired their own special powers.

In 1941, the Captain received his own comic book, which became very popular, even outselling the *Superman* comic books during the 1940s. However, by 1953, sales of comic books were down and Fawcett Publications was tired of defending the lawsuit filed by DC Comics which alleged that *Captain Marvel* was too similar to its *Superman* comic and therefore infringed on the *Superman* copyright. Fawcett settled the lawsuit, agreeing never to publish the character again. Thus, the initial run of *Captain Marvel* ended.

*The Adventures of Captain Marvel* (1941) was the first serial based upon a comic book character. It was also unusual in that it explained the creation of the character. Batman, Captain America and even Zorro were active crime fighters when their serials began.

When *Captain Marvel* opened, Billy Batson was just a young radio reporter, participating in a scientific expedition. Exploring an ancient tomb, Billy met a stranger with a long gray beard. It was Shazam, who in this story was the guardian of the secret of the Scorpion. That task was then handed over to Billy by Shazam. As in the comics, whenever Billy said the word, "Shazam," then, with a clap of thunder and a bolt of lightning, Billy was turned into Captain Marvel. As Captain Marvel, Billy looked more like Tom Tyler than Frank Coghlan, Jr. He had enormous strength and could fly. When he repeated the word "Shazam," he once again became Billy Batson.

After the initial transformation in the serial, the action of the serial returned to America, where Billy and his alter ego fought the masked villain, The Scorpion, who was after the golden scorpion, a device with lenses which could turn objects into gold. At the end of the serial, the Scorpion was defeated. The ghost of the wizard said," Shazam," Captain Marvel disappeared, and Billy was permanently returned to his original appearance. Thus, unlike the comic book stories, there could be no subsequent adventures for Captain Marvel.

## Spy Smasher (Republic)

*Spy Smasher* was created by Bill Parker and C.C. Beck, the writer and artist who also created *Captain Marvel. Spy Smasher* was introduced in the first issue of *Whiz Comics* books in February, 1940, which was the same issue in which *Captain Marvel* first appeared. The stories became so popular that Spy Smasher received his own comic book, which debuted in the fall of 1941 and continued in 11 issues through the summer of 1943.

The comic book stories began when Admiral Corby, from Navy Intelligence, phoned Alan Armstrong to advise him that a plane in which the Admiral's daughter, Eve, was traveling had been shot down and that Eve was presumed dead. Eve was Alan's fiancée. Alan refused to believe the news, particularly when he learned that the foreign spy known as the Mask was responsible for the plane crash. Alan suspected that Eve had been taken captive by the Mask.

Later that night Alan donned his Spy Smasher costume, which consisted of a cape, khakis and goggles, which concealed his identity. He then took to the air in his specially designed Gyrosub, a device that was a combination flying machine and submarine. He soon located the Mask's hideout and saved Eve. The Mask however managed to escape in the process.

In later stories, Spy Smasher finally killed the Mask. Also, Spy Smasher eventually disclosed his secret identity to Eve Colby. During World War II, Alan Armstrong did indeed smash spies, and in particular,

*Spy Smasher* (1942). Kane Richmond, as Alan Armstrong, a/k/a Spy Smasher, leaps into the ocean to chase Nazi collaborator, Tristam Coffin, in the exciting last chapter of this famous serial.

an evil German known as America Smasher. After the war, when employment for spy smashers became sparse, Alan Armstrong became a private investigator and called himself Crime Smasher. His last appearance in comic books during this original run was in *Whiz Comics* #83 in March, 1947.

The movie serial *Spy Smasher*, from 1942, stated that it was suggested by the character "Spy Smasher" appearing in Whiz Comics and Spy Smasher Magazines, publications copyrighted by Fawcett Publications, Inc. The serial was clearly inspired by the comic books, with Alan Armstrong dressed in the Spy Smasher outfit (an outfit somewhat similar to the comic book version with goggles hiding his identity), fighting the German spy known as the Mask. Admiral Colby was a significant character in the serial, as was his daughter, Eve. By the end of the serial, Eve learned the true identity of Spy Smasher. Alan's twin brother, Jack, a new character in the serial, assisted his brother in the fight against the German spies.

## Batman (Columbia)

*Batman* first appeared in *Detective Comics* #27, dated May, 1939, nearly a year after *Superman* first appeared in a comic book. In addition to Batman and his alter ego, Bruce Wayne, the only series regular to appear in that first issue was Commissioner Gordon. It was not until almost a year after Batman's debut, in *Detective Comics* #38, dated April, 1940, that Bruce Wayne took in Dick Grayson, whose parents, circus high wire performers, had been killed by gangsters. Thus, Batman's crime-fighting assistant, Robin, was born.

Batman was given his own comic book in 1940, although he continued to appear in *Detective Comics*. Alfred, the butler, did not appear until *Batman* #16, in April/May 1943. Alfred was originally drawn as an overweight figure but he was slimmed down after the debut of the 1943 serial, in which Alfred was played by a slimmer actor. The slimmed-down Alfred, with new mustache, first appeared in the comic books in *Detective Comics* #83 (January, 1944). The explanation for his change of appearance was that he had gone to a health farm to slim down.

In terms of favorite villains, the Joker, a prank-obsessed criminal with a clown like appearance, first appeared in *Batman* #1 (Spring, 1940). Catwoman, sometimes enemy and sometimes ally of Batman, debuted in the same issue but in a different story. The Penguin, with his crazy umbrellas, arrived in *Detective Comics* #58, in December, 1941. The Riddler, with his green, ?-covered costume, did not appear until *Detective Comics* #140 (October, 1948).

Originally in the comic books, Batman drove a red car, with nothing special about it. A vehicle that could be truly called the Batmobile was first introduced in *Batman* #5, in the spring of 1941. The car eventually became a dark blue, supercharged car with a large bat-shaped figure on the front, external exhaust pipes on the hood, and a tall, scalloped vertical fin extending from the rear edge of the roof to the tail.

The serial, *Batman*, was released in 1943, within four years of Batman's introduction into comic books. It was generally true to the comic book tradition, even bringing the newly introduced Alfred to the serial. The female interest, Linda Page, was a character from the comic books. In the comics, she was a socialite and nurse and Bruce Wayne dated her throughout the war years. Dr. Daka, a Japanese spy seeking to overthrow the United States, was original to the serial but was subsequently a character in a comic book story. However, Commissioner

Gordon, a true Batmobile, and Batman's utility belt, were missing. In fact, Commissioner Gordon was replaced by a character known as Captain Arnold, for no logical reason. The Bat Cave was created in this serial (called the "Bat's Cave") and then adopted by the comic books. Although the cave did appear earlier in the comic books, it was not called the Bat Cave until *Detective Comics #83* (January, 1944).

The sequel, *Batman and Robin* (1949), brought Commissioner Gordon and sometimes female interest of Batman, photo-journalist Vicki Vale, into the story, along with some use of the utility belt. The Batmobile was a basic convertible of the era and stately Wayne Manor appeared as a modest home. The villain was the Wizard, a master criminal. Though truer to some of the more outrageous villains from the comic books than Dr. Daka, from the first serial, the Wizard did not have the flair or outrageousness of characters like the Joker or the Riddler.

Artist Bob Kane created the Batman character but it was writer Bill Finger who contributed the original story lines, conceived of the character's costume and had the original idea for Robin. Kane, however, negotiated a mandatory credit on all Batman productions, leaving out Bill Finger's contribution. Thus, both serials now have the credit, "Based on the Batman Comic Magazine Feature appearing in Detective Comics and Batman Magazines, created by Bob Kane," although the reference to Kane was not in the original serial credits but was added later when the serials were reissued.

Batman never had his own radio show, although he and Robin appeared from time to time on the radio in *The Adventures of Superman*. Batman did have his own television show, which ran on ABC from 1966 to 1968 and Batman has been the subject of several full length motion pictures.

## Captain America (Republic)

This 1944 serial was, according to its credits, based on the character appearing in *Captain America Comics*. The comic book character, Captain America, was unusual in that it debuted in its own book, *Captain America Comics #1* (March, 1941). Joe Simon and Jack Kirby were the writers and artists for the first 14 issues. They then moved to DC Comics and other artists and writers took over the *Captain America* stories.

The story line of *Captain America* followed blond Steve Rogers, who was turned down by the Army because of his unfit condition. He then participated in an experimental project and received an injection of Super Soldier Serum, developed by famous scientist Professor Reinstein. The serum turned Rogers into a super hero, with greatly enhanced strength and reflexes. Because of enemy sabotage, Rogers was the only person to receive the injection.

In his everyday life, Rogers was a private in the Army. When Rogers used his super powers, he concealed his identity by donning a red, white and blue costume and a mask, becoming Captain America. The masked super hero also had a distinctive bulletproof shield that he used to protect himself. Later, the shield was modified so that it could be used by the Captain as a discus-like weapon. In the first issue, a boy named Bucky Barnes accidentally learned Rogers' secret, and so he became the Captain's sidekick. It was also in this issue that Rogers and Bucky first met their arch-enemy, The Red Skull, a former hotel bellhop whom Hitler personally promoted to the post of super villain. The initial run of the series ended in 1949.

*Captain America* (1944). District Attorney Grant Gardner, played by Dick Purcell, dresses in an unusual outfit to fight crime. Here, Captain America has the drop on one of the Scarab's henchmen, played by Jay Novello, and intends to make him talk.

The movie serial had no relationship with the comic book series, although many of the lobby cards used with the serial included a drawing of the comics Captain America, who never appeared in the chapter play. The serial involved Grant Gardner, a district attorney in a large American city, who was doing battle with the evil Dr. Maldor, also known as the Scarab. For some reason, Gardner sometimes dressed in a costume, wore a mask and was known as Captain America and in that guise, fought the forces of evil. However, the good Captain had no superpowers, no utility belt, no whip, no sword and no shield, so it was unclear why Gardner felt the need to dress in the silly costume.

None of the characters from the comic book were present. Bucky Barnes was nowhere to be found. Indeed, Steve Rogers was nowhere to be found. The serial was unconnected to the comic book series, except for the title.

### Hop Harrigan (Columbia)

*Hop Harrigan* debuted in the first issue of *All American Comics* (April, 1939). All American Comics was an independent company which was eventually purchased by DC Comics. DC continued to publish the *Hop Harrigan* stories through the 99th issue of *All American Comics*, in July, 1948.

Hop was an orphaned farm boy who ran away from a cruel guardian on an old biplane he restored. He landed on an airfield run by Prop Walsh, a test pilot. Another character there was chubby, red-haired mechanic, Ikky Tinker, whose name was later changed to Tank Tinker. It was Tank who gave Hop his nickname when, talking about the flight there, he remarked, "Some hop, Harrigan."

Hop obtained his pilot's license and started an aviation business with his friends. During World War II, he joined the Air Force and fought in both Europe and Japan. After the war, he continued his adventures as a civilian pilot.

America's Ace of the Airwaves, as Hop was known in radio, debuted on the Mutual Network in 1942. Chester Stratton played Hop and Ken Lynch (later replaced by Jackson Beck) played Tank Tinker. Initially, this was a war time program, with Hop fighting and spying in both Europe and the Pacific. After the war, Hop was involved in civilian mysteries and adventures. The radio series ended in 1948.

According to the credits, the 1946 serial was based on both the adventure strip created by Jon Blummer, appearing in *All American Com-*

*ics*, and on the radio program heard on the Mutual Network. The serial was a post-war adventure of Hop, who was hired by an eccentric inventor who wanted to be flown to his secret laboratory. Hop was assisted by friend and mechanic, Tank Tinker. Prop Walsh was missing but his girlfriend from the radio series, Gail Nolan, was present. The story was original to the serial.

## The Vigilante (Columbia)

*Action Comics* #42 (November, 1941) introduced a new masked hero to the comic book ranks. He was the Vigilante, the son of a western sheriff and the grandson of an Indian fighter. The Vigilante wore a fancy western outfit with a double button blue shirt and a white hat. The lower part of his face was covered by his crimson bandana. In real life, the Vigilante was Greg Sanders, a singing cowboy known as the Prairie Troubadour. He started his career in crime fighting when his father was killed by gold thieves and Sanders had to catch the murderers. Despite the western origins, many of the stories were set in an urban environment, where the Vigilante traded in a horse for a motorcycle.

The comic was created by writer Mort Weisinger and artist Mort Meskin. It was one of the longest running series in *Action Comics*, continuing until *Action Comics* #198 (November, 1954). Early in the series (*Action Comics* #45), the Vigilante picked up a youthful sidekick, Stuff the Chinatown Kid. Some of the stories were actual mystery plots, with clues and a surprise solution.

The 1947 serial was the modern version of the comic book story. Although the Vigilante was still Greg Sanders, in real life, Greg was now a western movie star. His dual identity was known only to his sidekick Stuff, who was now an adult. The serial, which was about a fight to obtain a string of valuable pearls, gave credit only to the adventure feature appearing in *Action Comics Magazine*.

## Tex Granger (Columbia)

According to the credits, *Tex Granger* (1948) was based on the famous *Tex Granger* adventures featured in *Calling All Boys* and *Tex Granger* comic magazines, published by The Parents Magazine Group. If *Tex Granger* were famous in 1948, he is hardly famous today, and the comic book probably did not deserve one of the longest source credits in serial history.

*Tex Granger* (1948). Robert Kellard, in his masked Rider outfit, does battle with Carson and his henchmen. In real life, the Midnight Rider of the Plains is Tex Granger, the town newspaper publisher.

In fact, *Tex Granger* was originally published in *Calling All Boys Magazine*, which was distributed by Parents Magazine Company. Granger was popular enough that in June, 1948, the title of the comic book was changed to *Tex Granger Adventure Comics*. The serial itself featured a masked hero, sometimes known in the serial as the Rider of Mystery Mesa, even though the subtitle of the serial was *The Midnight Rider of the Plains*. The serial was not based on the comic book, but rather, was purportedly loosely based on a silent movie, *The Last Frontier*, which had been previously turned into a serial in 1932 by RKO. The only aspect of plot that the serial, *The Last Frontier*, has in common with the serial, *Tex Granger*, was a masked newspaper reporter who fought the villains, so there is truly no relationship between the two works.

## Superman (Columbia)

The most famous comic book character of all time, Superman, debuted in the first issue of *Action Comics* (June, 1938). The character became so popular so quickly that Superman became the first comic book character to have his own title, when the comic book *Superman* debuted in 1939. Thereafter, Superman appeared in a newspaper strip, seventeen movie cartoons by the Fleischer Brothers, a novel by George Lowther, a television show in the 1950s and eventually full length movies and other television series. Other spin-off characters from the original concept who received their own comic book titles were Superboy, Supergirl, Lois Lane and Jimmy Olsen.

*Superman* was created by two Ohio teenagers, Jerry Spiegel and Joe Shuster. When DC Comics finally agreed to publish the comic book story, DC obtained all rights to the character. In 1947, Siegel and Shuster tried to regain legal control of their character, but they failed. They were then fired by DC Comics. In 1978, their cause was taken up again and after a large publicity campaign, DC Comics granted lifetime pensions to the two. Shuster died in 1992 and Siegel in 1996.

As part of the settlement, DC Comics also granted permanent credit to Shuster and Siegel on all Superman products. Thus, all recent movie and television shows have a credit for Shuster and Siegel. However, that was not the case at the time of the 1948 and 1950 serials. The credits stated simply that the serial was based on the *Superman* adventure feature appearing in magazines *Superman* and *Action Comics*. In addition, the credits stated that the serials were adapted from the *Superman* radio program broadcast on the Mutual Network.

The first *Superman* radio show aired on February 12, 1940. Bud Collyer, who hosted television game shows in the 1950s, such as *Beat the Clock*, portrayed both Superman and Clark Kent. Collyer portrayed Clark Kent as a tenor, dropping an octave in mid-sentence into Superman's deep baritone as he proclaimed: "This looks like a job—FOR SUPERMAN." Bud Collyer's portrayal of the Man of Steel remained the definitive interpretation throughout the 1940s. He also provided the voice of Superman for the well-respected series of Fleisher movie cartoons from the 1940s.

The *Superman* radio series ended on March 1, 1951, around the time the television series started. In all, there were more than 2000 shows broadcast. The show ran on the Mutual Radio Network, which received mention in the credits of the serial, and also on ABC and in syndication.

The *Superman* radio show was very influential in the development of the *Superman* series. The characters of Perry White, the editor of the Daily Planet and Jimmy Olsen, a copy boy (eventually to become a cub reporter), were first used in the radio series. Kryptonite was introduced in the radio adventures in 1943, years before it appeared in the comic books. In fact, Kryptonite did not appear in the comic books until *Superman* #61 (Dec, 1949), after the release of the first serial.

*Superman* (1948) was truer to its comic book (and radio) origins than any other serial based either on a comic strip or comic book character. It was also the first comic book serial since *Captain Marvel* to explain the character's origins. Indeed, the whole first chapter was devoted to the origins of the character, with the impending destruction of Krypton, the rocket ship sending the young child to Earth, his discovery by the Kents, his growing to adulthood and his leaving for the big city to make his fortune.

In the second chapter, Clark Kent applied for a job at the Daily Planet and then tried to earn that job by covering a news story. It was not until the third chapter that the actual story involving the Spider Lady began. Kryptonite was introduced shortly thereafter.

In terms of characters, the main ones were carried over from the comic book. Perry White was the editor of the Daily Planet and Lois Lane was a reporter who was always trying to "scoop" Clark Kent. One change from the comics was that Jimmy Olsen was no longer a copy boy; he was now a newspaper photographer. The story took place in Metropolis. The sequel, *Atom Man vs. Superman* (1950), featured Superman's arch-enemy, Lex Luthor.

The serials took the concept of Kryptonite from the radio show. By the time of the second serial, Kryptonite was a part of the comic books. Indeed, in a comic book story, (*Action Comics # 141*, February, 1950) Luthor developed synthetic Kryptonite, a story line used in *Atom Man vs. Superman*. The change in voice from Clark Kent to Superman, as he declared, "This is a job for Superman," was carried over from the radio series.

## Congo Bill (Columbia)

*Congo Bill* was the longest running series in DC's *Action Comics* other than *Superman*. *Congo Bill* debuted in June, 1940, in *More Fun Comics* #56. The regular series started in *Action Comics* #37 in June, 1941 and continued into the late 1950s, when it became more of a fantasy/ super hero adventure and was renamed *Congorilla*. The series was created by editor Whitney Ellsworth and artist George Papp. Ellsworth was a cartoonist, writer and editorial director of Detective Comics, Inc. from 1931 to 1953. Papp was best known as the creator of *The Green Arrow*. Ellsworth and Papp did not stay with the strip very long and other writers and artists carried the comic for most of its history.

The original comic book story was similar to that of the comic strip, *Jungle Jim*. Congo Bill was an adventurer and soldier of fortune who often worked for the African authorities. The 1948 serial, which credited Whitney Ellsworth and *Action Comics* magazine, was a standard jungle adventure about a white jungle goddess, Lureen, who was the potential heir to a $500,000 trust fund. Lureen was totally unaware of her incredible wealth. As the story line developed, if no one showed up to claim the fortune within a year, the money would go to the evil Bernie Macgraw.

If that plot sounds familiar, that was the basic outline of the serial, *Jungle Jim* (1937). Thus, both the comic book and the movie serial of *Congo Bill* were surprisingly similar to the earlier works.

## King of the Congo (Columbia)

This 1952 serial was the last serial in which Buster Crabbe appeared. It was the story of an air force pilot, Roger Drum, whose plane crashed in the jungle. Working even faster than Buck Rogers did in the 25th century, Drum was quickly anointed by the natives as Thunda, King of the Congo. Thereafter, Drum was involved in a jungle adventure with the Rock People, the Cave People and some foreign subversives.

The serial was based on an obscure comic book character, the dynamic hero of *Thunda* cartoon magazine, according to the credits. There were only five issues of the comic book published, which was titled *Thunda, King of the Congo*. The character's name was spelled Thun'da in the stories. The publisher was Magazine Enterprises and the issues were all from 1952, the year the serial was released. The first issue was drawn by Frank Frazetta, who drew many comic books and later became a paperback book cover illustrator. Because of Frazetta's involvement, the first issue of the series is considered special by comic book enthusiasts.

The beginning plot of the serial came from the original comic book, where the plane of spy, Roger Drum, went down over the continent of Africa. There he evolved into the vine swinging, Thun'da. In the comic books, Thunda had a mate named Pha. The character of Pha appeared in the serial but as the leader of the Rock People.

## Blackhawk (Columbia)

Blackhawk was a Polish aviator whose sister and brother were killed in a Nazi bombing raid. Blackhawk then formed a paramilitary group of fighting men from several of Europe's free countries who lived on an island of their own, called Blackhawk Island. There they were united into a band of anti-Nazi fighters that did not owe allegiance to any one nation. The other members of the group were named Andre, Olaf, Hendrikson, Chuck, Stanislaus, and Chop Chop.

The Blackhawk team dressed in dark blue uniforms and visored caps. Once the Nazis were defeated, they went after a variety of international villains, including Communists.

*Blackhawk* debuted in *Military Comics #1* (August, 1941), just a few months before the United States entered World War II. Will Eisner, who also created *Sheena, Queen of the Jungle*, is usually credited as the creator of the comic book heroes. However, Chuck Cuidera, who drew the first story, had substantial input. Another prominent cartoonist associated with the comic was Reed Crandall. In 1944, *Blackhawk* received its own title. Also, *Military Comics* changed its name to *Modern Comics* at the end of World War II and continued under that title until 1950, with *Blackhawk* remaining a part thereof, in addition to its own title.

The 1952 serial was the last serial based upon comic book characters. Credit was given to *The Blackhawk Comic Magazine* drawn by Reed Crandall and Charles Cuider. The serial followed the general concept of

*Blackhawk* (1952). Carol Forman, as the evil Laska, has the drop on Kirk Alyn, as the heroic Blackhawk. In *Superman* (1948), another serial based upon a comic strip, Forman starred as the evil Spider Lady and Alyn starred as the heroic Superman.

the comic book series, with Blackhawk leading the Blackhawks , "with no weapons but strong fists and alert minds," in their fight against a band of saboteurs. Olaf, Andre, Chop Chop, Chuck and Stan were part of the serial Blackhawks. Although the main story was original, the parts concerning the female spy Laska (Leska, in the comic book) and the impersonation of Stan came from *Blackhawk* #31 (June, 1950).

**The Masked Marvel (Republic)**

For the sake of completeness, *The Masked Marvel* must be mentioned here. The credits of the 1943 Republic serial do not cite any source material. There was a *Masked Marvel* comic book series, which debuted in the July, 1939 issue of *Keen Detective Funnies*. The hero was a mysterious masked crime fighter who, with the aid of three former government agents, was dedicated to the fight against crime. The Masked Marvel wore a red shirt, red riding breeches and a red domino mask. His partners wore business suits and green masks. The series was short-lived, ending in the summer of 1940, when *Keen Detective Funnies* ceased publication, although there were then a few issues of the series that came out under its own title later that year.

The serial involved a group of four insurance investigators, one of whom was The Masked Marvel. The Masked Marvel wore a double-breasted suit, white shirt, business hat and a dark mask. As the serial progressed, two of the candidates for The Masked Marvel were eliminated, until only two were left standing, one of whom was finally revealed as the masked crime fighter. There was no relationship between the comic book series and the serial.

## III. RADIO SERIES

The era of the sound serial generally mirrored the era of the radio drama or adventure show, with each being popular in the 1930s and 1940s, only to become overshadowed by television and ending their respective reigns in the 1950s. Also, many of the radio dramas told their stories in installments with cliffhangers at the end of each episode so that radio dramas were, in essence, audio serials.

Thus, it was natural for serial makers to adopt popular radio characters for their cliffhangers, obviously hoping to have a built-in audience for their weekly adventures. Here are the serials that were based primarily on radio shows.

## Chandu (Principal)

*Chandu, the Magician* first aired nationally on the Mutual Radio Network from 1932 to 1936 as a daily 15-minute serial. The series starred Gayne Whitman as Frank Chandler, a/k/a Chandu, who used his crystal ball and the powers of the occult that he learned from a yogi in India to fight the powers of evil. The scripts from the first run were reproduced in the 1948 to 1949 version, starring Tom Collins in the title role. The main villain in both runs of the series was a character named Roxor. This was truly a radio serial, with stories running over many episodes. Some stories involved Chandu's romance with Nadji, an Egyptian princess. Chandu's sister, Dorothy Regent and her two children, Bob and Betty, were also important characters.

Chandu was first brought to the movies in the 1932 feature, *Chandu the Magician*, with Edmund Lowe as Chandu, Irene Ware as Princess Nadji, and Bela Lugosi as the villainess Roxor. The next screen appearance was in the 1934 serial, titled *The Return of Chandu*, with Bela Lugosi playing the hero, Chandu. The credits to the serial stated that the serial was adapted from the radio drama written by Harry A. Earnshaw, Vera M. Oldham and R.R. Morgan.

The story involved a strange Egyptian religious sect which was after the Princess Nadji, the only living Egyptian princess, to use Nadji's body to restore to life the body of Ossana, the last high priestess of the Ubasti. Luckily for Nadji, her boyfriend, Chandu the Magician, was around to protect her.

Maria Alba played Princess Nadji. Chandu's sister and her two children were also important characters. Roxor did not make an appearance. The music under the credits was also used in the radio show, as was the gong which started each chapter of the serial. *Chandu* was also released as two distinctive feature films, *The Return of Chandu* and *Chandu on the Magic Island*.

## The Lone Ranger (Republic)

Radio's best-remembered drama, *The Lone Ranger*, debuted on January 31, 1933 in Detroit, Michigan on radio station WXYZ. George Trendle, who was the owner of the radio station, developed the premise of the show. However, the man who developed the story lines and wrote most of the scripts was Fran Striker, who was originally from Buffalo, New York.

After a slow start, the show became so popular that it was one of the reasons why several stations linked together to share programming on what became the Mutual Broadcasting System. The radio series continued on the air until September 3, 1954, long after the television series was also on the air. Beginning in 1941, the Lone Ranger was portrayed on radio by Bruce Beemer, who was the actor most associated with the radio role. Tonto was played by John Todd.

The first radio episode did not explain the origin of the Lone Ranger. Indeed, Tonto was not originally a part of the series. However, on radio, the Lone Ranger needed someone to talk to, since all of the action was conveyed by sound. Therefore, the Tonto character was inserted into the radio show in the very early days of the program.

Anyone familiar with the television series knows the origin of The Lone Ranger. Six Texas Rangers, on the trail of Butch Cavendish, were ambushed in a box canyon and left for dead. However, one luckily survived and he was nursed back to life by an Indian, Tonto, who

*The Lone Ranger* (1938) Three of the candidates for the masked man are pictured: Lee Powell (standing), Herman Brix (kneeling) and Lane Chandler (lying in the foreground). From left to right, the other performers are Chief Thundercloud, Lynn Roberts, George Cleveland and Sammy McKim.

happened to come along after the massacre. Indeed, Tonto knew the remaining ranger, as he had saved Tonto's life when they were both youngsters.

Once the only ranger who was still alive regained his health, he decided to make a career of ridding the west of outlaws. The ranger also decided to hide his true identity by wearing a mask, made from his dead brother's clothes, and to use only silver bullets, made at a hidden silver mine in which the ranger had an interest. Since he was the only ranger to survive the ambush, Tonto observed that he was the lone ranger and the masked hero adopted that name as his official moniker.

In their early travels, the Lone Ranger and Tonto came upon a white horse that was being attacked by a buffalo. The Lone Ranger saved the horse's life and in return, the horse became the Lone Ranger's mighty steed, Silver. The legend was complete.

*The Lone Ranger* radio show was the source material for two Republic serials, *The Lone Ranger* (1938) and *The Lone Ranger Rides Again* (1939). Fran Striker was mentioned in the credits of both of the serials. On some of the posters for the first serial, Station WXYZ Detroit was also mentioned. The serials took much from the radio program, which would be expected since the story of the Lone Ranger was so well known at the time. Thus, the characters in the serials included that fabulous individual, the Lone Ranger, his fiery horse Silver and his faithful Indian companion Tonto.

The origin of the Lone Ranger was told at the beginning of the first serial, and although it was similar to the classic version of the origin of the Lone Ranger, the story was not as fleshed out in the serial as it was at the beginning of the television show. Indeed, unlike the radio or television program, the gimmick in this serial was that one of five male leads was, in reality, the Lone Ranger, and the audience had to figure out who it was. The Lone Ranger's identity was finally revealed to the audience in the last seconds of the serial. This unmasking was a significant departure from the radio show, as the Lone Ranger never unmasked on the radio show, or, for that matter, on the television show.

In the sequel, Tonto and Silver returned with the Lone Ranger, whose real identity, Bill Andrews, was known from the beginning of the chapter play. This was also a change from the radio show, where the Lone Ranger's real last name was Reid. This was known because his brother, Dan Reid, was killed in the original ambush of the Texas Rangers. The Lone Ranger's first name, however, was not revealed in either the radio or television series. Nevertheless, the spirit of the serial was the same as the radio show, as the Lone Ranger led the fight for law and order in the early west.

## The Green Hornet (Universal)

The credits to *The Green Hornet* (1939) stated that the serial was based on the radio dramatic adventure serial entitled "The Green Hornet" owned and copyrighted by The Green Hornet, Inc. However, just before the action started in each chapter, there was a frame with the credit: "Adapted from the Radio Dramatic Adventure Serial by Fran Striker." The sequel also gave credit to Fran Striker.

*The Green Hornet* radio program was originally broadcast on WXYZ in Detroit, Michigan, just as *The Lone Ranger* was. The first broadcast was on January 31, 1936. After a few years on the air as a local program, it moved to a national broadcast on the Mutual Network, beginning on April 12, 1938. The show continued on the air through December 5, 1952.

The story of the Green Hornet is well known. The Hornet was a masked crime fighter whose real identity was Britt Reid, a famous playboy. His father was so concerned about Britt's future that he installed him as the publisher of the family-owned newspaper, the *Daily Sentinel*. The father also provided a bodyguard for his son in the name of Irishman Michael Axford, a former policeman.

As a result of his work at the newspaper, Reid was often alerted to ongoing criminal activity. Reid then transformed himself into the Green Hornet at night to battle crime in the city. Despite his efforts against crime, the police believed the Hornet to be a master criminal and therefore the masked crime fighter had to elude the police, while chasing the criminals. The Green Hornet's special equipment included his high-powered car, the Black Beauty, and a gun that fired knockout gas instead of bullets. The Hornet was assisted by his valet, Kato, who was a Filipino of Japanese descent. Kato drove the Black Beauty, kept watch out for the police or the bad guys and sometimes lent a hand in the pursuit of crime.

Fran Striker and George W. Trendle created *The Green Hornet*, just as they had previously created *The Lone Ranger* radio program. There was much similarity between the two shows, as each masked crime fighter was assisted by a faithful companion, be it Kato or Tonto. Even more significant, Britt Reid was actually the great-nephew of the Lone Ranger. Britt's

*The Green Hornet Strikes Again* (1940). The new Green Hornet, now played by Warren Hull, replacing Gordon Jones, is attacked by henchman James Seay.

father was Dan Reid, the nephew of the Lone Ranger. Britt Reid's family fortune supposedly came from the silver mine from which the Lone Ranger made his bullets. Of course, the Lone Ranger's last name was Reid.

The serials remained true to their radio origins. In the first chapter of *The Green Hornet* serial, the origin of the character was explained. As the serial opened, wealthy playboy, Britt Reid, and his valet, Kato, were experimenting with a chemical to be used in a car engine that Kato had invented. The engine had the strongest and fastest motor ever built and was to be installed in Reid's black car. Kato also showed the new horn he has installed in the black car, which sounded just like the giant green hornet the two once encountered in Africa.

Mention was made that Reid met Kato when Reid saved Kato from an attack by a native in Singapore, who tried to kill him only because he was a Korean. Kato's nationality was a change from the radio program and although the serial was made prior to Pearl Harbor, the change probably reflected Americans feelings about the Japanese at the time.

The serial then shifted to the offices of *The Sentinel*, a newspaper which was published by Britt Reid. The police commissioner and a judge asked Reid to write scathing editorials about the rackets, as Reid's father, the prior publisher, had done. Reid demurred. However, the discussion gave Reid an idea.

After a spate of racketeering activity in the city, Reid decided to become a modern Robin Hood. Kato designed a mask for him (adorned with a hornet drawn on the front) and to complete the costume, Reid wore a wide-brimmed hat and a dark overcoat with ascot. As to the other member of the duo, Kato turned in his valet outfit for a chauffeur's uniform with a dark cap, dark suit, bow tie, and goggles. Kato had also invented a gas gun which would not kill, but would render the victim unconscious for several moments.

On their first mission, one of the criminals was killed by other henchmen. For some reason, Reid then left a button on the victim, with the Green Hornet insignia on it, thereby convincing the police and the general public that the Green Hornet was a criminal. Throughout the serial, as the Green Hornet chased the racketeers, the police chased the Green Hornet. In this regard, the Green Hornet was like the Spider. Since the Green Hornet, in real life, was a wealthy playboy with a younger assistant, he was also like Batman. However, in the serial, the Green Hornet may actually have been most like Superman, as Reid's voice changed when he donned his crime fighting costume and the Green Hornet was able to survive every cliffhanger thrown at him, whether explosions, fires, falls out of windows or truck plunges over a cliff.

The radio origins of the serial were always evident. The theme music of the serial, which was re-used during much of the action, was Rimsky-Korsakov's "Flight of the Bumble Bee," just as it was in the radio show. The voice of the Green Hornet, once he donned the mask, was dubbed by Al Hodge, the actor who was then playing the Hornet on radio.

*The Green Hornet* serial was popular enough to spawn a sequel, *The Green Hornet Strikes Again*, released in 1940. The radio series also spawned several comic books and a television series in the 1960s.

### Captain Midnight (Columbia)

*Captain Midnight* was on the air from 1939 to 1949, first in syndication in the Midwest and then, beginning in 1940, as a national broadcast over the Mutual Radio Network and for a time, on the NBC Blue

*Captain Midnight* (1942). Dave O'Brien in his most famous serial role as Captain Midnight who, on many occasions, is not masked in the serial and therefore everyone knows he is actually Captain Albright, a famous aviator.

Network. In its syndication days, it was sponsored by Skelly Oil Company, and aired in Midwest and Southwest markets in which Skelly products were sold. When it went national, its sponsor became Ovaltine, which needed a replacement for its formerly popular program, *Little Orphan Annie*, which had been canceled after a ten-year run.

Captain Midnight's real name was Charles Red Albright, and he was a pilot during World War I. His code name, Captain Midnight, was given to him by a general when he returned from a dangerous secret mission precisely at midnight. When the radio show began in 1939, Midnight was a private flyer who assisted people in trouble. His main adversary was Ivan Shark, a master criminal who desired to control the world. Albright was assisted by Chuck Ramsey and Patsy Donovan.

When the show went on the national networks in 1940, the origin of Midnight was changed. Albright was now the head of the Secret Squadron, a paramilitary organization which fought espionage and sabotage. Midnight was still assisted in the Secret Squadron by Chuck Ramsey but Patsy Donovan was replaced by Joyce Ryan. Also helping was Ichabod "Ichy" Mudd, who was Midnight's mechanic. Albright reported to Major Steel. There was still an emphasis on flying.

The main villain at this time continued to be Ivan Shark, who was now assisted by his daughter, Fury Shark. During World War II, there was an emphasis on fighting Nazis and "Japs" with adventures all over the world.

Columbia turned the popular radio show into a fifteen chapter serial in 1942. According to the credits, *Captain Midnight* was based on the radio serial broadcast over the Mutual Network. Despite the fact that the serial was produced during World War II, the villain was Ivan Shark, who was assisted by his evil daughter, Fury. A substantial portion of the serial involved Shark's attempts to steal a range finder invented by John Edwards.

Most of the cast was carried over from the radio serial. The hero, Captain Albright, was still a famous aviator known as Captain Midnight. For part of the serial, the Captain Midnight character was used to hide Albright's true identity. That plot point seemed to disappear as the story moved forward.

Albright was assisted by Chuck Ramsay and Ichabod Mudd. He reported to Major Steele. The main character who was missing was Joyce Ryan, Albright's female assistant in the radio series. Professor Edwards' daughter, Joyce, was an important character in the serial but she was a true wimp, far from the commando that Joyce Ryan was on the radio.

With the success of the radio show, *Captain Midnight* was turned into a comic book, published by Fawcett Publications. It had a nice run, from June, 1942 to September, 1948. There was also a short-lived television show on CBS in the 1950s.

**Gang Busters (Universal)**

This radio show was originally titled *G-Men* and debuted on CBS in 1935. Its name was changed to *Gang Busters* the following year. The show stayed on the air through 1957. There was also a one season television show which aired in 1952.

The radio program was created by Phillips H. Lord, who was also the narrator. Each episode was a police procedural of some kind, based on a real FBI or police case. The series was an anthology, with no regular cast. However, people who later became famous in television worked on the radio show, such as Art Carney, who did regular voiceover work and Gale Gordon, who appeared in an episode. Each episode ended with a description of a criminal, which led to many arrests of real criminals over the 21 year history of the radio show.

The serial gave a credit to Lord as the creator of the radio program. It followed the general tone of the radio show, with the police chasing a gang of criminals led by Dr. Mortis and known as "The League of Murdered Men." Since the serial involved criminals who committed suicide and then were brought back to life by Dr. Mortis, it is believed that the plot was not based upon an actual crime.

The radio program had a distinctive opening, with a narrator, and then the sounds of shuffling feet, gunshots, a window breaking, machine guns and a police siren. The serial had a similar opening behind the credits with a police whistle, prisoners marching in jail, and then a siren and a machine gun. The movie narrator then stated, " Universal presents – Gang Busters." A voice then said, "Calling the police. Calling the G-Men. Calling all Americans to war on the underworld. Gang Busters, with the cooperation of law enforcement officers of the United States, presents a picture of the endless war of the police on the underworld, illustrating the clever operation of law enforcement officers in the work of protecting our citizens, the all-American crusade against crime."

This opening, with one of the longest sentences in serial history, set a tone similar to that of the radio program. The serial embodied the spirit of the radio show, even though the plot was hardly a true crime story.

**Chick Carter, Detective (Columbia)**

Chick Carter was the adopted son of the master detective, Nick Carter. Although Chick Carter did appear in some of the Nick Carter stories, Chick Carter was primarily famous from his radio adventures. In fact, the credits to the 1946 serial stated that it was adapted from the Street and Smith character appearing in *Shadow Magazine* and *Shadow Comics* but that it was based upon the radio program broadcast on the Mutual Network.

Although Chick was originally a part of the *Nick Carter* radio series, Chick's radio show was then spun off from the original and called *Chick Carter, Boy Detective*. The show was first broadcast on the Mutual Network on July 5, 1943, in a 15-minute, five-days-a-week serialized program. The show, however, only lasted a couple of seasons, leaving the airwaves on July 6, 1945. In all, there were 524 episodes that were broadcast.

In the serial, Chick Carter was no longer a boy detective. In fact, he was played by Lyle Talbot, who was 44 years old when the serial was released. Thus, to the extent this serial was based on a detective named Carter, it was really the master detective himself, Nick Carter. Apparently, this was originally supposed to be a Nick Carter serial, but when the copyright holder would not give permission to use the Nick Carter character, the name of Chick Carter was substituted.

The serial was a standard detective plot which could have starred Nick Carter, Chick Carter, or even Sam Spade. The plot was original to the serial, although given the number of Nick Carter stories in print and on radio, there was probably some overlap in plot.

## Jack Armstrong (Columbia)

One of the longest running radio shows with a juvenile hero, *Jack Armstrong, The All American Boy,* told the tales of Hudson High School student, Jack Armstrong, and his adventures all around the world. Apparently, as a result of these adventures, Jack had little time for his high school studies so he remained in high school from the debut of the radio program, on July 31, 1933, until the 1950-51 season when Jack Armstrong became a government agent. The show was generally broadcast in 15 minute daily episodes, at different times on all four major networks, including the Mutual Radio Network, which was referred to in the credits of the serial. The show ended its 18 year run on June 28, 1951, being last broadcast on the Mutual Radio Network.

The radio show was originally broadcast from Chicago and was produced by an advertising agency. The writer who developed the idea and turned out the initial scripts was Robert Hardy Andrews. Those initial stories had Jack, accompanied by friends Billy and Betty Fairfield, traveling around the world to places such as Canada, the Arctic, Brazil and Arizona on various adventures. The adult companion on many of their adventures was Captain Hughes.

In 1936, the writing duties were turned over to Talbot Mundy, an adventure novelist, who wrote the stories until 1940. Mundy introduced the character of Jim Fairchild, uncle of Billy and Betty Fairchild, who was an industrialist and an inventor. He then accompanied the kids on most of their adventures, such as ones to Egypt, Africa and Tibet.

The show was sponsored for many years by Wheaties cereal, the "Breakfast of Champions," transforming the product into a national phenomenon. The show was also famous for taking an object used in the show's current storyline, such as a Torpedo Flashlight, an Explorer Telescope, or an Egyptian Whistling Ring and offering it as a "premium" to listeners who mailed in a dime and a Wheaties box top.

The 1947 serial was clearly based upon the radio show, although John Hart, at 30 years of age, seemed to be too old to play a high school student. Jack, the Fairchilds and Uncle Jim traveled to a jungle island to fight criminals who intended to use cosmic radiation to conquer the Earth. The serial even included a new character that had been recently introduced on the radio program—renowned scientist and inventor Vic Hardy. With problematic jungle natives and even a rocket ship, this adventure was clearly inspired by the radio shows, as the teenagers eventually triumphed over the forces of evil.

**The Sea Hound (Columbia)**

This 1947 serial, according to its credits, was based on a "radio program and cartoon magazine." The radio program, *Adventures of the Sea Hound*, was broadcast on different networks from 1942 to 1951. There was also a comic book of the character which had six issues over four years. Some of those comics were drawn by Jon Blummer, the creator of *Hop Harrigan,* and written by Fran Striker, one of the creators of *The Lone Ranger* and *The Green Hornet.*

The hero of the radio series was Captain Silver, who, along with his young friend Jerry and other companions, had seagoing adventures on his ship, *The Sea Hound.* The concept was carried over to the serial, with most of the regular characters from the radio show included in the movie. The serial involved an adventure on the sea, much like the radio stories.

CAPTAIN SILVER'S
STRATEGY
Chapter 5
THE SEA HOUND
Daredevil Adventures of Captain Silver
A COLUMBIA SERIAL
Reprint

*The Sea Hound* (1947). This Columbia serial was based on a radio show called *Adventures of the Sea Hound* and as the lobby card indicates, involves the seagoing adventures of Captain Silver. Buster Crabbe stars as Captain Silver.

## IV. PULP MAGAZINES AND OTHER PERIODICALS

The pulps were inexpensive, all-fiction magazines printed double column on coarse, wood pulp paper. They were widely circulated from the beginning of the 20th century into the 1950s. The typical magazine measured seven by ten inches, contained 128 pages, had brightly illustrated covers and contained all types of fiction, including mystery, crime, science fiction and adventure. Each issue had some short stories and usually installments of several serials.

Prior to the circulation of pulp magazines, dime novels were a popular source of similar stories of fiction. Dime novels were first published in 1860. They lasted until around 1915. From about 1900 to 1915, the last dime novels and the first pulp magazines overlapped.

The earliest dime novels were small booklets, four by six inches, with about 100 pages. They eventually evolved into larger books, five by seven inches, containing 250 to 300 pages. These were published at regular intervals at a low price and since they had cover dates and numbers, they received the lower second-class postage rate.

With regard to pulp magazine characters, it is often unclear whether the serials were based on the original pulp magazine stories, the novels made from those stories or the radio shows developed from those stories. Other serials were based on characters first published in dime novels or regular magazines. In any event, stories originally published in periodicals were a significant source of material for serials during the sound era.

## Tarzan (Universal and Independents)

Most people believe that Tarzan originated in a series of books by Edgar Rice Burroughs, because that is how they are read today. In fact, *Tarzan of the Apes* was first published in a pulp magazine, *All-Story Magazine*, in the October, 1912 issue. What was unusual about this publica-

*Tarzan the Tiger* 1929). Philip Annersley, Tarzan's cousin, attempts to steal the title of Lord Greystoke from Tarzan and his mate. Pictured from left to right are Clive Morgan, Frank Merrill and Natalie Kingston.

tion was that instead of serializing the lengthy story, the magazine published the novel-length story in one issue. It was an immediate success.

Surprisingly, *All-Story Magazine* turned down the sequel, *The Return of Tarzan*, so Burroughs took it to *New Story Magazine* which did publish it, in seven monthly issues beginning in June, 1913. Burroughs then sought to have *Tarzan of the Apes* published in book form and after a number of rejections, a book of the original novel finally came out in June of 1914. In all, there were 26 Tarzan novels written by Burroughs, including one book, *Tarzan and the Tarzan Twins*, which was specifically written for younger audiences.

Tarzan was a success in all media. A historically important comic strip of *Tarzan* began in the newspapers on January 7, 1929, the same day that *Buck Rogers* was first published, starting the Golden Age of Comic Strips. A successful radio show debuted in September, 1932. However, Tarzan's greatest success outside of books was his movie career, in silent movies, silent serials and the very successful MGM full-length movie series originally starring Johnny Weissmuller. Tarzan was also a fixture in sound serials, appearing in three.

The first was the early sound serial, *Tarzan the Tiger*, released in 1929. This serial was based on the book, *Tarzan and the Jewels of Opar*, first published in a magazine in 1916 and in book form in 1918. Indeed, much of the plot of the serial came from that book. The serial was produced by Universal Studios. Tarzan was played by Frank Merrill, who had previously played the role in *Tarzan the Mighty*, a silent serial from the previous year. *Tarzan the Tiger* was really a silent film, with title cards. However, music and sound effects were added at the time of the release, including the Tarzan yell and the sounds of jungle animals.

The second Tarzan serial was *Tarzan the Fearless* released by Sol Lesser/Principal Picture in 1933. The credits referred to a story by Edgar Rice Burroughs. The serial was about a search for a missing professor and a lost treasure. Tarzan was played by Olympic athlete and soon to be star of many serials, Buster Crabbe.

The last Tarzan serial was *The New Adventures of Tarzan* which was released by Burroughs' own company, Burroughs-Tarzan Enterprises, Inc. in 1935. Burroughs was unhappy with the versions of Tarzan produced by MGM and wanted to do a picture more in keeping with his own vision of Tarzan. Thus, Tarzan was very articulate in this serial, unlike in the Weissmuller movies, where he had trouble completing whole sen-

*Tarzan the Fearless* (1933). Buster Crabbe plays Tarzan in the first all-talking serial concerning the jungle character.

tences. The plot involved a search through the jungle for the Green Goddess which contained a fortune in jewels and a formula for a powerful explosive. Tarzan was portrayed by Herman Brix, who a few years later, played a similar character in *Hawk of the Wilderness*.

### The Jade Box (Universal)

This early 1930 serial from Universal involved the theft of a jade box which held the secret of invisibility, and the attempt of an Oriental cult to take it back. The screenplay was based on a story by Frederick J. Jackson. The story was originally published in 1916 in *People's Magazine*, a short story magazine or pulp which published under various names from 1906 to 1924. It should not to be confused with *People* magazine, currently being published and having no relationship to the pulps. A number of Jackson's stories were adapted for the screen and he also write screenplays in Hollywood, such as *Stormy Weather* (1943), starring Lena Horne and Bill "Bojangles" Robinson, The serial is now lost and all that is left are some stills and plot summaries.

### The Call of the Savage (Universal)

According to the credits, this serial was based upon the "Argosy" story "Jan of the Jungle" by Otis Adelbert Kline. This reflects the fact that just like the early *Tarzan* stories, the *Jan of the Jungle* works were originally serialized in a magazine and only later were they published in book form. In the case of *Jan of the Jungle*, the magazine was *Argosy Magazine*, which was one of the first pulp magazines. The *Jan of the Jungle* stories appeared in the magazine in April and May, 1931. There was also a sequel, published in book form under the title *Jan in India*. The books and the serialized stories were written by Otis Adelbert Kline.

As the first book begins, the reader learns that 17 years before, the villainous Dr. Bracken had kidnapped Jan, the one day old red-haired baby of Georgia and Harry Trevor, and locked him in a cage with a chimpanzee named Chicma. Bracken was raising the boy to kill his mother, in revenge for Georgia spurning Bracken's love for that of Harry Trevor. However, early in the novel, Jan and Chicma escaped from Dr. Bracken's cages and through a series of strange circumstances, traveled from the Florida Everglades to a jungle in South America. Over the next several years, Jan acclimated himself to the jungle and became a Tarzan-like character, although one who was much more brutal than Tarzan as Jan fought real and mythical beasts of the jungle.

Eventually, where civilization touched the outskirts of the jungle, Jan met Ramona, the adopted daughter of Isabella and Fernando Suarez. She taught Jan how to read and write as they fell in love. In her right hand, Ramona had a blue tracing of a many-petaled flower, which meant that she was the missing princess of the lost civilization of Mu. Jan, who had become a leader of that lost civilization, finally reunited Ramona with her real parents in Mu just as Jan also became reunited with the Trevors. In the meantime, Bracken's hunt for Jan in the jungle was thwarted by Jan who was able to get his revenge against Bracken for 17 years of ill treatment.

The serial took almost nothing from the Kline stories. In the film, Dr. Trevor, along with other scientists, including Dr. Bracken, was in the jungle trying to discover a cure for infantile paralysis. Once Trevor found the cure, he wrote half of the formula on a metal wrist band which he placed on the wrist of his young son, Jan. At that point, a fire broke out and the caged wild animals escaped, apparently killing the entire Trevor family.

Many years later, Dr. Bracken and an associate returned to the jungle to attempt to obtain Trevor's medical formula so that they could collect a valuable prize for discovering the prescription. It turned out that the entire Trevor family had not been killed in the jungle disaster. Jan had escaped into the jungle and thereafter was raised by chimpanzees, including one named Chicma. Dr. Trevor had lost his memory but otherwise was in good health.

During the early chapters of the serial, Jan met Mona Andrews, who had a birth mark of a flower on her hand. Borneo (a minor figure in the book) realized that Ramona was the lost Princess of Mu and he, along with Jan, attempted to return her to that civilization with Dr. Bracken in pursuit. Eventually, Jan was reunited with his father and Bracken was killed.

While the serial and the stories had a superficial similarity, they really had little in common. Most of the book involved Jan's trials and tribulations in the jungle, much of the time spent with mythical beasts and strange civilizations. Dr. Bracken was a much more important character in the serial than in the book and most of the events in the book were not used in the serial. Since Universal did not even use Kline's clever title of "Jan of the Jungle" for the serial, it is not clear why any credit was given to Kline in the serial.

## The Adventures of Frank Merriwell (Universal)

Frank Merriwell was introduced by Street and Smith in its dime novel, *Tip Top Weekly*, which eventually became a pulp magazine under other titles. The original story was published on April 18, 1896. Merriwell's adventures continued on a weekly basis, for almost two decades. The creator of the stories was Gilbert Patten, using the pseudonym, Burt L. Standish. At the height of Merriwell's popularity, it was estimated that the circulation of the *Weekly* reached 200,000 copies per week.

*Tip Top Weekly* often came with a subheading, "An Ideal Publication for the American Youth." The Merriwell stories fit that description, with Merriwell a student at Yale, who excelled in football and baseball, and had many adventures, some in faraway places. Frank Merriwell was turned into a daily comic strip for a short period of time in the early 1930s and there were two radio programs starring the youthful hero, one in the 1930s and one in the 1940s.

The credits to the 1936 serial referred to the stories by Gilbert Patten. The movie Merriwell was a baseball player at Fardale College, which was a reference to the college preparatory school which Merriwell attended in the stories before moving on to Yale. After winning a baseball game at the beginning of the serial, Merriwell had to leave school to search for his missing father. He was successful in that endeavor and returned to school just in time to lead Fardale to victory in an important college football game.

Although the plot was original to the serial, it captured the spirit of the Merriwell stories. In the stories, Merriwell was deeply involved in football and baseball and, upon occasion, searched for his missing father. A character from the stories, Elsie Bellwood, played by Jean Rogers, appeared in the serial.

## Zorro (Republic)

Much like Tarzan, Zorro had his origin in the pulp magazines, before some of the stories were published in novel form. The first Zorro story was "The Curse of Capistrano." It was written by Johnston McCulley and published in *All-Story Magazine* in five parts, starting in the August, 1919 issue. After the success of the film *The Mark of Zorro* (1920), starring Douglas Fairbanks, Sr. as Zorro, the original Zorro story was published in book form, titled *The Mark of Zorro.*

Johnston McCulley was born in 1883. Although Zorro was McCulley's most famous creation, McCulley was a prolific writer of westerns, adventure tales, and detective thrillers for the pulp magazines and other publications. His stories were published from 1911 until his death in 1958, with one Zorro story published posthumously in 1959. In addition to Zorro, the stories featured colorfully named heroes including The Bat, Thubway Tham and The Black Star. His works included fifty novels.

When McCulley wrote the first *Zorro* story, "The Curse of Capistrano," he had no idea how successful his character would be. Since he never expected to be writing any more *Zorro* stories, Zorro's identity was revealed in the next to the last chapter of the story. Until that point in the tale, neither the reader nor the other characters knew the true identity of Zorro. In some of McCulley's later stories, Zorro's true iden-

*Zorro's Fighting Legion* (1939). Don Diego, played by Reed Hadley, and Ramon, played by William Corson, are stopped by two of Don Del Oro's men. The henchman on the right is played by Ken Terrell. Of course, the effeminate Don Diego is actually the heroic Zorro.

tity was, once again, unknown to most of the other characters. In all, McCulley wrote about sixty stories concerning the exploits of Zorro. Some were serialized in magazines but many others were short stories published in just one issue of a magazine.

McCulley's first *Zorro* story established the basic premise of the entire series, although some aspects of the character were modified in subsequent stories, movies and serials. Zorro's true identity was Don Diego Vega, an individual who was usually around the fringes of the action, often portrayed as cowardly and effeminate. However, to fight the forces of evil, Vega became Zorro, dressing in a black costume with a cape, a small flat-brimmed hat and a black mask that covered the top of the head from eye level up. Zorro was an accomplished swordsman, often using his sword to leave a distinctive large "Z" on the forehead of his victims. He also made excellent use of his black bullwhip.

There were four Zorro serials which carried over the basic concepts of the McCulley creation. They were: *Zorro Rides Again* (1937), *Zorro's*

*Fighting Legion* (1939), *Son of Zorro* (1947) and *Ghost of Zorro* (1949). Of the four, only *Zorro's Fighting Legion* had the original Zorro in the story. The other Zorro serials were about offspring of the original legend. All of the stories made use of the basic concepts of the original McCulley stories: dual identity and a masked hero. A fifth serial, *Zorro's Black Whip* (1944) had credits referring to Johnston McCulley, but Zorro did not appear in the serial. However, that serial did have many elements of the original McCulley works, including the dual identity, masked heroine, and the excellent use of the black bullwhip.

## The Spider (Columbia)

*The Spider's Web* (1938) and its sequel, *The Spider Returns* (1941), were, according to the credits, based on "The Spider" Magazine stories. *Spider Magazine*, which was a pulp, was a response to the success of the masked crime fighter, the Shadow, who became the hero of a Columbia crime serial in 1940. Indeed, much like the Shadow, the Spider wore a black hat and black cape and fought against crime. However, the Spider of the pulps was also hunchbacked and had fangs. When he caught or killed a criminal, the Spider stamped an image of a spider on his victim's forehead.

When he was not dressed in his costume, the Spider was Richard Wentworth, a wealthy socialite and amateur detective. He was assisted in his crime fighting by his fiancée, Nita Van Sloan, his Hindu manservant, Ram Singh, his old war colleague, Jackson, and his faithful butler, Jenkins. Since the police believed that the Spider was actually a criminal, he was chased by police commissioner Stanley Kirkpatrick, who was a friend of Wentworth. While the commissioner believed that Wentworth was the Spider, he could not prove it.

The first issue of *Spider Magazine* was published in October, 1933, by Popular Publications. The first Spider story was titled, "The Spider Strikes." Here the Spider story was not yet fully developed, as the Spider did not even wear a costume. After two issues, the series was handed over to Norvell Page, who wrote the stories under the house pen name, Grant Stockbridge. The first story he wrote was "Wings of the Death," for the December, 1933 issue. Starting with that issue, the character of the Spider began to be developed, including the introduction of his costume. From then on, the Spider stories focused on Wentworth's battles to foil some of the meanest and sadistic villains in pulp history. Indeed, the

*The Spider Returns* (1941). Prolific serial henchman Anthony Warde grabs the collar of Warren Hull, in his disguise as Blinky McQuaide, as other henchmen of the Gargoyle look on.

Spider stories have been called the most violent and action-packed of any of the major pulp series. In all, there were 118 *Spider Magazines*, with the last one published in 1944.

*The Spider's Web* was surprisingly true to the Spider's pulp magazine sources. Richard Wentworth was a noted criminologist who, upon occasion, dressed as the Spider to fight arch-villains, such as the Octopus, who was attempting to take over a city by destroying its transportation system and other infrastructure. The police, led by Commissioner Kirk (for some reason the name was shortened from the Kirkpatrick of the magazine), believed the Spider was a criminal and they were often out to capture or kill him. Wentworth was assisted by Nita Van Sloan who was still his fiancé, who called him "Dick," his Hindu manservant, Ram Singh, who addressed him as "Sahib" or "Master," his friend, Jackson, who addressed him as "Major" and his butler, Jenkins, who addressed him as "Sir." The Spider stamped an image of a spider on his victim's foreheads, whenever he remembered to do so. In the tradition of the pulps, the serial was particularly bloody, with many henchmen killed or wounded through-out the serial.

The sequel was *The Spider Returns* (1941). All of the series regulars returned. In this case, the Spider was attempting to defeat the masked villain, the Gargoyle, who was intent on sabotaging America's industrial facilities, at the behest of some unknown Power. This second serial was less bloody than the first, and also had more of a tongue in cheek atti-tude. Therefore, this serial did not evoke the true spirit of the original pulp stories as the first serial had.

**The Shadow (Columbia)**

The Shadow first came to the public's attention in 1930 on radio, as the narrator of the shows done for *The Detective Story Hour*, a mystery anthol-ogy whose stories came from a pulp magazine of the era, *Detective Story Magazine*. The publication was from Street and Smith and the intent was to have the radio show promote the magazine. Instead, listeners were more interested in the announcer with the deep and eerie voice, and they flocked to newsstands seeking issues of *The Shadow Magazine*, which did not exist. Street & Smith was smart enough to respond to the demand, and it quickly started a new magazine about the character, which magazine was called, ap-propriately enough, *Shadow Magazine*. It debuted with an April, 1931 issue.

Walter B. Gibson, at the time a free lance writer, was called in by Street and Smith to develop the character and launch the new publica-tion. Gibson came up with the idea of a suicidal man, Henry Vincent, who was convinced not to jump off a bridge by the Shadow. In return, Vincent would work for him as an agent in the fight against crime. The Shadow also had other agents helping him, such as socialite Margo Lane and taxi driver Moe Shrenitz. In the pulps, the Shadow was always an elusive crime fighter who disguised himself under a slouch hat and black cape. Contrary to popular belief, the Shadow was not Lamont Cranston in the pulps. He merely pretended to be the millionaire when Cranston was out of town. In the August 1, 1937 issue of the magazine, in a story titled "The Shadow Unmasks," it was finally revealed that the true iden-tity of the Shadow was Kent Allard, a World War I flying ace.

The pulp magazine was a huge success. Gibson wrote almost all of the more than 300 *Shadow* stories issued over the next twenty-years, using the pen name of Maxwell Grant. The success of the magazine led to a change in the radio program. By 1932, the radio show was renamed

*The Shadow* but the Shadow was still the narrator of mystery stories. These shows aired on CBS and on NBC's Blue Network. By the end of that run, however, the Shadow started participating in the stories. The first radio show featuring the Shadow as an adventure character debuted on the Mutual Radio Network on September 26, 1937. The catch phrase of the new radio show, which has become a part of American culture, was a deep, sepulchral voice intoning, "Who knows what evil lurks in the hearts of men? The Shadow knows!" followed by eerie laughter.

The radio program contradicted the pulps, and there, the Shadow's real identity was millionaire Lamont Cranston. The Shadow had learned to cloud men's minds in the Orient. Eventually, some of the wilder elements of the story were downplayed in the radio show, making the character more like the detective of the magazines.

For the new series, the Shadow was initially played by Orson Welles. Agnes Moorhead played Margo and Ray Collins played Commissioner Weston. Welles left the show in 1938. Many other actors played the Shadow over the next 18 years. The radio program ran on Mutual until 1954.

*The Shadow* (1940). This lobby card effectively conveys the noir aspects of the pulp magazine stories which were the source for this Columbia chapter play. Victor Jory is prominently shown in his guise as the masked Shadow.

According to the credits, the 1940 serial was based on the stories published in *The Shadow Magazine*. The serial was clearly based more on the pulps than on the radio show, with the Shadow a crime fighter with no special powers, He was assisted in the serial by Henry Vincent and Margo Lane. Commissioner Weston also made an appearance. The Shadow's use of disguises was inspired by the magazine stories. Even the Cobalt Club, a location from the pulps where the elite gathered, made an appearance in the serial. However, much like the radio program, there was no doubt that the Shadow was Lamont Cranston.

There was also a full length movie of *The Shadow* in 1994. It was not a success.

**Drums of Fu Manchu (Republic)**

The first Fu Manchu story, "The Zayat Kiss," was published in the magazine, *The Story-Teller*, in England in October, 1912. It was followed by nine more stories which were eventually combined into the novel, *The Mystery of Dr. Fu Manchu*, which was published in England in 1913.

*Drums of Fu Manchu* (1940). On the left is Dr. Fu Manchu, played by Henry Brandon. He has ordered his dacoit slave (John Merton) to tie up an Oriental importer (Philip Ahn) who is in possession of a document which could lead to the tomb of Genghis Kahn.

Soon thereafter, the book was published in the United States with a new title, *The Insidious Dr. Fu Manchu*. It then ran as a 10 part series in *Collier's, The National Weekly Magazine*, from February 15, 1913 through June 28, 1913.

The author was Sax Rohmer, a pseudonym for Arthur Henry Ward, who was born in 1883. In total, there were 13 Fu Manchu novels, a novelette and some short stories written by Rohmer. Most of the Fu Manchu novels were first serialized in the United States in *Collier's Magazine*. *Collier's* was hardly a pulp magazine but the Fu Manchu stories would have easily fit into the type of stories carried in pulp magazines of that era.

Rohmer also wrote a successful series of stories about detective Gaston Max and another series about occult detective Morris Klaw. For periods during the 1920s and 1930s, Rohmer was one of the most widely read and most highly paid magazine writers in the English language. Rohmer died in 1959.

The Fu Manchu stories were about an evil Asian master criminal, Dr. Fu Manchu, who was seeking to overthrow western civilization. He was sometimes assisted by his lovely daughter, Fah Lo Suee. His adversary in all of the stories was Sir Nayland Smith, an official of the British government. Smith was assisted by Dr. Petrie, who often narrated the stories.

The 1940 serial, *Drums of Fu Manchu*, was, according to the credits, suggested by stories by Sax Rohmer. In this tale, Fu Manchu, the head of a secret sinister society known as Si Fan, was trying to foment war in Asia and somehow then secure world domination. In order to do this, he needed to locate the lost sword of Genghis Kahn. Opposing the evil doctor was Sir Nayland Smith and his assistant, Dr. Petrie. They were aided by a new character, Allan Parker, whose father was killed by Fu Manchu early in the serial. Not to be outdone, Fu Manchu had his daughter, Fah Lo Suee, along for assistance.

While the serial was clearly inspired by the Fu Manchu stories and novels, the plot was original to the movie. There was a novel, *The Drums of Fu Manchu*, which was originally published in *Colliers Magazine*, in ten parts, from April 1, 1939 to June 3, 1939. However, that story had a different plot from the one used in the serial.

There were also several radio series based on the Fu Manchu character and a number of full length films. The most famous movie was *The Mask of Fu Manchu*, a 1932 film in which Boris Karloff played the evil doctor.

## Deadwood Dick

For the sake of completeness, *Deadwood Dick* is considered here. This was a fifteen chapter western directed by James W. Horne and released in 1940. It told the story of Dick Stanley, editor of the local Deadwood newspaper, who donned a mask and became the mysterious hero, Deadwood Dick, to fight the notorious Skull. The credits did not cite any source material for the serial.

In fact, a character named "Deadwood Dick" was the star of a number of dime novels written by Edwin L. Wheeler from 1877 to 1885. In these stories, Dick, whose real name was Ned Harris, was usually an outlaw who dressed in black and rode a black horse. Interestingly, one of the regular characters in the *Deadwood Dick* stories was Calamity Jane, who was also a character in the serial.

The name "Deadwood Dick" became so popular that a number of people claimed the name as their own. One was Nat Love, a Black cowboy born a slave in Tennessee, who lived from 1854 to 1921. His autobiography, published in 1907, is titled, in part, *The Life and Adventures of Nat Love Better Known in the Cattle Country as "Deadwood Dick" by Himself.* There was no relationship between the serial and Love's book, or, for that matter, none between the Wheeler dime novels and the serial.

## V. NOVELS AND OTHER LONGER WORKS

As noted above, many magazine characters, such as Tarzan and Fu Manchu, who are thought of today as characters from novels, actually debuted in the pulps or other periodicals. In addition, the studios based some serials on more traditional novels, including such famous works as *The Last of the Mohicans* and *The Three Musketeers*. Here is a review of serials based upon novels. While some of the following works actually appeared first in magazines, these works are discussed here because the credits of the serial specifically referred to the books.

## The Lightning Express (Universal)

The credits to this early talking serial stated that movie was suggested by the story, "Whispering Smith Rides" by Frank H. Spearman. Spearman was born in 1859 in Buffalo, New York and died in Hollywood, California in 1937. During his lifetime, Spearman was a traveling salesman, bank cashier and bank president. It was in the latter capacity that he became familiar with the economics of railroads. Spearman's most famous novels, many of which were set in the west, were about the railroad. The novel *Whispering Smith* was written in 1906 and became a best seller.

*Whispering Smith* was about a railroad detective who was fighting a gang of renegade employees who were wrecking and robbing trains. Universal filmed the book as a silent serial of the same name in 1926 and then produced a serial sequel the next year, titled *Whispering Smith Rides*. In addition, there were silent and sound feature films based upon the character of Whispering Smith. The serial, *The Lightning Express*, was inspired by the original book, as it involved a railroad, sabotage and a hero named Whispering Smith. However, there was no novel called *Whispering Smith Rides* and the reference was probably to Spearman's story for the 1927 silent serial with that title.

## The Indians Are Coming and.
## Battling With Buffalo Bill (Universal)

Both of these Universal serials gave credit to the story "The Great West That Was" by William F. "Buffalo Bill" Cody. Actually, the work was not exactly a story but was an autobiography of Buffalo Bill, although it was unlikely that Bill actually wrote the book. The autobiography was first published in *Hearst's International Magazine*, from August, 1916 through July, 1917, under the title, "The Great West That Was, Buffalo Bill's Life Story." The work was then published in book form, after Cody's death, in 1920, entitled *An Autobiography of Buffalo Bill.*

The title of the magazine article and the reference in the serial credits was to a portion of the text near the end of the book that read, "I have now come to the end of my story. It is a story of The Great West that was, a West that is gone forever." These were the only serials that were based upon a non-fiction work, assuming that Buffalo Bill did not exaggerate or embellish his life story in the book, which was a distinct possibility.

Universal made a substantial use of the Buffalo Bill name in its early western serials, first in two silent serials about Buffalo Bill, *In the Days of Buffalo Bill* (1922) and *Fighting with Buffalo Bill* (1926). The first all talking serial from Universal, *The Indians Are Coming* (1930) listed the Cody work as its source but since the serial had nothing to do with Buffalo Bill, there was likely little connection between the book and the serial.

The other sound serial that listed Cody's autobiography as its source was *Battling with Buffalo Bill* (1931). At least this serial involved Buffalo Bill, played by Tom Tyler. However, the serial had a typical serial plot concerning a villain after gold and the hero's efforts to protect the towns-people. Once again, the story was unrelated to Buffalo Bill's life.

## The Last of the Mohicans (Mascot)

*The Last of the Mohicans*, by James Fenimore Cooper, was probably the most famous novel to become the source for a sound movie serial with the exception, perhaps, of *The Three Musketeers*, by Alexander Dumas. In addition to the novelists being contemporaries and each book being the source for serials and other movies, the two novels have something else in common—no one reads them anymore. However, that was not the case when *The Last of the Mohicans* was first published in 1826. Cooper was one of the first popular American novelists of his time and his books sold well in both the United States and England.

The novel was set during the French and Indian War of the 1750s. It involved a French attack on Fort William Henry, a British outpost commanded by Captain Munro, the journey of Munro's daughters to reach the safety of the Fort, their interaction with different Native Americans such as the treacherous Magua, and an American scout known as Hawkeye.

The 1932 serial was generally based on the novel, with all of the main characters retained. The hero was Hawkeye, played by Harry Carey, and one villain was the treacherous Native American, Magua, played by Bob Kortman. A number of events from the novel were incorporated into the serial, such as Magua's antipathy toward Captain Monroe (Munro in the novel) as a result of a perceived past injustice, a slaughter of British forces when they withdrew from their fort and Magua's love interest in Cora Monroe. However, large sections of the plot of the serial were original to the serial.

## The Jungle Mystery (Universal)

This 1932 serial was based on *The Ivory Trail* by Talbot Mundy. Mundy was a British-born writer of adventure stories during the early twentieth century. He obtained much of his material during his world travels. His most famous book was *King of the Khyber Rifles*, which was set in India under British occupation.

In 1919, Mundy serialized *On the Trail of Tippoo Tib*, a novel about treasure hunting and ivory poaching in East Africa. It was published in book form as *The Ivory Trail* in that same year and subsequently reprinted under the name *Trek East*. In the novel, four westerners were on the trail of hidden ivory of Tippoo Tib, worth a veritable fortune if it could be located. They were in a contest with, and blocked in their efforts by, particularly vicious German conquerors of East Africa, a Greek named Coutlass who sometimes sided with them but often undercut their activities and a particularly evil and two-faced woman, Lady Saffren Waldon. After many twists and turns, including an exciting escape by sea from the German authorities, they finally located the ivory,

The serial retained much of the basic plot from the original novel, although the heroes, reduced in number to two, were changed from British to American and some of the villains changed from German to Russian. In serial tradition, the film added a subplot of searching in the jungle for the missing brother of Barbara Morgan, giving the film a female romantic lead which was missing from the book. There was another new character in the serial, but this was a jungle ape named Zungu who helped the heroes from time to time. *The Jungle Mystery* is a lost serial so it is difficult to compare the chapter play to the book. Suffice it to say, while the basic plot outline of the two works appears to be the same, most of the specific incidents in the serial appear to be original to the movie version of the story.

Interestingly, Mundy was one of the writers of the *Jack Armstrong* radio show, having those duties from 1936 to 1940. During that period, he used *The Ivory Trail* as the basis for one of Jack Armstrong's adventures.

**The Last Frontier (RKO)**

The credits to this serial simply stated that the story was by Courtney Ryley Cooper. However, the advertising for the serial used language such as: "Courtney Ryley Cooper's red-blooded drama of fighting men and fighting days."

Courtney Ryley Cooper was born in Kansas, Missouri in 1886. At the age of 16, he ran away from home to become a clown in a small circus. He continued to work in the circus for some time, both as a performer, sign painter, press agent and general manager. He eventually became a newspaper reporter for a number of different newspapers. Although forgotten today, during his life Cooper was most famous for his works about the circus and about crime. He also wrote a number of western novels and short stories, including *The Last Frontier*, a novel which was published in 1923. Cooper committed suicide in 1940.

In fact, the 1932 serial bears little resemblance to the 1923 novel. In the book, Tom Kirby had convinced Beth Halliday and her parents to relocate to Kansas, with the expectation that Beth would then marry Tom. However, the Hallidays' wagon train was attacked by Indians on its way to Kansas and Beth's parents were killed. Beth was then all alone in Kansas, and she had no choice but to move into the house of an apparently pious man, Lige Morris. She refused to talk to Tom Kirby ever again and started spending time with a man named Maitland. The plot of the story involved bringing the railroad westward, difficulties with the Indians and Kirby's eventually rapprochement with Beth. In the end, Morris turned out to be a true villain, including being involved with smuggling guns to Indians.

The serial used some of the same character names from the novel and it involved gun smuggling to the Indians. However, almost every incident in the serial was original to the film and the character of the masked hero, The Black Ghost, was entirely a creation for the serial. The filmmakers were simply trading on the name of Courtney Ryley Cooper when citing his work as the source for the chapter play.

## The Three Musketeers (Mascot)

The credits to this 1933 serial indicated that it was a "modern version of the story by Alexander Dumas." The Dumas novel of the same name was first published in a French magazine in 1844. It told the tale of D'Artagnan, a young man, who wanted to join the Musketeers but almost immediately, offended the three musketeers of the title, whose names were Porthos, Aramis, and Athos. However, when the four were attacked and D'Artagnan showed his courage in battle, the four became fast friends. Thereafter, they had adventures in both France and England which often involved historical figures.

The serial concerned a struggle by an American, Tom Wayne, to defeat a gun runner, El Shaitan, who was operating in the Sahara Desert. In the first chapter, Wayne saved the lives of three soldiers from the French Foreign Legion, who referred to themselves as the Three Musketeers. They all became good friends and the Musketeers dubbed Wayne their D'Artagnan.

As in the novel, the story revolved around the Wayne/D'Artagnan character, with the Three Musketeers having subsidiary roles (but for some reason, higher billing). This story took nothing from the original novel, except perhaps, the bravery and camaraderie of the four heroes.

## The Red Rider (Universal)

W. C. Tuttle was a prolific writer of western novels and short stories. He was known as the "world's champion thrill and action writer," at least in the trailer to *The Red Rider*, if nowhere else. Tuttle was born in the Montana Territory in 1883. His father was a lawman who told him many of the tales which were eventually incorporated into Tuttle's western stories. A number of movies were based on Tuttle's novels and stories, starting in the silent era and continuing well into the talking era.

*The Red Rider* (1934) was based on Tuttle's novel, *The Red Head from Sun Dog*, published in 1930. The book featured one of Tuttle's series characters, Brick Davidson. The Davidson character was carried over to the serial, but his name was changed to Red Davidson. He was played by Buck Jones. Even though the serial was shot in black and white and Buck Jones was not a red head in real life, Davidson was referred to in the serial as "The Redhead."

The plot of the novel and most of the incidents from the book were used in the serial. Thus, in the opening pages of the story, Silent Slade was convicted of the murder of Scotty McKee and condemned to death. Slade's girlfriend was the daughter of McKee and Slade's best friend was the sheriff of Sun Dog, Brick Davidson, who let Slade escape from jail before he could be executed. Davidson then quit his job and set out to find the real murderer of Scotty McKee.

The main plot of the novel involved the smuggling of diamonds near the Mexican border, with the disappearance of valuable gems after the killing of Del Harper, the ranch foreman of Bob Maxwell. Del was the man who was carrying the stones across the border. Brick took a job at Maxwell's ranch, eventually located the diamonds and cleared Slade's name. Large and small incidents from the book appeared in the serial, such as Brick winning a valuable horse and saddle in a card game, ranch hand Johnny being in love with Maxwell's daughter, McKee's daughter arriving at the ranch and eventually reuniting with Slade, and the surprise location of the missing diamonds.

In addition to novels, Tuttle wrote short stories, many of which were published in western pulp magazines. He died in 1961.

**The Amazing Exploits of the Clutching Hand (Independent)**

Arthur B. Reeve, who wrote mystery short stories and novels as well as the screenplays for several silent serials, was most famous for the series of detective novels and short stories that he penned about Craig Kennedy, a detective who was also a professor of chemistry at Columbia University. As was usual in detective fiction of the day, the stories were narrated by a Dr. Watson-like character, Walter Jameson, Kennedy's roommate and a newspaper reporter. In all, there were 26 novels and short story collections in the series, published from 1912 to 1936. They are noted for being some of the first mystery novels to combine science with detective work, and Kennedy was sometimes referred to as "The Scientific Detective" or the "American Sherlock Holmes." In their day, the Kennedy books were very popular, both in America and England.

Craig Kennedy was an important figure in movie serials. He made his first appearance in *The Exploits of Elaine* (1915), which, although it starred Pearl White as Elaine, was really about Craig Kennedy's battle with the evil Clutching Hand, who was trying to steal Elaine's inheritance. That serial was followed by two more in which Elaine and Kennedy appeared: *The New Exploits of Elaine* (1915) and *The Romance of Elaine* (1916). These were inspired by Reeve's three books on Kennedy and Elaine, *The Exploits of Elaine* (1915), *The Romance of Elaine* (1916) and *The Triumph of Elaine* (1916).

Kennedy also appeared in two other silent serials. He was the main detective in *The Carter Case* (1919) and a subsidiary character in *The Radio Detective* (1926). Kennedy was also the lead detective in a feature film, *Unmasked* (1929). Kennedy's only appearance in talking serials was in *The Amazing Exploits of the Clutching Hand*, a 1936 serial released by Stage and Screen.

This serial featured Jack Mulhall as Craig Kennedy and Rex Lease as Walter Jameson. They were employed by Gordon Gaunt of the United States Justice Department to investigate the disappearance of Dr. Gironda and his formula for producing synthetic gold. Their opponent was their arch enemy, the evil Clutching Hand, a shadowy figure who had a slew of henchmen at his beck and call. The serial was based, in part, on a novel Reeve wrote about Kennedy titled *The Clutching Hand* which was published in 1934.

While the novel was a detective story, to a degree, it reads more like an old-fashioned melodrama, more similar to the *Fu Manchu* novels of Sax Rohmer than a traditional whodunit. The basic plot of the novel and the serial are the same, as in the novel Kennedy was called in to investigate the death of Dr. Gironda and his missing formula for synthetic gold and a mystery ray useful in the development of television but which could also be employed to render all electricity useless. Many of the same characters appeared in both works and The Clutching Hand was the villain in each medium. However, the events in the serial were considerably different than those in the novel and the two works are substantially dissimilar. In fact, the Clutching Hand in the serial was identified as a surprise character from the story while in the novel, the Clutching Hand remained a criminal mastermind.

There was also a short-lived television show about Kennedy, entitled *Craig Kennedy, Criminologist*, which ran in syndication in the 1952-1953 television season, for 26 episodes. It starred Donald Woods (*Sky Raiders*) as Craig Kennedy and Lewis Wilson (*Batman*) as Walt Jameson.

## The Mysterious Pilot (Columbia)

The credits to this serial indicated that the source material was the novel, *The Silver Hawk*, by William B. Mowery. Mowery was born in Ohio in 1899 and died in 1957. In addition to being a professor of English at New York University, Mowery wrote many novels and short stories, a number of which were about Canada and the Canadian Mounties. Indeed, the serial, *The Mysterious Pilot*, was set in Canada and the heroes were Mounties although in this case, there was an emphasis on flying pontoon planes which could land on Canadian lakes.

The hero of the serial, Jim Dorn, was played by Frank Hawks, in only his second appearance in films. Frank Hawks was a familiar name to filmgoers of the era. He was a famous aviator who set many transcontinental and city-to-city speed records. Indeed, the advertising for the serial identified Captain Frank Hawks as the fastest man alive. This was the only serial in which Hawks performed, as he was killed in a plane crash the year after the serial was completed.

## Wild West Days

There were some excellent novelists, like James M. Cain, who are now best known for the movies which were based on their books rather than on the books themselves. Another example of this is W.R. Burnett, who specialized in books about crime, corruption and gangsters, usually in the big city. While his novels are seldom read today, some of the mov-

*Wild West Days* (1937). This serial was based on a work by W.R. Burnett, better known then and today for his crime novels. Pictured from left to right are Robert McClung, George Shelley and Johnny Mack Brown.

ies based on his novels are classics. Who can forget *Little Caesar* (1931), starring Edward G. Robinson, *High Sierra* (1941), starring Humphrey Bogart, and *The Asphalt Jungle* (1950), starring Sterling Hayden?

Less well-known are the western stories written by Burnett. During a three week stay in Tombstone, Arizona, in the early 1930s, Burnett met people who could describe the Old West to him through personal experience. Tombstone was also the site of the gunfight at the OK Corral. This led to Burnett writing *Saint Johnson*, published in 1930, his most famous western work. The book was about a former lawman, Frame Johnson, who, with three of his friends, arrived in Tombstone to bring law and order to the wild frontier town. The story included a fictionalized account of the gunfight at the OK Corral. Universal based several movies on the book, including its 1937 serial, *Wild West Days.*

Only the beginning of the serial incorporated elements of the book, as retired lawman Kentucky Wade and three friends came to the town of Brimstone, to help a friend keep control of his mine. There was no Saint

Johnson in the story as John Mack Brown played the hero, Kentucky Wade. Interestingly, when Universal next filmed Burnett's novel, as *Law and Order* (1940), John(ny) Mack Brown still had the lead, this time playing a character named Bill Ralston. In the 1953 version, also titled *Law and Order*, Ronald Reagan had the role of the hero, finally using the name from the novel, Frame Johnson.

### Hawk of the Wilderness (Republic)

There is no mystery about the source of this serial. The credits proudly announced on a separate frame, "Based on the novel of the same name by William L. Chester." Also, there was a picture of the book behind the writing. The novel, *Hawk of the Wilderness*, was part of a four book series which was originally serialized in *Blue Book Magazine* in 1935. The other books in the series were *Kioga of the Wilderness*, serialized in 1936, *One Against a Wilderness*, serialized in 1937, and *Kioga of the Unknown Land*, serialized in 1938. *Hawk* was first published in book form in 1936, but the others were apparently not so published until the 1970s.

*Hawk of the Wilderness* (1938). Kioga, played by Herman Brix, is about to be burned at the stake by some natives, whose leader is Yellow Weasel, played by Monte Blue.

These stories were clearly influenced by the *Tarzan* novels. The hero was Kioga, the child of Dr. Lincoln Rand and his wife, Helena. The Rands and their Indian friend Mokuyi were shipwrecked on the island of Nato-wa above the Arctic Circle. Despite the location, the island had a temperate jungle setting, caused by warm ocean currents, hot thermal springs and volcanic pools. The island was inhabited by warlike Indians who were cut off from the outside world. Early in the novel, the Rands had a son they named Kioga. After his parents were killed, Kioga was raised by Mokuyi and Mokuyi's wife as part of the Shoni tribe. When Mokuyi and his wife were eventually killed, Kioga essentially raised himself among the jungle animals.

Kioga's white skin earned him the nickname, "Snow Hawk," which explained the title of the book. Much like Tarzan, Kioga developed a rapport with the animals of the jungle, having been partially raised by bears when he fled the Shoni tribe at a young age. However, unlike Tarzan, he invented a whip and grapple hook to aid his climbing and swinging.

The serial was clearly inspired by the book. In the first chapter, the Rands, along with their baby Lincoln and their servant Mokuyi, were caught in a storm on a ship and the Rands were thrown overboard. Mokuyi and the baby survived and landed on an island. Mokuyi then raised the Rands' son on a jungle island. As the serial moved to present times, the son, now known as Kioga, had grown up and become a Tarzan-like figure. Just as in the novel. Kioga could swing from tree to tree with his ropes and grapples. He was also in perpetual battle with some of the native Indians on the island. The leader of those Indians was Yellow Weasel, also a character from the novel.

The true plot of the serial, involving a bottle with a message thrown into the water by Dr. Rand before dying, a band of thieves on the island, and the hunt for a treasure was not based on the original book by Chester. There were some interesting carryovers from the book, though, such as appearance of a minor Indian character from the book, Kias the Lame, use of some of the other character names and Kioga's discovery of a chest of valuables from an old shipwreck buried in the sand. However, most of the first half of the book involved Kioga's growth to manhood in the jungle and his ascension to power as the leader of the Shonis, events not shown in the serial.

In the last third of the book, a new shipwreck brought some westerners onto the island, including Beth LaSalle, with whom Kioga fell in love. At this point, the action in the book has some relation to the events in the serial, with the character of Beth Munro in the serial somewhat inspired by the character of Beth LaSalle from the book. The serial ended with Kioga leaving the island with the surviving westerners. A similar event occurred near the end of the novel.

## The Green Archer (Columbia)

Edgar Wallace was born in England on April 1, 1875 and died at the age of 57 in Hollywood on February 10, 1932. He was a prolific British crime writer, journalist and playwright, who wrote over 170 novels, and many plays, short stories and articles in newspapers and journals. In the 1920s, one of Wallace's publishers claimed that a quarter of all books read in England, exclusive of Bibles and textbooks, were written by Wallace.

Over 150 films have been made of his novels, more than any other author. One was the silent serial, *The Green Archer*, which was a 10 chapter serial issued by Pathé in 1925. The remake was a 15 chapter serial released by Columbia in 1940. Both serials were based upon Wallace's 1924 novel of the same name.

The book was about the search by Valerie Howett for her birth mother. She believed that the person who may have killed her was Abel Bellamy, who was living in a Gothic castle in England named Garre Castle. Valerie moved to an adjoining house with her stepfather to try to learn the secret of Garre Castle. She was aided by Spike Holland, a newspaper reporter and, more importantly, by Jim Featherstone, a police detective, who fell in love with Valerie. Garre Castle was filled with eerie hallways, dungeon rooms and a ghost-like figure known as The Green Archer, whose very real arrows killed at least three people during the course of the book.

The sound serial had plot elements similar to the book, although much of the plot was original to the movie. In the serial, Michael Bellamy inherited Garre Castle but his brother Abel, the leader of a gang of jewel thieves, framed him on burglary charges. Michael was then killed in a train crash on the way to prison. Abel moved into the castle and when Michael's wife Elaine appeared, Bellamy had her imprisoned in the castle dungeon. Elaine's sister, Valerie Howett, and her father moved to an adjoining property in an attempt to investigate their suspicions about the castle. They were assisted by Spike Holland, who was now an insurance investigator. The Jim Featherstone character was missing from the serial.

*The Green Archer* (1940). Victor Jory, as Spike Holland, assists Iris Meredith, as Valerie Howett, in investigating the evildoings at Garr Castle. Note the shadow of the Green Archer in the background.

Garre Castle was filled with eerie hallways, dungeon rooms and many death traps which were appropriate for cliffhanger endings. The Castle was haunted by two mysterious green archers, one who could be real and the other who was one of Bellamy's henchmen, posing as the mysterious figure.

### Jungle Girl (Republic)

This is a difficult one, as this serial was not really based on any novel, despite the fact that the credits specifically stated, "Based on the famous novel by Edgar Rice Burroughs." The novel was apparently *Jungle Girl*, a conclusion based mainly on the name of the serial. If that book were really famous in 1941, when the serial was released, it is surely forgotten today.

Much like *Tarzan of the Apes*, the first printing of *Jungle Girl* was in a magazine. It was serialized in five parts in *Blue Book Magazine* in 1931 under the title, "The Land of Hidden Men." It was first published in book form in 1932. It was the story of Dr. Gordon King, who explored the jungles of Cambodia and discovered a lost civilization. The jungle girl that he did meet was named Fou-Tan. King eventually rescued Fou-Tan from a forced marriage to a Leper King.

The serial, *Jungle Girl*, had no relationship to that story. The jungle girl was named Nyoka Meredith and the story took place in the African jungle. The story involved a dispute over tribal diamonds. Nyoka was a female Tarzan-like character, with a rapport with the jungle animals.

The alleged serial sequel was *Perils of Nyoka* (1942). It was presumably also based on *Jungle Girl* because the female lead in this serial was also named Nyoka. Once again, however, there was no relationship between that se-

*Jungle Girl* (1941). Frances Gifford plays the title character, Nyoka Meredith. This was Gifford's only serial.

rial and the Burroughs' book. The setting appeared to be in the Middle East. The parties were in search of the Golden Tablets of Hippocrates, which contained the only known cure for cancer.

Both of the Nyoka serials traded on Burroughs' name to draw in viewers without incorporating the plots or concepts of any of his original works. Neither of these serials had a source in novels; they were both original works. However, after the release of the serials, the Nyoka character did become a regular in comic books, once in the 1940s and once again in the 1950s.

**Haunted Harbor (Republic)**

The credits to this serial listed the source material as the novel by Dayle Douglas. Douglas was the pseudonym for film writer Ewart Adamson. Adamson wrote over 145 movie shorts and also contributed stories and screenplays for features at several studios. His first film work was in the silent era.

Adamson was born in Scotland in 1881 and went to the sea as a teenager. As an adult, he spent five years managing a tin mine. *Haunted Harbor* was published in 1943 and the serial followed the next year. Adamson's early experiences came in handy for the parts of the story about boats, the sea and a gold mine.

The main plot of the serial was based substantially on the book. Thus, in the novel, Captain Jim Marsden was falsely convicted of the murder of the banker, Voorhees, and sentenced to death. With the help of some of his friends, Marsden escaped from jail and headed to the island of Pulau Mati, in search of a man named Lawson who was probably the real killer. Along the way, Marsden rescued Lispeth Harding and her father from a boat trapped in a major storm. Once on the island, Marsden met Kane, the owner of a local mine, who turned out not to be Lawson but who was a major villain in his own right. It later turned out that Marsden's servant Olivia was secretly working for Kane. The natives were frightened by several sea monsters in one of the harbors, giving the area the name "Haunted Harbor." At one point, Marsden went out to sea to challenge the monsters. All of those incidents were very similar to incidents in the chapter play.

In many other ways, the novel and the serial differed. For example, the novel emphasized the growing relationship between Lispeth and Marsden, something missing from the serial. Obviously, the serial created many new events which could lead to cliffhangers and their resolutions, something that was not needed for the book. Toward the end of the novel and the serial, however, the plots converged once again, with the sea monsters being electrically controlled from a hut on the island by Kane's men, to guard against anyone discovering a sunken boat containing a hoard of gold.

For serial fans, there was an interesting moment at the end of the book, when Marsden's men attacked and then killed or wounded several of Kane's men. When Lispeth suggested that the violence was not necessary and that Kane's men could have been taken prisoner, Marsden replied that that was all right in story books, but he never said "Stick 'em up!" or "Drop that gun!" when he was up against murderers. Marsden said, "That's fine when the story teller wants the assassins to escape so that the chapter ends with, 'To be Continued.'"

Despite this obvious rebuke to Republic Pictures by the lead character in the novel, Dayle Douglas and Republic got together and Republic released the serial version of the book in the year after it was published. Even though he had substantial screen writing experience, Douglas did not contribute to the screenplay of the serial.

## Mysterious Island (Columbia)

This was the second serial inspired by a French novel, the first being *The Three Musketeers*. The author of the novel, *The Mysterious Island (L'ile Mysterieuse)*, was Jules Verne, who was well-known to American audiences for his science fiction works, such as *Journey to the Center of the Earth* and *From the Earth to the Moon*, and his adventure novels, such as *Around the World in Eighty Days*. Published in 1874, *The Mysterious Island* was, in part, a sequel to another famous Verne novel, *Twenty Thousand Leagues under the Sea*.

The novel was set during the American Civil War, when five Northern prisoners, along with a dog, escaped captivity in Richmond, Virginia by stealing a hot air balloon from the Confederacy. Once in the air, however, the fugitives encountered hurricane winds and the balloon drifted far across the Pacific Ocean, eventually crash landing on an unknown island in the Pacific. The first half of the book detailed the castaways' efforts in turning the island (which they named Lincoln Island) into their home, including building quarters in a cave in a granite hill, making their own tools and weapons, cultivating the ground, collecting sheep and other farm animals and even building a small boat. They also discovered a man named Aryton on a nearby island, who was left there by himself many years before as punishment for his piratical activities. When the castaways first met Aryton, he was a slightly demented wild man but over the course of the story, he returned to his more civilized nature.

Throughout the novel, there was a mystery as to what unknown person or force was assisting the castaways in times of crisis. For example, as the hot air balloon was first about to land on the island, the leader, Cyrus Smith (Harding in some translations), was swept overboard and apparently lost. His body was later discovered on shore but it was not clear how he got there. At another time, pirates invaded the island but just when events started to go badly for the castaways, the pirates' ship was blown up by a mine, which was not placed in the harbor by any of the castaways. Late in the novel, the castaways finally came to learn that Captain Nemo, with his famous submarine, the Nautilus, was on the island and that he was their mysterious benefactor. At the end of the story, the island was destroyed by a volcanic eruption.

The beginning of the serial came from the novel as during the Civil War, five prisoners and a dog took off in a balloon and after being swept away by hurricane winds, landed on a strange, uncharted island. There, just as in the novel, the castaways eventually met Ayrton who was a former pirate who had been living in the wild, they had to deal with pirates who attempted to take over the island, and Captain Nemo helped the castaways several times, such as rescuing Captain Harding when he jumped out of the hot air balloon as the castaways first reached the island. The serial, however, introduced a new science fiction element, with visitors from Mercury on the island who were hoping to find radioactive material as part of a plan to destroy the Earth. Other new characters were some hostile natives known as the Volcano People. At the end of the serial, the island was destroyed by the volcano, but this time the volcanic eruptions were started in some way by those outer space visitors. Thus, the serial did take many elements from the novel but freely adapted them into an inventive premise, but ultimately, into a typical serial plot.

Verne's novels were turned into many well-known movies, including several versions of *Mysterious Island*. The most famous version was the 1961 feature, noted for the special effects created by the legendary Ray Harryhausen.

## VI. SHORT STORIES AND MISCELLANEOUS SOURCES

### The Lost Special (Universal)

Although Arthur Conan Doyle is obviously most famous for the Sherlock Holmes stories, he also wrote a number of short stories which were not part of the Sherlock Holmes series. One such short story was "The Lost Special" (1908). This was an intriguing tale of a man who was in a rush to travel from Liverpool to London and then on to Paris, France. He had missed the regular train to London and therefore ordered a special, a train that would be specially run for him to take only the man and his companion to London. The two boarded the train but somewhere between Liverpool and London, the entire train disappeared.

The only remnants of that special train trip were the dead body of the train driver, found with a broken neck along the tracks. Later, a letter from a guard on the train sent from America to his wife in England also became a clue. Nevertheless, no one was able to determine what happened to the train and its two passengers, until a confession, eight years later, from the man who perpetrated the disappearance.

The 1932 serial started with a similar concept. A special train carrying a gold shipment disappeared without a trace. It turned out that robbers have forced the train off the main line by laying down portable tracks. They then hid the train in an abandoned mine shaft and took the gold. The villains then removed the portable track, creating a mystery as to the disappearance of the special train.

The opening chapter was clearly based upon the Conan Doyle short story, even though the short story had nothing to do with a gold shipment. The remainder of the serial involved the hunt for the gold shipment and the search for the villains who had engineered the theft.

## Heroes of the West, Gordon of Ghost City and Flaming Frontiers (Universal)

The two serials, *Heroes of the West* (1932) and *Flaming Frontiers* (1938) credited the story, "The Tie That Binds," by Peter B. Kyne, although the earlier serial stated that it was based on the serial, with the later serial saying the movie was only suggested by the story. The 1933 serial, *Gordon of Ghost City*, according to the credits, was suggested by a story by Peter B. Kyne. A number of Kyne's novels and short stories were made into films, including a 1923 silent film also based on "The Tie That Binds," these three serials and the John Wayne movie, *Three Godfathers* (1948). The story upon which *Gordon of Ghost City* was based was apparently "Oh Promise Me."

Kyne was a novelist and short story writer, who wrote about ranchers, loggers, businessmen and seamen. He was born in 1880 in San Francisco, California and died in 1957. He was originally a lumber company bookkeeper. During the middle decades of the 20th Century, Kyne was one of the most popular American writers. Many of his short stories originally appeared in *The Saturday Evening Post*.

## Other Short Stories

According to the credits, *The Roaring West* (1935) was based upon a magazine story by Edward Earle Repp. Repp, who lived from 1900 to 1979, was originally in advertising and newspaper reporting. He then turned to screenwriting, authoring scripts for a number of B-westerns. Repp also wrote western stories for pulp magazines. This serial was apparently based on one of those stories.

According to the credits, *The Great Adventures of Wild Bill Hickok* (1938) was based on a story by John Peere Miles. Miles wrote several western short stories for magazines such as *Blue Book* magazine, a popular magazine in print from 1905 to 1975, although under several different names. In 1931, he wrote a multi-issue story about Wild Bill Hickok for *Triple X Western*, also known as *Fawcett's Triple X Magazine*, a magazine with western stories which was published from 1924 to 1936. These stories were apparently the basis for the plot of this serial.

According to the credits, *Scouts to the Rescue* (1939) was based upon an original story written by Irving Crump of *Boy's Life* magazine. That makes sense since this serial involved the adventures of a group of Boy Scouts. *Boy's Life* magazine was first published in 1911 and soon became the official magazine of the Boy Scouts of America. Irving Crump wrote a number of stories for the magazine over the years.

According to the credits, *Overland Mail* (1942) was based on a story by Johnston McCulley. Of course, McCulley, who lived from 1883 to 1958, is most famous for creating the masked hero "Zorro," but McCulley was a prolific writer, authoring many stories and books, including a number of westerns. He also wrote original stories for the screen and it is believed that this serial was based on one of those original stories.

## Clancy of the Mounted (Universal)

A serial based upon a poem? That seems hard to believe. Yet, according to the credits, this 1933 serial was suggested by a poem by Robert W. Service. Robert William Service was born in Lancashire, England in 1874. In 1895, at the age of 21, Service moved to Canada, where he traveled west to Vancouver Island. He then worked for the Canadian Bank of Commerce in the Yukon. Here he became familiar with the Canadian West, the subject of many of the more than 1000 poems he wrote during his lifetime. His poems were collected in 45 volumes of poetry. His most

*Clancy of the Mounted* (1933). This is the only serial supposedly based upon a poem. Pictured is the stalwart title character, portrayed by Tom Tyler, in one of his seven starring serial roles.

famous western poem is probably "The Shooting of Dan McGrew" which was published in 1907.

The poem, "Clancy of the Mounted," was written in 1909. It was the tale of a Canadian Mountie, who, using his dog sled, rescued a man caught in a blizzard. The serial, on the other hand, was about a Canadian Mountie named Tom Clancy, who was trying to prove the innocence of his brother, who had been framed for murder. What the poem and the serial had in common was the heroism of Clancy of the Mounted.

## Adventures of Sir Galahad (Columbia)

The credits to this serial did not cite any source material for the chapter play. Nevertheless, the writing credit was phrased in an unusual manner, "Written for the screen by George H. Plympton, Lewis Clay, David Mathews." Most serials provided the writing credit as "Screenplay by" or "Written by." There was therefore an implication that the serial was based on other material, even though it may not have been mentioned in the credits.

One source of the legend of King Arthur and the Round Table was *Idylls of the King*, a cycle of 12 epic poems by Lord Alfred Tennyson published between 1856 and 1885. Tennyson's epic poem has its origins in the story of *King Arthur and the Knights of the Round Table*, written by Sir Thomas Malory in 1485. Malory himself had adapted the Arthur story from a variety of 12th-century French romances. In addition to Tennyson's famous work, there were many other literary renditions or variations on the story, including *A Connecticut Yankee in King Arthur's Court*, by Mark Twain, published in 1889.

Tennyson's 12 poems began with the coronation of Arthur, his ascension to the throne and his marriage to Lady Guinevere. They conclude with Arthur's death after he received a mortal wound in combat with the treacherous Mordred. In between, the reader met Merlin, the famous wizard with his magical powers, the brave Knights Sir Lancelot and Sir Galahad, and the Lady of the Lake who gave Arthur his famous sword, Excalibur. In some versions of the King Arthur story, Excalibur was stolen by Morgan le Fay, a powerful sorceress and foe of King Arthur.

The movie serial may or may not have been based on *Idylls of the King*. If it were, it would be the second serial based on a poem, albeit in this case, really 12 separate poems. More likely, the screenwriters took elements from many different versions of the Arthur legend and then created a serial plot on their own. Thus, at the beginning of the film, Sir Galahad was guarding Excalibur when it was stolen by agents of Ulric, the Saxon king who desired to invade Camelot. Throughout the serial, Galahad sought to recover the magical sword and prove his bona fides to King Arthur.

Also present in the serial were Merlin, who seemed to be allied with Ulric but then, maybe not, Sir Lancelot, a brave knight, Queen Guinevere, wife of King Arthur, Modred, a traitor in King Arthur's Court and even the Lady in the Lake, who assisted Sir Galahad from time to time. Also present was the sorceress Morgan La Fay in an ambiguous role. While the serial was surely not an accurate retelling of the Arthur legend, it at least respected its origins with this tale about jousting, sword fights, magic, Excalibur and heroic knights, along with employing many familiar characters from the stories about the Knights of the Round Table.

**Captain Video (Columbia)**

A serial based on a television show? That is even harder to believe than a serial based upon a poem. Yet, in 1951, when television was well on its path to making serials extinct, Columbia Pictures did just that. The television show was *Captain Video and His Video Rangers*, which ran on the Dumont Network from 1949 to 1955.

*Captain Video* was a very popular children's program from the early days of television. Done live, it was the first science fiction show on television. It was set hundreds of years into the future. The title character was a master of science who invented a number of devices helpful to mankind such as the opticon scillometer, which allowed the Captain to see through walls at a long distance, the atomic rifle which could destroy anything in sight, and the electronic strait jacket, which

*Captain Video* (1951). This is the only serial based on a television program. Pictured are Judd Holdren and Larry Stewart as Captain Video and Ranger, respectively.

placed opponents in invisible restraints. Captain Video fought inter-planetary foes, such as Nargola, Mook, and the Moon Men. The Captain's most persistent adversary over the years was Dr. Pauli, a great inventor in his own right.

Captain Video was originally played by Richard Coogan, but Al Hodge took over the role in late 1950. Hodge was the radio voice for the Green Hornet, and he also supplied the voice for the serial Green Hornet once Britt Reid donned his mask. The Captain's assistant was The Ranger, who was much younger than Captain Video and closer in age to his young viewers. The show also featured the first television robot, named Tobor.

In retrospect, the idea to base a movie serial on a television show was forward thinking. The serial, *Captain Video, Master of the Strato-sphere* (1951), was the first movie based upon a television show. Other movies based on 1950s television shows were *Dragnet* (1954) and *The Lone Ranger* (1956). The practice has gone on continuously since that time, up until today, with recent examples being *Mission: Impossible* (1996), *Charlie's Angels* (2000) and *Get Smart* (2008).

For the 1950s movies based on television shows, the movies were a huge step-up in budget from their television counterparts. For example, *Dragnet* was no longer set indoors and the movie actually had some ac-tion, in contrast with the all talking television episodes. *The Lone Ranger* movie was shot on new and varied locations, and, unlike most of the television shows, was not based on old radio scripts. Similarly, the *Cap-tain Video* serial carried an increased budget, but only because the live television show was done so cheaply. The television series was reputed to have had an original prop budget of only $25 per week. Even though the serial obviously had a larger budget, the serial still seemed to be low budget, with cardboard sets and weak special effects. One unique aspect of the production was that the scenes on the planet Atoma were tinted in color. Even with the tinting, this serial paled in comparison to *Flash Gordon* and even *The Phantom Empire*, which were completed 15 years before *Captain Video*.

The plot of the serial did not come from the television series, al-though it probably had a similarity to some of the many plots used in the series. Judd Holdren played Captain Video and Larry Stewart played the Ranger. Dr. Pauli was not present, although he is mentioned several times in the serial, probably to the delight of fans of the television program.

The main villain was Vultura, who, not unexpectedly, was interested in conquering the Earth. Vultura was assisted by Dr. Tobor, who was not the robot from the television series but was an evil scientist in his own right. The serial surely captured the spirit of the television series but both seem dated in today's world of sophisticated science fiction television and movies.

# Chapter 3
# The Structure of a Serial

## I. CHAPTER INTRODUCTIONS

Each serial chapter after the opening chapter began with a recap of the events of the prior week's episode, both as a reminder of the storyline for the person who saw the episode and also as a concise summary of the plot for someone who was new to the serial or missed the last chapter. Every serial chapter then picked up the action with film from the prior week's episode. However, each studio had a different approach in recapping the prior episode's action.

### Mascot

In the early Mascot serials, from *The Lone Defender* (1930) through *The Devil Horse* in 1932, the chapter opening was a detailed narration of the prior episodes of the serial, with clips from those prior episodes. The narrator even made an appearance on-screen in *The Lone Defender* (1930). The Mascot narration was more detailed, less hysterical and therefore more helpful than the narrated introductions of the later Columbia serials. The clips that were used often showed scenes from multiple episodes, which could be very helpful in following Mascot's convoluted plots.

After *The Devil Horse*, the chapter recaps of all Mascot serials used drawings of several of the serial characters, with a short description of the character or the action of the story written below. One difference from the later Republic serial introductions was that in some of the Mascots, such as *The Three Musketeers*, the description of the picture was extended by the use of a rolling text, permitting a more detailed plot recap than could have been contained in just a few words of text.

**Republic**

When Republic Studios was formed by the merger of Mascot with other independents, the use of a picture with a character or plot description was carried over into the chapter introductions. This approach continued through all of the Republic serials from the 1930s into the 1950s. An example of a character description from *Dick Tracy* for the villain is:

> THE LAME ONE – brains of the Spider Ring
> declares war against the G-Men.

The drawings were fabulous, being an accurate rendering of the actor playing the role. Oftentimes, the drawings actually looked like photographs and, indeed, may have been photographs made to look like drawings. The last drawing in the sequence was almost always that of the hero, leading to the footage of the prior episode's cliffhanger. For example, in *Zorro's Black Whip*, a caption for The Black Whip in one chapter was:

*Dick Tracy vs. Crime, Inc* (1941). This is a typical Republic introduction frame, with a drawing of the star, some interesting background, and then a terse recap of the action.

> The Black Whip races to overtake the stolen wagon
> and rescue Vic Gordon from Hammond's men.

This was an excellent technique for Republic. In just a few short frames, the viewer was re-acquainted with the action and could also put a face on a character, once the film resumed.

In the introductions to the earlier Republic serials, it seemed as if a drawing of every possible character in the serial was used. In *The Painted Stallion*, for example, there were as many as eight pictures used at the beginning of each chapter. Often, Oscar and Elmer, the "comic" relief, had a frame together even though they contributed little to the plot and less to the previous cliffhanger. There was also a joint frame of Davy Crockett and Jim Bowie, which was used beginning with Chapter Two, even though Davy Crockett did not appear in the serial until Chapter Five. Similarly, *Dick Tracy* used the same seven drawings at the beginning of each chapter of that serial.

These lengthy introductions sometimes slowed down the beginning of a chapter. It seemed that once Republic put the effort into making a drawing of a character, it did not want to waste the drawing and therefore used it over and over again. As time went on, however, Republic tended to move towards shorter openings. This can be seen in the evolution of the *Zorro* serials.

*Zorro Rides Again* (1937) generally used about six frames for each chapter opening. By the time of *Zorro's Fighting Legion* (1939) generally only about four frames was used, although they were drawings of a variety of characters throughout the length of the serial. In *Zorro's Black Whip* (1944) generally only one frame was used. Throughout the serial, there were only three different drawings shown.

By the mid-1940s, Republic's serials almost always used only one frame to introduce the serial chapter, with very few different drawings used throughout the serial. By that time, Republic serial chapters were shorter and the studio may have been cutting costs by using only one frame at the beginning of the chapter. At that point, since only one drawing was being used, more information than just a description of the character was inserted in the frame. Here is an example from *G-Men Never Forget* (1948):

> Ted learns of Murkland's plan to sabotage Cook's ship, and
> races to warn the workmen.

If this were an earlier Republic serial, this frame would have been divided into three parts, i.e., one for Ted, one for Murkland and one for Cook.

From time to time, Republic, even though it only used one frame for the introduction, used two drawings in the frame. Thus, in the introduction to Chapter Four of *Perils of Nyoka*, a double drawing of Kay Aldridge and Clayton Moore was shown, with the following caption:

NYOKA AND LARRY – Are trapped by Cassib in the
Tunnel of Bubbling Death

This one frame approach for recapping the action from the prior episode did move the serial faster into the action but at the cost of limiting the extent of the recap of the serial's plot. Often, the serial characters themselves had to recap some of the important plot points of the serial, during the chapter, by talking among themselves.

**Columbia Serials**

Most people associate the beginning of Columbia serial chapters with a narrator and scenes from the prior week's episode. Surprisingly, that was not always the case. For example, some serials simply had a written introduction, with the screen rolling through the language. *Deadwood Dick* was an example of this. *Terry and the Pirates* and *The Shadow* were similar but in those serials, the first several paragraphs of the text were identical in each episode. Only the last paragraph was different, being more specific to the events of the prior episode. Indeed, if the viewer looked closely, the viewer could see the line where the new paragraph was spliced onto the prior text.

Most Columbia serials did have a narrator but not necessarily over scenes from the prior week's episode. *Holt of the Secret Service* and *Captain Midnight* had the narrator reading one screen of text.

*Jack Armstrong*, *The Phantom*, *Batman and Robin* and the *Superman* serials were examples of narration over scenes from the last episode. This was effective in re-introducing the viewer to the characters and plot of the serial, although unlike the long text introductions, the plot recap tended to be limited to the prior week's action.

*Mandrake, the Magician*, *Flying G-Men* and *The Spider's Web* had a variation on this. The narrator talked over some scenes from the prior chapter, then the action continued without narration, and then there was additional narration leading up to the cliffhanger. This was effective in pushing the chapter forward to the cliffhanger resolution with a sense of excitement.

The one irritating ingredient of the Columbia introductions was the sometimes melodramatic nature of the narration or text. The narrator stated that Captain Midnight would meet his doom, or Mandrake had been left to certain doom, or the Shadow was doomed to a certain death. While this might have worked at the end of chapters, to bring people back to the theater next week, it seemed silly in the opening of a chapter, when all of the audience knew that the hero would not suffer certain doom in the next few minutes but rather, would survive.

*Holt of the Secret Service* had a different type of hysteria associated with its chapter openings. A typical one started like this:

> The Secret Service is on the march! Crime shall never pay,
> yet the underworld despoils and murders to the bitter end!
> Is Jack Holt next on the list?

Fortunately, this type of hysteria was missing from many of the later serials, such as *Jack Armstrong* and the *Superman* serials.

By the 1950s, the opening narrations of the Columbia serials became shorter, parroting Republic's use of shorter chapter openings of that era. Once the Columbia narration became shorter, the narrations were less hysterical than they had previously been because they now had to quickly convey the recap information to the viewers and there was no time for excesses.

Unlike other studios' serials, on each frame of a Columbia serial where the title of the serial chapter was shown, there was usually a certificate of approval from the Motion Picture Association of America (MPPA), with a number. The MPAA adopted a Production Code, which came into prominence in 1934, which set forth specific restrictions on movie language and behavior. All films had to obtain a certificate of approval before being released. For some reason, Columbia highlighted the certificate at the beginning of each serial chapter. The certificate number on each chapter was usually different, so the code enforcement personnel must have evaluated each chapter separately.

**Universal Serials**

The signature Universal chapter opening was scrolling text, similar to that of some of the Columbia serials. However, there were significant differences. The Universal titles were captioned, "Foreword Chapter Number." The name of the chapter was not given. The text scrolled but it scrolled away from the screen, with both sides of text angling in as the text rolled upward. This gave the impression of the text rolling to infinity, giving more significance to the words. This style was also used at the beginning of *Star Wars* and satirized at the beginning of *Airplane 2: The Sequel.*

The last sentence of the text was usually not completed, leading directly into the action. Thus, in Chapter 3 of *Flash Gordon Conquers the Universe*, the last sentences of the introduction read, "They drop a bomb. It misses but starts an avalanche which…"

This style of opening was used in many Universal serials, starting in 1939 with *The Green Hornet* and continuing with serials such as *Buck Rogers, The Oregon Trail* and *Sky Raiders.* This type of opening was done by an optical special effect and could be expensive. (The use of glass in the optical effect can be seen in *Airplane II: The Sequel.*)

Prior to this opening, Universal often used one or more non-scrolling slides of text to introduce each chapter. When this was done, the plot recaps were very detailed, often going on for 10 lines or more. Whether using scrolling or non-scrolling texts, Universal often used very long and convoluted sentences to recap the action, like this one from the opening to Chapter Three of *Tailspin Tommy in the Great Air Mystery*:

> Unknown to them, war has broken out in Nazil over possession of the oil fields Tommy and Skeeter are to survey, and an armed plane sent to prevent their arrival, after forcing Betty down on Mandragos Island, is battling Tommy and Skeeter when….

Try to diagram that sentence.

Also, in either style of Universal written plot recaps, the summaries were often directed to audience members who had missed the last chapter. Before summarizing the new action of the last chapter, the cliffhanger resolution from the previous chapter was explained.

In some of the very early Universal sound serials, an onscreen personality introduced each chapter. For example, in the western, *The Indi-*

*Scouts to the Rescue* (1939). This is the signature Universal opening, with the text scrolling to infinity. For some reason when this opening was used, the title of the chapter was not given.

*ans Are Coming* (1930), a cowboy set the scene for the upcoming chapter, relating the story in a folksy, down-to-earth manner.

Universal sometimes used a comic strip opening when a serial was based on a comic strip. Hands unfolded a Sunday paper, the camera moved into the strip in question and then there was a dissolve into the strip that recapped the prior chapter. This was a clever way of reminding the viewer of the origin of the serial and since comic strips have much in common with films, as both are done in frames and varying points of view, it was an excellent way of re-telling the story of the prior chapter.

In the Universal openings, it was disappointing that the strip that the supposed newspaper reader had in his hands was different than the actual recap strip that was shown each week. Also, the drawings were very basic and did not have the realism or accuracy of the drawings that started the Republic chapters.

But, there was a special joy in this type of opening and that was to identify the other comic strips on the page. In *Ace Drummond* (1936), the comic strip above was *Jungle Jim*, which then returned the favor

*Jungle Jim* (1937). This shows the comic strip style of opening which was used by Universal in the middle and late 1930s for a serial based on a comic strip. Note the credit given to Alex Raymond, one of the creators of *Jungle Jim*.

because in *Jungle Jim* (1937), the comic strip just below was *Ace Drummond*. Additionally, in some chapter openings of *Jungle Jim*, if the viewer looked really close, he could see some lines that indicated that the strip above *Jungle Jim* was *Secret Agent X-9*, even though when the newspaper unfurled, *Jungle Jim* was the top strip on the page. In *Secret Agent X-9* (1937), the comic strip just above was *Radio Patrol*, although that did not become apparent until later chapters when a new set of hands opened the newspaper in a slightly different manner. Of course, all of the other comic strips shown on the page were also turned into Universal serials.

Universal sometimes varied this approach, with the comic strip appearing in other forms. In *Radio Patrol* (1937), the strip was in a book, in *Red Barry* (1938), the strip was in a police file and in *Flash Gordon's Trip to Mars* (1938), the strip was on a television screen.

Republic used a variation on the comic strip opening at the beginning of *The Adventures of Red Ryder* (1940). Before the credits of the serial, there was a Sunday Red Ryder comic strip. The camera then focused on one frame which was clearly a drawing of Red Barry playing

Red Ryder. The drawing then dissolved into film of Red Barry riding a horse. Similarly, *Dick Tracy* (1937) also showed a comic strip before the opening credits. The chapter recaps in both of those serials, however, were the typical Republic drawings.

Universal's true innovation was to have no recap at all. This started with *Gang Busters* (1942), and continued in *The Master Key* (1945), *Lost City of the Jungle* (1946) and most of the later Universal serials until Universal went out of the serial business. For example, in *The Master Key*, each chapter opened with the voice of the Master Key piped into a meeting, asking his henchmen to report on the status of their nefarious activities. The report summarized enough of the plot to lead into the footage from the prior week's cliffhanger, even though, on many occasions, there was no way that the particular henchmen or the Master Key could have known what had happened, particularly since the cliffhanger was taking place as they spoke.

This approach reached its zenith in *Secret Agent X-9* (1945). At the beginning of each chapter of the serial, two or more serial characters

*Secret Agent X-9* (1945). Here, two of the actors who played Charlie Chan's sons appear in the same scene, introducing the plot in the introduction to Chapter Nine of the serial. To the left is Keye Luke, still on the side of the law, and to the right is Benson Fong, who has turned to the side of evil.

were talking to each other and they recapped the action in their own words. These characters ranged from bit players talking to a scientist played by Benson Fong, the main villain, Nobura, recapping the action in talks with her assistant, and two governmental employees in Washington recapping some of the action, although they were half a world away from the story.

This approach by Universal brought its special joy. Obviously, the main draw to come back to a serial week after week was to see the cliffhanger resolved. In *Secret Agent X-9*, and other serials with similar openings, it was also to see which characters or bit players would narrate the story and how the writers managed to weave their knowledge into the plot.

For some reason, when Universal used this opening, it did not number the chapter or give the title of the chapter. That was provided at the end of the previous week's episode. Also, some Universal serials combined types of openings. In *Lost City of the Jungle*, the credits were shown by the scrolling text into infinity. The chapter introductions were done by the characters in the serial.

## Independents

The independent studios, being independent by definition, did not have a specific pattern for recapping the events of the prior week's action. Some, such as *The Return of Chandu* (1934) and *The Lost City* (1935), simply used a screen or screens of text to do the job. This was similar to the method used in the Universal serials of the day.

Others were more inventive. For example, in *The Sign of the Wolf* (Metropolitan, 1931), each episode starting with Chapter Two began with a pretty maiden placing a fortune tellers' globe on a ceremonial table. Then a wizard-like figure appeared who gestured over the globe. Suddenly, a stranger used a blow dart to crack the globe. There was a burst of smoke and then the wizard reached into the globe and unfolded a note. That note contained the handwritten summary of the prior week's episode.

Another example occurred in *The Mystery Trooper* (Syndicate, 1931). In the introduction to the chapters starting with Chapter Two, the masked title character rode in on his horse. He then threw a rock with a note wrapped around it through a window, breaking the window. The recipient picked up the rock, took the message off, unfolded it and flattened it out. Then there was a cut to the recap text which was supposed to be on the message.

*The Sign of the Wolf* (1931). The chapter recap is hidden in the crystal ball, which is about to be broken by a henchman with a blowpipe.

In both of these serials, the use of rocks or darts to deliver messages occurred during the actual serial so their use in recapping prior chapters was consistent with the flavor of the serials. It added a nice touch to the chapter introductions and gave these serials a distinctive look. However, the other major studios, with the exception of Universal with its comic strip openings, never followed this practice of the independents and never individualized their serial openings.

**Best Opening**

What serial had the best opening to its chapters? Hands down, it was *Flash Gordon's Trip to Mars* (1938). In the story, Queen Azura had a closed circuit television which she used for communication with her soldiers. There were several dials at the bottom of the set which controlled the screen. In the chapter openings, there was a similar television which showed a comic strip of the story from the previous week's chapter. There was only one dial to control the screen. As the recap opened, a soldier turned the dial to move the frame from drawing to drawing.

Obviously, the actor playing the soldier could not see the screen and could not match the movements of the dial to the movements of the frames. Thus, for one of the frames in Chapter Two, the frame moved before the soldier touched the dial. In Chapter Four, on two occasions, the soldier touched the dial but the frame was slow in moving. In Chapter Ten, an entire frame move was almost completed before the soldier touched the dial. Again, while cliffhanger resolutions were obviously important, the success, or lack of success, of the soldier in moving the frames in conjunction with his hand on the dial, was an added joy of this second *Flash Gordon* serial.

## II. NUMBER OF SERIAL CHAPTERS

During the silent film era, there was no set pattern to the number of chapters contained in each serial. While most serials of that era contained 15 episodes or less, there were a number of exceptions. For example, *The Perils of Pauline* (1914) contained 20 chapters, *The Diamond from the Sky* (1915) had 30 chapters, and even as late as 1924, *Fighting Ranger* had 18 chapters. Toward the end of the silent era, most serials contained only ten chapters.

The early sound serials tended to contain either 10 or 12 episodes. By around 1932, however, a pattern was established and serials were always 12, 13 or 15 chapters in length. The only exception to this rule was *Robinson Crusoe of Clipper Island* (1936) which had 14 chapters.

Of the 57 serials produced or released by Columbia, all but two were 15 chapters in length. The exceptions were *Brenda Starr, Reporter* (1945) which was 13 chapters and *Mandrake, the Magician* (1939), which was 12 chapters. That means that even in the 1950s, when Universal had stopped producing serials and Republic was producing short 12 chapter serials, Columbia was still producing its standard full length cliffhangers.

Of course, one of the common criticisms of the Columbia chapter plays was that they were too long and tended to fizzle out at the end. Many of the Columbias would have been far better had they only been 12 chapters in length.

Of the 66 serials produced by Republic, the substantial majority (44) were 12 chapters in length. Republic did produce another 17 serials which were 15 chapters in length, including such well-remembered seri-

**Chapter 8. DOOMED CARGO**

*Adventures of Frank and Jesse James* (1948). This is the middle serial in Republic's Jesse James trilogy and the last 13 chapter serial for Republic. Clayton Moore (right) reprises his role as Jesse James from *Jesse James Rides Again* (1947) and Steve Darrell plays his brother Frank James, a character who did not appear in the previous serial.

als as the four *Dick Tracy* serials, the two *Lone Ranger* serials, the two Nyoka serials (*Jungle Girl* (1941) and *Perils of Nyoka* (1942)), and the two Rex Bennett serials (*G-Men vs. The Black Dragon* (1943) and *Secret Service in Darkest Africa* (1943)). In 1947 and 1948, Republic turned out four 13 chapter serials, the last one being *The Adventures of Frank and Jesse James*. The remaining 18 Republic serials were all 12 chapters in length.

Mascot Pictures produced a few silent serials and then released 24 serials during the sound era. All of its serials were either 10 or 12 chapters, with the exception of *The Miracle Rider* (1935) which contained 15 chapters. Presumably, Mascot invested in a longer serial, since it was able to obtain Tom Mix for the serial, and the chapter play was expected to be very marketable with Mix as the star.

Other independent studios also produced 15 chapter serials. Stage and Screen Productions produced three such serials in 1936: *The Black*

*Coin*, *The Clutching Hand*, and *Custer's Last Stand*. These are among the least-liked serials of all time so the fact that they extend out to 15 chapters hardly added to their appeal. Victory Pictures also produced two 15 episode serials: *Shadow of Chinatown* (1936) and *Blake of Scotland Yard* (1937). The very earliest independent releases, *Voice from the Sky* (Ben Wilson, 1930), *Mystery Trooper* (Syndicate, 1931) and *Sign of the Wolf* (Metropolitan, 1931) were only ten chapters in length. RKO's only serial release, *The Last Frontier* (1932), was 12 chapters in length.

The serials of Universal never fit a pattern and neither did the number of episodes in its serials. Universal did have more 13 chapter serials than the other studios, having produced 20 cliffhangers with that odd number of chapters out of the 69 serials released by Universal during the sound era (although not all of them were talking serials). Universal also released ten 15 chapter serials in the sound era, which tended to be westerns, such as *The Oregon Trail* (1939) and *Riders of Death Valley* (1941). Universal also produced six serials of ten chapters in length through 1931. The rest of the Universal serials were 12 episodes in length, for a total of 33 such serials.

Apparently, Universal had trouble making up its mind as to the appropriate number of chapters in a serial, even during the same series. Thus, *Flash Gordon* (1936) had 13 chapters, *Flash Gordon's Trip to Mars* (1938) had 15 chapters, and *Flash Gordon Conquers the Universe* (1940) had only 12 chapters.

## III. LENGTH OF SERIAL CHAPTERS

The longest chapter of most serials was the opening chapter. The reason for this appears to be twofold. For serials with very complicated serial plots, it took a longer period of time to introduce all of the characters, set up all of the plot lines and build to a good cliffhanger which would convince the viewer to come back weekly for the remaining chapters of the serial. The second reason may simply have been that the studio budgeted for the longer first chapter and therefore the filmmaker used that budget to attempt to immerse the viewer in the plot, characters, stunts and/or special effects that were impliedly promised throughout the remainder of the serial to convince the audience to return on a weekly basis.

Mascot employed long first chapters for its serials. For example, the first chapter of *The Vanishing Legion* (1931) was over 35 minutes long and the first chapter of *The Phantom Empire* (1935) was about 30 minutes long. When Mascot merged into Republic, those long first chapters carried over, at least during the early years of Republic. Thus, there were many examples of first chapters of Republic serials which timed at around thirty minutes in length. They included *The Vigilantes Are Coming* (1936), at over 31 minutes, *SOS Coast Guard* (1937), at 30 minutes, *Dick Tracy* (1937), at more than 29 minutes, and *Zorro Rides Again* (1937), at around 29 minutes. The later chapters in those serials ran in the 17 to 20 minute range.

Over time, the length of the first chapter of the Republic serials decreased and the later chapters were then in the 14 to 16 minute range. By the middle of the 1940s and into the 1950s, the chapter length of the first episode of a Republic serial was 20 minutes and the other chapters were all around 13 minutes and 20 seconds in length. These later Republic serials were among the shortest twelve chapter serials ever made. They ran about 167 minutes, which was slightly over 2 ½ hours. That was shorter than many feature films.

Much like the early Republics, Columbia often had very long first chapters. The first chapter of *Deadwood Dick* (1940) ran over 32 minutes, the first chapter of *The Green Archer* (1940) ran over 31 minutes, the first chapter of *Captain Midnight* (1942) ran over 30 minutes and the first chapters of *The Phantom* (1943) and *Terry and the Pirates* (1940) ran about 29 minutes Much like the serials of Republic Pictures, first chapters of later Columbia serials were shorter. For example, the first episode of *Superman* (1948), which had a lot of ground to cover, ran slightly less than 20 minutes.

Universal's first chapters were longer than the later chapters, but Universal's first chapters seldom ran outside the 20 minute range. There were, however, exceptions to this rule, as for example, *Gang Busters* (1942), whose first chapter ran over 27 minutes. However, even in a serial with an action-filled first chapter, such as *Flash Gordon* (1936), Universal seldom went for a very lengthy first chapter.

The longest serial chapter in sound serials was the first chapter of *The New Adventures of Tarzan* (1935), which was sometimes released in a 60 minute format. The film was intended to be released in many different formats, one being a 70-minute feature film known, oddly enough, as *The New Adventures of Tarzan*. That film included the entire first chapter of the serial, about five minutes of the second chapter which included the cliffhanger resolution from the first chapter, and then a short conclusion to the movie. Most commonly, however, the first chapter of the serial was released at 42 minutes in length. In that format, it did not include all of the padding from the first chapter which was included in the feature and the 60 minute chapter format.

The longest serial chapter for a serial that was not also intended to be a feature film was the first chapter of *The Miracle Rider*, the 1935 serial from Mascot Pictures. The first chapter, titled "The Vanishing Indian," ran almost 43 minutes. This was one of the strangest chapters in serial history. It started with the history of the Indians from 1777, showing them being pushed over time into smaller and smaller areas. The chapter portrayed historical figures, such as Daniel Boone, Davy Crockett, and Buffalo Bill.

The actual plot of the serial did not begin until the story reached the year 1935, which came almost 14 minutes into the chapter. Indeed, and partly because of this long first chapter, *The Miracle Rider* was one of the longest sound serial ever made, running approximately 5 hours and 9 minutes.

*The Miracle Rider* was not, however, the longest sound serial. *Custer's Last Stand* and *The Black Coin*, each 1936 releases from Stage and Screen and each with first chapters of almost 40 minutes in length, ran for a total of around five hours and 20 minutes. *Flaming Frontiers* (1938) and *The Jungle Menace* (1937), at slightly more than five hours each, were among the longest serials for Universal and Columbia, respectively. For Republic serials, *Dick Tracy* (1937) was the longest, running about 4 hours and 50 minutes in length.

## IV. RECAP FOOTAGE

The use of economy or recap chapters started with Mascot and some of the other independent studios. Indeed, there was flashback footage (although not an economy chapter) in the first serial with sound, *King of the Kongo*, released by Mascot in 1929. Among all of the studios, Republic embraced the idea of using economy chapters the most, employing them sporadically before and during World War II. After World War II, each of Republic's already shortened serials contained a recap chapter.

Universal generally did not use recap footage in its serials. However, Chapter Nine of *Buck Rogers* (1939) was an unusual recap chapter where, at the insistence of Buddy, Dr. Huer used his television screen to bring back events that happened to Buck Rogers, Buddy and Wilma Derring on Saturn. The footage came from Chapter Two of the serial. (There was also one bit of recap footage in Chapter 11 of the serial.) Another example occurred in *The Red Rider* (1934), where the plot fizzled out about two minutes into the 15th and last chapter. To finish the serial, two flashbacks from earlier chapters were shown, ending an already boring serial in a very tiresome manner.

Unfortunately, *The Red Rider* was not the only serial which had an economy chapter for its last chapter. The same poor plotting occurred in the independent serial, *The New Adventures of Tarzan* (1935) where the writers also ran out of ideas a few minutes into the last chapter, which in this case was only the 12th chapter. There, a fortune teller ran out the clock by recounting prior events of the serial that she was able to call up by way of her crystal ball and then show to all of the people around her.

Universal's *Flash Gordon's Trip to Mars* (1938) did not contain an economy chapter as such. However, in Chapter Six, Flash explained to the ruler of the Clay People why he hated Ming, and the invisibility footage of Flash from the first serial was shown, for no apparent reason. This was particularly disconcerting, as Jean Rogers was shown with long blond hair in the flashback while her hair was short and dark in *Trip to Mars*. In Chapter Ten, Prince Barin gave some history of his relationship with Ming to the ruler of the Clay People, which precipitated a repeat of Barin's fight with Flash from the first serial. In Chapter 14, Flash Gordon explained to the people of Mars why they should not accept Ming as their leader, recalling events from Chapters 7 and 8 of the original serial, including events that occurred in the world of King Vultan in the city in the sky.

Originally, Columbia did not use economy chapters but then began employing them on a regular basis in the 1950s. An example occurred in Chapter 12 of *Cody of the Pony Express* (1950), where Jim Archer and Bill Cody told Major Walker about their attempts to thwart the villains who were trying to destroy the Pony Express. A number of flashbacks from the serial were shown.

The difference between the Columbia flashbacks and the Republic flashbacks was that the Columbias tended to be narration over multiple

*Atom Man vs. Superman* (1950). Pictured is Lyle Talbot as Lex Luthor. He somehow found out the origin of Superman and related it to a henchman in flashback footage in the serial.

prior scenes from the serial while Republic usually showed large chunks of earlier footage, often encompassing prior cliffhangers and their resolutions. Given the shorter length of the Republic chapters of the post-war era, the Republic recap footage tended to consume a larger percentage of the chapter than that of a Columbia serial chapter. Even when Columbia used recap footage in two chapters of the same serial, such as Chapters 10 and 11 of *Gunfighters of the Northwest* (1954), the total length of the recap footage was less than that used in one chapter of a Republic serial.

Interesting recap footage appeared in Chapter Seven of *Atom Man vs. Superman* (1950), where Lex Luthor explained the origin of Superman to one of his henchmen. He somehow learned the history from coded messages sent from the Planet Krypton which were picked up on Earth and finally given to Luthor. The chapter incorporated footage from the first chapter of *Superman*.

*Trip to Mars* and *Atom Man* were the only serials which showed flashback footage from another serial. Of course, there may have been one or two instances where serials used uncredited footage from prior serials but those are the subject of a different chapter of this book.

If the insertion of one economy chapter into a serial was irritating, two or three economy chapters in one serial became particularly outrageous. *Fighting with Kit Carson* (1933) had four economy chapters; Mascot's last serial, *The Fighting Marines* (1935), had three. Each one of those economy chapters contained recap footage of interminable length.

An interesting variation on the use of economy chapters and repeat footage occurred in the 1936 serial, *Robinson Crusoe of Clipper Island*, which was originally supposed to be 12 chapters in length. When it became clear to the filmmakers during production that the serial was going over budget, two additional chapters were added. One was a traditional economy chapter, retelling incidents from earlier chapters, and the other extra chapter was created by repeating earlier scenes and footage, as if they were new scenes. With the use of these techniques, there was now a hope of possibly producing a profit on the enterprise, by amortizing the production costs of the serial over a total of 14 chapters instead of just 12.

Unfortunately, *Robinson Crusoe* was not the last Republic serial to reuse prior footage in the serial in multiple chapters. Republic used that easy way out to fill the 12 chapters of *The Fighting Devil Dogs* (1938), which had two economy chapters. The second one was interesting, however, in that it was a lesson in how to create an interesting economy chapter, if one must be employed at all.

In Chapter 11, all of the principals were lured to an abandoned warehouse to see a demonstration of a new invention. When they got there, the inventor was not present so that characters sat down and discussed the question of who might be the insider disclosing secret information to the Lightning. That was an excuse for showing footage from prior episodes of the serial. While the clips were being shown of the various suspects and opinions as to the guilty party were given by other members of the group, the Lightning's men were filling the locked room with carbon monoxide gas. As the clip series ended, the characters were dropping, one by one. The result was an economy episode, with suspense building throughout, resulting in an interesting chapter.

In addition to recap chapters, recap footage was shown at the beginning of each serial chapter. After the introduction, each serial chapter contained footage from the prior episode, which led to the cliffhanger and now, the cliffhanger resolution. This entailed a delicate balancing act on the part of the filmmaker. The amount of old footage shown must be long enough to set up the cliffhanger, but not too long so that it bored the viewer.

The record for longest recap footage at the beginning of a chapter appears to go to *The Return of Chandu* (1934). At the end of Chapter Nine, there was a mild cliffhanger where Chandu was seized by his enemy. In the next chapter, over six minutes of footage from the prior episode was shown, with no other justification than to extend the length of the episode. In fact, given the time spent on the credits and the written foreword to the chapter, the new footage in the chapter did not begin until almost the eight minute mark. Amazingly, shortly thereafter, the episode turned into an economy episode, with about four minutes of footage from earlier chapters of the serial. For a chapter that had about 19-1/2 minutes of film in it, only about 7-1/2 minutes was new footage.

Perhaps the most unusual recap footage at the beginning of a chapter occurred at the beginning of Chapter Seven of *Fighting with Kit Carson* (1933). The cliffhanger at the end of the prior chapter was the shooting of Kit Carson by Reynolds, an outlaw whose gang had just turned on him. The recap footage in Chapter Seven started long before the shooting, showing the gang turning on Reynolds. However, during the recap footage, Reynolds tried to stop the double cross by telling the gang how important he had been to them, segueing into long recap footage from earlier chapters. In other words, there was recap footage within recap footage! The cliffhanger resolution did not occur until after the 11 minute mark of the chapter.

## IV. ACTING CREDITS

Most serials had mundane credits, simply listing the stars of the serial and the producer, director and the technical crew, the same as other motion pictures. Upon occasion, however, short clips of the main stars, with their names and characters were employed. This process was sometimes referred to as the opticals.

Many of the older Universal sound serials had the lead player opticals for every chapter of the serial. This can be seen, for example, in *The Red Rider* (1934) where six clips of the lead actors were shown at the beginning of each chapter. One of the clips was for Silver, Buck Jones' horse.

Starting in the mid-1930s the lead player opticals were only shown in the first three chapters of a Universal serial. An example of this occurred in *Tim Tyler's Luck* (1937) where clips of six actors were shown in the first three chapters only and some of the actors were shown in pairs to save time. By the early 1940s, the lead player clips were eliminated by Universal in their entirety. For example, in *The Green Hornet Strikes Again* (1940), there were no lead player opticals even though *The Green Hornet* (1939) had used them in the first three chapters.

Republic employed introduction footage of the actors beginning with its first serial, *Darkest Africa* (1936) and continued the practice until *Haunted Harbor* (1944), with the exception of *Hawk of the Wilderness* (1938). The opticals were shown in the trailer for *Zorro's Black Whip* (1944), but for some reason they were not used at the beginning of the first chapter of the actual serial. Unlike Universal, Republic only used the opticals for the first chapter and reverted to written credits for the later chapters. For example, in *The Fighting Devil Dogs*, seven actor clips were used at the beginning of the first chapter. The rest of the chapters only had written credits for the actors who were called "The Players."

Columbia used the clips of the lead actors sporadically, in serials such as *Overland with Kit Carson* (1939) and *Mandrake the Magician* (1939). Its last use by Columbia was in *Brenda Starr, Reporter* (1945). In the opening to *The Spider's Web*, which used lead player opticals, Warren Hull received three separate credits, as Richard Wentworth, the Spider, and as Blinky McQuaide, a disguise Wentworth employed several times in the serial. Similarly, in the cast listing for *The Shadow* (although there were no opticals), Victor Jory was listed as playing Cranston, Li Chang and the Shadow. Li Chang, much like Blinky McQuaide for the Shadow, was an alias that Lamont Cranston used from time to time.

Mention should be made of that great actor who specialized in playing masked villains at Columbia. The actor billed only as "??" played the Octopus in *The Spider's Web*, the Gargoyle in *The Spider Returns*, and the Wasp in *Mandrake the* Magician. He even played the Black Falcon, the masked hero of *Flying G-Men*. A different actor was listed as playing the Black Tiger in *The Shadow*. It was "???."

Republic billed their masked villains differently. The character's name was sometimes listed in the cast and if opticals were used at the beginning of a chapter, the masked villain was shown with his character name at the bottom. Thus, the cast of *Dick Tracy vs. Crime, Inc.* included "The Ghost," the cast of *Fighting Devil Dogs* included "The Lightning" and the cast of *The Adventures of Captain Marvel* included "The Scorpion."

Turning to the independents, Mascot employed the opticals a few times, such as in *Law of the Wild* (1934) and *The Fighting Marines* (1935). However, the most incredible use of the opticals was in Stage and Screen Productions' lengthy 1936 serial, *Custer's Last Stand*. There, clips of 27 members of the cast were shown at the beginning of the first chapter, although they were done two, three, four and five at a time. Incredibly, after that, twelve more actors were given a written credit only. The actor credits took well over a minute of screen time. By the second chapter, only 14 clips of the actors were used. However, along with the written credits, there was still over a minute of screen time devoted to the actor credits.

Mercifully, the lead player opticals were gone by Chapter Four and the number of written actor credits was severely limited. The amount of time provided for the actor credits in *Custer's Last Stand* may explain why that serial had such a long running time.

Masked villains and masked heroes provided other problems in the serial credits. Obviously, many serials had a masked villain, whose real identity was revealed in the last chapter to be one of the apparent good guys in the serial, such as a prominent townsperson in a western, or one of a group of scientists or university professors in a modern story. One of the joys of serial viewing was to guess which good guy was really a bad guy. In order to disguise the true identity of the hidden villain, his voice was often dubbed by an actor who did not play any character in the film. When that was not done, such as in *Dick Tracy vs. Crime, Inc.* (1941), the distinctive voice of the Ghost made it easy for any avid serial fan to determine which one of the suspect businessmen was the true Ghost.

The earliest example of dubbing in the villain's voice occurred in *The Vanishing Legion* (1931). In that serial, the Voice, an unknown villain, communicated with his henchmen via electronic devices. His words were spoken by Boris Karloff. However, when the Voice was identified in the last chapter, he was played by an actor other than Karloff, and Karloff did not otherwise appear in the serial. Karloff was not yet a star and he received no billing in the credits.

Other examples of unbilled voices for masked villains included Gerald Mohr dubbing the role of the Scorpion in *The Adventures of Captain Marvel* (1941), Edwin Stanley voicing the role of The Lighting in *Fighting Devil Dogs* (1938) (although Stanley Price did the voice in the first chapter) and Forrest Taylor dubbing the voice of the Octopus in *The Spider Returns* (1941). I. Stanford Jolly dubbed the voice of the title character in *The Crimson Ghost* (1946) and also played a bit part in the serial. He did, however, receive a billing in the credits, for either or both roles.

Turning to masked heroes, the voice of the Lone Ranger, while masked, was dubbed by Billy Bletcher in both of the movie serials. Bletcher had substantial experience providing the voices for cartoons produced by Disney, Warner Bros. and MGM. He received no screen credit. Similarly, when Brit Reid turned into the Green Hornet, in *The Green Hornet* serial (1939), his voice was dubbed by Al Hodge, who played the role on radio. No screen credit was given to Hodge. Also, the Masked Marvel, when wearing the mask, was portrayed by stunt man, Tom Steele,

Superman (Kirk Alyn) doing what he likes to do best. Alyn did not receive a screen credit in either of the *Superman* serials.

but the voice was that of Gayne Whitman, who, like Al Hodge, had substantial experience on the radio. Whitman did not receive any screen credit either.

Indeed, Tom Steele was not mentioned in the credits to *The Masked Marvel* (1943) either, even though he played the masked crime fighter under the mask. It was a large part, with significant dialogue. This lack of billing was particularly amazing because, in Chapter Eight, Steele also had a significant bit playing a henchman of Sakima, the main villain.

While unusual, there were other instances in serials of actors who had a significant role in a serial but received no billing in the credits. For example, despite his important villain's role as Jason Grood in *Jack Armstrong* (1947), Charles Middleton did not receive any screen credit. Actors with far less important roles in the serial, however, did receive a credit. This occurred despite the fact that Middleton was well-known to serial audiences of the time, particularly from his performances in the *Flash Gordon* serials.

Kirk Alyn, who played Clark Kent and Superman in the *Superman* serial (1948), did not receive any credit in the cast list. Noel Neill, as Lois Lane, received the top credited billing. Even after Kirk Alyn became well-known for his portrayal of Superman in that serial, he still did not receive any credit in the sequel, *Atom Man vs. Superman* (1950). Noel Neill still received the top credited billing. However, the top name listed in the credits in each serial was simply "Superman." This was apparently because Columbia promoted the serial on the basis that it was unable to find a suitable actor to play Superman and therefore the real Superman had to be hired for the role. Even the trailer to the serial indicated that the star was Superman.

One final billing seems very strange, particularly looking backward after many years. John Wayne was clearly the star of *The Three Musketeers* (1933), as he fought El Shaitan's evil doings in the Arabian Desert. Yet, he only received fourth screen billing, after the actors who played the Musketeers, even though each of them had far less screen time than Wayne and, of course, Wayne ended up being the biggest star ever to appear in serials. Wayne did, however, receive a top billing in his other two serials.

## VII. CHAPTER CONCLUSIONS

### Universal and Republic

The chapter conclusions of serials were far less interesting than the chapter introductions. Indeed, Universal, which had the most variety of chapter introductions, used the least interesting chapter conclusions. The cliffhanger came, the film ended and Universal concluded with one screen of text. This was a typical conclusion:

SEE

DEATH'S

SHINING FACE

Chapter Six of

LOST CITY OF THE JUNGLE

AT THIS THEATRE NEXT WEEK

As to the final chapter, Universal sometimes failed to announce that an upcoming chapter was the last chapter of the serial, simply giving the name and chapter number of the ensuing episode. This occurred, for example, in *Scouts to the Rescue* (1939). The following week, it may have come as a surprise to some viewers that the serial had concluded.

Republic serials were not much different, although the end titles were generally much simpler. Here is a typical Republic slide from *The Crimson Ghost* (1946):

Next Week

Chapter 7

Electrocution

A Republic Serial

When it came to the final chapter, however, Republic usually signaled the end of the serial by the screen announcing the upcoming chapter as either the final episode or final chapter.

The difference from the Universal conclusions was that sometimes, after the cliffhanger and after the text, Republic would show additional credits for the serial, usually over some scenes from the serial. Thus, in *The Adventures of Captain Marvel* (1941), the viewer had a chance to see some of the flying sequences once again. In *King of the Royal Mounted*

(1940), the viewer had another chance to hear some of the excellent score for the serial. However, in the later Republic serials, these additional credits and scenes were eliminated and the conclusion was the simple slide announcing the next week's chapter title.

## Columbia

Of course, Columbia had the most attention-grabbing and most irritating chapter conclusions. After the cliffhanger ended, there was usually a cymbal crash and then scenes from the next chapter were shown, usually over some breathless narration raising questions about the next episode. Here is an example:

> There is Blackie, the most dangerous man in the gang.
> What does he see? Who is he shooting at? And what
> about Kay? Can she escape his evil clutches? Don't miss
> "Ramparts of Revenge." Next week's exciting chapter of
> "Holt of the Secret Service."

In the earlier Columbia serials, the cliffhanger was actually undercut by showing the hero alive and well in the next chapter, even though he was about to die at the end of the prior chapter. Thus, in *Mandrake, the Magician* (1939), at the end of Chapter Two, both Betty and Mandrake were involved in separate cliffhangers. Both showed up in the clips for the next chapter. This occurred chapter after chapter, with Mandrake facing certain death at the end of an episode and then appearing in the clips for the next episode. Where was the cliffhanger?

Similarly, *Terry and the Pirates* (1940), Chapter 11, had an excellent cliffhanger with sliding floors forcing Terry and Pat into a pit filled with deadly swords. Yet, the clips for the following episode showed the two alive and well, undercutting the suspense of the cliffhanger. This happened throughout the serial.

Columbia eventually caught on to this problem and in later serials stopped making that mistake. Thus, in the *Superman* serials, if Lois Lane were in trouble at the end of the episode, she was not shown in the preview clips but Superman was. If Superman were on the brink of death at the end of the chapter, then Lois Lane would be seen in the preview clips but not Superman. This was a vast improvement over the earlier serials.

After the scenes from the next episode, Columbia, much like the other studios, ended the chapter with a slide touting the next week's episode, but with a difference. For Columbia, the upcoming episodes were either thrilling or exciting or both. Thus, in *The Phantom* (1943), the slide said "Don't Fail to See" or "Don't Miss" the next episode or, referring to the questions raised in the preview clips, "Learn the Answers in" or "See What Happens in" the next chapter. The narrator also described the next chapter with an interesting adjective, such as "absorbing," "smashing," "action-packed," "action crammed," "exciting," "thrilling," "breath-taking," "thrill-packed," "dynamic," "excitement-laden," or, of course, "gripping." By the time Columbia was done, it had a thesaurus full of these types of adjectives.

As usual, with regard to the upcoming final chapter, Columbia usually promoted the conclusion with breathless excitement, while signaling that it was the final chapter. Here is part of the narration from the conclusion to Chapter 14 of *The Green Archer* (1940):

> Learn the identity of the real Green Archer, in
> "Green Archer Exposed," Next week's concluding
> chapter of *The Green Archer*.

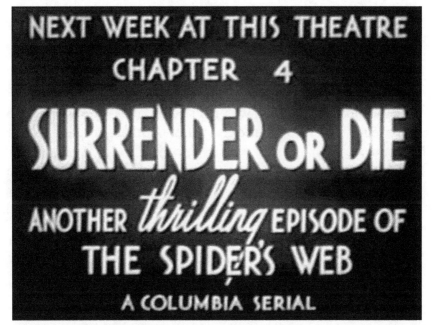

*The Spider's Web* (1938). This is a typical final title card for a Columbia serial, with the narrator promoting the next chapter with his typical hyperbole.

The slide referred to it as "Another thrilling episode of *The Green Archer.*"

Of course, however the studio chose to write the conclusion of an episode, it was the cliffhanger that brought the moviegoer back to the theater next week, not the serial conclusion. The serial fan knew that Republic and Universal also had thrilling, exciting or even dynamic serial chapters upcoming, even though they did not say so in their chapter conclusions.

**Independents**

Sometimes the independent studios used written questions at the end of a chapter to entice the viewer back for the following week's episode. For example, at the end of Chapter Six of *The Clutching Hand* (1936), the question read, "What happened to Kennedy and Shirley?" At the end of Chapter Seven of *The Black Coin* (1936), the question was, "What happened to Virginia?" Those were both productions released by Stage and Screen Productions.

At the end of Chapter One of *Shadow of Chinatown* (1936), from Victory Pictures, the text read:

> Will Martin's and Joan's search for Willy Fu lead
> to their capture by Poten's Giant God? Witness
> the interesting answer in the Second Chapter
> "The Crushing Walls."

The more interesting question with regard to that chapter is whether Columbia would have ever promoted one of their upcoming chapters as merely "interesting."

Perhaps the best way to end a serial chapter was with the simple but clichéd ending that everyone knew. Each chapter of the independent serials *Sign of the Wolf* (1931) and *The Mystery Trooper* (1931) ended with the short statement: "To Be Continued."

# Chapter 4
# Serial Cliffovers

[*Author's Note: The next three chapters contain a detailed look at the cliffhangers in serials. In order to do the subject justice, many of the cliffhanger resolutions must also be discussed. This obviously results in some spoilers. However, to preface each spoiler with a warning, such as "Spoiler Alert," would disrupt the flow of the chapters and make them hard to read. Therefore, if you do not want to read a spoiler, carefully skim over those parts of these chapters. But, don't skim over too much, as these are the most gripping chapters in the book.*]

**The cliffhanger** was the moment at the end of the serial chapter when the hero was in grave danger, or, indeed, may already have been dead. The action stopped, to be continued next week, before the viewer could learn the fate of the hero. Cliffhangers were such an important element of the serial that serials themselves became known as cliffhangers.

The term itself is not limited to serials. For example, with the success of the television show *Dallas* in the 1980s, wherein the last episode of each season left the story in doubt, to be resolved many months later when the new season began, the term "cliffhanger" became commonly used in television. Perhaps the greatest cliffhanger of them all, movie serials to the contrary notwithstanding, was the "Who Shot J.R.?" cliffhanger and resolution on *Dallas*.

The term "cliffhanger" derived from silent serials where the heroine might find herself hanging from a cliff or a high ledge as the serial chapter concluded. Surprisingly, it was rare in talking serials for the end of the episode to actually have the hero or heroine hanging from a cliff. One example occurred in Chapter Six of *The Red Rider* (1934) with hero Red Davidson holding onto a henchman's leg on the side of a perilously high cliff as the chapter concluded. Another occurred at the end of Chapter Ten of *The Last Frontier* (1932) when Tom Kirby and Betty Halliday were hanging on a rope over a side of a cliff, with the rope about to break. For a modern take, there was the ending to Chapter 13 of *Superman* (1948), when Perry White found himself hanging from a high ledge on the Daily Planet building, having landed there after a fight with a henchman.

Talking serials replaced the cliffhanger with, to coin a term, the cliffover. A cliffover may be defined as a chapter ending where the hero went over a cliff in a stagecoach or motor vehicle, or sometimes, simply on his own, to a certain death. Except for the other world type of serials such as *Flash Gordon* (1936) or *Buck Rogers* (1939) or the jungle or island type adventures such as *Jungle Girl* (1941) or *Jack Armstrong* (1947), a large majority of serials had a chapter which ended in a vehicle or individual cliffover. However, there were many exceptions, such as *Dick Tracy* (1937), *The Shadow* (1940), *Daredevils of the Red Circle* (1939) and *Son of Zorro* (1947).

*Federal Operator 99* (1945). Here is Jim Belmont, played by George J. Lewis, at the piano, concocting another cliffhanger for Jerry Blake or his secretary. The others are, from left to right, LeRoy Mason, Lorna Gray and Hal Taliaferro.

## I. CITY VEHICLE CLIFFOVERS

In serials set in modern times, the cliffover usually involved a car going over a cliff. However, there were also trucks (*The Great Alaskan Mystery* (1944) and *The Vanishing Legion* (1931)), armored trucks (both *Batman* serials), trains (*Mandrake, the Magician* (1939) and *The Master Key* (1945)), runaway train cars (*Hurricane Express* (1932) and *Raiders of Ghost City* (1944)), railroad hand cars (*Deadwood Dick* (1940)), motor-cycles (*The Galloping Ghost* (1931) and *Burn 'em Up Barnes* (1934)), a mine car (*Tiger Woman* (1944)), and even a laundry hamper (*Federal Operator 99* (1945) and *Radar Patrol vs. Spy King* (1949)).

There were two basic resolutions (or takeouts) to these cliffovers, both of which were cheats. The most common resolution was that the hero managed to jump out of the vehicle before the car went over the cliff. Examples of this occurred in *The Fighting Devil Dogs* (1938), *The Crimson Ghost* (1946), *King of the Royal Mounted* (1940), *Spy Smasher* (1942), *Drums of Fu Manchu* (1940), *The Green Archer* (1940), *Radar Men from the Moon* (1952), *Batman and Robin* ( (1949) (two times) and many other serials. In *SOS Coast Guard* (1937) (Chapter Eight), a record was set (and later tied in Chapter 13 of *Flying G-Men* (1939)) when three people jumped out of a moving car before it went over a cliff. Surprisingly, none of the three was hurt.

In Chapter Two of *The Phantom Creeps* (1939), the hero accidentally fell out of the car before it went over the cliff, but at least he was saved. Saunders in Chapter Seven of *The Tiger Woman* (1944) and the Green Hornet in Chapter Seven of *The Green Hornet* (1939) were similarly and luckily saved in each of their respective predicaments when fights spilled out of the back of a truck and onto the road, before the vehicle went over the cliff. In Chapter Four of *The Phantom Empire* (1935), there was an interesting variation on this takeout when Gene Autry jumped out of a vehicle but onto a horse ridden by Frankie Darro, before the car went over the cliff.

The second common resolution was the "lived through it" scenario. The vehicle went over the cliff with the hero in it. The vehicle may then have fallen many feet down the hill, yet the hero survived. In Chapter Three of *Secret Agent X-9* (1945), X-9 was in a truck that rolled over a steep cliff. Luckily, X-9 only suffered some pain in his upper arm, which disappeared early in the next chapter. In Chapter Ten of *Secret Agent X-9* (1937), Pidge and Shara went over a cliff in a car. Even though the car rolled over several times, Pidge suffered no injuries. Shara was knocked unconscious but she was recovering nicely by the end of the next chapter.

Other trips over a cliff have produced no discernible injuries, despite the severity of the crash. In *The Fighting Marines* (1935) (Chapter Ten), the two marines were in an open convertible, which went over a cliff and rolled over at least four times until it landed at the bottom. The marines suffered no apparent injury from the crash.

*The Green Hornet* (1939) had a classic in this regard in the resolution to the Chapter Ten cliffhanger. The Green Hornet was driving an armored truck and the villains were bombing it from above. An explosion caused the truck to go over a cliff. Kato rushed down the hill to the Green Hornet's rescue and the following dialogue occurred:

> KATO: Are you hurt badly?
> GREEN HORNET: No. These armored cars are built
> for protection.

Never mind that being bounced from side to side in an armored truck as it fell down a hill would cause serious injury to anyone.

On a rare occasion there were real injuries suffered in a vehicle cliffover. In Chapter Four of *Radio Patrol* (1937), Molly Selkirk went over a cliff in a car. Although she survived, at least she spent a night in a hospital before returning to her heroine duties. Similarly, in *The Vanishing Legion* (1931) (Chapter One), two people went over a cliff in a truck and although both survived, at least one suffered some serious injuries.

*The Adventures of Smilin' Jack* (1943) (Chapter Nine) had an interesting combination of cheat resolutions to a cliffhanger involving a car over a bridge. One person jumped out before the fall and the two other people in the car survived the fall. Thus, viewers saw two cheat resolutions for the price of one.

Water resolutions were another version of the lived through it resolution. In the second cliffover in *SOS Coast Guard* (1937) (Chapter 10), a burning truck rolled over a cliff and landed in water. Not only were the occupants saved but the fire was put out. In *Captain Midnight* (1942) (Chapter 11) and *Federal Operator 99* (1945) (Chapter Three), the hero was also saved by water when he went over a high cliff on a motorcycle. In *Secret Service in Darkest Africa* (1943) (Chapter 13) and *Daughter of Don Q* (1946) (Chapter Five), both the hero and heroine were saved when their car plunged over a high cliff into water.

*Daughter of Don Q* (1946). This is an unusual cliffover, with the henchmen cutting a tarpaulin on his truck, which then covers Dolores Quantero's car which was in hot pursuit, causing the car to go over a cliff. In the resolution, there is a water save, as can be seen in this photo.

Were there other resolutions to vehicle cliffovers in modern serials? No. Unless your name was Lois Lane and you were friends with a strange visitor from another planet with powers and abilities far beyond those of mortal men. Or, there was Chandu, in Chapter Two of *The Return of Chandu* (1934), who suddenly lost control of his car for no reason other than the fact that the end of a chapter was coming. As Chandu's car headed for the cliff, the chapter ended. At the beginning of the next chapter, Chandu managed to stop the car before it went over the cliff. Perhaps that was the biggest cliffover cheat of all time.

## II. WESTERN WAGON CLIFFOVERS

Westerns also had vehicle cliffovers. Heroes might be trapped in wagons or stage coaches drawn by horses. A fight ensued, the hero was knocked out, the horses broke away from the vehicle, and the vehicle always headed toward a steep cliff. Over it went.

The same two takeouts from the city serials were also employed in western serials. Often, the hero was able to jump out of the wagon or stagecoach before it went over the cliff. This could be seen in the resolution to the Chapter Four cliffhanger to *Cody of the Pony Express* (1950) and the Chapter Three cliffhanger to *Raiders of Ghost City* (1944). A record was set for western wagon cliffovers in the resolution to the Chapter 12 cliffhanger of *The Lone Ranger* (1938) when three people, including the masked rider himself, jumped off of an out-of-control stagecoach before it went over a cliff. All three managed to survive the bumps along the road.

Sometimes, as occurred in the resolution to the Chapter Four cliffhanger of *Tex Granger* (1948), the heroine who was trapped in a runaway coach jumped onto a horse ridden by the hero and thus was saved without having to take a perilous bump on the road. Also, there was a unique variation on this type of resolution to the Chapter Eight cliffhanger of *The Lone Defender* (1930). Ramon was tied up on an out-of-control wagon which fell over a steep hill and crashed. In the takeout, Rin–Tin-Tin jumped onto the wagon and untied Ramon, so that Ramon could jump off the wagon before it went over the hill.

*Adventures of Red Ryder* (1940). Vivian Coe, as Beth Andrews, and Don "Red" Barry, as Red Ryder, survive a Western stagecoach cliffover after a fall into water.

The other type of western wagon cliffover resolution was the "lived through it" scenario. For example, in Chapter 11 of *Gordon of Ghost City* (1933), a stagecoach went over one of the highest cliffs in western serials but all aboard somehow miraculously survived even though the wagon landed on hard ground. Often, in western wagon cliffovers, there was a water resolution, with the wagon going over the cliff and landing in water. The water apparently cushioned the blow and the hero was saved. This could be seen in the resolutions to the cliffhangers in Chapter Ten of *Zorro's Fighting Legion* (1939) and Chapter Four of *Zorro's Black Whip* (1944).

Even though the stagecoach landed in water, a fall from that distance should have caused some injury to, say, Vic Gordon, in Chapter Four of *Zorro's Black Whip* (1944). It did not. The coach came out of the water and Vic floated to the surface uninjured. While this may seem unrealistic, Red Ryder, in Chapter One of *Adventures of Red Ryder* (1940), also fell into the same lake over the same cliff in the same stagecoach from Mesquite Stage Lines and was also uninjured, so apparently a fall into water from such height was not a problem. Or, Mesquite Stage Lines had padded stage coaches.

## III. INDIVIDUAL WESTERN CLIFFHANGERS

Westerns also had individual cliffhangers, where the hero went over the cliff on his own or on a horse and not in a vehicle. For example, Red Ryder tried to jump a high canyon on his horse for the second time in Chapter Ten of *Adventures of Red Ryder* (1940). He should not have tempted fate twice as his horse could not quite make the jump. Horse and rider plummeted to the earth below.

In the next chapter, the horse and rider landed in water and were therefore uninjured. They rode out together. In *The Oregon Trail* (1939) (Chapter One) and *The Painted Stallion* (1937) (Chapter Three) there were similar cliffover resolutions with a fall over a cliff into water although in the latter serial, the hero was knocked unconscious and had to be rescued by the Rider. The most spectacular one of all occurred at the end of the first chapter of *The Last Frontier* (1932), where Lon Chaney and Dorothy Gulliver went over a cliff on the back of the horse, the horse did a 360 in the air and then landed in a river of raging rapids, yet riders and horse all survived.

*Adventures of Red Ryder* (1940). This is a spectacular jump by horse and rider over a high gorge, used several times in Republic serials. However, in this serial, the jump is not successful, sending horse and Red Ryder into a spectacular cliffover.

Sometimes the western cliffovers came close to being real cliff hangers. In Chapter Nine of *The Law of the Wild* (1934), Alice Ingram was fighting with some henchmen when she was knocked off a steep cliff. As the chapter ended, her scream was heard over the closing frame.

In the resolution, as she slid down the hill, she grabbed onto a puny-looking branch sticking out of the rocks. Then, as she hung from the branch, it started to come loose from the mountain. Luckily, she was inexplicably saved just in time by the same henchmen who had tried to kill her at the end of the prior chapter. Since she was not hanging from the branch at the end of the prior chapter, this cannot be deemed to be a true cliff hanger.

There was a similar ending in Chapter One of *Riders of Death Valley* (1941), with the cliffhanger being a wagon over a cliff. In the next chapter, the hero was saved by jumping out before the wagon went over the cliff. However, he then rolled down the hill and then found himself hanging from the side of a cliff, part way down the hill. He then had to be rescued by his friend. Although close, this was still not a true cliff hanger ending.

## IV. INDIVIDUAL CITY CLIFFOVERS

There are no cliffs in the city, but there are the next best things: high buildings. Serial heroes have been falling out of windows, or off roofs and ledges, since serials were invented. These have led to some interesting resolutions.

First, however, was the simple "lived through it" resolution. Logically, this would not work if the fall was from a high office building but it was sometimes plausible in smaller drops. Dick Tracy, in Chapter Five of the serial of the same name, survived a fall from the roof of a house. At least there was an explanation. The fall was broken by some branches and what appeared to be a patio roof.

The Green Hornet, on the other hand, survived a fall without any explanation at all. At the end of Chapter Six of *The Green Hornet* (1939), the villains were shooting at the Green Hornet. He tried to escape but in so doing, fell out a second story window. In the next chapter, he landed on a stone walkway and, nevertheless, got up uninjured. There was no explanation for this serial miracle.

Jungle Jim had similar luck to the Green Hornet. In Chapter Nine, he fell out of a second story window backwards after being shot, but in the resolution, landed on his feet uninjured. He stated that his fall was cushioned by a balcony, but the balcony was unseen in any of the footage.

Although *The Mystery Trooper* (1931) was actually a western, it had a city-style cliffover at the end of Chapter Nine. The hero and villain were fighting on top of a high roof, when they both fell off together. In an unusual development, they were both saved in the next chapter when they landed on a group of henchmen who were watching the fight.

Other "survived through it" city cliffovers involved an awning save. Spike Holland, in Chapter Six of *The Green Archer* (1940), was pushed out of a high window but survived by landing on the entryway awning of the building. The resolution was foreshadowed cleverly because the location of the awning was shown several times before the fall. In *Gang Busters* (1942) (Chapter Five), Bill Bannister was saved from a push over a building ledge when his fall was slightly broken by an awning near the ground. However, the awning appeared to be so flimsy that it could not have protected a baby, much less an adult, yet Bannister survived with nary a scratch.

The most spectacular awning save occurred in the resolution to the Chapter Two cliffhanger of *Pirate Treasure* (1934). Dick Moreland was fighting with villains back and forth across high building roofs when he was finally caught alongside a ledge. As he was about to be lifted over, a long shot showed there were a series of five awnings at windows on each of the floors just below Moreland. Once Moreland was pushed over, his fall was broken by three of the awnings and he did an acrobatic roll over two of the awning poles, landing in safety on the sidewalk below.

A variation on the awning save resolved the cliffhanger to Chapter Four of *Junior G-Men* (1940). Billy Barton was rescued from a fire in an apartment building by an FBI man, who carried Billy to a window. As he tried to climb down with Billy on his back, they both fell. Luckily, they landed in a firemen's net and were saved. Once again, this resolution was set up nicely, with the prior episode containing lots of stock footage showing the firemen racing to the scene of the fire.

*Batman* (1943) had a spectacular ending to Chapter One. The Caped Crusader was thrown off a high office building, and as the chapter ended, he was plummeting to the ground. In the next chapter, he was saved when he landed on a window washing platform, which broke his fall. Even the two window washers apparently hung on, thus letting three people defy the laws of physics. There was no shot of the platform at any time during the prior chapter so there was no foreshadowing of the resolution. Nevertheless, the resolution was quite spectacular.

Another spectacular takeout occurred when the title character in *The Masked Marvel* (1943) was pushed off a high gasoline tank in Chapter One and his fall was luckily broken by the roof of a truck below. Similarly, the title character in *Captain America* (1944) survived a fall out of a building in Chapter 13, "Skyscraper Plunge" by falling through the roof of a truck, apparently onto some laundry bags, which cushioned the fall. In the resolution, however, the skyscraper looked to be about two stories high.

In those three examples, the saves by the trucks came as a complete surprise, as the trucks were not shown in the prior episode and therefore, the resolutions were less convincing than the serials which foreshadowed the save. However, masked crime fighters, such as Batman, the Green Hornet, the Masked Marvel and Captain America, seemed to have a lot of luck when it came to city cliffovers. Or, maybe it was just the uniform and not the mask. In Chapter Ten of *Scouts to the Rescue* (1939), Boy Scout Bruce Scott, played by Jackie Cooper, fell from a high building

*Batman* (1943). In this spectacular resolution to a fall off a high skyscraper, Batman is saved by a window washing platform. Even the man in white on the right is not injured. Batman is played by Lewis Wilson.

roof as he was throwing ammunition into an adjacent building to help a federal officer. Luckily, there was a huge water tank below and Scott emerged uninjured.

Of course, much like a western, a fall in the big city into water from a high ledge was surely safe for the serial heroine and hero, but then, maybe not. In Chapter Seven of *The Perils of Pauline* (1934), Warde and Pauline, on a high hotel balcony, were in a fight with Dr. Bashan and his henchmen for possession of the sacred disks, when the railing broke and Warde and Pauline fell into the hotel pool. Unfortunately for them, the pool contained man-eating sharks. This was a somewhat unusual facility for a big city hotel, but then, this was the Mandarin Hotel in exotic Singapore. Luckily, Warde and Pauline were able to escape, with some help from a courageous hotel employee.

City serials often moved to the country for some of their cliffhangers, thus permitting western-style cliffovers. In Chapter Three of *Batman and Robin* (1949), Batman was forced off a cliff by the Wizard's long distance villainy. Luckily, Batman's fall was stopped by a tree, which Batman grabbed with his legs as he was upside down. Despite the great fall and the sudden stop, Batman was not injured at all, not even in his knees.

Jack Holt in Chapter Two of *Holt of the Secret Service* (1941) was wrestling a henchman on top of a high cliff when they both rolled off and plummeted to the ground. The next chapter revealed that the hench-man died in the fall but Holt was not even scratched. His suit, however, was terminally scuffed. When you were as tough as Holt, you could easily live through any cliffover.

Commando Cody, in *Radar Men from the Moon* (1952), was hit with a rock and fell off a high cliff at the end of Chapter Six. Luckily, he was wearing his flying suit at the time.

## V. SUBSTITUTION RESOLUTIONS

One of the cleverest of all cliffover resolutions was the substitution, where it turned out that the hero did not actually take the fall. Probably the cleverest use of this resolution occurred with the cliffhanger in Chap-ter 11 of *The Crimson Ghost* (1946). The Crimson Ghost's henchman, Ashe, and another man wearing a light suit, forced Diana (heroine) to remove the Cyclotrode plans from a safe and give them to the Ghost's men. However, Diana tricked them and threw the real plans out the window. There was a shot of the henchmen, looking out of the window, watching the plans flutter to the ground, several stories below. (This was the first notice to the viewer that the apartment was on a high floor and a fall out the window would be deadly.)

As the two henchmen started to leave to retrieve the plans, Duncan (hero) arrived and a fight ensued. Ashe left Duncan and the other to fight while he went down to retrieve the plans. The film cut away from the fight to show Ashe retrieving the plans. When the film cut back to the fight upstairs, Duncan was punched out the window and fell to his death. Unlike most other serials, the viewer was given a shot out the window, showing Duncan hit the ground.

How could Duncan possibly survive? The takeout was clever. Just before the camera cut to Ashe retrieving the plans, Duncan was the closer of the two fighters to the window. During the shot of Ashe, the fighters changed positions. It was the henchman who was now closest to the window, and Duncan punched the bad guy out the window, to his death. The resolution used widely accepted movie techniques to make this work—action did take place in movies when cuts were made back and forth during a fight (or chase scene or battle scene, etc) but the audience often forgot that. The resolution also made use of a negative in 1940s movies and particularly serials, i.e. that the male actors, especially if they were wearing similar clothes, often looked alike.

This same resolution was used earlier for the Chapter Six cliffhanger in *Secret Agent X-9* (1937). However, the setup and execution were not done nearly as well as in *The Crimson Ghost*.

*Batman and Robin* (1949) had an interesting substitution resolution of the cliffhanger at the end of Chapter Ten. Batman was in a fistfight with three villains by an open window in a tall building, when Batman was punched out the window. Batman was seen falling and then landing behind a car in the street. Clearly, Batman could never have survived such a high fall. In the next chapter, the resolution was told in flashback. Earlier, Batman was knocked out and one of the minor characters changed clothes with Batman and went on to impersonate the super hero. He was the one who lost his life in the fall, not Batman.

*Federal Operator 99* (1945). One car contains the heroes; the other car contains the villain. If one goes over a cliff, whose car will it be?

Another interesting variation occurred in Chapter 11 of *Federal Operator 99* (1945), when villain Jim Belmont sent a henchman to force Jerry Blake and his secretary off the road. Coincidentally, the henchman chose a car which was very nearly identical to Blake's car. In the ensuing chase on a mountain road, the two cars changed position several times. Then, after a scream by Blake's secretary, one car was pushed off the high mountain, crashed to the ground below and exploded. Although not unexpected, the resolution involved the henchman's car actually taking the dive, and not the car of Jerry Blake.

Substitution resolutions were not limited to cliffovers. Substitution resolutions could be seen as resolutions to a car crash and a plane crash in *The Green Archer* (1940) (Chapter 11) and *Sky Raiders* (1941) (Chapter One), respectively. In those two cases, the substitutions were obvious and the resolutions came as no surprise. Substitutions related to guns could be seen in the resolution to a long range shooting which occurred in Chapter Nine of *The Lightning Warrior* (1931), and a close range shooting through a door in Chapter Seven of *The Masked Marvel* (1943).

In *The Black Widow* (1947) (Chapter Four), two trunks were in an airplane, with an open door. The heroine was trapped in one of the trunks, which apparently fell out of the plane at the end of the chapter. The resolution was an obvious substitution resolution. In *The Adventures of Frank and Jesse James* (1948) (Chapter Ten), Jesse, who was involved in a fight with two henchmen in a barn, was punched onto a metal knife-like object sticking through some wood, causing instant death. In the resolution, the viewer learned that it was actually the similarly-dressed henchman who had been punched onto the knife, not Jesse. Again, this was not much of a surprise to the viewer.

However, *Spy Smasher* (1942) (Chapter Two) had a clever one where the hero was trapped by enemy agents and apparently machine-gunned to death at the end of the chapter. In the resolution, it turned out that Spy Smasher had forced an enemy soldier to dress in his outfit and it was the enemy who was killed, not the hero. That resolution came as a true surprise.

More controversial substitution resolutions were those that involved a different hero being killed than the primary hero. A prime example occurred in Chapter Eight of *The Masked Marvel* (1943). The masked title character, who was actually one of four insurance investigators, was fighting with henchmen on top of a roof of a high building. As the

Marvel was climbing back onto the roof after a short fall onto a fire escape, he was shot and fell off the high building. The dummy that was used looked like it fell all the way to the street.

In the resolution, there was a long time expansion cheat wherein Jim Arnold, one of the other insurance investigators, arrived. He was dressed just like the Marvel, except for the mask. It turned out that Arnold took the fall, not the Marvel, and that Arnold was killed. This was hardly a satisfying resolution since Arnold was one of the heroes of the serial, just like the Masked Marvel. That actually meant that the cliffhanger had no resolution at all.

The most famous substitution resolution of this kind occurred with the cliffhanger at the end of Chapter 11 of *Spy Smasher* (1942). The caped and goggled crime fighter was shot off a high roof and as the chapter ended, his body landed on a concrete sidewalk. Clearly, there was no way that he could survive.

In the new footage shown at the beginning of the next chapter, it turned out that Jack, the Spy Smasher's identical twin, had knocked out the Spy Smasher and taken his place on the deadly mission. Thus, it was Jack who was killed and not Alan, the real Spy Smasher. However, Jack had been as heroic as Spy Smasher throughout the serial and this was hardly a satisfying resolution. Indeed, Chapter 11 of the serial was titled, "Hero's Death," which reinforced how heroic Jack had been throughout the serial.

Although not a substitution resolution, *Gunfighters of the Northwest* (1954) had a similar unsatisfactory resolution to a cliffhanger which should be mentioned here. At the beginning of the serial, it appeared that the story would be about two Royal Mounties, Sgt. Joe Ward, played by Jock Mahoney, and Constable Arch Perry, played by Tom Farrell. In addition to being co-employees, they were best friends. Then, at the end of Chapter Two, the Mounties were attacked by Indians and Perry tried to escape by climbing a tall, wooden structure. One Indian followed him to the top. The two fought on top of the structure and once Perry knocked the Indian off, Perry was shot from a long distance by a rifle used by one of the White Horse Rebels. As the chapter ended, Perry fell off the structure to certain death.

For once, that turned out to be true. Perry's fall was not miraculously broken by some previously unseen object; he did not just survive a 30 foot drop. In fact, he simply died. In some ways, it was the most startling cliffhanger resolution of all time. In other ways, it was no resolution at all.

Substitution resolutions (except, perhaps, where a different hero was killed) made some of the cleverest cliffhanger resolutions of all time. While they usually came as a surprise, there was an underlying logic to them.

## VI. CONCLUSION

*Zorro's Black Whip* (1944) hit the trifecta on cliffovers. A wagon over a cliff, a stagecoach over a cliff and an individual over a cliff made this serial a roadmap for resolving cliffovers. However, some modern day serials had even more. For example, in *Batman and Robin*, a car and then a truck went over a cliff, Batman individually went over a cliff and Batman was pushed out of the window of an office building. However, the record has to go to *Holt of the Secret Service* (1941), who went over a waterfall in an open canoe, rolled off a high cliff in a fight and appeared to go over a cliff in a car, not to mention two falls in a ship and one fall climbing a ladder on a high building.

Individuals falling out of buildings or over cliffs and wagons or cars propelled over steep hillsides were the most familiar cliffhangers of the sound movie serials. While often resolved by cheats or absurd resolutions, they were still some of the most spectacular cliffhangers in any serial. They truly deserve a new word to describe them, and the appropriate word is "cliffover."

# Chapter 5
# Cheat Cliffhanger Resolutions

**The high point** of the serial was the cliffhanger and its resolution the following week. The cliffhanger distinguished a serial from any other form of motion picture. When it was done well, with an exciting cliffhanger from which the hero could not possibly escape, and then a clever, yet plausible resolution in which the hero, in fact, survived unscathed, the serial really delivered.

Too often, however, the filmmaker provided a cheat resolution, which could only disappoint the viewer. In fact, when it came to cars over cliffs or airplane crashes, the experienced serial viewer knew that the resolution would always be a cheat. Why rush back to the theater the following week to see the next chapter when the resolution was already known, and already known to be a cheat?

Cheat resolutions fell into three categories: time expansion cheats, "survived through it" cheats, and re-shot footage cheats. There were also resolutions that strained credulity, such as absurd resolutions and "too close for comfort" cheats.

## I. TIME EXPANSION CHEATS

The villains jumped into a car and took off at high speed. The hero followed in his own car as fast as possible. As the cars proceeded up and down hills and around bends with reckless indifference to safety, shots were exchanged between the two vehicles. Finally, the villain took close aim, fired and hit the front tire of the hero's vehicle. The vehicle careened out of control, through a fence, over a steep cliff, and dropped at least 100 feet to the ground, where it burst into flames. There was no way that the hero could survive such a catastrophe. Or was there?

151

In fact, most members of the audience knew that at the beginning of the next chapter, it was likely to be learned that the hero managed to jump out of the vehicle to safety, before it crashed over the cliff. This technique has been referred to as "time expansion," in the sense that more footage was shown the following week, and in the time of the new footage, the hero had the chance to jump out of the vehicle before the crash. The term "time expansion" is simply a fancy expression for "cheat."

Time expansion was one of the most common serial cheat resolutions. It was a cheat because if the serial were shown the first time with all of the footage in the proper time sequence, there would have been no cliffhanger at all.

Cars or other vehicles over cliffs were not the only cliffhangers where time expansion was used. Another common serial cliffhanger was an airplane crash with the hero trapped in the plane. The next week, it turned out that the hero had the time to find a parachute, put it on, and dive from the airplane before the crash. The airplane time expansion resolu-

*The Masked Marvel* (1943). This is a set up for a time expansion cheat resolution. Henchman Ken Terrell fights with Tom Steele, playing the Masked Marvel, as the boat with explosives on board crashes into a concrete bank. In the next chapter, it turns out that the Marvel jumped out of the boat before the crash.

tion was even worse than the vehicle over the cliff cheat, because the amount of new footage inserted into the next chapter for the airplane cheat was usually quite lengthy.

There was an interesting variation on this airplane time expansion cheat in the resolution to the Chapter One cliffhanger of *Flying G-Men* (1939). The heroic Black Falcon was flying one of the new piggy-back planes, with a smaller plane being carried on top of a larger plane. The Falcon deliberately flew his plane into an out-of-control drone plane, which was about to drop bombs on a crowded city. There was a terrific mid-air explosion. In the resolution, the Falcon escaped by flying off in the smaller plane, while his larger plane was destroyed. While this was still a time expansion cheat, it was a refreshing change from a parachute escape.

Time expansion was also used in other cliffhangers, such as buildings which exploded with the hero inside. The following week it was discovered that the hero had time to exit the building before the explosion. A clever variation on this occurred in Chapter One of *Captain America* (1944) when the hero was trapped on a high floor in a collapsing skyscraper, so simply running out the back door would not work. In the added footage shown the next week, the Captain managed to find a window. He jumped into the adjacent skyscraper before the total collapse of the structure in which he was originally trapped.

One of the longest time expansion inserts occurred in Chapter 15 of *Batman* (1943). At the end of the prior chapter, Batman had been locked in a pine box and tossed into a pit filled with deadly alligators. The resolution included over two minutes of time expansion footage, to explain how Batman survived. The explanation itself was a clever substitution resolution.

## II. "SURVIVED THROUGH IT" CHEATS

Another type of common cheat resolution was the "survived through it" cheat. The hero was put in a catastrophic situation at the end of a chapter, from which no one could survive. Yet, the following week, the hero simply lived through the event and walked away, barely scratched.

If the hero did not escape from that car over the cliff, he simply walked away from the crash the next week with no injuries, or with only minor injuries. Even if there were some minor injuries, they would be forgotten within a few minutes. No honest explanation was given for these seeming miracles. It is true that upon occasion in real life, people do walk away from horrific auto or other accidents with nary a scratch. But, serials were not real life and a "survived through it" resolution was always a cheat, because if that were an acceptable resolution of a cliffhanger, then it could be used for any cliffhanger in any serial, defeating the suspense of the cliffhanger and, indeed, the purpose of the cliffhanger.

Survived-through-it cheats were not limited to cliffovers. Another bad example of a "survived through it" resolution occurred in *The Green Archer* (1940) (Chapter Ten). Spike Holland opened a booby-trapped safe and was shot by two revolvers straight into his body. He fell to the floor. In the next episode, Spike simply got up and participated in a fist fight. There were no ill effects of the shotgun blasts and not even an attempt at an explanation as to how he survived being shot at such close range. With a resolution such as that one, why have any cliffhanger at all?

Another bad example occurred in *Sky Raiders* (1941). At the end of Chapter Four, Captain Dayton was trapped in a plane which crashed into a mountain. In the time expansion cheat in the next chapter, Dayton simply jumped out of an airplane without a parachute and rolled on the ground, as if he had jumped out of the ubiquitous fast moving automobile of serial cliffhangers. Dayton was knocked unconscious but when he woke up, he had no injuries at all. Presumably, the explanation was that the plane was going so low at the time he jumped that the fall did not hurt him. However, the plane was still going very fast at the time of his jump and it is hard to understand why the fall did not result in, at a minimum, many months of hospitalization for Captain Dayton. This type of "survived through it" cheat was used in many other serials, including the takeout to the Chapter Seven cliffhanger of *The Green Hornet Strikes Again* (1940), when the masked hero was able to survive a crash in a burning plane by jumping out at a low altitude.

A particularly outrageous airplane-related "survived through it" cheat occurred in Chapter Eight of *Burn 'em Up Barnes* (1934) when Barnes was involved in his new job doing movie stunt work, this time on an airplane with a double wing. As the cameraman filmed from another airplane, Barnes walked out on the lower wing and then pulled himself up to the top wing. Unbeknownst to Barnes, the villains had damaged the rudder on the plane, causing the pilot to lose control. That knocked Barnes off his feet, causing him to lie flat on the top wing and holding on as hard as he could. The plane then did a complete 360 degree roll and crashed into the ground.

This was a particularly well-done cliffhanger by Mascot, with a live stunt man on the wing and the shots of Jack Mulhall as Barnes taken from such an angle that a process screen did not have to be used. Barnes somehow survived the crash, after somehow hanging onto the wing as it did its roll. After rubbing his right wrist slightly, Barnes was able to chase after the henchman who caused the accident, the ill effects of the crash quickly forgotten. There were no explanations given for how Barnes did not fall off the plane when it looped and then how Barnes survived the crash to the earth when he was not even inside the plane.

One of the strangest "survived through it" cheats occurred in the resolution to the Chapter Four cliffhanger of *The Indians Are Coming* (1930). Jack Manning sent his dog Pal through Indian lines to attempt to obtain help for a besieged wagon train. An Indian chased after him and as the chapter ended, shot Pal in the side with an arrow. In the next chapter, Pal sat up, pulled the arrow out with his teeth and continued on his journey. This was truly a jaw-dropping cliffhanger resolution,

Sometimes, explanations were attempted for these types of resolutions. A wagon or motorcycle over a cliff landed in water, apparently cushioning the blow. The hero's fall over a cliff or off a roof was broken by trees or a patio or a laundry truck. Usually, however, there was no explanation attempted. If the hero in a plane which was about to drop could not find the parachute, he would simply survive the plane crash. If the hero could not find a way out of a building before it exploded, he would simply survive the explosion.

The problem with these cheat resolutions was that because the cliffhanger is such an integral part of the serial, enough cheat cliffhanger resolutions can seriously detract from the quality of the serial. A famous case in point was *The Shadow*, a 1940 serial from Columbia. *The Shadow* had much going for it, including some clever plot twists and good performances, especially by Victor Jory playing the title character. Yet, the cliffhanger resolutions sabotaged the effectiveness of the serial.

*The Shadow* had 15 chapters so there were 14 cliffhangers. Six of those cliffhangers (Chapters 1, 4, 7, 10, 12 and 14) involved the Shadow trapped in a building or a cave when there was some type of explosion and the roof collapsed. As the narrator would say, the Shadow was doomed to die.

The following week, the Shadow merely picked himself up, dusted himself off, and started all over again. There was no attempt at an explanation as to why he survived the explosion and roof collapse. In fact, in the last explosion and collapse that occurred in the serial, four other characters also survived the explosion along with the Shadow, making the whole scenario even more ludicrous.

The Shadow also survived a rollover car crash (Chapter 13), and there were also several time expansion cheats. For a major serial, *The Shadow* may have had more cheat resolutions than any other serial. That was why, in the end, despite all of its virtues, *The Shadow* was a disappointing serial.

An incident in *The Green Archer* (1940) described this type of cliffhanger best. In Chapter Five, Spike Holland was tied in the back of a truck which crashed into some high voltage electric towers. There was an explosion, the truck turned over and a fire ensued. Surprisingly, in the next chapter, Spike survived, unhurt. When Valerie came back to find him, this dialogue occurred:

VALERIE: Spike. I thought you had been killed.
SPIKE: I thought so too for a minute. Only a miracle saved me.

Unfortunately, too many serial makers relied on miracles for cliffhanger resolutions.

## III. RE-SHOT FOOTAGE CHEATS

This was the worst cheat of all. A chapter ended with an excellent cliffhanger, from which the hero could not survive. In the next chapter, that turned out to be true. The filmmaker could not figure out how the hero could survive, and so the supposed footage from the prior episode that was shown in the new chapter was actually different footage, changing the cliffhanger and allowing the hero to survive. There were a number of examples of this in serial history. These are just five:

1) *Undersea Kingdom* (1936) had several cheat cliffhanger resolutions of this type. The most famous occurred in Chapter Eight, "Into the Metal Tower." Crash Corrigan was secured to the front of the Juggernaut, a tank-like vehicle run on a battery that sounded like it came from a golf cart. If Crash did not tell his friends in the walled city to hand over

the priming powder which was needed to propel Unga Kahn's tower to the surface, the gates would be rammed by the Juggernaut with Corrigan at the front. Corrigan's response? "Go ahead and ram."

As the chapter ended, the gate was rammed. There was noise of the collision and dust from the collision spilled out. Crash's friends inside the city, including little Billy, were standing together on the second floor of the palace veranda and were alarmed.

In the next chapter, different footage was shown. Little Billy took command, directing that the gates be opened. The guard followed the commands of the little tyke and the gates were opened before the juggernaut hit. There was no crash, noise or dust. A great cliffhanger had turned into no cliffhanger at all.

2) *Zorro Rides Again* (1937) was an otherwise excellent serial which had one of these cheats at the end of Chapter 10, entitled "Trapped." Zorro was in the city where he was searching for documents in an office in a high building. He was discovered and was chased. He decided to escape by jumping from the roof of one office building to another. He made the jump, landing on his feet on the ledge of the second office building. Then he fell backwards. As the chapter ended, Zorro had clearly fallen backwards off the ledge.

At the beginning of the next chapter, Zorro made the same jump but grabbed the ledge of the other office building with both hands. His feet never landed on the ledge. Zorro then lost his grip on the ledge with one hand but that gave him the opportunity to pull out his whip, fling it around a pole and then swing to safety.

The sad part of this cheat was that if, in the cliffhanger, Zorro had caught the ledge of the second building with both hands and then lost his grip with one hand, that would have been cliffhanger enough. (Also, it would have been an actual cliff hanger.) There was no reason to create this colossal cheat, severely disappointing any viewer who could remember what had happened at the end of the prior week's episode.

3) *Buck Rogers* (1939) proved that these cheat resolutions were not limited to Republic serials. In this science fiction adventure from Universal set on Earth in the $25^{th}$ century, the heroes had to worry about deadly ray guns in addition to other serial menaces. In Chapter Nine, "Bodies without Minds," Buddy, who was Buck Rogers' youthful assis-

tant, climbed into Killer Kane's lair to search for information concerning Buck Rogers' whereabouts. He was discovered by the Killer himself. As Buddy rushed to the window to try to escape, he was struck by the ray of the deadly ray gun. He started falling back as the chapter ended.

In the next chapter, Buddy rushed to the window and jumped out. He was not hit by a deadly ray. In fact, the ray gun was never even shot at him. There was simply no excuse for this cheat resolution. It is hard to believe that an audience member in the 1930s, even after waiting a week for the cliffhanger resolution, would not recognize this resolution for the cheat that it was.

4) *Secret Service in Darkest Africa* (1943) was filled with re-shot footage cheats. The worst one occurred at the end of Chapter Seven, titled "Murder Dungeon." Janet, the heroine, was knocked unconscious in a small pit. Above her was a heavy metal slab on chains which could

*Secret Service in Darkest Africa* (1943). Noted for its re-shot cliffhanger cheat resolutions, this is the second Rex Bennett serial, with the lead played both times by Rod Cameron, pictured at the bottom right. He is with the female lead, Joan Marsh. This lobby card emphasizes the villains, who are, from left to right, Lionel Royce, Kurt Krueger and Frederic Brunn, the latter playing the main henchman, Wolfe.

drop on her and kill her if the slab were released from the chains. Unfortunately for Janet, a vicious fist fight very near to the pit ensued between Rex Bennett and several henchmen. As Janet regained consciousness, one of the henchmen grabbed a sword, swung it wildly at Bennett and accidentally hit the switch which released the slab. As the chapter ended, Janet was rolling to her right but she was still in the pit as the slab dropped on her.

In the next chapter, the same events were faithfully re-shown until just before the switch was hit. In this new version, Janet quickly jumped out of the pit on her left (for no apparent reason), just before the sword hit the switch and dropped the block. Janet survived because an interesting cliffhanger was turned into no cliffhanger at all.

5) *Perils of Nyoka* (1942) may have had the most clever re-shot footage cheat cliffhanger resolution of all time. During Chapter Seven, titled "Monster's Clutch," Larry and Nyoka decided to sneak into Vultura's hideout to rescue her father. In case of a problem, they devised a clever escape route. The two tied a strong rope to a tree and flung it over a high cliff. If either or both had to escape quickly, they would not have to make a difficult climb down some rocks but instead could go quickly down the rope to safety.

Later in the chapter, Nyoka and Larry were discovered and Nyoka was chased out of the temple by the giant ape Satan. Nyoka headed quickly to the escape route and started to rappel down the cliff on the rope. Satan, not to be outsmarted and emulating his distant relative King Kong, started to pull up on the rope, dragging Nyoka toward him. Just as Nyoka was in his grasp, she let go, and with arms flailing, fell down the cliff to her apparent death.

In the resolution, it turned out that Nyoka fell into the lake at the bottom of the cliff and was easily able to swim to safety. That was a common resolution to these types of cliffhangers, so where was the cheat? It was clever. Earlier in the prior chapter, when Nyoka and Larry first threw the rope over the cliff, there was clearly no water under the cliff. There was a point of view shot of Larry looking over the cliff, surveying the rocky landing below. Then, once again, right at the end of the prior chapter, as Nyoka was almost in the grasp of the giant ape, she looked down and in another point of view shot, there was only a rocky landing below, with no water. The first and only time the water appeared was in the cheat resolution. Few viewers, after a week of waiting, would have consciously remembered the shots of solid ground below the cliff which were used in Chapter Seven and they would therefore feel it was a clever takeout and not a cheat.

There were many more examples of re-shot footage cheats. In Chapter One of *The Red Rider* (1934), Buck Jones fell off his horse and was trampled by onrushing riders while in the next chapter the line of horses stopped before it reached the fallen hero. In Chapter Six of *Tim Tyler's Luck* (1937), the young hero was chased through the jungle by a lion, which caught Tim as he was about to climb into a tree and pulled him to the ground. In the next chapter, a tiger prevented the lion from attacking, Tim made it to safety in the tree and the lion never touched him. In Chapter Ten of *The Adventures of Rex and Rinty* (1935), Frank Bradley was shot in the right chest as he was leading Rex up a gangplank. Bradley fell off the gangplank into the water. In the next chapter, Pasha saw the shooter, saved Bradley by pushing him off the gangplank into the water, and Pasha was the one who was shot. Finally, Chapter 11 of *The Mystery of the River Boat* (1944) was a particularly exciting serial episode involving a bus trip beset by sabotage, ending with the bus, as it turned over, skidding into an electricity tower, knocking part of the tower down and sending volts of electricity into the bus. In the next chapter, while the bus did hit the tower, the bus never turned over, it did minimal damage to the structure and no electricity hit the bus.

It is hard to determine which serial had the most re-shot footage cheat resolutions. Leading candidates are *The Fighting Marines* (1935), *Perils of Nyoka* (1942) and *Secret Service in Darkest Africa* (1943). A sure entrant into this Hall of Shame was *The Vigilantes Are Coming*, a Republic serial from 1936. It seemed that every resolution had some re-shot footage. For example, there was a fall off a high cliff which turned into about a ten foot jump (Chapter Five), a piece of heavy machinery landing on the Eagle's chest which turned into the Eagle being rescued before the device hit him (Chapter Four), five soldiers whacking the Eagle with swords as he laid on the floor turning into nothing at all, i.e., the footage was skipped in the next chapter (Chapter Seven), and a fall off a high bell tower into water which was clearly not there in the prior chapter and never appeared again in the serial and, in any event, hardly seemed deep enough to break his fall (Chapter One).

The true shame was that the footage leading up to the cliffhangers in *The Vigilantes Are Coming* was usually very well done, being both exciting and suspenseful. However, after a few chapters, the viewer, knowing each cliffhanger was likely to end in a cheat, hardly rushed back to the theater the next week to learn the resolution.

## IV. "TOO CLOSE FOR COMFORT" CHEATS

A variation on the re-shot footage cheat was, for want of a better term, the "too close for comfort" cheat. Here, the hero was inches from death at the close of the chapter. On a conveyor belt, he might be a second away from being chopped to bits, in a room with closing walls, he might be inches away from being crushed, or in a train cliffhanger, the train might be a foot away and about to smash the hero. There was absolutely no chance for the hero to be saved.

In the resolution, however, the footage was slightly altered so that the hero never got quite as close to the blades or the wall or the train as the scene was shown at the end of the prior chapter. Thus, there was now time for an escape or a rescue.

A continuity error in *The Spider's Web* (1938) highlighted this cheat. In Chapter Ten of the serial, Richard Wentworth and Nita Van Sloan were trapped in a room with fire and closing walls containing spears. As the chapter ended, they were about to be crushed and speared. In the resolution, the first time Wentworth and Van Sloan were shown, the walls were still about to touch them. Then there was a time expansion cheat allowing for a potential rescue and when there was a cut back to the trapped victims, the walls were not as close as they previously were in that chapter, not to mention at the end of the prior chapter. The "too close for comfort" cheat allowed for a rescue, which could not possibly have occurred without the walls suddenly appearing farther away than they previously were.

In the usual case, the cheat was not so obvious. The continuity error actually came between the end of the chapter with the cliffhanger and the start of the chapter with the resolution. For example, at the end of Chapter Three of *Zorro Rides Again* (1937), Zorro was doing battle near a railroad track with El Lobo. As the fight went on, El Lobo pulled a switch bar by the tracks, thus trapping Zorro's foot between two rails.

*Zorro Rides Again* (1937). This is an example of a too close for comfort cheat. As the cliffhanger chapter ends, the train is almost upon Zorro and there is no time for escape. In the resolution, the train never comes quite so close to Zorro, giving Zorro added time to free his leg which is trapped in the tracks. Zorro is played by John Carroll.

Zorro could not get out and unfortunately for him, a high speed train was on the way. As the chapter ended, through a process screen shot, the train was almost upon him.

This was an absolutely excellent cliffhanger, set up by a good fight and then cross cutting between the approaching train, Zorro, and his foot caught in the rails. During the fight, the sound of the train could be heard in the background. The resolution was also clever. Zorro used his bullwhip to lasso the switch bar and pull on it to move the switch track. Zorro was then able to jump out of the way.

The cheat in the resolution did not involve re-shot footage. Simply put, the train in the resolution never got quite as close to the trapped Zorro as it did in the previous chapter. This cheat allowed Zorro to escape by use of the whip. Zorro would never have had the time to escape in that manner if the train had come as close to him in the resolution as it had in the previous chapter.

Another name for the "too close for comfort" cheat is "the missing footage" cheat. A good example occurred in Chapter Two of *Radar Patrol vs. Spy King* (1949). Chris Calvert had trailed some henchmen to Tami's Garage, where one man was holding a lit acetylene torch and there were barrels of chemicals lying around. The cliffhanger was obvious. After a fight, Calvert was knocked unconscious, and the acetylene torch was dropped to the ground near the chemicals. As the chapter ended, there was a shot of Calvert lying on the ground. The camera then panned over to the torch and chemicals without a cut. There was an explosion and then a cut to the outside of the garage, which showed the entire building being destroyed.

Given the few seconds between the shot of Calvert lying unconscious on the floor of the garage and the explosion, there was no time for Calvert to escape from the building before the explosion. So, in the resolution, the panning shot from Calvert lying on the floor to the explosion was eliminated, giving Calvert plenty of time to escape from the building.

Another example occurred at the end of Chapter 11 of *Mysterious Dr. Satan* (1940), where the Copperhead was trapped in a cell with the walls closing in. As the chapter ended, the Copperhead was unable to push the wall back and he fell to the ground, about to be crushed by the wall. In the next chapter, the fall to the ground was eliminated and the Copperhead was able to use the reflection from a cigarette case he happened to be carrying to obtain a view of the wall mechanism in order to shoot it out of commission. No explanation was given for the missing footage of the Copperhead's fall.

The "too close for comfort" cheat was actually one of the most common cheats in serial resolutions. It was always used in combination with a time expansion cheat. It was not exactly a re-shot footage cheat. Rather, in the resolution, some of the footage from the previous chapter's cliffhanger miraculously disappeared, giving the hero the chance to escape.

## V. ABSURD RESOLUTIONS

These were not really cheats because the filmmaker provided a reason why the hero survived the preceding week's cliffhanger. It was just that the resolution was absurd and unconvincing. Luckily, it was also often quite amusing. Indeed, those types of cliffhanger resolutions were one of the small joys of watching serials.

*Jack Armstrong* (1947) had an absurd resolution to its cliffhanger at the end of Chapter Five, entitled "The Space Ship." The villains invented a rocket ship which they intended to use to conquer the Earth. The rocket ship took off from Earth from a hole in the ground, where most of the ship was in the ground and the nose of the ship was above the ground. After the rocket ship took off with a burst of flame, Jack and his friend were trapped in the hole from which the rocket ship lifted off. The villains realized this and directed the rocket ship back to earth, to crush the intruders. The ship came down vertically, fitting perfectly into the hole, apparently squashing Jack Armstrong and his three companions.

In the next chapter, just before the rocket ship landed, Uncle Jim told everyone to flatten themselves against the wall. They did that and the rocket ship landed so perfectly that no one was even nicked. Forget the effects of the heat from the bottom of the rocket caused by the ship recently taking off and returning to the earth's atmosphere. Jack and his friends should have been burned to a crisp but instead, there were no lingering effects from the cliffhanger.

*Batman and Robin* (1949) seems like a deliberately camp serial by today's standards. Batman's "Batmobile" was a regular Mercury convertible, stately Wayne Manor was smaller than many middle class homes, and Batman and Robin kept their costumes in a filing cabinet. Batman did not even appear to have a utility belt, until…

In Chapter Six, "Target: Robin," Batman and Robin were trapped in a room which was filling with deadly carbon monoxide gas. In the next chapter, Batman pulled two breathing devices out of his utility belt and then, with the ease of a magician, pulled an acetylene torch from the same belt. He used the torch to escape through a metal door. Where these devices came from, nobody knows.

*The Phantom* (1943) had an excellent cliffhanger at the end of its first chapter. The Phantom fell into quicksand and was trapped. An alligator crawled along the ground, ready to attack the trapped hero. The chapter ended with an effective special effect with the shot of the real alligator in the same scene with the Phantom.

In the next chapter the Phantom was rescued by—his dog. First, the dog barked at the alligator, scaring it away. The ferocity of the jungle was not what it used to be. Then the dog tried to pull the Phantom out by his sleeve. When that did not work, the dog grabbed a tree vine and dropped it by the Phantom so the Phantom could pull himself out. The dog even

*The Phantom* (1943). The Phantom, portrayed by Tom Tyler, is trapped in
quicksand and about to be attacked by an alligator. Luckily, he is saved by his dog
Devil, who is played by the aptly named Ace, the Wonder Dog.

pulled on the vine to assist the much larger man. For all his trouble, the
dog just got a scratch on the neck and a slight pat on the head. Hopefully,
there was an extra treat in the dog's dinner that night for his actions that
went far beyond his responsibilities as man's best friend. The Phantom's
dog, Devil, was played by Ace, the Wonder Dog, and at least in this case,
Ace was aptly named.

In *The New Adventures of Tarzan* (1935) (Chapter Six), unbeknownst
to Tarzan, there was a jungle spike trap set up by natives to kill a wild animal.
Tarzan, travelling through the jungle, heard a cry from a companion and ran
to rescue him. However, a panther attacked Tarzan, knocking him into the
trip wire, causing the trap to fall. At the end of the chapter, it appeared that
the trap fell all the way to the ground, impaling Tarzan. In the resolution, it
turned out that the trap did, in fact, fall the way to the ground, but the only
injury Tarzan suffered was a small scratch to his arm. The viewer is apparently
supposed to believe that Tarzan's body was lying in such a perfect position
that all of the sharp wooden stakes missed the jungle hero. It is a wonder that
the natives caught any animals in their traps.

Other absurd resolutions in serials included Tom Grayson with his air hose cut while underwater in heavy diving gear, walking along the ocean floor to safety on the shore, in the resolution to the Chapter Five cliffhanger of *Fighting Devil Dogs* (1938), the Spider, high in the air in a plane which was on fire in Chapter Ten of *The Spider's Web* (1938), flying the plane faster in order to have the wind extinguish the flame, Zorro being shot at point blank range by an arrow in Chapter Nine of *Zorro's Fighting Legion* (1937), only for the viewer to find out in the next chapter that the arrow was actually shot at Zorro's image in a full length mirror, the Copperhead, thrown out of a truck and landing on the road in front of a fast pursuing vehicle in Chapter Eight of *Mysterious Dr. Satan* (1940), instead of rolling out of the way, ducking down and allowing the car to drive over him without hitting him in any way, Blackhawk jumping out of a burning plane in Chapter Seven of *Blackhawk* (1952) and his parachute not opening, being caught in the air by another member of the Blackhawks who had parachuted out of the plane first, and Kent Fowler being dropped out of a Martian flying disc and plummeting to the ground at high speed, only

*Secret Agent X-9* (1945). X-9, portrayed by Lloyd Bridges, is literally having the floor pulled out from under him by the evil Nabura. If he falls, he will be impaled on some sharp spikes. Luckily, he saves himself with an incredible acrobatic feat.

to be saved by landing in a hay stack (which he later referred to as a "soft spot"), in the Chapter Five cliffhanger of *Flying Disc Man from Mars* (1950). The latter cliffhanger and resolution was courtesy of archive footage from Chapters Seven and Eight of *King of the Mounties* (1942).

A variation on the absurd resolution was the incredible acrobatic resolution. A good example was in *Secret Agent X-9* (1945), in Chapter Eight aptly titled "Dropping Floor." X-9 was trapped in a room. The villainous Nabora pulled the concrete base floor out of the room by use of a machine specifically designed for that purpose. X-9 looked down and saw that once the floor disappeared and he fell down, he would land on steel knives protruding up from the pit. As the chapter ended, there was only about a foot of floor remaining. X-9 was facing the left side of the screen and fell to the left.

In the next chapter, there was a time expansion cheat. A friend came to X-9's aide, forcing Nabora to slide the floor back. However, X-9 had already fallen at the end of the prior chapter. Luckily, as the floor came back, X-9 managed to catch the edge of the floor. He was now facing the right side of the screen, holding onto the floor.

In the piece of footage not shown between the two chapters, X-9 must have twisted in the air and at the same time, tumbled right side up, so that he could be turned around to catch the edge of the floor. This was a feat of acrobatics that defied many of the laws of physics. Of course, the laws of physics often did not apply in serials.

Another incredible acrobatic resolution occurred in Chapter One of *Flash Gordon Conquers the Universe* (1938), where Flash tumbled into a bottomless pit with a henchman of Ming. The drop was straight down and they were falling at a high rate of speed. Nevertheless, Flash was able to grab onto a solid horizontal bar on the side of the pit and stop his fall without injury. This topped any stunt done on the horizontal bar at the summer Olympics. Perhaps Buster Crabbe should have competed in gymnastics rather than swimming if only gymnastics were an Olympic sport in 1928 and 1932.

Of course, it may just be that great athletes were able to do this. That is the only explanation for Red Grange, in Chapter 11 of *The Galloping Ghost* (1931), being pushed off a roof yet saving his life by catching onto a fire escape railing at least four floors below.

Another variation on the absurd resolution was the ESP or extra-sensory perception resolution. The hero, in danger without knowing it, suddenly took action to escape from trouble, for no apparent reason. In

Chapter 11 of *Holt of the Secret Service* (1941), there was a trap set in the jungle where someone, running down a path, would fall over a rope, dropping a set of spikes on him. Holt knew nothing about this trap. At the end of the chapter he tripped over the rope and fell, right under the trap. In the next chapter, he fell but immediately rolled away, avoiding the trap. No explanation was given for this sudden move. It could only have been ESP.

At the end of Chapter Five of *The Great Alaskan Mystery* (1944), Jim Hudson was driving a truck on a back road. Unbeknownst to him, the villains had partially sawed the cables on one side of a bridge, knowing that the weight of Jim's truck would cause the weakened bridge to collapse and that Hudson will fall to his death in a high ravine. The plan worked to perfection and at the end of the chapter, the bridge had fallen with the truck on it.

In the next chapter, it turned out that just before the truck started across the bridge, Hudson jumped out, thus saving his life. However, why did he do that? The henchmen were nowhere in sight. Hudson was driving at night so he could not see the weakened bridge cables. There was nothing to indicate to Hudson that there would be a problem with the bridge. There is therefore only one explanation for Hudson's prescient action of jumping out of the truck. It was ESP.

## VII. CONCLUSION

Were there any serials that had no cheat cliffhanger resolutions? Probably not. As inventive as the serial creators could be, it is hard to imagine a serial without at least one time expansion cheat.

Indeed, the most famous sound serial of them all, *Flash Gordon* (1936), is likely to be the serial that came closest to being free of cheat cliffhanger resolutions. The serial was 13 chapters in length, so there were 12 cliffhangers. In the takeouts to the first 11 cliffhangers, there were no cheats. In some cases, Flash Gordon was rescued from the chapter ending peril by his allies (and even on one occasion by Emperor Ming), or he defeated one of the beasts of Mongo on his own or with some help, or his falling rocket ship was saved by the anti-gravity ray which held Vultan's kingdom floating above Mongo. However, at the end of Chapter 12, Flash and the gang were trapped in a turret house and Ming and his men, in a rocket ship,

CHAPTER 2. "DEATH'S CHARIOT"

*Perils of Nyoka* (1942). This serial has many great cliffhangers. Pictured is Kay Aldridge in a torture rack, being watched by Charles Middleton, Lorna Gray and George J. Lewis.

were firing on them from above. The chapter ended with a loud explosion, obviously killing all of our heroes.

The next chapter started with a time expansion cheat, which showed Flash luckily locating a trap door in the house. Everyone was able to escape just before the explosion occurred. Thus, the blast did no harm, except for ending a record of 11 straight cliffhanger takeouts without one cheat resolution.

Some serial fans do not mind cheat resolutions, believing they are just a part of the genre. Others merely tolerate them; others loathe them. Whichever category the viewer falls in, cheat cliffhanger resolutions are a fact of life in the sound movie serial. They are never going away.

# Chapter 6
# A Variety of Cliffhangers

**The most common cliffhanger** was probably the cliffover. The next most common cliffhangers were probably the airplane crash with the hero inside or the exploding building, once again, with the hero inside. Much like the cliffover, those two types of cliffhangers tended to be resolved with cheats.

When you have seen five cars or wagons going over cliffs or ten factories blowing up, you have seen them all. Luckily, there were a variety of other cliffhangers that were exciting and suspenseful, drawing the moviegoer back into the theater for the following week's chapter.

## I. SPECIAL TYPES OF CLIFFHANGERS

### Railroads

Trains were often involved in serial cliffhangers. The most common use was in a cliffover where the train jumped the tracks or there was an explosion in front of the train, in both cases causing the train to go down a steep hillside. This type of cliffhanger could be seen in *Winners of the West* (1940) (Chapter Two), *Mandrake the Magician* (1939) (Chapter Nine) and many others.

People who are not serial fans might expect that there would be many chapter endings with a damsel in distress tied across the tracks as a train approached. However, while that may have happened many times in the silent era, it was a rare occurrence in the talking era and when it did happen, it was the male lead who was in the predicament. For example, at the end of Chapter 13 of *Deadwood Dick* (1940), the masked hero was lassoed off his horse and pulled over to the railroad tracks, just as a train was coming by. Luckily for Dick, the villains did not have enough time to tie him to the tracks so it was easy enough for Dick to roll out of the way just in time.

In *The Hurricane Express* (1932) (Chapter Four), John Wayne was knocked out on tracks and run over by a train. In the resolution, it turned out that Wayne was luckily lying within and exactly parallel to the tracks, and the train was able to pass over his body, without causing even a scratch. A particularly exciting train cliffhanger occurred in Chapter Three of *Zorro Rides Again* (1937), with the masked hero's foot caught in a railroad switch track as the train was rapidly approaching. This was resolved with a "too close for comfort" cheat as described in the previous chapter.

A spectacular variation on a hero-across-the-tracks cliffhanger occurred in Chapter Five of *Dick Tracy's G-Men* (1939). The evil Ghost was after a train which was carrying a gold shipment. He intended to derail the train at Lethal Gorge and steal the gold. Tracy overheard the plans but was too far away to reach the train by land. Tracy's only hope was to reach the speeding train by plane and somehow convince the engineer to stop the locomotive.

As Tracy and Steve Lockwood approached the train from the air, Tracy kept waving his arms and pointing to the ground, trying to convince the engineers to stop the train. They misunderstood and merely waved back at him, thinking it was a friendly greeting. Tracy was desperate. He decided to parachute out of the plane and convince the train to stop once he was on the ground. Tracy bailed out, but unfortunately, he appeared to land right on the track, falling down in front of the speeding locomotive. At the fadeout, the train ran over the parachute, apparently killing Tracy.

The resolution was clever. While the parachute was lying across the track, Tracy was lying on the other side of the rails, off the track. Although Tracy had passed out after the hard landing, he was not in harm's way. The train ripped the parachute but did no other damage. The take-out was a slight cheat but still a clever hero-across-the tracks cliffhanger. Republic used this cliffhanger again in *Federal Agents vs. Underworld, Inc.* (1949) and *Government Agents vs. Phantom Legion* (1951).

*The Galloping Ghost* (1931) had an unusual train cliffhanger at the end of Chapter Five. Buddy tried to escape from some henchmen in a cab driven by his friend and roommate, Red Grange. However, Buddy had amnesia and did not recognize the great football star. As the two were driving down city streets, chased by other cabs, Buddy and Red got into a fight in the front seat of the taxi. They then somehow ended up on a railroad track, and drove the car straight into the front of an oncoming train. Luckily, in the resolution, it turned out that the two fell out of the cab before the vehicle hit the train. As Red and Buddy rolled on the ground, there was a nice, lingering shot of the train as it just passed them by.

Of course, the more traditional car/train crash, and frankly, the more effective one, was the train hitting a car as it attempted to cross the tracks at an at-grade crossing. In Chapter Five of *The Phantom Creeps* (1939), hero Bob West was in a car on a road which ran parallel to a railroad track. West was being chased and shot at by a carload of henchmen. There were fast cuts back and forth between West, the train and the henchmen, and there was an excellent long shot of West's car and the train in a dangerous race. The air was punctuated by the loud whistle of the train. Suddenly, and without any warning to West, the road turned toward the track. West tried to brake but he was too late. As he crossed the track, the rear of the car was hit by the train and turned around in a full circle as the scene faded out.

One of the directors of *The Phantom Creeps* was Ford Beebe, an experienced serial director who had the wherewithal to make that cliffhanger exciting. In the hands of a less experienced director, the result could be quite disappointing. The independent production, *The Black Coin* (1936), had a very similar cliffhanger ending to Chapter 11. Hero Terry Navarro was driving a stolen car and was being chased by the police down a dirt road, when suddenly a train came into view. The road ran perpendicular to the tracks and when Terry tried to outrace the train to the crossing, the car was hit broadside.

This may have been one of the most boring train-car collisions in serial history. There was almost no cross-cutting between different scenes and there was only one close-up of Terry throughout. Since the cliffhanger was shown almost entirely in long shot, there was little personal involvement in Terry's predicament. Without a montage of different shots to add to the excitement, the cliffhanger was as boring as the rest of the serial.

The resolution was no help either. In the next chapter, the car was absolutely demolished by the train. There was a shot of scrap and a tire and not much else. Yet Navarro survived and by the middle of the chapter was doing quite well. While Bob West also survived his train collision in *The Phantom Creeps*, there was at least a shot of him being thrown out of the car, giving some explanation for that medical miracle.

There were other interesting variations on a train cliffhanger. In Chapter Three of *Dick Tracy Returns* (1938), FBI agent Steve Lockwood chased Pa Stark and his sons to the top of a train where Lockwood unluckily was clearly outnumbered. Lockwood was knocked out, and he ended up lying unconscious on the top of the train. The Stark boys then handcuffed Lockwood to the top of the car, with his own handcuffs, and then threw away the key. Making matters worse, the train was on a collision course with a passenger train coming the other way on the same track.

Dick Tracy jumped into a tank that happened to be sitting near a train station and took off in pursuit of the train. The tension increased with cross-cutting back and forth between the trains and the tank (which looked somewhat incongruous riding through a western background). Lockwood woke up on top of the train but was unable to escape his predicament. Finally, Tracy reached the train and in a great stunt without cuts, leapt from the tank onto a ladder on the side of the train and climbed to save Lockwood. At the same time, Tracy's train was just diverted from a head-on crash with the passenger train, but before anyone could feel relief, the diversion caused Tracy's train to hit the end of the line, go off the tracks and crash.

This was one of the great cliffhangers of the Republic serials. From the time Tracy jumped into the tank, there was another four minutes of film until the end of the chapter, which included many surprises such as Tracy reaching the runaway train and the crash with the passenger train being suddenly avoided. The resolution involved a time expansion cheat but did not detract from the excitement that went before it. This spectacular cliffhanger was used several times again by Republic.

Another interesting variation on the railroad cliffhanger occurred in Chapter Four of *Daughter of Don Q* (1946). Hero Cliff Roberts was knocked out and tied up on a railroad work car filled with explosives. The original intention was to have a train carrying a large gold shipment crash into the explosive-filled work car and then the villains would rob the train of the gold during the confusion of the crash. However, the police caught up to the villains, who were then caught in a shootout. The henchmen decided to send the work car down the tracks toward the oncoming train, so that they would not be caught in the explosion. Quantero set off in her automobile, to somehow stop the work car at a crossing, preventing the destruction of the train.

Luckily, the road ran parallel to the train tracks. There was a rapid montage of clips of the speeding work car, the pulsating train, Quantero in her car and Roberts trapped in the work car, contrasted with longer shots of the work car and Quantero's vehicle in the same shot traveling at high speed. Suddenly, the road turned, Quantero's car hit the work car and there was a massive explosion.

In the resolution, there was a double escape. Cliff managed to loosen his bonds and then jump off the work car. Quantero managed to jump out of her automobile just before she directed it to hit the work car. Everyone was saved and the train passed safely by.

**Bridges**

In addition to rope bridges, which will be discussed later in this chapter, bridges for cars and railroads were an immense source of material for cliffhanger endings. Usually, the cliffhanger involved an explosion on the bridge, whether it was a car, railroad or even a wagon train trying to make the journey across.

A famous example occurred at the end of the first chapter of *Adventures of Captain Marvel* (1941). The Malcolm Expedition was trying to escape an attack by some natives on their camp by leaving the area by car. That necessarily meant a trip across a high road bridge, apparently made of wooden supports. The natives anticipated that move and determined to dynamite the bridge.

The first car made it across. However, as the second car with Whitey and Betty aboard was about halfway across, the explosion occurred. The bridge did not fall immediately but the wooden supports were weakened. Whitey tried to back the car up but he was not fast enough. The supports broke and as the chapter ended, the car fell into a high ravine.

This cliffhanger was quite exciting, with long shots of the high bridge intercut with the failing bridge supports and Whitey and Betty panicking in the car. The miniature of the bridge falling and the car following after it were quite impressive. Whitey and Betty were saved when the car landed in water and Captain Marvel was able to drag them to safety.

Most exploding bridge cliffhangers were done on a smaller scale. In Chapter Three of *Radar Men from the Moon* (1952), titled appropriately enough, "Bridge of Death," a bomb was set by the villains, designed to kill Commando Cody as he rounded a bend in his car and started onto the bridge. In Chapter Six of *The Crimson Ghost* (1946), a bomb was set on a bridge to destroy a truck carrying uranium but instead, it was Diana, racing toward the truck to prevent the disaster, who was trapped on the bridge when it exploded. In both cases, the hero and heroine were able to jump out of the vehicle, before the bridge explosion.

Explosions were not limited to city car bridges. In Chapter Seven of *Scouts to the Rescue* (1939), a bridge across a river which was made of a single log on which to walk with rope sides much like a traditional rope bridge was dynamited with Boy Scout Bruce Scott (Jackie Cooper) on board. He somehow managed to hold onto a part of the log, swing to safety and then when that log broke off and fell into the water, Scott was able to ride it through some serious rapids to safety. Unfortunately, most of the resolution was unconvincing, as it used poorly matched stock footage, probably from a silent film.

Even wagon trains in the Old West were not immune from this problem. *Overland Mail* (1942) involved the attempts of villain Frank Chadwick to destroy the overland mail service provided by Tom Gilbert, so that Chadwick could receive a lucrative government contract. At the end of Chapter Four, titled "The Bridge of Disaster," Chadwick's men dynamited a bridge across the Yellow River in an attempt to destroy a wagon train that was carrying equipment necessary for Gilbert's company.

The villains used one of the longest cords in dynamite history, so that much of the wagon train made it across the bridge safely. However, once the wagon driven by the hero, Jim Lane (Lon Chaney, Jr.) started across, the viewer knew an explosion was coming. It happened and Lane's wagon appeared to be destroyed in the blast. In the next chapter, through the use of stock footage, the wagon fell into the river and all of the passengers were rescued.

While there were many similar explosions on railroad bridges, with the train carrying the hero caught half way across the bridge, there were some interesting variations. In Chapter Two of *Flying Disc Man from Mars* (1950), Kent Fowler was fighting henchman Drake on a railroad bridge which Drake has previously dynamited, so that he could recover the uranium which was being carried in the train. Fowler was knocked below the bridge where he ended up hanging from a railroad cross-tie, as the train rapidly approached. That gave Drake the chance to run off the bridge and hit the switch blowing up the train.

In the exciting resolution, the train actually rolled across the bridge, with Fowler hanging on below. However, Fowler could not hang on forever and he finally let go, falling into the water under the bridge. The explosion then occurred, the train was wrecked but Fowler was saved.

Of course, not all train/bridge cliffhangers involved an explosion or a destruction of the bridge. In Chapter Three of *Batman* (1943), while the villains were attempting to blow up a train bridge, Batman and Robin arrived just in time to thwart their efforts. As a train was bearing down on them, a fight ensued on the bridge, with the caped heroes getting the better of the battle. However, when Batman bent down to throw away the bomb, he was hit over the head with a thrown wrench and fell unconscious on the track. As the chapter ended, the train was upon him.

In the takeout, Robin ran over to rescue Batman, something Robin did several times in this serial. There was a nice projection screen shot, as they jumped off the bridge just in time. A landing in the water saved them.

In Chapter One of *Law of the Wild* (1934), John Sheldon (Bob Custer) on the back of Rex, the King of Wild Horses, with Rinty running alongside, were chased by villains in a car. In order to escape, Sheldon decided to ride across a railroad bridge. It turned out to be a bad decision, as a train was just coming through a tunnel on the other side. As Sheldon turned his horse around and tried to ride back to safety, the train just caught up to him, forcing Sheldon and Rex to take a spectacular dive into the river below. Rinty was nowhere in sight so unlike Sheldon, Rinty must have been smart enough to get off the bridge as soon as he heard the train whistle.

It is fitting to end this section with what was probably the most spectacular bridge cliffhanger of them all. At the end of Chapter One of *Dick Tracy* (1937), the Lame One, using Gordon Tracy as his assistant, decided to destroy the Bay Bridge on the day of its dedication. The villain's technique was clever. By the use of loud sound waves directed at the bridge from the flying Wing, the bridge would be destroyed much like an opera singer's voice could shatter a crystal glass. When Tracy found out, he directed the FBI to order as many trucks as it could onto the bridge, hoping their weight would counter the sound waves and prevent the bridge from collapsing.

The Lame One was smarter. He had three of his own truck drivers block the bridge, thus preventing any other vehicles from providing a counter-force to the sound waves. Dick Tracy ran onto the bridge, trying to encourage the truckers forward. However, the cables and supports from one of the towers started to collapse and Tracy was pinned below some small girders. As the chapter ended, a large part of a crane or support structure started to fall, aimed right at Tracy's body.

The special effects were excellent and the suspense was heightened by the loud screeching sounds from the Wing. Tracy was saved when the falling bridge pieces hit a bridge support and missed Tracy. By then, the other truck drivers were able to move the stalled trucks out of the way. The trucks were then able to move into place on the bridge, effectively countering the sound waves. This was a clever cliffhanger with an exciting resolution, emblematic of many of the exciting chapter endings from Republic's golden era of serials.

**Boats**

Much like trains and planes, boats were commonly used in cliffhangers. Usually, the cliffhanger involved a boat crashing into something solid, such as a pier or another boat, with the hero on board. An example of that occurred in Chapter 13 of *Dick Tracy Returns* (1938). On other occasions, the villains might be flinging explosives at the boat or the boat hit a mine, causing it to explode with the hero on board. An

*Dick Tracy's G-Men* (1939). A photo of the spectacular cliffhanger where Dick Tracy drops into the boat in an attempt to prevent it from crashing into the Industrial Canal.

example of this occurred in Chapter Nine of *Secret Service in Darkest Africa* (1943). In the resolutions, the hero always jumped out before the crash or the explosion. Nevertheless, these water cliffhangers were usually exciting as the cross-cutting in the boat chase heightened the tension, and there was usually a grand explosion at the end to top off the episode.

Probably the most complex and exciting exploding boat cliffhanger was first shown at the end of Chapter One of *Dick Tracy's G-Men* (1939), when the evil Zarnoff decided to blow up the Industrial Canal in California. His plan was clever. First, he tricked the canal patrolmen to send a boat down river to investigate potential sabotage and when they arrived on shore, they were killed by Zarnoff's men. The henchmen then loaded the boat with explosives, placed dummies in the seats so that it appeared that the boat was still being driven by the patrolmen, and then set the boat off in the direction of the canal, with Zarnoff controlling it by a remote control device. The device included a television camera which permitted Zarnoff to see in the boat and also to see where the boat was going.

Tracy set off in pursuit by air, with Steve Lockwood flying the plane. They spotted the patrol boat on its way to the locks. Lockwood flew the plane low and in a feat of daring do, Tracy jumped into the craft, after hanging from below the plane. Tracy then covered the television camera in the boat so that Zarnoff could not see what he was doing. Zarnoff countered by deciding to blow up the boat, at least killing Tracy if not destroying the canal. As the chapter ended, the boat crashed with a loud explosion.

This cliffhanger was enhanced by the obvious time and expense that went into creating it, the quick cross-cutting to enhance the suspense, and the real life thrill of the plane flying low over the speeding boat. It ended with one of those patented Republic explosions. Of course, the resolution was obvious, as Tracy probably simply jumped out of the boat, before the explosion. But no, there was an innovative twist. Steve Lockwood flew the plane back down low again, Tracy was able to grab the axle between the wheels and fly to safety just before the explosion. The cliffhanger and resolution were innovative enough that Republic repeated it in the next *Dick Tracy* serial.

Another boat cliffhanger that was used from time to time was a canoe or kayak ride on a river that suddenly turned into a treacherous ride through rapids and then over a high waterfall. A good example of this occurred at the end of Chapter One of *Holt of the Secret Service* (1941), when Holt and Crimp Evans were floating down river in a canoe in order to reach the villain's hideout. During the trip, the previously calm river turned into at least Class III rapids. The long shots were exciting, as Holt and Evans (or more than likely, their two stunt men) were clearly navigating a treacherous river. Quick cuts to the upcoming waterfall created intensity for the scene. The close-ups were marred, however, by obvious process screen shots. During the trip, a fight ensued between Holt and the henchmen. Therefore, no one was steering the canoe as it reached the high waterfall. Over it went.

This canoe-over-the-waterfall cliffhanger after a ride through rough rapids was used several times in serials. It could be seen in Chapter Four of *Scouts to the Rescue* (1939) and once again in Chapter Four of *Royal Mounted Rides Again* (1945). The latter instance was an excellent example of this type of cliffhanger. Heroine June Bailey along with Latitude Bucket and Lode Mackenzie were attempting to escape a forest fire by taking a canoe downriver. At times the river itself appeared to be ablaze, as burning trees fell near their path. Just as Bucket mentioned that the falls were upcoming, there was a terrifying point-of-view shot of the wild rapids leading to a void where the waterfall must be. As the canoe approached the falls, there was a terrific shot from high above showing the relentless progress of the boat toward the upcoming danger. The scene was capped off with a shot from just behind the canoe, as the passengers were flung out of the boat and into the churning water. The directors, the stunt people and the special effects department for *Royal Mounted Rides Again* (or the serial from which the archive footage may have been taken) had turned the mundane over-the-waterfall cliffhanger produced in Universal's *Scouts to the Rescue* into one of the best Universal chapter endings of the 1940s.

By serial convention, any landing into water, whether off a high cliff, in a plane crash or over a waterfall, resulted in the hero surviving the predicament and swimming to safety. The over-the-waterfall cliffhangers mentioned above were no different so the resolutions did not come as a surprise to the viewer. Nevertheless, the lead-up to the cliffhangers, with the action shots through the rapids and the cuts to the upcoming waterfall, were always exciting.

From time to time, there were novel cliffhangers involving boats. One of Republic's favorite cliffhangers was the "boat squeeze" cliffhanger, used in Chapter Eight of *The Fighting Devil Dogs* (1938). Heroine Janet Warfield had been taken prisoner by the Lightning, who then had a henchman remove her by motor boat to a new location. Hero Tom

Grayson was in hot pursuit, in a boat of his own. The henchman decided to elude Grayson by driving his boat between two huge ships, one of which was gradually floating closer to the other so that they could be lined up parallel to each other. There was only a small window to go through but the henchman's boat made it.

Grayson, coming around the first boat and not realizing the problem at first, thought that he could also make it through. However, a quick look to the left and a quick look to the right quickly convinced him that he might not be correct. As the chapter ended, his tiny boat was being crushed between the two large ships.

The resolution was nothing special as Grayson merely jumped out of the boat and swam to safety. However, Republic liked this cliffhanger so much that it used it at least two other times in serials.

Interestingly, the concept of the boat squeeze cliffhanger was first used at Mascot Pictures, although on a much smaller scale. In Chapter Two of *The Galloping Ghost* (1931), Buddy was spirited away in a boat by his secret wife, Irene, and the mysterious hunchback. He was being chased in another boat by Red Grange and Buddy's sister. The chase wound in and around the harbor and even under a pier. Buddy then tried to sneak past a ship that was pulling into the harbor. Buddy made it! Red then tried the same stunt but it was too late. There was not enough daylight between ship and harbor and Red's boat got stuck between the two immovable objects. As the chapter ended, Red's boat was crushed to pieces. The resolution, which was substantially similar to the one that Republic would use for the same cliffhanger, did not come as a surprise.

This last boat cliffhanger involved a shanty boat in the Cajun river adventure serial *The Mystery of the River Boat* (1944). A shanty boat is an old shack permanently built on a raft. During a severe storm, hero Steve Langtry's father, Charles, and his girlfriend, Jenny Perrin, were on a shanty boat which was attached to trees on the shore by huge ropes. Langtry was concerned about his father and Jenny and therefore jumped off the riverboat and swam to the shanty in order to help his father and Jenny. Just as Steve was about to reach the shanty, two off the villains cut the last rope holding the boat to the shore, letting the shanty boat loose on the rain swollen river upon which the levee had already washed away.

As the shanty boat broke loose from the shore, Steve swam after it. Also, the riverboat led by Captain Perrin was in hot pursuit. The excitement increased as there was cutting between the debris in the river, the lolling of the shanty boat, Steve swimming after it and the riverboat racing at top speed. The special effects with the riverboat and the shanty boat, which may have been done with miniatures, were startling. The background music was exciting.

Then the shanty boat hit some tree debris in the river and suddenly stopped. Steve climbed on board. Just when things appeared to be under control, the shanty boat was itself hit by floating debris. Off it went down river toward the broken levee. As the chapter ended, the shanty was headed toward a trip over the levee.

The resolution was as exciting as the cliffhanger. Captain Perrin chased after the shanty boat in his riverboat and caught up with just as it was about to go over the levee. A rope was thrown to the shanty and quickly tied. The riverboat was then able to pull the smaller boat back up the river. This was a beautifully conceived and executed cliffhanger, with additional quick cutting during the resolution to continue the excitement. This was an excellent cliffhanger for a 1944 serial so late in the Universal cycle of serial production.

**Elevators**

Elevators provided exciting cliffhangers in many serials. Sometimes, the hero was trapped inside a rapidly falling elevator. On other occasions, the hero was trapped in an elevator shaft, with the descending elevator about to crush him.

*Zorro's Fighting Legion* (1939) provided an excellent example of the latter. In Chapter Three, Zorro was below ground, in a sword fight with some henchmen. He lost his footing and fell backwards into an elevator shaft, but only a drop of ten feet or so. He was knocked out, near some explosives with a lighted cord attached. It looked like an explosion would be the cliffhanger but when Zorro awoke, he put out the flame.

The elevator itself had been lifted up by natives on the surface turning a wheel. However, there was an attack above ground and the natives let go of the wheel, allowing the elevator to drop. As Zorro looked up, it was rapidly falling on him just as he was trying to escape from the elevator pit up a ladder.

In the next episode, Zorro merely squeezed himself behind the ladder he was on, avoiding the elevator cage. This was a unique cliffhanger, first with the fake explosive cliffhanger and then the unexpected danger from above which Zorro cleverly avoided. Also, the resolution did not involve a cheat.

*Spy Smasher* (1942) (Chapter Five) also had an adventure with a falling elevator. In order to escape from some henchmen, Spy Smasher jumped onto the cable of an empty elevator shaft and slid to the bottom, where he was temporarily knocked out. The villains sent the elevator car down to crush him. This was an excellent cliffhanger because as the elevator dropped lower, a shadow began to descend on Spy Smasher. As the chapter ended, the last shot was looking up, with the car almost upon the Smasher. The resolution was also excellent as in the next chapter, Spy Smasher saved himself by putting his gun into the machinery of the elevator, stopping the car with only inches to spare. In Chapter Seven of his 1943 serial, Batman was knocked down an elevator shaft and fell onto concrete, about 20 feet below. To ensure that he did not survive, the henchmen started the freight elevator down. There were chains hanging loose from the elevator and they were touching Batman as the chapter ended. Luckily, Robin awoke after being knocked unconscious in a fight just in time to save his mentor.

*Junior G-Men* (1940) (Chapter One), *The Great Alaskan Mystery* (1944) (Chapter Six) and *Riders of Death Valley* (1941) (Chapter Eight) involved elevator cliffhangers where the hero or heroes were trapped inside or on the falling elevator car. Somehow, the heroes survived the fall, even though the drops were from high distances. A similar example occurred in Chapter Five of *Scouts to the Rescue* (1939), where the elevator, which was operated on some kind of rope pulley system, provided passage down a high cliff in the wilderness. The heroes tried to use the elevator to escape from some modern day Indians. Instead, the Indians chopped at the elevator rope, cut it in two and the elevator hurtled toward the ground. Just as in the city, however, the heroes were able to survive the nasty drop without explanation.

Better takeouts were provided in the cliffhangers to *Mandrake, the Magician* (1939) (Chapter Two), and *The Spider's Web* (1938) (Chapter Nine) which also involved situations wherein the hero or heroines were trapped inside an elevator, which was falling out of control to the ground. In these two serials, the falling elevator was stopped by its automatic brake. Logically, that should have been the resolution to all of those types of elevator cliffhangers.

## Conveyor Belts

People who are not familiar with sound serials probably assume there were many chapter endings with a woman trapped on a conveyor heading to a buzz saw in a saw mill. This impression probably comes from silent films and, in particular, early silent serials where a woman was usually in peril during an episode. In sound movie serials, conveyor belt cliffhangers were often used but they usually did not involve a woman in peril.

Chapter Three of *King of the Royal Mounted* (1940), captioned "Boomerang," involved the traditional saw mill ending. The hero, Sergeant King, was knocked out in a fight and set on a conveyor. Slowly, he moved closer and closer to the whirling buzz saw. As the chapter ended, death was imminent. The resolution involved a rescue and a somewhat clever one at that, with King escaping unharmed although someone else lost his life.

The classic body in the saw mill cliffhanger was also used in Chapter Four of *Captain Midnight* (1942). The masked hero lost a fight with three henchmen and fell unconscious on a log. Ivan Shark pulled a switch and the log started moving toward a circular saw. Once again, the resolution was a rescue.

Machinery other than that a whirling saw was often used as a trap for the serial hero on a conveyor belt in sound motion picture serials. In *Spy Smasher* (1942) (Chapter Six), after an exciting fight in a plant, Spy Smasher was knocked off a ledge and onto a conveyor belt, which led to a wheel that was used to cut pipe. The wheel went round and round and sliced anything on the conveyor belt, even solid block. This was similar to a buzz saw but was actually a more spectacular peril. In the next chapter, Spy Smasher was saved by a clever move by his brother.

In *Jungle Girl* (1941), Stanton was the one who was secured to the conveyor belt in the hope that he would tell the location of some valuable diamonds. At the end of the conveyor belt was a crushing block, which went up and down, crashing to the belt as Stanton was pulled to his death. Here, the machine was operated by hand cranking, which made sense in a jungle setting, but also related to Stanton's rescue.

An interesting variation on the a conveyor belt cliffhanger occurred in Chapter 12 of *Dick Tracy vs. Crime, Inc* (1941) where Dick Tracy was knocked unconscious on a conveyor belt which would then dump him into a blazing furnace. The same happened to Jimmy Olson in *Superman* (1948), Chapter Seven. Of course, Jimmy Olson was likely to be rescued by a famous superhero. So was Jimmy Carter, in Chapter 11 of *The Lightning Warrior* (1931), when he was knocked unconscious on a mine conveyor belt. In this Jimmy's case, the famous superhero who rescued him was none other than Rin-Tin-Tin.

However, the most unusual conveyor belt cliffhanger probably occurred in Chapter Ten of *The Phantom Empire* (1935) when Gene Autry, trapped in Murania, was knocked unconscious in a fight and landed on a conveyor belt. The belt had some cylinder-shaped parts on it and a robot periodically brought a welding torch down onto the parts, in some kind of advanced production line. As the chapter ended, the robot was just about to burn Autry with a torch. In the takeout, Autry was saved with little time to spare by the two of the Junior Thunder Riders.

**Machines and Other Devices**

Upon occasion, the scene of the serial took place in an industrial building, whether on location or on a realistic set built in a studio sound stage. The machines regularly used in the manufacturing process made great devices for disposing of the hero, and the villain was quick to realize this.

Jerry Blake's secretary, Joyce Kingston, in *Federal Operator 99* (1945), had a particular run of bad luck in industrial buildings. At the end of Chapter Three, she was trapped in an incinerator which burned the waste products of a tannery. As the door closed, the incinerator filled with gas,

*Federal Operator 99* (1945). Helen Talbot, playing Joyce Kingston, who is hero Jerry Blake's secretary, is tied up, with a whirling airplane motor advancing on her while Jerry is otherwise engaged in fisticuffs.

knocking her unconscious. Outside the incinerator, hero Jerry Blake was fighting with villain Jim Belmont and a henchman when Blake accidentally hit the switch which ignited the gas in the chamber. Presumably Kingston was burned to a crisp.

At the end of the very next chapter, trouble ensued at an airplane repair factory. Kingston's hands were tied to a hook hanging from the ceiling. A plane motor test block, with a whirling propeller, was gradually moving toward her. At the same time, Blake was involved in another fight with a Belmont henchman and appeared to be too busy to save Kingston. Hopefully, if Kingston somehow survived this peril, she would have learned to stay away from other industrial buildings, at least for the remainder of the serial.

The plot of *The Hurricane Express* (1942) revolved around trains and much of the action took place on trains or in train stations or railway yards. That led to an exciting cliffhanger in Chapter Six where Larry Baker was fighting a group of henchmen in a train repair facility. During the course of the fight, a switch was accidentally pulled and a locomotive, which was in the air on a hoist, gradually started coming to the ground. Baker was then knocked unconscious and unfortunately for him, he fell right below where the locomotive was headed. As the chapter ended, the locomotive was about to crush him. While the resolution was nothing special, the cliffhanger, shot in a real railroad yard with what appeared to be a real and heavy locomotive, was quite exciting.

Industrial device cliffhangers were not limited to city serials. *Son of Zorro* (1947) was a western and yet it had an exciting cliffhanger related to an interesting industrial device. In Chapter Two, Zorro decided to take a gold shipment from a mine and deliver it to a town to raise needed cash. In the first scene in the mine, there was footage of an ore crushing machine, with a heavy stone wheel that went around a circular table, crushing ore and anything else in its way. The camera lingered on the machine, as if to say, this would be a great device for a cliffhanger.

Sure enough, the action returned to the mine toward the end of the episode. A fight broke out and Kate Wells was knocked onto the table, unconscious. Hopefully, the machine would not be set in motion. But no, during the fight, the lever was accidentally hit, and the wheel started its slow movement around the table. At the fadeout, Zorro was down and Wells was about to be crushed.

*Captain Midnight* (1942). Surely this is one of the most diabolical and expensive devices ever created by a villain to trap a hero. What was Ivan Shark thinking? Pictured is Dave O'Brien as Captain Midnight.

The resolution was not that surprising. Nevertheless, the ore crushing wheel was an unusual cliffhanger device for a western and made the chapter ending quite exciting.

*Captain Midnight* (1942) had one of the most unusual devices ever to appear in a serial cliffhanger. At the end of Chapter Ten, the Captain was trapped in a room with a pole in the middle. The floor started to rotate and the walls came out, revealing that the floor was above a pit of fire. Captain Midnight tried to hang onto the pole and not slip off the rotating floor into the fire. Then the roof started to come down. How could the Captain survive?

The resolution was clever. The gang was busy destroying evidence in the rest of the building, because the police were on the way. In the process, one gang member threw a chair into electrical coils, terminating the power to the building, including the death trap. The floor stopped spinning and the Captain was saved. Of course, this death trap probably cost Ivan Shark a bundle of money to build. If he had skipped the building of this device and saved the money, he may never have had to turn to a life of crime in the first place.

In Chapter Nine of *Drums of Fu Manchu* (1940), Mary Randolph was placed in a hypnotic trance by the evil doctor and then placed on an alter. Using two large lenses in the ceiling, Fu Manchu directed a power- ful, laser-like ray along the ground. It gradually worked its way toward Mary's prone body, burning a line through solid bronze. It was just reaching Mary when the chapter ended.

This was a very effective cliffhanger, beautifully filmed from novel angles, with interesting cross-cutting. For today's audiences, it invokes memories of a similar predicament for James Bond in *Goldfinger* (1964). The resolution involved a rescue and a destruction of the device and although it used a slight cheat, it was a logical way to resolve the situation. There was a somewhat similar cliffhanger in Chapter 11 of *The Lost City* (1935), when Zolok used a death ray on Bruce Gordon, which burned through a metal table toward Gordon, much like a laser burns through metal. Once again, the resolution involved a rescue.

In Chapter Four of *The Adventures of Smilin' Jack* (1943), Jack was trapped in a cage along the floor by Fraulein von Teufel. Below Jack's body was a bed of knives, on a board, floating on sea water. As the tide came in, the board rose and the knives got closer to Jack's back. Unless he revealed the Mandon secret to the Fraulein, Jack was doomed. However, in the resolution, two of Jack's associates came to his rescue and the Fraulein's plans were thwarted.

**Gun Traps**

One of the best of the gun trap cliffhangers occurred in Chapter Nine of *Adventures of Captain Marvel* (1941). Professor Lang had re- vealed that the location of one of the lenses of the Scorpion was in a safe behind a picture in his study. The Scorpion's henchmen reached the room first. Once they lifted the picture, opened the sliding doors to reveal the safe and then started to enter the combination to the safe, unbeknownst to them, a panel opened on the other side of the room and two machine guns flipped into place, to go off, once the safe was opened. Luckily for them, the henchmen heard Billy Batson and Betty Wallace arriving. The henchmen returned everything in the room to their prior condition and hid. The machine guns disappeared.

Billy and Betty also had the combination to the safe. They moved the picture on the wall and opened the doors to the safe. Billy started to turn the combination to the safe and once again, the panel on the oppo-

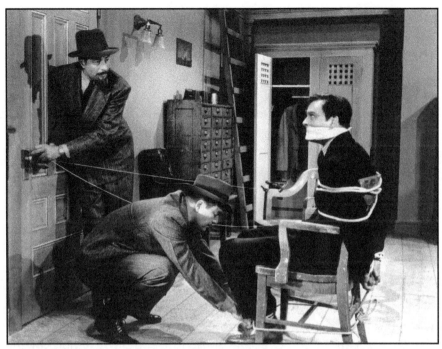

*Dick Tracy's G-Men* (1939). A photo of an innovative gun trap cliffhanger with Zarnoff (Irving Pichel) by the door and Dick Tracy (Ralph Byrd) tied in the chair.

site wall opened and the machine guns flipped into place. They rotated back and forth, ready to shoot when the safe was opened. Sometimes the scene was shot from behind and between the guns, as Billy continued to enter the combination. At other times, the camera focused on the guns themselves, as Betty read the combination to Billy and he turned the knob on the safe. Finally, with the camera turning to the guns, Betty announced the last number. The guns went off and the chapter ended.

This was one of the most suspenseful cliffhangers of all time, with the filmmakers first presaging the cliffhanger by showing the henchmen at the safe. Next, with Billy and Betty in harm, the camera viewed the scene from many different angles, with Betty's voice announcing the impending flash of guns. The resolution was clever, as the Scorpion's henchmen came back into the picture just in time.

*Dick Tracy's G-Men* (1939) had an interesting variation on a gun trap cliffhanger, at the end of Chapter Two. The evil Zarnoff tied Dick Tracy to a chair which was bolted to the floor. Tracy's mouth was gagged. A gun was bracketed to another chair, and a rope was attached from the trigger to the door knob. The gun was not aimed at Dick Tracy. Rather, it was set up so that when the FBI agents came to rescue Tracy, they would have to turn the door knob. The first agent in would then be shot by the rigged gun. The G-men would retaliate, thus killing Tracy who was bound and gagged on the other side of the door.

Zarnoff's plan almost worked perfectly. The door knob was turned and the first FBI agent was shot. The G-men retaliated by shooting through the door with a machine gun, killing Tracy for sure. Luckily, however, in the next chapter, it turned out that Tracy was able to cut the ties that bound him and escape from the death chair just before the guns went off.

Unfortunately, this type of cliffhangers was not immune from cheat resolutions. In *Jungle Girl* (1941), Chapter 13, a plane was rigged by the villain to prevent Stanton and Nyoka from escaping from the jungle. A gun was set with string so that the person pulling back on the steering wheel of the plane would be shot in the stomach, preventing his escape. The trap worked to perfection and at the end of the chapter, when Stanton tried to escape in the plane, he was apparently critically wounded by the rigged gun. However, in the next chapter, although Stanton did feel some of the effects of the wound, when it turned out he was shot in the shoulder, by the 15th chapter, Stanton had recovered so quickly that he was able to hold onto the bottom of a plane, as it flew through the sky.

An interesting variation occurred in Chapter Two of the *Daughter of Don Q* (1946). The heroine, Dolores Quantero, was hung by some henchmen from a ceiling in a fishing net. A harpoon gun with the trigger tied by rope to the room's only door was ready to strike Quantero once the hero, Cliff Roberts, opened the door by turning the door knob. Roberts was on his way to the room where Quantero was being held, as Quantero had unknowingly led him into the trap. Nevertheless, apparently as a result of extra sensory perception, Roberts made it through the door without turning the door knob.

Unfortunately, a fight ensued, and it was only a matter of time before someone would fall on the rope, shooting the harpoon at the helpless heroine. Indeed, that was what happened. Roberts shot one of the henchmen, who then fell on the rope, shooting the harpoon directly at Quantero. Luckily, in the resolution, Roberts acted quickly, shooting the rope holding the fishing net from the ceiling. Quantero dropped to the floor just in time, with the harpoon barely missing her.

Gun traps made some of the most exciting and suspenseful cliffhangers, because the audience knew the trap had been set, and the hero did not. So long as there was not a cheat resolution, these were often the best-remembered cliffhangers from a serial.

## Rushing Waters and Mine Tunnels

The first chapters of serials were almost always the longest, as the filmmaker used the extra time to introduce the characters and lay out the plot that would consume the next eleven or more chapters. Often, the first chapter also contained one of the best cliffhangers, to entice the viewer to invest his time in the entire serial.

One of the best-remembered cliffhangers of all time occurred in the first chapter of *Daredevils of the Red Circle* (1939). One of the daredevils, Gene Townley, attempted to stop 39013's plan to destroy the new Channel Tunnel, which had just been constructed under the ocean. While Townley was inspecting the tunnel, it started to fail. Townley jumped on his motorcycle to warn others of the impending disaster. As he rode, the daredevil was being chased through the narrow tunnel and around the tunnel curves by a rushing wall of water. The tension mounted as the hero seemed doomed to a drowning death as the waters overtook him. The chapter ended.

Luckily, in the takeout, Townley discovered a large valve that had been installed in the tunnel that could close doors in the tunnel, effectively blocking the water. Townley thereby averted the destruction of the tunnel and his own death.

Most rushing water cliffhangers were not as spectacular as the one in *Daredevils* and did not take place on such a large scale. The hero was usually exploring a cave or tunnel, when the water was let loose. The hero appeared to be trapped. The suspense increased with the mix of claustrophobia from the close confines of the tunnel and a fear of drowning.

An example of this occurred in Chapter Eight of *Zorro's Fighting Legion* (1939), where Zorro was trapped in a cave. A dike was broken and the cave filled with water. The waters rushed in, filling the cave, leaving no exit for Zorro and his companion. They were apparently drowned. In the next chapter, Zorro was luckily saved by finding an air pocket. He was then able to swim back to safety.

Another example was in *Jungle Girl* (1941), Chapter One, when Nyoka and Stanton were trapped in a tunnel with rushing water. Their only way of escape was through a door, which closed to block their way.

They then kept running in a desperate attempt to save their lives. Finally, they reached a point in the tunnel where the water rushed out of the mountain, through a hole, creating a high pressure water fall. Nyoka and Stanton were sucked out of the mountain, presumably to their death.

In this case, the special effects were only fair, as the back projection of the water seemed artificial. However, the chase through the tunnel, with one exit suddenly blocked, was exciting. The shot of the waterfall from below increased the tension. The cliffhanger resolution was not unexpected but was reasonable and not a cheat.

Another example occurred in *Flash Gordon Conquers the Universe* (1938) in the Chapter Nine cliffhanger. Flash Gordon and friends attempted to sneak into Ming's palace by way of a tunnel to try to rescue Princess Aura. They did not realize, however, that Ming could monitor their activities by use of his closed circuit television. Ming ordered the flood gates opened, and water came rushing into the tunnel, sweeping Flash and his comrades toward a bottomless pit. In the resolution, Ming, believing Flash and his friends had drowned, walked away from the television screen which showed Flash, and that error on Ming's part permitted a rescue of Flash.

Mine tunnel cliffhangers combined the claustrophobic effect of being in a narrow tunnel with a low ceiling and then usually the rush of a fireball, which rapidly overtook the hero as he tried to escape. The combination provided thrilling cliffhangers and they tended to be resolved without cheats.

As was often the case, the first chapter of a serial provided an excellent example. In this case, the serial was *Spy Smasher* (1942). The hero was chasing after some henchmen down a mine tunnel. The henchmen had rigged the situation so that once Spy Smasher reached the end, there would be an explosion. Also, they had blocked any escape from the direction Spy Smasher had come.

As our hero reached the end of the tunnel, the explosion occurred. Spy Smasher jumped in a mine car and started pumping the handle, in a desperate attempt to outrun the fireball that had been unleashed by the explosion. The special effects were excellent, especially in the shots from the front of the mine car, looking over Spy Smasher's shoulder, with the fireball gaining on the vehicle. To make matters worse, there were grenades in the back of the car, which were sure to explode once fire and car collided.

The resolution was unexpected and not a cheat. Spy Smasher grabbed a grenade, pulled the pin and threw it into the fire. The explosion halted the onslaught of the fire and Spy Smasher was saved. It was an excellent cliffhanger with a clever resolution and it was a great way to start a serial.

Another example of a mine tunnel cliffhanger occurred in Chapter 11 of *Zorro's Black Whip* (1944). Vic Gordon and the Black Whip were trapped at the back of a mine tunnel, by three villains. The villains sent a leaking barrel filled with coal oil down the mine, on a mine car. Then the villains lit the coal oil, sending a trail of flames shooting down the mine toward Vic Gordon and the Black Whip. An explosion occurred.

In the next chapter, it turned out that Vic and The Whip had turned over a metal coal cart and had hidden under it before the explosion occurred. They were unhurt. In addition, the explosion blew a hole in the roof of the cave and they were able to escape.

In Chapter Five of *The Black Widow* (1947), Steve and Joyce were ambushed in a cave when they tried to trap Sombra, the Black Widow. They attempted to escape on a mine car but Sombra directed her men to start a chemical file, to cremate Steve and Joyce. This was a particularly spectacular cliffhanger as the chemical fire spread down the tunnel quickly,

*The Black Widow* (1947). This is a typically spectacular Republic mine tunnel cliffhanger, with a fireball racing down the tracks after the trapped heroes.

seemingly engulfing the mine car in its flames. As the chapter ended, the mine car was about to reach a blocked doorway. In the clever resolution, Steve and Joyce jumped off the mine car, which then crashed through the door. Steve and Joyce then ran to safety through the hole in the door that had been created by the speeding mine car.

**Rope Bridges and City High Wires**

The hero stood on one side of a cliff with the villain on the other side. The only way to cross the high canyon was by a flimsy plank bridge, held together by ropes. The hand rails themselves were ropes. The bridge bounced with the weight of each step. The bridge swayed with each gust of wind. The villain was sawing the rope on the other side and there were only a few seconds left to cross the bridge in safety.

The crossing of a rope bridge was suspenseful in and of itself, even if the villain were not trying to cut the support ropes. Add the villainy of the henchman and those cliffhangers were always exciting.

*Zorro's Fighting Legion* (1939) had an excellent rope bridge cliffhanger. At the end of Chapter Four, Zorro had to escape from a horde of riding

*Rustlers of Red Dog* (1935). John Mack Brown and Joyce Compton are saved from a rope bridge cliffhanger in the classic manner. They hang onto the bridge and then ride it over to safety.

Yaquis by running across a rope bridge. Unbeknownst to the masked hero, there was another Yaqui on the other side of the bridge, whom Zorro had to shoot. As Zorro continued to proceed across the bridge, the fallen Yaqui cut one of the bridge's two support ropes, tipping the bridge in a perilous manner. Zorro just managed to hang on. Then the Yaqui cut the second rope, causing the bridge to drop into the high gorge.

The suspense of the cliffhanger was enhanced by the excellent use of process screen shots and shots from different angles, with both techniques increasing the feeling of peril to Zorro. The masked hero was saved when he managed to hold onto the bridge and then swing on the rope to safety on the other side of the gorge.

That was a common resolution to a rope bridge cliffhanger. It could also be seen in *The Rustlers of Red Dog* (1935) (Chapter Eight) and *Jack Armstrong* (1947) (Chapter Four). The latter serial probably holds the record with four people trapped on the rope bridge when the rope broke. Suffice it to say, no one was injured.

The rope bridge cliffhanger was surely one of the most exciting cliffhangers in serialdom. It was hard to blow that type of chapter ending. Yet, Universal managed to do just that in Chapter Four of *Winners of the West* (1940). There, hero Jeff Ramsay and his partner, Tex, started across a bridge. An Indian rolled a boulder down onto the bridge, causing it to collapse with the heroes still on it. While this was a clever variation on the usual rope bridge cliffhanger, the director missed every opportunity to create suspense.

The only true close-up shot came when Jeff and Tex took their first step onto the bridge. The rest of the scene was shown in a long shot. Therefore, the viewer felt no suspense from the bouncing bridge. The Indian throwing the boulder was shown but there was no point of view shot from the individuals on the bridge which would create some suspense. The boulder simply hit the bridge in a long shot and the bridge fell. In Chapter Five of *Overland Mail* (1942), a similar rope bridge cliffhanger was handled a little better. There, the heroes were shooting at the Indians while on the bridge and there were at least some tight shots of the heroes on the bridge before the large rock fell on them.

Did the hero ever make it safely across a rope bridge? In *The Adventures of Red Ryder* (1940), in the last chapter, Red managed to cross the bridge even though the villain was cutting the rope. However, a fight then ensued and the two ended up struggling back on the rope bridge.

The double weight then caused the bridge to fall, with hero and villain apparently dropping to their death. No true explanation was given as to how Red Ryder survived the fall.

In *Jungle Jim* (1937), at the end of Chapter Five, "The Bridge of Terror," there was a rope across a canyon, which was not exactly a rope bridge, although it was apparently the only means of bridging the ravine. To cross, a person had to go hand over hand, hanging from the rope. This scene was shot from below and from a distance, giving a convincing picture of height and terror. Here, Jungle Jim was halfway across when the villain shot the rope, and Jim fell to his apparent death. In the next chapter, Jim landed in a river and was saved. Looking back, the river was shown in the prior scene and this was therefore not a cheat.

*Flash Gordon's Trip to Mars* (1938) contained a high tech rope bridge. It was a bridge of light between two high buildings. While it did not sway or bounce, it also had no hand rails of any kind on the side and the floor was see-through. Each walk across the bridge was suspenseful. Surprisingly, the light bridge was not involved in any cliffhanger.

There were no rope bridges in the city but there were the next best things—high wires. For example, at the end of Chapter Three of *The Crimson Ghost* (1946), Duncan was in a fight with the title villain, who escaped from a high office window across electrical wires. Duncan immediately followed him. There were several shots of the street, far below. When the Crimson Ghost reached the top of the opposite building, he used a torch to burn the wires. Just as Duncan was almost across, the wires broke and Duncan fell. Luckily, however, he hung onto the wires and conveniently swung onto a ledge of the original building. This was the same resolution that was commonly used for rope bridge cliffhangers.

Another good example of a city high wire cliffhanger occurred in Chapter 12 of *The Spider's Web* (1938). The Spider was being chased across a roof by several henchmen of the Octopus, when the masked hero was apparently shot. The Spider slid down the roof and grabbed onto the ledge. He was then trapped, with men above and below shooting at him. He then saw a suspended electric wire, leading from the building. The Spider grabbed it and traveled across the wire by hand, hanging from the wires. The Octopus' men then broke the wires, as they connected to the roof, causing the Spider to fall. Luckily, and, again, much like the rope bridge resolution, the Spider was able to hang onto two of the wires as he fell. He swung into a brick wall and then was able to drop safely to the ground.

*The Undersea Kingdom* (1936) is not thought of as a city serial, but it did take place in the lost city of Atlantis. At the end of Chapter Six, Crash Corrigan escaped from Unga Khan's castle by walking across a high wire, one foot after the other. To add to the suspense, he was carrying Billy Norton on his back. Kahn fired a rocket at the duo and as the chapter ended, the wire broke and the two plummeted to their death.

This was an interesting variation on the city high wire, with excellent long shots of Corrigan crossing the wire, contrasted with close-ups of his feet as he tried to make the treacherous walk. Unfortunately, *The Undersea Kingdom* was known for its cheat cliffhanger resolutions and this one was no exception, thus undercutting the excellent cliffhanger that came before it.

## Pits and Pendulums

Once again, the first chapter of a serial had a spectacular cliffhanger and probably the best of the bottomless pit chapter endings. The serial was *The Tiger Woman* (1944), which was sometimes known as *Perils of the Darkest Jungle*. Chapter One was titled "Temple of Terror." Towards

*The Tiger Woman* (1944). This is a publicity photo of the famous bottomless pit cliffhanger at the end of the first chapter. The cliffhanger did not develop in exactly the same way in the serial. The Tiger Woman (Linda Stirling) is on the throne and Allen Saunders (Allan Lane) is hanging over the pit.

the middle of the chapter, in a scene which took place in a temple in an elaborate cave, the natives were executing an intruder whom they had captured. The intruder was hung by a rope, over a deep pit of fire. The rope went through a pulley on the ceiling and then was attached to the wall by three threads of the rope. A native girl did a dance, each of the threads was cut and on the third thread, the intruder fell to his death. (This was notice to the viewer that when the hero fell into that same trap, he would die.)

Allen Saunders (hero) was then captured by the natives and believing he had hurt the Tiger Woman, the natives prepared for his execution. Saunders was hung by a rope over the fire pit. The ceremony began. The Tiger Woman was on the way to the rescue. Two threads were cut. The Tiger Woman entered the temple. The third strand was cut and Allen Saunders plummeted to his death. The cliffhanger ending was beautifully set up, with cuts back and forth between the ceremony, Saunders hanging, and the Tiger Woman.

The resolution was not a cheat. After the third strand was cut, the Tiger Woman leapt across the pit, grabbed the rope before all of it went through the pulley, and stopped the fall of Saunders, who was then pulled out of the pit.

At the end of Chapter One of *Flash Gordon* (1936), a guard was shot, a trap door opened, and Flash was sent hurtling to his death in a bottomless pit, accidentally accompanied by Ming's daughter, Princess Aura. Flash was saved by an unlikely person. As it turned out, the pit was not actually bottomless but appeared to have deadly alligators or other Mongo beasts at the bottom.

Similarly, at the end of Chapter One of *Flash Gordon Conquers the Universe* (1940), Flash was fighting on the surface with one of Ming's henchmen when they both fell into a bottomless pit. Flash was saved in the next chapter with a feat of acrobatic skill and the suspension of disbelief on the part of the filmgoer.

After pits must come pendulums. Edgar Allan Poe's "The Pit and the Pendulum" inspired several exciting cliffhangers. In the story a prisoner was subjected to several torture devices, including a swinging pendulum sword, which dropped closer to the prisoner with each swing.

Probably the best pendulum cliffhanger occurred in *Drums of Fu Manchu* (1940) (Chapter Twelve). Fu Manchu had Alan Parker in a pendulum trap, in order to force him to reveal secret information. The pendulum itself was curved on the ends and seemed to be particularly sharp. The direction was excellent. There were shots of the swinging pendulum from the front and above. These were interspersed with views of the pendulum from the side and lower, and scenes of the pendulum as it went past Fu Manchu's face. As the chapter ended, the pendulum was almost slicing Parker's body. As with all of these swinging pendulum cliffhangers, the resolution involved a rescue.

There was an interesting variation on the pendulum trap in Chapter 12 of *Secret Service in Darkest Africa* (1943). Rex Bennett was thought guilty of a crime and placed in a pendulum torture. This time he was attached to a wheel, and each time the wheel came around, the pendulum dropped closer. The suspense was enhanced by the sound element, i.e., the beating of kettle drums and the creaking of the pendulum each time it dropped a bit lower. Luckily, in the next chapter, Bennett was rescued by an unexpected person.

*Perils of Nyoka* (1942) had another interesting variation in Chapter 11, when Nyoka and Larry were attacked by Cassib's warriors in the Temple of the Moon God. Nyoka was putting up her usual good fight when she was knocked unconscious, falling on a platform below an unmoving pendulum. Larry continued the fight and eventually a pedal was accidentally pushed, starting the pendulum in motion. The platform on which Nyoka was lying then began to rise, coming closer and closer to the pendulum. As the chapter ended, Nyoka was moments away from death.

This was another excellent cliffhanger, with shots of Nyoka and the blade from above and shots from below the platform looking toward the blade, interspersed with shots of the fight and other activities. Once again, the resolution was a rescue but a very exciting one involving Larry and Nyoka's dog.

The most unusual pendulum cliffhanger befitted the serial from which it came. In Chapter 12 of *Adventures of Sir Galahad* (1949), the famous knight was captured by Modred and tied to a table. A spiked iron ball was then swung above Galahad's body, lowering toward the victim with each swing. At the end of the chapter, the ball fell off its chain, apparently crushing Sir Galahad. The effectiveness of this cliffhanger was enhanced by Spencer Bennet's direction, with the spiked iron ball swinging ominously into the camera and the shadow of the ball crossing back and forth over Galahad's panic-stricken face.

*Adventures of Sir Galahad* (1949). Here, George Reeves as Sir Galahad, is about to be tortured by the swinging spiked iron ball.

Unfortunately, and as was typical for this serial, the takeout was disappointing and involved a cheat. Galahad's aide, Sir Bors, rescued Galahad by releasing the rope holding the spiked ball, causing it to drop to safety behind Sir Galahad. However, in the previous chapter ending, it was clear that the ball had dropped onto the middle of Sir Galahad's body.

## Jungle Spike Traps and Other Sharp Objects

Jungle spike traps were usually traps which were set up by natives to catch and kill wild animals. They consisted of a platform of logs or wood, with spikes protruding downward. The platform was held above the ground, out of sight, by a rope. Another rope was pulled across a path near the ground. As a wild animal ran by, it would hit the rope, drop the knives and be instantly killed. In serials, of course, in addition to accidental peril to the hero from these devices, the spike trap was often used by villains in a deliberate attempt to kill the hero.

*Jungle Girl* (1941) had the classic use of this device in Chapter 12. A native set a device in place, which consisted of logs with spikes protruding downward. Nyoka's young friend, Kimbu, accidentally tripped the device but the native grabbed the support rope before Kimbu was impaled. The device was then re-set. Later in the chapter, Nyoka was running for her life, when she accidentally tripped the device. As the chapter ended, the spikes fell. Nyoka was about to die.

Luckily, Nyoka was as quick as she was beautiful. In the next chapter, she managed to roll out of the way, saving herself from a very painful death.

In *Hawk of the Wilderness* (1938), the natives set up an animal trap in the jungle. A log held up five wooden logs strapped together with sharp spikes on the end. When the log was hit, the trap was intended to swing down on the animal, spearing it. Of course, Kioga got into a fight with several henchmen near the trap. He was punched in the face, fell backward, hit the trip log and as Chapter Six ended, the logs with the sharp spears had fallen on Kioga's prone body. In the resolution, Kioga grabbed another short and stout tree branch that happened to be lying in the right place and blocked the complete fall of the trap just in time.

*Hawk of the Wilderness* (1938). This is a particularly menacing jungle spike trap, sure to end the life of the courageous Kioga, played by Herman Brix.

*Holt of the Secret Service* (1941) is not thought of as a jungle serial but, in fact, the last several chapters took place in an island jungle. At the end of Chapter 11, Holt accidentally tripped a wire, causing a spike trap to fall on his prone body. If not for his incredible instincts, the federal agent from the city would have died a nasty death in the jungle. Based upon the experiences of Nyoka, Kioga and Holt, these jungle traps probably fell too slowly to capture any kind of animal, much less a fast jungle beast.

Spike traps were not limited to the jungle. *King of the Royal Mounted* (1940) was set in the Canadian west but that did not prevent some henchmen from using a trap in the woods to attempt to kill Tom Merritt. It was the standard jungle spike trap, set in place by a rope across the trail. (There was no explanation of why the trap was there in the first place since there did not seem to be any lions or tigers prowling this part of Canada.) Merritt was not fooled but Sergeant King, in hot pursuit, got into a fight with a henchman under the trap. One big punch and King was knocked backward, tripped the rope and fell to the ground. The trap was released and at the fadeout, it was dropping quickly to King's body.

The resolution was clever and was similar to the save at the end of the first chapter of *The Tiger Woman* (1944). Luckily, Linda Merritt was trailing close behind to King. As the trap dropped, she jumped up and grabbed the rope that was originally holding the trap in place, preventing the trap from falling all the way to the ground. The spikes ended up about a foot from King's prone body.

In addition to pendulums and spike traps, there were other sharp objects that menaced the heroes of serials. One example was the guillotine used in the Chapter 11 cliffhanger of *Lost City of the Jungle* (1946). The hero, Rod Stanton, was trapped by some natives, who believed he intended to harm them. Stanton protested his innocence. The natives therefore secured Stanton's head under a guillotine blade, which was held up by three ropes. A globe was strategically placed to focus the sun's rays onto those ropes. If the ropes held, Stanton was innocent. If the ropes broke, well, the result was obvious.

The first rope burned and broke and the blade dropped slightly. Then the second rope broke and the blade dropped even further. Finally, as the chapter ended, the last rope broke and the blade fell with a thud. Stanton was presumably killed. The resolution was clever as Stanton was rescued when the final rope was grabbed after it broke but before the blade was allowed to pierce Stanton's body. However, there was no thud

*Lost City of the Jungle* (1946). Russell Hayden, playing hero Rod Stanton, is trapped by natives and placed in a guillotine.

of the blade, as occurred in the prior chapter, providing at least a small cheat. Nonetheless, this was a very exciting and scary cliffhanger.

Chapter 11 of *Daughter of Don Q* was entitled "Glass Guillotine," so it was not unexpected that the peril at the end of the chapter was a sharp object. Dolores Quantero and Cliff Roberts, heroine and hero, were in the fight of their lives with two henchmen, one of whom was in an armored suit which made him practically invincible. During the fight, the outside window was broken. Then Dolores, who was standing near the window, was hit by a thrown object, knocking her out. Her neck came to rest on the edge of the window, with her head outside and her body inside the room. Above Dolores, a very sharp portion of the window glass hung in the frame.

The fight between Roberts and the armored figure continued and each time an adversary hit the wall, the glass in the window dropped, threatening Quantero's life. Finally, as the chapter ended, the glass dropped the whole way, becoming a glass guillotine, presumably splitting Quantero's neck. While the takeout was not unexpected, this was an interesting and inventive cliffhanger, making excellent use of most people's fear of sharp objects.

In Chapter 11 of *The Phantom* (1943), the masked hero was in a fight with two guards near the outside wall of the forbidden domain of Tartar. The Phantom was finally knocked unconscious, directly below a portal gate, which had sharp, protruding spikes at the bottom. Rather than kill the Phantom with his sword, the guard decided to lower the portal gate onto the Phantom's prone body, essentially spearing him to death. However, in the resolution, it turned out that the guard had delayed a little too long. The Phantom woke up and just managed to roll out of harm's way before the spikes skewered him.

## Closing Walls and Sliding Floors

So, you've decided to conquer the world with your newly invented ray of destruction. First, you need a base of operations. You hire an architect to design a house for you. It must have a laboratory, a jail to hold any heroes that discover your location, and multiple bedrooms or a dormitory for your henchmen to sleep in, so they do not have to take the bus home each night. And, you need a room in which the walls close together, so that you can crush any hero who sneaks into the house and also accidentally ends up in that room. Cost is not a factor.

It is hard to explain why the room with the closing walls was originally built for *The Fighting Marines* (1935) (Chapter Eleven), since it was located in a warehouse. It is even harder to understand why one was built for the room in *Ace Drummond* (1936) (Chapter Three), particularly since the room was located in a monastery. Indeed, in Chapter Two of *Shadow of Chinatown* (1936), when Victor Poten (Bela Lugosi) showed his closing walls death trap to his ally in crime, Sonya Rokoff (Luana Walters), she commented, "I see no practical use for that."

Apparently Sonya never watched many serials in her lifetime. In a number of serials the walls were there for whatever reason and they came in very handy as a way to try to destroy the serial hero.

In Chapter Six of *Zorro's Fighting Legion* (1939), Zorro was trapped in a room much like a jail cell when the walls started to slide together. Zorro was about to be crushed. In the next chapter, Zorro tried to prevent his death by placing the cot between the walls, to stop the sliding. The cot was not strong enough and snapped in two. The walls kept closing in. Then Zorro found a loose and large stone in the floor, propped it between the walls and the walls stopped. It was a clever solution to Zorro's problem. His first attempt failed but the second one succeeded.

In *Batman* (1943) (Chapter 13), the Caped Crusader fell through a trap door into a pit, which had walls with protruding knives. Dr. Daka pushed a button and the walls started to close. At the fadeout of the chapter, Batman was about to be impaled on the knives. Luckily, in the resolution, the Boy Wonder arrived just in time to save Batman. This was an excellent and imaginative cliffhanger and resolution.

An interesting rescue resolved a closing walls cliffhanger at the end of Chapter Two of *Shadow of Chinatown* (1936), an otherwise dismal serial. Joan was trapped in one of Victor Poten's death traps, a room with the ubiquitous closing walls. Martin Andrews and Willy Fu learned of the predicament and set off to rescue Joan. In an unusual directorial approach to the situation, much of the action with Joan in the room was shot from directly above through what, for film purposes, was an invisible ceiling. This actually undercut the peril to Joan, as more suspense would have been created by cross cutting within the room between Joan and the closing walls, conveying the claustrophobic effect of the situation. Shooting through the open ceiling actually lessened the feeling of peril to Joan. Perhaps that is why the other serials that had this type of cliffhanger seldom shot the predicament from above.

Andrews and Fu finally located Joan and while Andrews could not open the door to rescue her, he realized that cutting off power to the room would have the same effect. The power line was high on the ceiling of the hallway and Andrews needed to lift Fu to reach the lines. Just as Fu was about to get there, henchman Grogan discovered the two and threw a sword at them, to prevent the rescue. As the closing chapter caption asked, "Will Martin's efforts overcome Poten's cunning?"

The resolution was clever. The sword thrown by Grogan missed, cutting the power lines. The closing walls stopped and Joan was saved. Thus, in a surprising development, Poten's evil plan was thwarted by his own henchman.

One of the most frightening of these cliffhangers occurred in Chapter Ten of *The Spider Returns* (1941). Richard Wentworth and Nita Van Sloan were trapped by the Gargoyle in a cave. The Gargoyle pulled a lever and stakes came down on two walls. He pulled another lever and fire came from the floor in the front and the back. Then the walls started to close and as the chapter ended, death was imminent. While the cliffhanger was resolved in the next chapter with a particularly long time expansion cheat, the cliffhanger itself was still unique.

*The Green Archer* (1940) had an interesting variation on this. In Chapter Four, Spike Holland was trapped in a room in a castle. A switch was pulled and suddenly it was revealed that the ceiling had a series of knives protruding downward. The ceiling gradually lowered and as the chapter ended, Spike was squeezing as low as he could, with only about a foot between him and the knives, and the ceiling was still dropping. There seemed no possible resolution to this death trap, except, perhaps, if there were a rescue by the title character.

*Secret Agent X-9* (1937) had another interesting variation on this cliffhanger at the end of Chapter Three, which was actually set up in Chapters One and Two. To enter or leave the grounds of a large mansion, a car traveled over a switch which opened a sliding metal gate. Once through, the car went over another switch which closed the gate. This was shown several times in the first two chapters of the serial.

At the end of Chapter Three, the hero was on the running board of a car, fighting with the driver. The car drove over the switch, opening the gate. The hero was then knocked off, falling unconscious, just where his neck would be snapped by the closing gate. The car then traveled over the other switch, and the gate started to slide, to close across the hero's neck.

This cliffhanger was interesting because it was unusual and was set up several chapters in advance. The resolution was nothing special, although it was not the expected one.

Sliding floors were closely related to closing walls. As the floors gradually slid away, the hero had no standing room and was destined to fall into a dangerous pit. An example of this occurred in Chapter Eight of *Secret Agent X-9* (1945). The hero, Phil Corrigan, was trapped in a room by the evil Nabura, who then started withdrawing the concrete base of the floor out of the room, slowly eliminating all of the standing space for Corrigan. Once the floor was totally gone, Corrigan would fall into a pit which contained spears or knives sticking straight up, ready to impale him. As the chapter ended, Corrigan started to fall. Luckily he was saved in the next chapter by a rescue and an incredible acrobatic move.

In Chapter Nine of *Jungle Girl* (1941), Nyoka, Stanton and Curley were trapped in a room in a temple. A switch was pulled and the floor started to retract into the wall. No explanation was given as to what was powering the floor, as there was no evidence of electricity in this jungle, Nevertheless, as the floor pulled back, Nyoka could see that there was a drop into a bottomless pit. As the chapter ended, the floor had retracted

*Terry and the Pirates* (1940). This is a combination sliding floor and closing walls cliffhanger. Granville Owen, as Pat Ryan, saves the day with a metal bar he happened to be carrying with him. In the back is William Tracy, playing young Terry Lee.

all the way into the wall. The resolution in the next chapter, while unrealistic, was nevertheless as suspenseful as the cliffhanger.

*Terry and the Pirates* (1940) combined closing walls with a sliding floor in Chapter 11, entitled "Walls of Doom." Terry and Pat were locked in a room in a temple. The floor in the middle dropped away to reveal a pit with knives protruding from the floor, similar to the situation in which Agent X-9 found himself. In this case, the walls started to close in from both sides, forcing both Pat and Terry to the center and a dangerous drop. Luckily, in the next chapter, Pat managed to save the two when he blocked the closing walls with a metal bar he happened to have with him.

*The Green Archer* (1940) had an interesting variation on this trap when Spike Holland, along with three others, was locked in a room. The floor boards fell off in series, revealing a pit of fire below. Spike and his friends were trapped with their backs against the wall, as the last board was about to drop.

This trap actually occurred in the middle of the last chapter and was therefore not technically a cliffhanger. The serial itself took place in an old castle with secret passages, surprise doors and other deathtraps, so whatever faults the serial had, there were some interesting cliffhangers. Once again, Spike Holland was luckily saved from the floor trap by a rescue by the Green Archer.

## Wild Animals

Wild animals were a source of exciting cliffhangers starting with the very first sound movie serial. In *King of the Kongo*, a jungle serial from 1929, there were numerous attacks on the heroes by gorillas, leopards, and lions. Over the years, other wild animal attacks in serials included tigers, gorillas, alligators, mountain lions, bears and some very strange creatures on the Planet Mongo. *Call of the Savage* (1935) even replaced the standard western cliffhanger of the hero apparently being crushed by stampeding horses or cattle with Jan of the jungle apparently being trampled by a horde of stampeding elephants.

*The New Adventures of Tarzan* (1935), an obvious jungle serial, had several cliffhangers which involved wild animals in some way, but the cleverest one was in the ending to Chapter Nine. Tarzan (Herman Brix) and Ula Holt were captured and thrown into separate but adjacent prison cells. Tarzan's hands were tied behind his back and then to the wall and on the other side of the cell, a ferocious lion was chained to the wall. The lion constantly swatted at Tarzan and each time the beast did so, the chain that was holding the lion started to break, little by little. At the end of the chapter, just as Tarzan was managing to come loose from the wall, the lion's chain broke and the beast leaped at Tarzan.

The resolution was almost more exciting than the cliffhanger. Holt managed to escape her captor in her cell and then dug through the wall with a small knife. She was able to help Tarzan cut his ropes through the hole in the wall. When the beast leaped at Tarzan, Tarzan's hands were free. It was then a life and death struggle between man and beast, with the two rolling over and over, Tarzan's arms caught in the lion's mouth from time to time and then Tarzan finally trapped beneath the king of the jungle. At the last instant, Tarzan grabbed the knife that was lying on the floor and was able to stab the beast repeatedly, ending the titanic struggle. The wrestling match between the two jungle icons was one of the best in jungle serial history. Tarzan was surely justified with emitting his patented jungle yell at the end of the fight, to signal his victory.

Herman Brix was involved in more trouble with jungle animals in his second jungle serial, *Hawk of the Wilderness* (1938). Towards the end of Chapter Three, the natives of the area were shown preparing a tiger trap: a large hole in the ground covered by brush with a small lamb tied to the top. The hope was that the tiger would attack the lamb, falling into the hole. Hawk and Beth Munro then came along and rescued the lamb. The tiger still attacked and as planned by the natives, fell into the trap.

All would have been well except that Hawk then got into a fight with the natives. The fight ended with Hawk being flipped into the tiger's hole. As the chapter ended, the tiger leaped at the unarmed jungle warrior. The suspense was increased by the cuts to the stalking tiger during the fight and the sounds of the tiger growls, interspersed with exciting music. In the takeout, Hawk grabbed a wooden stake lying in the trap and speared the leaping tiger, just as it was about to reach him.

Lions and tigers were not the only jungle animals to menace the serials' heroes and heroines. At the end of Chapter 11 of *Tarzan the Tiger* (1929), Jane was off on her own in the jungle, being chased by Princess La's men. She was trapped against a stream, which was filled with ferocious alligators. Jane had no choice but to attempt to cross the stream, on a flimsy tree branch that had fallen across the water. She reluctantly started across but about half way to safety, the branch broke, Jane fell in the water and her foot became trapped under the log. The alligators quickly swam to where their victim was trapped.

This was a very realistic cliffhanger ending, without obvious stock footage or process screen effects. It was also helped by the fact that it was the beautiful Natalie Kingston who was in trouble. Luckily for Jane, in the resolution, Tarzan heard her screams, leaped into the water, dislodged her foot from under the log and saved Jane, but not before wrestling and killing one of the alligators, a fight in which Tarzan exploited his own brute strength.

An unusual wild animal cliffhanger occurred in Chapter Two of *Tim Tyler's Luck* (1937). Tim and an ivory safari were walking along a path halfway down a huge cliff when suddenly a rock fell by. Then, at least eight gorillas, high on the mountain, started throwing huge stones at the group, hoping to knock them off the cliff. Despite the best efforts of the safari to avoid the rocks, there were too many gorillas throwing too many stones and eventually the leader of the safari was knocked off the cliff. He saved himself by hanging onto a branch but he was injured and knew that he could not hold on for long. Tim lowered himself down on a rope to try to rescue the man. Unfortunately, the native who was holding the rope for Tim was then himself hit by a rock and over they both went.

This was surely one of the most unusual cliffhangers of all time. Clearly, it set the record for most men in a gorilla suit at one time in a serial. In the resolution, Tim was luckily saved when the rope caught in a crevice and he did not fall all the way down the mountain.

Wild animal cliffhangers were not limited to jungle serials. They appeared from time to time in western serials. In Chapter 12 of *Overland Mail* (1942), Barbara Gilbert, the daughter of the owner of the overland mail company, decided to substitute for a fallen Pony Express rider and attempt to timely deliver the U.S. mail. While it was a courageous action on her part, she was immediately captured by Puma and his band of renegade Indians, some of whom were whites dressed as Indians. She was tied up in a cave but then cleverly escaped by tricking the woman who was watching her. Barbara then set out on her own, through the back country of the Wild West.

Suddenly, a mountain lion was spotted high on a hill. Barbara, slightly lost, was walking below the animal, unaware of the danger. With small warning the lion leapt down, landing right on Barbara. As the chapter ended, Barbara was knocked off her feet by the animal. In the takeout, the lion rolled off Barbara and as he was about to attack again, the lion was shot by friendly Indians who were luckily in the area. Barbara survived without a scratch.

There were apparently lots of mountain lions roaming the Wild West, as can be seen in the cliffhanger to Chapter Ten of *White Eagle* (1941). Janet Rand escaped from some henchmen and fled to safety in a cave. Unfortunately for her, a mountain lion spotted her and followed her into the cave. It trapped her in the back of the cave and came prowling after her. Luckily, White Eagle recognized the danger and came into the cave to rescue her. The lion, which seemed to have some of the longest and sharpest teeth of any serial animal, leaped at White Eagle as the chapter ended.

This cliffhanger was expertly done, with stock footage seamlessly intercut with new footage, making this one of the great western chapter endings. In the takeout, White Eagle fended off attack after attack by the lion, finally killing it with his knife. One lesson to be learned from many of these serials was how easy it was to dispose of a large ferocious beast with a very small knife.

The silliest wild animal cliffhanger occurred at the end of Chapter Seven of *Sign of the Wolf* (1931). Ruth received a note to come to the abandoned cabin in Red Rock Canyon to receive news about her missing father. Ruth followed the directions in the note and went to the cabin. Nearby, the good guys and the bad guys got into a fight and the mysterious Kuva was captured by some henchmen. However, the chapter was about to end and there was no cliffhanger in sight.

Suddenly, and inexplicably, a bear approached the cabin and started to enter. Ruth tried to block the door but to no avail and as the chapter ended the bear had entered the cabin. In the takeout, the bear did not actually make it into the cabin. Instead, a strange man came to the cabin window, shot at the bear and frightened it away. The bear was never seen again in the serial. This was an example of having a cliffhanger just for the sake of finding a way to end a chapter without the cliffhanger making any sense in the story line of the chapter play. The fact that it also contained a re-shot footage cheat hardly added to its effectiveness.

## Avalanches

In the real world, avalanches usually involve cascading waves of snow from mountainous areas in a cold country. In serials, however, avalanches generally involved boulders falling from mountains, as a result of explosions set by henchmen. Snow avalanches were seldom found in serials because serials seldom had scenes in snow areas. Even the majority of *The Great Alaskan Mystery* (1944) seemed to take place in a temperate climate.

There were some exceptions. Frigia was the frigid sounding name for the location of a number of chapters of *Flash Gordon Conquers the Universe* (1938). Frigia was just as it sounded. It was a cold, snowy and desolate area on the planet Mongo. And, it did have snow avalanches. In the serial, at the end of Chapter Two, one was started by bombs fired by Ming's henchmen. The resulting snow avalanche was shown through the use of stock footage which was cleverly intercut with shots of the live actors. The resolution was not unexpected as the heroes survived the snow and were eventually rescued.

Another example of a snow avalanche occurred in Chapter One of *Lost City of the Jungle* (1946), although this one was started by natural causes. While the serial took place in the Himalayan Mountains, only the first two chapters involved scenes in a snowy area, but those snow scenes allowed for a rare snow avalanche cliffhanger. Once again, the resolution involved the hero and heroine surviving the snow avalanche and being rescued.

Chapter Four of *The Painted Stallion* (1937) was entitled "Avalanche" so that even though there was no snow in the serial, there was no surprise when the cliffhanger occurred. A wagon train was traveling beneath a high mountain which some henchmen intended to blow up. Clarke Stuart discovered the situation but was unable to stop the fuse. He ran down the mountain, ordering the wagon train to turn around. Most of the wagons were able to do so but Stuart was trapped with one troublesome wagon when the rocks started rolling. The special effects were spectacular. It looked as if the hillside was actually blown up. Stuart's escape was reasonable and it was an exciting cliffhanger.

Chapter Five of *Riders of Death Valley* (1941) was entitled "The Avalanche of Doom," so, once again, there was no surprise as to what the cliffhanger turned out to be. What was surprising was that such a spectacular avalanche could be created by rolling just one large rock off a hill. Of course, it was also helpful to have stock footage of a huge avalanche available. Jim and Mary were saved when they hid in a cave.

The Phantom was trapped when a mountainside was blown up by the villains in Chapter Eight of the serial of the same name. An avalanche of rocks was cascaded toward him. The Phantom cleverly escaped by rolling into a recessed area, with the rocks falling safely in front of him. It helped that, since this was a Columbia serial, with its low budget, the avalanche was somewhat tiny in nature, and the Phantom may never have been in any real danger at all. However, the weakest avalanche of them all surely occurred at the end of Chapter Four of *Mysterious Island* (1951), when two of the castaways were subjected to an avalanche of wrapped packages containing food and other supplies which were pushed off a high mountain. Somehow they survived.

Possibly the most spectacular avalanche cliffhanger of them all occurred at the end of Chapter One of *Haunted Harbor* (1944). Jim Marsden and two friends were caught in a hurricane on their sailing ship when they noticed a small sloop swamped at the edge of the sea. Marsden swam over to rescue the occupants who turned out to be Patricia Harding and her injured father. All the while, the sea was bouncing the two boats and all of the occupants were being drenched in waves of water. To add to the tension, there was no background music in the film as the howling of the wind and the crashing of the waves was sufficient accompaniment for the tension-filled scenes.

Suddenly, a few rocks, loosened by the heavy downpour, fell from the adjacent cliff. The rescue continued and then a few larger rocks fell from the cliff. As the father was saved, there were a few more shots of the cliff with a few more rocks coming loose and then suddenly the entire cliff came down in one massive drop, burying the Harding boat with Jim and Patricia on board.

The special effects, along with the clever use of sound, made this one of the most spectacular and realistic avalanche cliffhangers in serials. Even the usual time expansion resolution in the next chapter did not detract from the excitement that came before.


## II. A VARIETY OF CLIFFHANGERS

This chapter was not intended to be an all inclusive list of serial cliffhangers. There were other mundane cliffhangers used repeatedly in serials, such as car crashes, airplane crashes, fire traps, and explosions.

On the other hand, there were many imaginative cliffhangers, used only once or twice by the studios, which remain in the serial aficionado's memory long after other parts of a serial are forgotten. All of the major studios and the independents can claim credit for several of these special cliffhangers. Here are a few of them.

### Republic

Republic emphasized the cliffhangers in its serials so it is no surprise that Republic had many memorable cliffhangers in its 66 serials. For example, in Chapter Four of *Secret Service in Darkest Africa* (1943), the Nazis had hidden a substantial amount of explosives in a grave yard located in a desolate area. There was an intricate wiring arrangement between the crosses in the graveyard and the explosives. Once the first explosive was triggered by pulling down on a cross, other explosives in other graves would ignite in an unknown pattern, blowing everyone to bits. Rex Bennett found the graveyard and got into a fight with two henchmen, in and around the open graves and crosses. Then, one of the henchmen was shot. He fell onto a cross and then into a grave, setting off the first huge explosion. That set off the series of other explosions from the other graves, while Bennett was trapped in a hole with the other henchman. As the chapter ended, the screen was filled with black smoke and Bennett was apparently killed.

This was a truly spectacular cliffhanger, with the explosions shot from above and with any background music drowned out by the large booms. No other serial had this particular cliffhanger. While the resolution was not unexpected, it did not take away from the inventiveness of this unique and suspenseful chapter ending.

Another impressive Republic cliffhanger took place at the end of Chapter Nine of *King of the Royal Mounted* (1940). Sergeant King's search for hollowed out logs which were being used to smuggle Compound X into the area led him and Mountie Tom Merritt to a dam under a bridge, where they immediately discovered some henchmen. This led to the requisite fight where Tom was knocked out, and King and a henchman went over the side of the bridge into a pool of water, in pursuit of a briefcase carrying Compound X. As the two fought in the water, the briefcase fell over a spillway into the next level of pool. There were cuts to the bridge above the dam from below, showing the high drop from that pool into churning water below. The henchman and King followed the briefcase into the second pool and when the briefcase fell over the high spillway, the henchman was also dragged over to a certain death. As the chapter ended, King was also about to go over.

In the takeout, King was rescued just in time by Merritt, who threw a rope to King and pulled him out of the water just as he went over the spillway. King was actually partially over the spillway when he caught the rope. The resolution was as exciting as the cliffhanger, as the stunt of rescuing King was shot from below the spillway, guaranteeing that it was a true stunt and not a special effect. Indeed, there were no process screen shots in either the cliffhanger or the resolution. The location shooting added to the effectiveness of the scene.

In *Perils of Nyoka* (1942) (Chapter Three), Nyoka and Larry entered the Tunnel of Bubbling Death on their quest for the Golden Tablets. The Tunnel was quite a frightening place. It had a labyrinth of footpaths which squeezed around pools of chemicals, which emitted clouds of smoke and from time to time, flared into a deadly fire. To make matters worse, a fight ensued with some of the villains, which involved running over and around pits of the boiling substances, gunfire, falls perilously close to the bubbling death and timely rescues. The musical score by Mort Glickman was particularly exciting; the special effects were awesome.

Suddenly, as Nyoka was about to shoot one of the henchmen, she was hit by a large object and knocked backward into one of the pits. The chapter ended with a shot of the flames surrounding Nyoka. In the take-out in the next chapter, there was a slight cheat as it turned out that Nyoka landed on the side of the pit, close to the flames but not into them. This resolution did not detract from the amazing cliffhanger that had gone before.

Chapter Three of *Daughter of Don Q* (1946) had one of those "small" cliffhangers which were often more exciting than the cliffhangers with stunts and special effects. Dolores Quantero (Adrian Booth) agreed to go under-cover and become the assistant in a knife throwing act at the El Diablo café which Donovan, the henchman (Ray Barcroft), was known to frequent.

*Daughter of Don Q* (1946). Heroine Adrian Booth went undercover in a knife throwing act, not realizing that the person throwing the knives was the evil Roy Barcroft. Here she is, along with Kirk Alyn, just before she goes on stage.

Quantero was on the lookout for Donovan so that she and Cliff Roberts (hero) could capture him and make him talk. In the act, Quantero wore a fetching outfit and the knife thrower, Romero, wore a mask. Unbeknownst to Quantero, Donovan was also quite an expert with the knives.

For the second performance of the night, Donovan decided to take the place of the Romero, in an attempt to make the act more realistic and give it a grisly ending. Because Donovan was masked, Quantero did not know of the substitution and innocently performed in the act, unaware of its potentially deadly ending. First, Donovan threw three quick knives perfectly to the left of Quantero's body, sticking into the backdrop. Two more knives were thrown just to the right of Quantero's body and then two just above and to the left of her head. To add to the suspense, Donovan took more time between the subsequent throws and there were cuts to hero Roberts slowly returning to the café by car, as Roberts was also unaware of any problem in the act. More knives were thrown, the background music pulsed louder and Donovan brought out the last knife. As he let it fly toward Quantero's body, the chapter ended.

Quantero was saved by a sudden rescue by Cliff Roberts, who was able to get back to the café in time and block the final knife with a large serving tray. It was sometimes the small cliffhangers like this one, cleverly executed, that remain in the serial viewer's mind long after the spectacular explosions have been forgotten.

### Universal

Universal's serials also had many imaginative cliffhangers. In Chapter 12 of *The Adventures of Smilin' Jack* (1943), hero Jack Martin had to return to Mandon in China to prove his innocence of a murder charge. In Mandon, when a defendant protested his innocence, Mandon law could not punish him, but the accused must undergo the Mandon Ordeal. If he survived, then he was innocent; if he died, he must have been guilty. Unfortunately, for an individual not of the Mandon faith, survival was unlikely.

The next morning, Jack was brought out to meet his fate. A gong was struck; natives beat their drums. The concrete on which Jack was standing slid backward, to reveal a pit of flaming hot coals. Jack was required to walk across them barefoot. Just before the chapter ending, he took several steps. The sweat was glistening on his face. At the fadeout, Jack appeared to fall.

*Adventures of Smilin' Jack* (1943). Having survived the Mandon Ordeal, Smilin' Jack is on his way to defeating the villains. Pictured from left to right in the foreground are Philip Ahn, playing Wu Tan, an aide to Mah Ling, Jay Novello as Kushimi, a captured henchman who may not live for long, and Tom Brown as Smilin' Jack. As was common with publicity photos, the scene developed slightly differently in the serial.

This was an excellent example of a plot-oriented cliffhanger from Universal. The cliffhanger was a logical part of the story and actually moved the tale along. In the resolution, Jack walked slowly and stoically across the coals and made it to the end. He had survived the Ordeal! (The apparent fall at the end of the prior chapter was not repeated.) It turned out that overnight, Wu Tan had explained the secret of surviving the Ordeal to Jack, allowing him to smile once again. What added to the interest to this chapter ending and resolution was the fact that the Mandon Ordeal was the type of cliffhanger that could not be repeated in another serial because it was integral to the serial's plot.

Generally, some of the most boring cliffhangers in westerns were the hero falling in front of a rushing line of horses or being caught in the middle of a cattle stampede. Universal loved to use that type of cliffhanger in its western serials, probably because it had loads of silent film archive footage on the subject. However, in Chapter Two of *Riders of Death Valley* (1941), Universal finally made this type of cliffhanger work.

Jim Benton and Tombstone were being chased by some of Wolf Reade's men. As they were forced into a canyon, the gunfire set off a horse stampede. The stock footage used was of one of the largest horse stampedes ever filmed. It was cleverly intercut with shots of Benton and Tombstone with about 20 horses following on their heels. Thus, it really seemed as if the two heroes were in the same shots with the hundreds of stampeding horses. Also, close-ups of the horses were interspersed among medium and long shots of the horses, and that, combined with the loud sound of the horses' hoof beats, added to the intensity. At the fadeout, there was the standard ending of Benton falling in front of the horses and being trampled. In a classic absurd resolution, although 200 horses may have passed over Benton's body, none of them even nicked him.

One of the most suspenseful cliffhangers in all of the serials occurred at the end of Chapter Six of *Lost City of the Jungle* (1946). Two of the henchmen finally reached the sealed Tomb of the Glowing Goddess. When they learned that there was a curse on anyone who entered the Tomb, they decided to send a tribesman in first. The native walked in but when he stepped on the first step of a stairway, the stone went down, the door closed behind him, and a swivel door opened in the opposite wall. A few seconds later, the main door opened again and the henchmen walked in. There they discovered the tribesman dead, from no apparent cause. Because the filmmakers did not show the viewers how the native died, the suspense increased.

Hero Rod Stanton came along next and the henchmen decided to let him go into the tomb, to a certain but unknown death. Unaware of the danger, Stanton entered. When he hit the first step, the door behind him closed and the swivel door in the opposite wall opened. This time, however, the cause of death was revealed—poison gas being piped into the Tomb. As the chapter ended, Stanton was gasping for his breath.

The resolution was also quite interesting. Stanton finally got his wits about him and sneaked out of the tomb room through the swivel door. There he found an important broken plaque. The henchmen tried to come in to see what happened to Stanton but were stopped by the poisonous gas. Stanton got away. This was a rare cliffhanger that relied on suspense and the fear of the unknown rather than on stunts or special effects.

## Columbia

Columbia also had its share of interesting cliffhangers. For example, in Chapter 12 of *Holt of the Secret Service* (1941), Holt became involved in a fist fight with six henchmen. Even for Holt, that was one henchman too many and the federal agent was knocked unconscious. He was then ordered to be executed by a firing squad for a crime he was alleged to have committed. Holt, with his hands tied behind his back, was marched out in front of the jungle natives so that they could see what would happen. Holt was then stood up in front of a block wall. Four men with rifles made up the firing squad. Holt was stoic. Upon command, the four riflemen fired and Holt fell to the ground. There was no way for Holt to survive this cliffhanger.

The resolution was clever. Kay Drew, another federal agent, had learned about the firing squad in advance. She replaced the bullets in the rifles with blanks. It was an innovative resolution although it had been used at least one time previously, in the takeout to the Chapter Six cliffhanger of *The Three Musketeers* (1933). It was not done quite as well in the earlier serial as it was in *Holt*.

*Holt of the Secret Service* (1941). Hero Jack Holt stands stoically and without fear, despite the fact that he is about to be shot by a firing squad.

One of the problems in concocting a cliffhanger for Superman in his serials was that since the Man of Steel was invincible, it was difficult to put him in a convincing life-threatening situation. Similarly, if Lois Lane were in trouble, Superman was always available to save her. That was why the ending to Chapter Four of *Atom Man v. Superman* (1950) was so clever. Atom Man captured Lois Lane and then used her to lure Superman to his hideout. Once there, Atom Man threatened Lois' life unless Superman agreed to enter a machine which would send him to the Empty Doom, a kind of phantom zone world from the comic books. Superman reluctantly agreed, a button was pushed and Superman disappeared.

Then, reneging on Atom Man's promise to free Lois, Atom Man's henchmen ended up placing the unconscious body of Lois in a car, which as the chapter ended, went over a high cliff. As the narrator said, "With Superman gone into the Empty Doom, who will save Lois?"

The resolution was clever. Superman never went to the Empty Doom. When Atom Man pushed the switch, Superman used his super speed to rush out of the hideout. He therefore appeared to have disap-

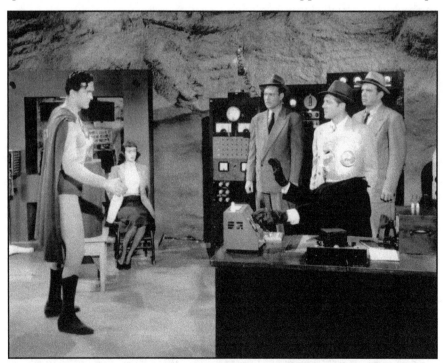

*Atom Man vs. Superman* (1950). Atom Man (Lyle Talbot) has trapped Lois Lane (Noel Neill), in order to send Superman (Kirk Alyn) to the Empty Doom. Also pictured from left to right are Don Harvey, Terry Frost and Rusty Wescoatt.

peared into the Empty Doom. He was then able to rescue Lois from her predicament. Of course, later in the serial, Superman did actually make it to the Empty Doom.

Surely, one of the most unique cliffhangers of all time occurred at the end of Chapter One of *Adventures of Sir Galahad* (1949). The heroic knight was on the trail of the stolen sword Excalibur which he believed was hidden in the Enchanted Forest. However, when Galahad started into the forest, the magician Merlin appeared and told him to leave, stating, "The way is not for you." When Sir Galahad refused to turn back, Merlin used his magic to freeze Sir Galahad in place in front of a tree. Then he blinded Sir Galahad and started a fire in front of him. As the chapter ended, the branches of the tree came to life and held Sir Galahad in place by the fire.

Obviously, this was one cliffhanger which was not going to be re-used in another serial. The cliffhanger was so unusual and Merlin appeared so powerful that the predicament of Sir Galahad was quite effective as a chapter ending. In Chapter Two, Sir Galahad was surprisingly saved by a character who had not yet appeared in the serial, the Lady of the Lake, whose power was the equal of that of Merlin.

During Chapter Ten of *Gunfighters of the Northwest* (1954), Sgt. Ward tried to capture Anders but in the ensuing first fight, Ward was knocked unconscious. Anders changed clothes with Ward and then placed Ward's prone body in a rowboat, stretched under the cross-seats. Anders shoved the boat into a lake and then from a ledge, threw heavy rocks into the boat, poking holes in the same and causing it to sink. As the chapter ended, the boat was sinking with Ward inside.

The resolution was not unexpected, as all water cliffhangers tended to have a similar resolution. However, the cliffhanger itself was quite suspenseful, once again highlighting the fact that simple cliffhangers could often be more exciting and suspenseful than the spectacular cliffhangers, such as explosions or plane crashes.

**Mascot and the Independents**

Mascot also had a surprising number of unique cliffhangers. For example, at the end of the first chapter of *The Galloping Ghost* (1931), Barbara Courtland (Dorothy Gulliver) decided to fly to Coynsville to be with her brother Buddy, not realizing that the rudder wire to her plane was broken. When Red Grange learned of the problem from an airport mechanic, he raced along the ground with the speed of a running back and managed to jump onto the back of the plane. He then inched along the plane to the front and told Barbara of the problem. This was an excellent stunt with a long shot of the plane in the air as Red climbed to the front, and the close-ups with Barbara and Red were cleverly shot so that there was no obvious projection screen.

The two had no choice but to parachute out of the plane, but unfortunately, there was only one parachute and Barbara was wearing it. They decided that Barbara would jump out with Red hanging on. They did so and at first, the idea seemed to be working. The chute opened. The plane crashed beneath them. Suddenly, the strings from the parachute started to break, because of the double weight in the air. Red, much like a quarterback on a screen pass, sacrificed his body for the good of the team and let go, hoping to at least save Barbara. As the chapter ended, there was an excellent special effect of Red hurtling toward the ground.

It was hard to believe that Red survived this cliffhanger but then, it was only Chapter One. As it turned out, George Elton (Walter Miller) was also flying to Coynsville and he spotted Red dropping from the plane. Elton quickly flew his plane below Red's body and Red landed on the wing of the plane. The plane was then able to land with only a minor crash but Red survived. Luckily, Red was not a lineman in college so his weight hitting the plane's wing from a freefall did not knock Elton's plane out of the air.

*The Galloping Ghost* cliffhanger was one of the best ever by Mascot. The following year, Mascot produced another stunning airplane cliffhanger. At the end of the first chapter of *The Shadow of the Eagle* (1932), Jean Gregory (Dorothy Gulliver) chased after a mysterious figure in an overcoat and hat who was impersonating her father. She was unable to prevent the man from boarding a plane and taking off. Jean's calls brought Craig McCoy (John Wayne) to her rescue, but he was also unable to stop the plane.

Since Jean had hurt her leg, McCoy started to carry her back to the circus. Suddenly the plane looped around and started after them. McCoy turned and started to run, with Jean in his arms. There was a particularly stunning shot at the fadeout with the plane flying very low, just about to overtake them and knock them to the ground. Was this cliffhanger the inspiration for the fake crop dusting plane chasing Cary Grant in Alfred Hitchcock's *North by Northwest* (1959)?

*Shadow of the Eagle* (1932). An unknown assailant, posing as Dorothy Gulliver's father, boards a plane which he will then use to chase John Wayne and Dorothy Gulliver across the ground from the air, in one of Mascot's best cliffhangers.

If so, at least Hitchcock did not make the mistake of the directors of *The Shadow of the Eagle*, as the serial cliffhanger was undercut by an inconsistency from shot to shot as to how close the plane was to Jean and Craig. Nevertheless, the chapter ending was quite exciting and the resolution kept up the intensity. The first attempt by the plane at hitting the two was a miss, but the plane came around for one more shot. In the second try, Jean and Craig landed in a hole in the ground, preventing a collision. The plane flew off.

In Chapter Seven of *The New Adventures of Tarzan* (1935), an independent serial, Tarzan dove into a river to recover a notebook containing important information about the Green Goddess. While the jungle hero was able to grab the notebook, he was caught in a strong river current. This cliffhanger made great use of the swimming skills of Olympian Herman Brix and the location shooting in Guatemala. Shots of an incredibly high water fall were intercut with Brix attempting to fight the current, at one point even grabbing onto a rock but being unable to hold on. Eventually, the current was too strong and over Tarzan went.

There were many more great cliffhangers that could be mentioned here. Everyone has their favorites. A special cliffhanger, even if the resolution was not perfect, was often the highlight of a serial.

## III. ANTICIPATION CLIFFHANGERS

With most cliffhangers, the hero was dead or very close to death as the chapter ended. If the hero's car went over a high cliff and then exploded, the hero must surely be dead. If the hero was on a conveyor belt heading toward a saw, and he was inches from the rotating blades as the chapter ended, then death must be imminent.

Those were the typical types of cliffhangers employed in serials. There was however, a different type of cliffhanger used in some serials, which brought some variety to the genre. This type of cliffhanger can be called, to coin another term, an anticipation cliffhanger. This is also often referred to as a plot cliffhanger. In this type of chapter ending, the hero was not dead or even close to death. The plot had merely taken an interesting twist and there was an anticipation of further suspenseful or dangerous activities in later chapters. Surprisingly, anticipation cliffhangers tended to be more interesting than regular cliffhangers.

### No Cliffhanger

Before looking at anticipation cliffhangers, they have to be contrasted with serial chapters that ended without a cliffhanger. This occurred most often in earlier serials, such as *Return of Chandu* (1934) and *Secret of Treasure Island* (1938). Some of the chapter endings were traditional cliffhangers, but other chapters simply ended, without any cliffhanger at all. They seemed more like episodes of television series or chapters of books, rather than chapters of movie serials.

Some cliffovers ended with the vehicle or hero landing in the water, before the chapter ended. An example of this occurred in *Rustlers of Red Dog* (1935) (Chapter 11) where a horse and two riders fell over a cliff but landed in water before the chapter ended. Obviously, by serial convention, any fall into water, no matter what the height, would not result in any injury. Thus, the chapter effectively ended with no cliffhanger at all.

This same unfortunate chapter ending also occurred in *The Oregon Trail* (1939) (Chapter One), *Winners of the West* (1940) (Chapter Six), *The Painted Stallion* (1937) (Chapter Three), and many other serials.

Then there were those Columbia serial chapters which ended in an excellent cliffhanger. Unfortunately, right after the ending, scenes from the following week's episode were shown, to entice the viewer back to the theater next week. Those scenes included clips of the hero, alive and active, thus undercutting any cliffhanger that there may have been.

**Anticipation Cliffhangers**

An excellent example of an anticipation cliffhanger occurred at the end of Chapter Seven of *Atom Man vs. Superman* (1950). Lex Luthor was determined to capture Superman and he had obtained some kryptonite to accomplish the task. Superman was speaking at a public function. The henchmen were sitting in the front row. Secretly, they pulled out the piece of kryptonite.

Superman started to become dizzy. He had no idea why. Then he collapsed. A call was made for an ambulance, which arrived surprisingly quickly. Superman was placed on a stretcher and put in the ambulance. That turned out to be a ruse. The ambulance was being run by Luthor's men. As the chapter ended, they were holding the kryptonite next to Superman, rendering him helpless.

Superman was not dead. He was not near death. The cliffhanger, however, was more effective than if he were. The viewer wanted to know: what did Luthor have in mind for Superman? How could Superman escape? Would this finally be the end of Superman? The excitement was not in the cliffhanger itself but, rather, in what the viewer anticipated might occur in the next episode or next several episodes.

An anticipation cliffhanger was often more effective than the traditional cliffhanger, partly because it was usually unique to the serial in question. In *Atom Man,* this cliffhanger worked because Superman was generally invulnerable but now, due to the cleverness of Luthor, Superman was in the hands of his arch rival. If the man in the ambulance was a mere mortal, such as Jack Holt, for example, and there was only a gun directed at him, the anticipation would not have been as great.

Chapter 14 of *Drums of Fu Manchu* (1940), captioned "Satan's Surgeon," had another plot cliffhanger. The nemesis of Fu Manchu, Sir Nayland Smith, was captured and brought to Fu Manchu. Instead of killing Smith,

Fu Manchu decided to turn him into a mindless zombie (a Dacoit) to help Fu Manchu escape. As the surgery was about to begin, Fu Manchu glee-fully announced, "Sir Nayland Smith, dacoit slave of Fu Manchu." It was the idea of Fu Manchu turning Smith into a slave, rather than killing him, that made this cliffhanger ending particularly chilling.

As the chapter ended, Fu Manchu was not even reaching for Smith. It was the anticipation of what was to come that made this cliffhanger work. Would Smith be rescued? If he was turned into a Dacoit, what would happen? Was the operation reversible? This anticipation cliffhanger was also unique to the *Fu Manchu* serial. It would make no sense in any other serial. The cliffhanger worked, not just because of the anticipation but also because it was well integrated into the plot of the serial.

Although a different type of operation was involved, there was a similar type of anticipation cliffhanger at the end of Chapter 12 of *Gang Busters* (1942), entitled "The Long Chance." As the chapter ended, Dr. Mortis was threatening to do an unusual medical procedure on police-man Bill Bannister, involving Bannister's death and subsequent return to life. Again, this cliffhanger was unique to the plot of *Gang Busters* and could not be used in any other serial.

There was another good anticipation cliffhanger at the end of Chap-ter 10 of *The Adventures of Smilin' Jack* (1943), titled "Blackout in the Islands." Mah Ling, the leader of Mandon, a province of China, who was finally ready to disclose the secret route across China to India, was mur-dered by a henchman of the Nazi, Fraulein Von Teufel. The evil Fraulein had rigged a record so that it appeared that Smilin' Jack was the one who murdered Mah Ling. As the episode ended, the Honolulu police were about to arrest Jack for the murder. The lights went out and there was shooting.

Again, Jack was not presumed dead or close to death as the chapter ended. The suspense came from the audience wondering how Jack would defeat this new roadblock from the Fraulein and clear his name in time to travel to China to learn the secret of the passage to India. Although not handled as well, there was a similar anticipation cliffhanger at the end of Chapter Eight of *The Galloping Ghost* (1931), when it appeared that Red Grange would be charged with a murder he did not commit.

An interesting variation on this type of cliffhanger could be called the "Take Off That Mask!" cliffhanger, based upon the title to Chapter Five of *Zorro's Black Whip* (1944). As the chapter ended, the Black Whip had been captured and she was ordered to remove her mask, so the hench-

*Zorro's Black Whip* (1944). The Black Whip has been ordered to take off her mask or else. As the chapter ends, she is about to do so.

men could learn her real identity. At the fadeout, the Black Whip was beginning to remove the mask.

A variation on the "Take Off That Mask!" cliffhanger occurred in Chapter Nine of *Adventures of Frank and Jesse James* (1948). The James Brothers were using aliases so that the sheriff and townspeople would not learn that they were the reputed criminal duo. However, in "The Eyes of the Law," there was a hearing in the sheriff's office to determine the rightful owner of a mine and the only documentary evidence was a deed witnessed by Frank and Jesse James. Unless Frank could bring another witness to the hearing in time, the deed would have to be produced and the James brothers' identities exposed. At the fadeout, it appeared that Frank would be too late.

A clever "Take Off That Mask" cliffhanger occurred at the end of Chapter Four of *The Masked Marvel* (1943). The villainous Sakima knew that one of four insurance investigators was the Masked Marvel and that the masked crime fighter was a long distance away, having just escaped from an exploding building. Sakima had the investigators called into a room, knowing the one who did not appear must be the Masked Marvel. As the chapter ended, three of the investigators had arrived and one, Jim, was missing. Sakima had discovered the real identity of the Masked Marvel!

Of course, in the resolution, the fourth investigator arrived just in time, just as Frank James arrived in time, and just as the Black Whip did not remove her mask. It was not that these unmasking cliffhangers were particularly special or very difficult to guess the resolution. It was that they were a welcome change from the standard cliffhanger used at the end of most serial chapters.

True anticipation cliffhangers in movie serials were the exception, rather than the rule. When done, and done well, they truly added to the effectiveness of the overall serial.

# Chapter 7:
# Stock Footage and Serial Bloopers

## I. STOCK FOOTAGE

While stock footage was inserted into many types of Hollywood films over many years, its use virtually disappeared from the movies by the late 1950s and it is no longer used at all in today's big budget movies. Serials, however, were low budget films and stock footage was always used to a great extent in the movie serial. Indeed, there was stock footage in just about every serial, no matter which studio produced the serial.

"Stock footage," which is sometimes referred to as "archive footage," may be defined as footage used in a movie that was not originally made for that movie. Stock footage came from many sources. One source was newsreel footage or documentary footage of events that actually occurred in real life, as contrasted with events specifically shot for a movie. In *Dick Tracy's G-Men* (1939), for example, some newsreel footage from the *Hindenburg* disaster was interspersed among special effects of a dirigible fire to add to the scope of the disaster that befell Dick Tracy at the end of Chapter Nine of the serial.

Another source of stock footage was film shot for a particular movie or serial and then re-used in a subsequent movie or serial. For example, in the first chapter of *The Black Widow* (1947), the hero's car was forced off the road. It crashed into a gas station which exploded. The footage was previously used in Chapter One of *Federal Operator 99* (1945), when the hero was apparently shot, causing him to lose control of his car, resulting in the same gas station explosion. The footage was then used one more time in Chapter Seven of *Federal Agents vs. Underworld, Inc.*(1949) when a henchman's car crashed into the same gas station. It was clearly the same footage in each of the three serials because the gas

*Federal Operator 99* (1945). This is a reused Republic cliffhanger, with the hero's car about to crash into a gas station, causing a huge explosion.

station was unusual in that it did not have a brand but instead had the large sign at the top which read, "Stop Your Motor."

The amount of stock footage varied substantially from serial to serial. By the 1950s, it sometimes seemed that there was more stock footage than new footage in many of the serials of the decade.

**A. First Chapter Use**

In serials, short clips of film often appeared in the introductory chapter of the serial as a montage of the nefarious acts of the villain. This montage was usually a collection of stock footage, culled from many sources.

A good example of this occurred in the *Flash Gordon* trilogy. As the first serial opened, the Planet Mongo was rushing to Earth, causing massive destruction. There were shots of crowds in London, Rome, Paris, Shanghai, India, Africa and Arabia, supposedly panicking. All of this was stock footage as the studio hardly provided enough money in the budget for the director to travel the Earth to obtain this film, which only appeared for a few seconds in the serial. Interestingly, the original *Flash Gordon* comic strip story had similar scenes from Africa, Arabia and Times Square.

In the second serial, *Flash Gordon's Trip to Mars* (1938), Ming was depleting nitron from the earth's atmosphere, causing destruction over the planet. Stock footage of buildings falling, high waves at sea, flooding, and hurricane winds were shown. In *Flash Gordon Conquers the Universe* (1940), Ming sent a black plague known as the purple death to earth. Stock footage of people running, large crowds and racing ambulances were used.

The same technique was used in the opening chapters of westerns. For example, in the opening chapter of *Adventures of Red Ryder* (1940), villains were trying to buy up land along the proposed track of a new railroad, by intimidating the owners to sell at a low price. This permitted the insertion of archive footage of shootings, burning of buildings and barns and driving off of cattle.

The use of stock footage in the first chapter was not limited to science fiction or western serials. In *The Secret Code* (1942), sabotage by the Nazis seemed rampant in America. Therefore, footage of buildings and industrial plants exploding, trains being wrecked, bridges being blown up, ships sinking, airplanes crashing and fires burning were shown. All of the clips were stock footage. If new footage had to have been created for this serial, just to show the vast sabotage activities of the Nazis, before the true plot of the serial unfolded, the entire budget for the serial would have been expended in the first three minutes of the serial. Thus, stock footage was an important tool for the serial maker, particularly in the first chapter, to set the scene for the remainder of the serial.

## B. During the Chapter

### (i) From Older Films

During a serial, stock footage was often used as background material, to give the serial a more expensive look than it could ever hope to achieve on its small budget. A good example was a clip used several times in *Flash Gordon* (1936), where a number of scantily-clad women danced in front of a huge statue of a sitting man, with a large head and moving arms. The figure had some relationship to the great god, Tao.

This stock footage came from a Universal feature from 1930, *Just Imagine*. To recreate this footage for the serial would have been prohibitively expensive. However, simply using a clip from an old feature that no one remembered achieved the same result. In fact, the producers of *Flash Gordon* liked the clip so much that they used it under a portion of the credits to the opening of each chapter of the serial. They then used the footage again in the first chapter of *Flash Gordon Conquers the Universe* (1940).

Another example of Universal's use of footage from an earlier feature occurred in *The Phantom Creeps* (1939), a Universal serial with Bela Lugosi as the main villain. Part of the story arose from a meteorite that the Lugosi character found in Africa. As luck would have it for Universal, Bela Lugosi had appeared with Boris Karloff in the 1936 science fiction film, *The Invisible Ray*, which also involved the discovery of a meteorite in Africa. That permitted the serial makers to use archive footage from *The Invisible Ray* in Chapter Three of the serial, with Bela Lugosi in a scene with a native, putting on a protective suit. (This bit of footage did not actually appear in *The Invisible Ray* so it may have been footage shot for the film but deleted from the release print.) Oddly, the individual in the protective suit in the serial who was then lowered into the pit in the stock footage was actually Boris Karloff, not Bela Lugosi, (which was footage used in the film) so essentially, Karloff was Lugosi's stunt double in *The Phantom Creeps*.

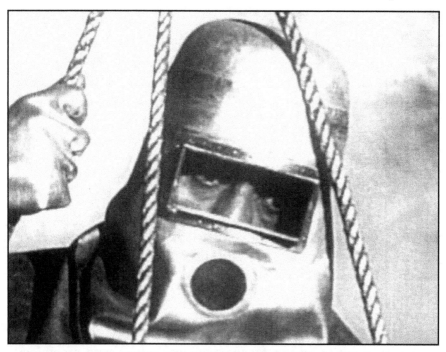

*The Phantom Creeps* (1939). This is stock footage from *The Invisible Ray* (1936). However, the actor about to be lowered into the pit is Boris Karloff and not Bela Lugosi.

In Chapters Two and Three of *Flash Gordon Conquers the Universe* (1940), mountain climbing and snow footage from *White Hell of Pitz Palu* were used. The original was a German film made in 1929, about a woman disappearing on a mountain. A few years later, her husband and two newlyweds found themselves in a similar predicament. The three skiers and their rescuers then found themselves in a number of perils, including an avalanche. The movie was filmed on location in the Swiss Alps. The film was later distributed in the United States by Universal.

In *The Black Coin* (1936), there were two cliffhangers involving an ocean liner at sea. In Chapter Four, the ocean liner hit a submerged derelict and eventually overturned. In Chapter Seven, another ocean liner caught on fire. In both cases, the passengers had to flee in a hurry. If the stock footage used in either cliffhanger reminded the viewer of the *Titanic* disaster, that made sense since the archive footage came from *Atlantic,* a fictionalized film account of the *Titanic* disaster, released in 1929.

In *The Great Alaskan Mystery* (1944), the first story arc involved a ship floundering on an iceberg and the efforts of the heroes to reach safety. Much of the iceberg footage came from Universal's 1933 film, *S.O.S. Iceberg*, a joint production with a German film company, which related the tale of a party traveling to Greenland to recover lost records. The party itself was then trapped on an iceberg. The movie was filmed on location in Greenland. This iceberg footage from the older film was melded seamlessly with the main story of the serial, giving *The Great Alaskan Mystery* a unique flavor, at least in those early chapters.

In *Lost City of the Jungle* (1946), starring Russell Hayden and Keye Luke, Universal attempted, on several occasions, to match shots of those actors with footage of Jon Hall and Sabu from *White Savage*, a 1943 island adventure movie with Maria Montez. For example, in the cliffhanger at the end of Chapter Two and its resolution in the next chapter, Hayden and Luke jumped from a high cliff into water, a bomb went off causing them to be sprayed with dirt and the two eventually swam to safety after an underwater rescue of Luke. For purposes of the jump, Luke removed his suit and was suddenly wearing native garb, no shirt and many beads. Hayden, on the other hand, did not remove his clothes, which included a loud print shirt. This clothing that Luke and Hayden wore in the serial was intended to match the clothing of the actors in the older film, although it was easy to see that the back of Hayden's shirt in the serial did not quite match the back of Hall's shirt in the movie.

Universal's archives were stocked, so to speak, with loads of stock footage from the westerns it made during the silent era. This footage appeared in all of Universal's western sound serials. *Flaming Frontiers* (1938) had many examples of this. In Chapter Three, footage of buffalo on the rampage was used. In Chapter Four, a wagon train was attacked and most of the shots of the hordes of Indians attacking, and the many wagons racing for safety was archive footage, creating an image of vast prairies filled with wagons and Indians. Chapter Eight, "The Savage Horde," had stock footage of Indians attacking a frontier town en masse. This was only a small part of the stock footage used in that serial.

Columbia did the same. In Chapter Nine of *Deadwood Dick* (1940), the henchmen started a cattle stampede, hoping to tear up the town of Deadwood. The footage of a horde of horses starting the cattle on their rampage was from an earlier film, as none of the *Deadwood Dick* cast appeared. Then, the longer shots of the townspeople running from the cattle appeared to be from a silent film, based on the speed of the film. Also, the town in which the cattle were running looked nothing like the town of Deadwood of the serial, clearly indicating that stock footage was being used.

Similarly, in Chapter 14 of *Cody of the Pony Express* (1950), the cavalry was called to rescue Cody and some friends from a gunfight at a telegraph camp. All of the footage of the cavalry, which contained at least 20 riders, was from a prior film; there were no shots with Cody and the cavalry together. In the next chapter, another rescue by the cavalry was made but since the cavalry had to interact with the actors from the serial, the cavalry footage was new. To save costs, the cavalry in the new footage had only six members.

There was a similar occurrence in the last chapter of *Raiders of Ghost City* (1944) which contained substantial stock footage of an Indian raid on a town. When stock footage of the cavalry was shown, it had many riders. In the new footage shot just for the serial, the cavalry suddenly only had a few horsemen.

This contrasting use of new and stock footage illustrates how the serial maker could paint a much broader picture than he could ever create on the limited budget of a serial, simply by using stock footage. Unfortunately, and particularly in westerns, the stock footage was often substantially older than the new footage and often did not match well.

Unlike Universal, Republic did not have many feature films from which it could purloin stock footage. However, in Chapter One of *Dick Tracy vs. Crime, Inc.* (1941), the Ghost dropped bombs into volcanic fissures in the Atlantic Ocean, causing a huge tidal wave to engulf New York City, resulting in spectacular damage. The footage came from *Deluge*, a disaster film released by RKO in 1933. Republic apparently purchased parts of the movie for use in its serials and other B-movies, employing the footage once again in the last chapters of *King of the Rocket Men* (1949).

## ii) From Well-Known Films

Since the heyday of the sound serial was in the 1930s and 1940s, the feature film footage that was used in serials was from feature films that, for modern audiences, seem very obscure. For example, and as noted above, *White Hell of Pitz Palu*, was a 1929 German film released in America by Universal, *S.O.S. Iceberg* was a 1933 film jointly produced by Universal and a German film company, and *Deluge* was a disaster film released by RKO in 1933. Even if available on home video or shown from time to time at film festivals, these films are little watched today and relatively unknown. Also, there was substantial re-using of silent film footage in sound serials and even if the silent film footage could be traced to a specific film, that movie might well be lost.

There were some exceptions to this rule and upon a rare occasion, the archive footage used in a serial was from a well-known film. One such example was the 1943 movie that is usually known as *War of the Wildcats*, but which was originally entitled *In Old Oklahoma*. Produced by Republic, it starred Republic's biggest mainstream movie star, John Wayne. The last half of the film involved the attempts of John Wayne and some other cowboys to find oil on Indian land. Once they were successful in that endeavor, they still had to bring the oil to Tulsa by 6:00 PM the next day or they would lose their rights to the oil fields.

Unfortunately for Wayne, his arch rival, played by Albert Dekker, bought all the rights to the oil pipeline to Tulsa and would not let Wayne use it. Wayne then came up with the idea of transporting the oil over land, in old tankers pulled by horses and new oil barrels they would build themselves and transport by wagon. However, on the way, their path was blocked by a huge fire. Wayne forced everyone to drive through, but in the process, some of the tankers caught on fire and burned. Then, the cowboys' way was blocked by logs and other sabotage, causing other tanker wagons to flip over and even burn. Despite all of these hardships, the wildcatters somehow made it to Tulsa just in time to save the business.

The last two chapters of *Jesse James Rides Again* (1947) had a similar story line. Clayton Moore and some cowboys had to deliver oil to the oil refinery by its close of business or they would default on a loan and lose the oil fields. Moore came up with the idea of using old tankers and new barrels to transport the oil. Footage from *War of the Wildcats* showed the building of the barrels. Once the cowboys set off on their journey, a spectacular shot of the line of horses and wagons in front of a magnificent mountain was shown, courtesy of the prior film.

Then, Moore and his gang had their travels blocked by a huge fire. Moore directed them to ride through as quickly as they could. They then had problems with a stretch of land with the wagons turning over. All of this exciting footage came from the John Wayne movie. Interestingly, at one point in the movie, a tanker wagon rolled off a high cliff and exploded in mid-air. It would have made an excellent cliffhanger for the serial because a similar event occurred in the serial during the mass wagon ride. For some reason, however, in the serial, the standard Republic serial footage of a wagon going over a cliff was used instead of the more interesting feature film footage.

In any event, to make this all work, Clayton Moore changed from the clothes he had been wearing throughout the serial into a black shirt and bandana, to match the clothing that Wayne wore in the movie. There is therefore a chance that John Wayne appeared in this serial, in some of the long shots in the stock footage.

*War of the Wildcats* is shown on television from time to time, probably because it stars John Wayne and has a built-in following for that reason alone. It is one film that is easily recognizable when its footage shows up in *Jesse James Rides Again*.

Who was the most famous director to work in serials? Was it William Witney or John English, the directors of some of the best serials that Republic produced during the Golden Age? Was it Richard Thorp, who directed some early Mascot serials and then went on to direct feature films at MGM? Few people would guess Alfred Hitchcock and yet he did contribute footage to a serial, albeit in an in advertent manner.

One of the first films Hitchcock made when he came to America at the beginning of World War II was *Foreign Correspondent* (1940). It told the story of reporter Johnny Jones, who, using his pseudonym Huntley Haverstock, travelled to Europe at the beginning of 1939 to assess the threatened outbreak of a world war. There he became involved with spies who were working with the Nazis. Toward the end of the film, the plane on which Haverstock was travelling was attacked by Germans and crashed into the sea.

While *Foreign Correspondent* was far from Hitchcock's most memorable film, few people ever forget the plane crash into the sea at the end of the movie. As described by Hitchcock in *Hitchcock by Francois Truffaut*, the camera was inside the cabin, above the two shoulders of the pilots. Between them, through the glass cabin window, the audience could see the ocean coming closer. Then, without a cut, the plane hit the ocean, the water rushed in and the two men were drowned.

The whole scene was done in a single shot, without a cut. There was a transparency screen made of paper, and a glass tank behind the screen. Footage of the plane approaching the water, taken prior thereto when a stunt pilot flew a plane as close to the ocean as he reasonably could, was projected onto the transparency screen. The plane in *Foreign Correspondent* dove and as soon as the plane got close to the water on the screen, Hitchcock pressed a button and the water burst through, tearing the screen away. By this method, Hitchcock had turned a mundane screen event, a plane crash, into a spectacular piece of footage.

*Foreign Correspondent* was released by United Artists. Universal must have been so impressed with the plane crash footage that it purchased the footage from the producer for use in its serials. In Chapter Six of *The Master Key* (1945), hero Tom Brent captured two foreign agents in an airplane, which was then shot out of the sky. As the plane was about to hit the water, there was a shot from behind the pilot and the co-pilot out the large front window of the plane, as the flyers ran back for safety. The plane hit the ocean and the cockpit became filled with water.

Avid serial watchers knew that the same clip was previously used in the Chapter Six cliffhanger of *The Adventures of Smilin' Jack* (1943) when the Honolulu Clipper on which Smilin' Jack was riding was shot out of the sky. The cockpit footage and some other clips from the scene in *Smilin' Jack* and *The Master Key* were originally from the climax to *Foreign Correspondent*, which was a big budget film compared to the Universal serials of the 1940s. The use of the footage from the Hitchcock film in those Universal serials created a great special effect at little cost. It also meant that Alfred Hitchcock was the most famous film director who contributed footage to a sound movie serial.

## (iii) Documentary or Newsreel Footage

Footage of real industrial work was often inserted into serials. In the first chapter of *The Green Hornet* (1939), real footage of workers installing a tunnel was mixed in with footage of the actors referring to the same. It was even used in the background when actors were talking. In Chapter Eight of *Tailspin Tommy in the Great Air Mystery* (1935), archive footage of the operation of an oil well facility was inserted into the action. One character even narrated the footage, pretending it was his own employees doing the work, as he explained to other characters the process being used. In Chapter Six of *The Green Hornet Strikes Again* (1940) a steel plant manager explained the operation of a steel mill to Britt Reid, standing in front of a process screen showing stock footage of real workers in a real steel plant.

In *Winners of the West* (1940) Chapter Ten, Jeff Ramsay and Jim Jackson traveled to a lumber camp to see why they had not received the timber they needed for railroad track repairs. That gave Universal the opportunity to insert documentary footage of workers cutting timber in the forest and then sending the timber down shoots into the river, so that

*Tailspin Tommy in the Great Air Mystery* (1935). This is an example of stock footage of an oil well seamlessly incorporated into the new footage of the serial.

*Winners of the West* (1940). Here, the man in the middle, lumberman Charlie, played by James Pierce, wears unusual clothing to match the stock footage of lumbermen previously incorporated into the serial. Also pictured are James Craig and Dick Foran.

the wood could float down the river to where it was needed. In the archive footage, there was one man who stood out, because he was wearing a light cap and a checkered shirt. So, when Ramsay and Jackson met Charlie Nelson, the timber operations manager, the actor was also wearing a white cap and checkered shirt, to match the stock footage.

Footage of real disasters was sometimes used as archive footage. As mentioned above, *Dick Tracy's G-Men* (1939) used footage from the Hindenburg disaster to augment the cliffhanger in Chapter Nine of the serial. In that same year of 1939, even more footage of the Hindenburg tragedy was used in the last chapter of *The Phantom Creeps*, as Dr. Zorka deliberately bombed an air ship in his maniacal reign of terror. It was interesting that two different studios, Republic and Universal, used the same archive footage in the same year.

Another example of the use of newsreel footage occurred in Chapter One of *Atom Man vs. Superman* (1950), where the famous footage of the incredible swaying of the Tacoma Narrows Bridge in Tacoma, Washington and its eventual fall into the river was incorporated into the serial.

The disaster occurred in 1940. There was one car on the bridge when it collapsed, with a dog trapped in the vehicle. In the serial, there was supposed to be a woman in the car. Superman rushed to the bridge and held a pier in place, which stopped the swaying and allowed the woman to be rescued. (Actually, the newsreel footage was put into freeze frame mode.) Once the woman was saved, Superman let go of the pier and the real footage of the actual collapse of the bridge was shown.

In Chapter 11 of that same serial, newsreel footage of extensive flooding was incorporated into the chapter, creating very realistic scenes. Then, special effects footage of a dam breaking, from an old cowboy movie, *Avenging Waters* (1936), was also incorporated. At very little expense, a spectacular chapter had been created.

### C. New Footage Becomes Stock Footage

Sometimes, original footage for a serial became stock footage during the serial. In *Zorro's Black Whip* (1944), the footage of the Black Whip entering or leaving her hideout on horseback under a waterfall was

*The Purple Monster Strikes* (1945). In many of the chapters, the Purple Monster (Roy Barcroft) takes over the body of Dr. Cyrus Layton (James Craven). The scene is pictured in this lobby card.

used over and over again in the serial. In *The Purple Monster Strikes* (1945), the footage of the Purple Monster entering Dr. Layton's limp body was exactly the same in each chapter in which the transformation occurred. Also, footage of the Green Hornet and Kato entering their laboratory and starting off in the Black Beauty, along with driving the fast car through city streets and around bends on squealing tires was re-used several times in *The Green Hornet* (1939) In an interesting cost-cutting move, some of the same footage was then re-used in *The Green Hornet Strikes Again* (1940).

In *Superman* (1948), each time Superman flew into an empty Daily Planet storeroom and changed into Clark Kent, the footage was identical. This was given away by the smile on Superman's face just before he ducked out of sight to change his clothes. In fact, the footage was used twice in the last chapter of the serial. Producer Sam Katzman, ever interested in reducing costs, used the same technique in *Atom Man vs. Superman* (1950), although in reverse. In that serial, the footage of Clark entering that storeroom and changing into his Superman costume was repeated over and over again. It would have been nice, in a few of those cases, if the same footage had to be used, that the same activities could have been shot from different angles.

Sometimes, this reuse of serial footage was amusing. In the first chapter of *The Lone Defender* (1930), Ramon cut out part of a wanted poster for the Cactus Kid, put the scrap in his pants, and got on his horse. The exact footage was shown during Chapter 11. It was easy to see that the footage was a repeat as in both chapters as Ramon almost hit his head on a tree branch.

In *The Miracle Rider* (1935), the same footage was used in Chapters Five and Ten when Tony, Jr., with Tom Mix on his back, jumped a fence. It was clearly the same footage in both chapters because in both pieces of film, the horse's hoofs clipped the rail, even though the horse did make the jump successfully.

Another common example of new serial footage becoming stock footage in the same serial occurred with establishing shots. These were shots where a short piece of film was used to show the location of the next scene. In serials, these were usually shots of the outside of a building where the heroine lived or where the villain had a hideout. An example of this occurred in *G-Men Never Forget* (1948), where every time the story moved to the house where Police Commissioner Murkland was being held by the villains, a shot of the outside of the building was used. In *Daredevils of the Red Circle* (1939), every time the action moved back to the Granville mansion, a shot of the outside of the house was shown.

### D. Reused Cliffhangers

When a studio put the time and expense into creating a spectacular cliffhanger for a serial, it made sense to amortize the cost of producing that cliffhanger over one or two other serials. Although the studios always used this approach to cost cutting, it became more common after World War II, when budgets for serials were cut sharply.

A good example of this reused footage occurred in *Daughter of Don Q* (1946). At the end of the first chapter, Cliff Roberts (hero) and Dolores Quantaro (heroine) were in a car chasing after the villains who were fleeing in a truck. One henchman was driving and the other was in the back of the truck. Quantaro drove the car close to the back of the truck, and Roberts jumped into the back, to do battle with henchman Donovan. They fought in the back and then accidentally, a revolver went off, shooting the driver in the front. He slumped over and his foot jammed the accelerator, sending the vehicle down the road at a high speed.

Roberts was knocked out. Donovan jumped off the back of the truck and then the truck crashed through a fence, on which there was a sign stating: "DANGER KEEP OUT 100,000 VOLTS." The truck hit the electrical plant, resulting in a spectacular explosion. The chapter ended.

While this may not have been Republic's most memorable cliffhanger, it did take substantial time and expense to shoot it. First, the real shots of the truck racing down real streets had to be filmed. Then the process screen shots, used when Roberts jumped into the truck and when scenes of the driver were shown, had to be filmed. Finally, the miniature work with the truck crash and explosion had to be created.

Given that expense, it was clear that the cliffhanger had to be used at least one more time. And, that new usage occurred just two years later, in *G-Men Never Forget* (1948), in Chapter Two titled, appropriately enough, "100,000 Volts." Here Agent O'Hara jumped into the back of a truck, had a fight with a henchman, the gun went off, the driver slumped, his foot jammed the accelerator, O'Hara was knocked unconscious, the henchman jumped out and the truck crashed through the gate with the sign, causing a terrific explosion at the electric plant.

The only new footage shot was the fight in the back of the truck and the slumping of the driver, because new actors were involved. Even the footage of the jamming of the foot on the accelerator and the footage of the henchman landing on the road were old. All of the new footage was shot in the studio, in front of the process screen, at little expense. Yet, a spectacular cliffhanger was created and if the viewer did not remember the older serial, there was no way to tell that old footage was reused.

In fact, ever cost effective, Republic then used the very end of this cliffhanger, with the truck crashing into the electrical plant with 100,000 volts, for the Chapter Six cliffhanger of *Radar Patrol vs. Spy King* (1949). Interestingly, just as in *Daughter of Don Q*, it was actor Kirk Alyn who was in trouble.

In any discussion of reused cliffhanger footage, mention must be made of the most overused snippet of old footage used in Republic serials. Almost every time a car, motorcycle or wagon or even a chariot (in *Perils of Nyoka* (1942)) went over a cliff, a point-of-view shot from the vehicle was inserted, going right to the edge of the cliff and looking down from a great height. Tire marks at the edge reminded viewers that they had seen this shot many times before. Then, the vehicle went over the cliff.

Have you ever seen this frame before? This is stock footage used in almost every Republic serial that had a cliffover.

It is interesting that at the very end of this shot, looking over the cliff, it was clear that there was no water under the cliff. Yet, the resolution to some of these cliffhangers had the vehicle falling into a deep lake, cushioning the fall and saving the hero. Where the lake came from, nobody knows.

It would take a lifetime of study to catalog all of the reused footage in serial cliffhangers. Here are four more examples.

### (i) The Motorcycle in the Tunnel

One of the most spectacular cliffhangers of all time occurred in the first chapter of *Daredevils of the Red Circle* (1939). The villain, 39013, promised to destroy the new Granville Channel Tunnel, which connected an island to the mainland, on the opening day of the tunnel. His technique was unusual. 39013's gang was operating an oil derrick in the ocean, which had been chipping away at the roof of the tunnel. The gang had timed its work so that the roof of the tunnel was set to fail just as the inaugural car trip proceeded through the tunnel.

One of the daredevils, Gene Townley, was in the tunnel. He became suspicious concerning a noise he heard. Then the roof started to leak. He drove off on his motorcycle to warn the motorcade. He was chased by an increasingly fast wall of water, which followed him through the tunnel. As the chapter ended, the tunnel was filled with water.

The special effects were fabulous. It was particularly thrilling as the water followed the motorcycle around bends, with the water flowing high on the side, turning over and filling the screen. Even though the motorcycle was clearly being ridden in front of a process screen, the entire cliffhanger was believable.

The model work must have been very expensive. Thus, it made sense to use the cliffhanger again. First, it was shown one more time in Chapter 11 of *Daredevils of the Red Circle*, which was the economy chapter. Then, in the first chapter of *G-Men Never Forget* (1948), the villain, Murkland, decided to destroy the new Cook Channel Tunnel. It was very similar to the Granville Channel Tunnel, also costing $6,000,000 dollars and connecting that same island to the mainland. Here, the villains exploded a powerful bomb, causing the tunnel to leak.

The hero, Ted O'Hara, happened to be on a motorcycle in the tunnel, so the shots could match those from *Daredevils of the Red Circle*. Even the footage of the motorcade entering the tunnel came from the prior serial. All of the special effects were the same. The resolution was identical. Once again, *G-Men Never Forget* had a spectacular cliffhanger, at little cost to the studio.

### (ii) The Woman on the Running Board

*The Master Key* (1945) had one particularly interesting cliffhanger. At the end of Chapter Two, Janet Lowe, a newspaper reporter, was sitting in a police car when a henchman sneaked out of a building and forced her to drive him away in the police car. With the police in hot pursuit, the crook forced Janet to stand on the running board of his car so the police would not shoot at him. As he turned onto a bridge, his way was blocked by two police cars. The villain panicked and turned the wheel sharply, crashing the car through the concrete bridge railing and over the side, onto a road with moving traffic. This was an excellent special effect.

Janet could hardly survive that fall, since she was standing on the running board when the car started to crash. Nor could she do what was usually done in serials in this situation, i.e., jump off the vehicle. She would surely be injured on the bridge's hard, concrete surface. The reso-

The Woman On the Running Board. This cliffhanger ends with a spectacular special effect with a car crashing through a concrete bridge wall, onto a highway with traffic. No wonder Universal used this footage more than once.

lution was therefore interesting. In the time expansion cheat, a police car pulled alongside the vehicle. Janet managed to shift into the police vehicle before the crook's vehicle crashed. While this did involve a cheat, it still showed some ingenuity on the part of the filmmaker.

It seemed unusual that Universal would put such effort into creating a spectacular cliffhanger for a serial that late in the Universal serial cycle. And, the studio did not. The cliffhanger footage came from *Gang Busters* (1942), Chapter Three. There, a newspaper photographer, Vicki Logan, got into a police car being driven by a henchman. The police car was of the same standard design that would be used later in *The Master Key*. When things looked bad for him, the henchman forced Janet out onto the running board of the car. The same set of events occurred as would happen later in *The Master Key*. The car crashed through the bridge railing and onto the road below, but Vicki was luckily saved beforehand.

The cliffhanger and resolution in each serial were identical. All of the outdoor footage in the two serials was identical and probably the same process screen footage was used in each. The only new film that had to be shot was footage in front of the process screen, including the transfer of the heroine between the two cars. All of that could be shot indoors. The cliffhanger was quite spectacular, and without seeing both serials, the viewer of *The Master Key* would never know that the cliffhanger footage was archive footage from the earlier serial.

### (iii) The Melting Mountain

Captain Marvel in *The Adventures of Captain Marvel* (1941) and Commander Cody in *Radar Men from the Moon* (1952) had very similar tunnel cliffhangers. In Chapter Five of *Captain Marvel*, the Captain was deceived by a fake Scorpion into entering a cave. Once there, the villains used the lenses of the Scorpion device to melt the mountain, causing molten lava to flow through the cave, trapping Marvel at the back.

In Chapter Two of *Radar Men*, Commando Cody and Ted were fleeing from two moon security guards so they hid in a cave. The guards used the ray guns on their vehicles to melt the mountain, causing a lava flow into the cave, trapping the heroes at the back. Despite the fact that one cliffhanger occurred on Earth and one on the Moon, the situations seemed almost identical. All of the special effects and process screen footage were the same. The resolutions, however, were different. Captain Marvel escaped by use of his super powers. Commander Cody escaped by finding a surprise exit.

Indeed, Republic liked this cliffhanger so much that it was repeated in Chapter Ten of *Radar Men*, which was the economy chapter. Thus, Republic was able to re-use a cliffhanger from *Captain Marvel* twice in another serial, making Chapter Ten of *Radar Men* a true economy chapter.

### (iv) The Building Implosion

In the 1940s, Universal obtained newsreel or other footage of the actual implosion of a multi-story building. In addition to being spectacular footage on its own, the building was imploded in two blasts, with the right side of the building falling first, and then the left side of the building falling second. It was obvious that this would make excellent cliffhanger footage, especially because the hero could be trapped in the building when the right side fell, forcing him to rush out of the building before the second part fell. The only problem was that before the implosion, all of the glass was removed from the building and there was some demolition work done in the front of the building. These anomalies had to be explained away in the serial plot.

The Imploding Building. This cliffhanger footage was used multiple times in Universal serials and it was stock footage to begin with. Here, the right side of the building implodes first.

In *Junior G-Men* (1940), Chapter Five, Billy Barton and the gang discovered one of the Torchies' hideouts. They went there to investigate and two of them were immediately captured. Luckily, the G-Men arrived, overpowered two of the henchmen, and rescued the boys. Unfortunately, one of the henchmen managed to escape and he called the Torchies' headquarters. The leader, Brand, decided to blow up the building by remote control, which he could do because, for some reason, the building was loaded with explosives.

The deed was done and the stock footage of the building implosion was used. First the right side went and then the rest of the building was destroyed, with the heroes inside. The explanation for the condition of the building to be destroyed was that it was a big apartment building that was never finished.

In *Gang Busters* (1942), Chapter Six, Professor Mortis issued a challenge to the police. He said, "Tonight, at 8:00, I shall destroy the nearly completed City Hall, and I defy the police to stop me." When the action cut to City Hall, it looked exactly like the big apartment building that was never finished in *Junior G-Men*. That could only mean another building implosion.

The police rushed to the site and entered the building. They searched the place for bombs, could not find any and prudently left. However, newspaper photographer Vicki Logan, not realizing the time, entered the building to take photographs. Bill Bannister rushed in to get her out before 8:00. However, he was too late and at 8:00 sharp, Dr. Mortis set off the first bomb planted by his henchmen, destroying the right side of the building. As Logan and Bannister tried to leave, Mortis set off the second bomb, destroying the rest of the building.

In Chapter Seven of *The Master Key* (1945), the Master Key discovered that the police were close to one of his hideouts so he ordered his henchmen to move the captured Professor Henderson "to the deserted loft building we have already chosen for this emergency." There was a quick cut to the deserted loft building which could pass for a big apartment building that was never finished or a nearly completed City Hall. Obviously, an implosion was upcoming.

The police obtained a clue to Henderson's location and proceeded to the building. The henchmen found out and one set a series of time bombs in the building. The police arrived and a fight broke out. The first bomb went off and the right side of the building fell. The second bomb exploded and the rest of the building fell, apparently with the police inside.

Universal's work here would have impressed even Sam Katzman from Columbia Pictures. The same footage was used for three cliffhangers and the original footage itself was stock footage. To top it off, the building implosion created a very impressive cliffhanger.

### E. Mismatched Footage

Sometimes the stock footage did not match the new footage as well as the filmmaker might have hoped. An amusing example occurred in Chapter Six of *Secret Agent X-9* (1937). The government agents were in hot pursuit of four henchmen traveling in a convertible. The car was racing along a road, next to a fast train. The henchmen's only hope of escape was to beat the train to a crossing and get to the other side, with the train then blocking the government agents.

For no reason, three of the four henchmen decided to duck down in the car. Then, stock footage from an old, probably silent film was inserted, showing a car just crossing the tracks in front of a train. The car barely made it across safely. Suddenly, the reason why the henchmen ducked down was made clear. It was to match the stock footage, which showed only a driver in the car, with no passengers. Even with that effort, however, the stock footage was a poor match for the new footage.

In Chapter 11 of *Dick Tracy vs. Crime, Inc.* (1941), villains decided to roll an automobile down a hill onto some policemen. The scene was in an outdoor area, with very few trees or plant growth but with several large rocks. Once the car was rolled, stock footage of a car going down a steep hill covered with vegetation, was shown. The hill was substantially larger than the hill in the prior scene, there were no large rocks and there were no policemen in sight. It was as if an entirely new movie were being shown in the middle of the *Dick Tracy* serial. In fact, that was the case, as the footage came from the cliffhanger at the end of Chapter Eight of *SOS Coast Guard* (1937).

## II. BLOOPERS

### A. Continuity Bloopers

Most people understand that a film, unlike a play, is often performed out of sequence. In other words, to save costs, for example, all scenes at one location are filmed around the same time, even if the scenes will appear at many different points in the final film. Also, if there are multiple camera angles in a scene, such as some long shots and some close-ups, the same scene is shot two or three times and then the film from the different versions is edited together to create one continuous scene. If care is not taken, when all of these scenes are put together, there can be continuity errors.

Despite all of the precautions taken by filmmakers, continuity problems occurred in even big budget films. For example, in *The King and I* (1956), when Yul Brynner was singing "Is A Puzzlement," in some shots, he was wearing a ring in his ear and in some he was not. In *Tea and Sympathy* (1956), a pair of china dogs on a mantel above a fireplace were back-to-back in long shots of a room in which Deborah Kerr and John Kerr were having a conversation, but face-to-face in the close-ups of Deborah Kerr during the same conversation and then face-to-face again for all of the later action in the scene.

Since there were continuity problems in big budget films, it is not surprising that they also occurred in serials. In fact, what is surprising is that there were not more continuity problems in serials, since serials were usually two to three times the length of a feature film and produced in far less time.

One way the serials avoided some continuity problems was to have the actors wear the same suits throughout the serial and the actresses to wear the same dresses. Then, no matter the order in which the scenes were filmed, once they were edited together, the clothes would always match.

*The Black Widow* (1947) illustrates why that was a good plan by the filmmakers. In this serial, the heroine wore two outfits throughout the serial, one dark and one light. Toward the beginning of Chapter Five, there was a scene in the editor's office at The Daily Clarion, with Joyce Winters, a newspaper reporter, wearing her dark outfit. At the end of the scene, she was walking out with Steve Colt who was going to an airport. A short time later, Joyce appeared at the hanger at the airport in her light outfit. Very little time had elapsed since she was last seen in the film and there was no reason for her to change clothes in the middle of the day. This was a classic continuity error.

There were a number of other instances of continuity errors in serials which involved clothing. In Chapter Two of *Daredevils of the Red Circle* (1939), there was a fight on an oil derrick between the three daredevils and some henchmen. As the fight started, one of the daredevils, played by Charles Quigley, was wearing a suit with a vest. Suddenly, near the end of the fight, the vest disappeared and remained missing for the rest of the scene.

In Chapter Five of *The Vigilantes Are Coming* (1936), the heroic Eagle, a Zorro-like figure, gave his cape to a wounded person to keep him warm. Later, when his group was about to be attacked by the villains, the Eagle decided to trick them into riding away. When he jumped on his horse, the Eagle was still not wearing his cape. As he rode around a bend, the cape had mysteriously appeared on his back and remained there, as he tricked the villains into riding off. However, when the Eagle returned to the outside of his church hideout, the cape was gone once again. But, when he rode into the cave beneath the church, the cape had magically reappeared. Upstairs in the church, the cape was once again missing.

Obviously, the shots without the cape were specifically shot for Chapter Five. However, probably most if not all of the outdoor riding shots in the serial were shot at one time, and the Eagle wore his cape in all of those shots. The footage inside the cave was original footage for the serial that turned into stock footage because the same footage was used many times in the serial. Someone simply forgot that there was going to be a point in the serial when the Eagle would not be wearing his cape and that new film would have to be shot to match the plot.

At the beginning of Chapter Three of *Who's Guilty?* (1945), the cast was investigating a scream from Ruth Allen's room. Nephew Curt was dressed in a bathrobe. Then there was another scream from Sister Sara's room, and Curt rushed in, still in his bathrobe. The cast then went back into the hall, to open Ruth Allen's room. Suddenly, Curt was wearing a suit with a bow tie. When the group entered Ruth Allen's room, Curt was back in the bathrobe. When the actors left the room, Curt was back in the suit with a bow tie. During this entire period, Curt's wife was consistently wearing a dressing gown and all of the other male characters were wearing day clothes.

In Chapter Two of *Flash Gordon* (1936), Flash and Princess Aura fell into a deep pit. Ming saved them by pulling a switch, thereby providing a net on which the two landed in safety. As Aura hit the net, her crown was thrown off. In the next shot, showing Flash and Aura from above, the crown was back on Aura's head. In the remainder of the shots in the scene, the crown was gone again.

Not all continuity errors involved clothing. Here are examples of some non-clothing continuity errors in serials. In Chapter Six of *The Green Archer* (1940), Spike Holland (Victor Jory) was sitting at a table, talking to Mr. Howett (Forrest Taylor). In a close shot, Holland lifted a cup of coffee to his mouth. The film then cut to a longer shot where

Holland completed drinking from a glass of water and put the glass back down on the table. Through a continuity error, a cup of coffee was transformed into a glass of water.

A more serious continuity blooper occurred in Chapter Nine of *Captain Midnight* (1942). Ivan Shark, a master of disguises, captured the local constable and decided to impersonate him. Shark used make-up to change the shape of his face and used a head piece to look partially bald, literally becoming the constable. In that guise, Shark arrested Captain Midnight. Midnight realized the ploy and grabbed Shark. The film cut away to Shark's henchmen and when it cut back, Midnight punched Shark to the ground. However, between the two shots of Captain Midnight and Shark, Shark suddenly had a full head of hair, no makeup, and was no longer wearing the sheriff's vest. Although he still appeared to have a pillow under his shirt, to match the sheriff's heftiness, Shark looked suspiciously like James Craven, the actor who played Shark, rather than the actor who played the constable. It is hard to imagine how this continuity mistake occurred.

*Captain Midnight* (1942). In a continuity error, James Craven, the second actor from the left, who was made up to resemble the local constable, suddenly appears in the same scene without the constable's makeup but still wearing some of his clothes. On the ground is Dave O'Brien, portraying Captain Midnight. The henchman on the left is Charles Hamilton and the one on the right is Al Ferguson.

*The Adventures of Captain Marvel* (1941) had two unusual continuity errors. At the end of Chapter One, Whitey and Betty were traveling across a bridge in a car when there was an explosion under the bridge. Betty yelled, "Back up, Whitey. Back up." There was a shot of a bridge support collapsing, a long shot of the car backing up, and then another shot of the bridge support. Then the same footage was repeated, and Betty once again yelled "Back up, Whitey. Back up." It is hard to understand how this mistake could have remained in the final print.

In Chapter Six of the same serial, Billy Batson made a long drive out to the country to the home of Professor Bentley. It was a one story house. When Batson walked in, there was a fight going on, so Batson changed into Captain Marvel. He then chased the crooks out a window, which was now in a high skyscraper in the city. The rest of the action took place in the city. This was a combination continuity and writing mistake.

## B. Mistakes in the Writing or Production

Another form of serial blooper was not caused by a continuity problem but rather, was caused by a mistake in the production. Probably the most famous mistake in serials came at the beginning of *Flash Gordon's Trip to Mars* (1938). As Dr. Zarkov's spaceship was returning to Earth from the first adventure on the Planet Mongo, Dale Arden was suddenly a brunette, with short dark hair. In the original ending of *Flash Gordon* (1936), she had long blond hair. How did this sudden conversion take place? Did Ming do something to Dale before she left Mongo?

One can argue that this was not a mistake because, for whatever reason, Jean Rogers had to be a brunette in the sequel, and no one would remember the ending of the original serial from two years before. Maybe not, but it is hard to believe anyone would forget Jean Rogers from the first serial. In any event, the serial makers compounded the mistake by later showing two flashbacks from *Flash Gordon* in the sequel. In both flashbacks, Dale Arden had long, blond hair. Still, no explanation was given.

Transitions between two serials in a series did seem to be trouble for the makers of serials. At the end of *Jesse James Rides Again* (1947), Sheriff Mark Tobin from Kentucky had chased Jesse to Tennessee but decided not to arrest him because he finally realized that Jesse was a good guy. The excuse Tobin told Jesse was that Tobin's eyesight was too poor and he did not recognize whoever Jesse was.

At the beginning of the sequel, *Adventures of Jesse James* (1948), Jesse recounted the story to his brother but stated that the sheriff did not arrest him because Jesse was outside the sheriff's jurisdiction. This mistake is hard to understand. The serials were made within a year of each other. Clayton Moore played Jesse in both films and Fred C. Brannon was a director on both films. Three of the writers were the same. Yet no one could remember how the prior serial ended.

Another inconsistency between a serial and its sequel occurred with the two *Green Hornet* serials. In both serials, there was a secret passage located behind a dresser in Britt Reid's apartment to the secret laboratory where the Black Beauty was located. In the first serial, the dresser opened from the right side; in the sequel the dresser opened from the left side.

Columbia was known for ending its serial chapters with scenes from the next episode. Sometimes, however, the scenes did not actually appear in the next chapter. At the end of Chapter Nine of *The Green Archer* (1940), there was a shot of the butler, standing outside the window, leaning into the house and holding an arrow. The narration cast doubts on the butler's honesty. In the next chapter, that scene did not appear and the butler did not act suspiciously.

At the end of Chapter Ten, there was a scene shown from the next chapter where the Green Archer searched for Elaine and found her place of captivity empty. The narration suggested that the Green Archer should have made an appointment to see Elaine. Yet, the entire scene was missing from the next chapter. Perhaps the person who wrote the preview should have made an appointment to see the whole next chapter before doing his work.

Speaking of scenes not in serials, the opening footage of each chapter of *Perils of Nyoka* (1942), before the credits, had a shot of men riding camels in the desert. The first chapter of the serial was titled "Desert Intrigue." Yet, there was no sand, camels or deserts anywhere in the serial. In fact, the primary means of transportation was horses and the location of the serial looked surprisingly like the Old West of the Iverson Movie Ranch and not the desert of the Middle East.

*Flash Gordon's Trip to Mars* (1938) had a mistake in its recap of a previous chapter. In Chapter Seven, Prince Barin revealed to Flash and the gang that the source of Azura's power was the sacred white sapphire that she wore around her neck. However, anyone who held the sacred black sapphire of Kalu could render Azura's magic powerless. Despite this clear explanation, the comic strip introduction to the next chapter got it wrong. One of the frames to the introduction to Chapter Eight read, "Flash learns that the black sapphire is the secret of Azura's magic power." By Chapter Nine, someone finally caught up to the plot because one frame of that introduction read, "Flash succeeds in obtaining the black sapphire with which to combat Azura's magic power." Sometimes it was just hard to keep those sapphires straight.

*The New Adventures of Tarzan* (1935) was about a quest to retrieve a native idol known as the Green Goddess. The original plot was quite different and involved the character of Ula Vale being revealed as a secret agent in the last chapter. Even though the plot was changed, the chapter titles remained the same and therefore they have little relationship to the actual plot of the serial. For example, the last chapter was titled, "Operator 17," which had nothing to do with the events which occurred in the last chapter of the serial.

*Tex Granger* (1948) had a mistake in the credits. A significant role in the serial was the part of the young boy, Jimmy. He was played by teenager, Buzz Henry. However, the credits listed the character's name as "Tim."

*Batman* (1943). This is one of the most amusing of all the bloopers.
When did Batman move from Gotham City?

In the first chapter of *Superman* (1948), a grown up Clark Kent was told by his father that he should move to the big city where he could use his super powers to help others. At that point in his life, Clark had not yet become Superman so he did not need to disguise his identity. Presumably, someone with x-ray vision had better than 20-20 vision and did not need glasses to see. Why, then, was Clark wearing glasses in this scene?

Sticking with super heroes, in Chapter Five of *Batman* (1943), Alfred handed Bruce Wayne the mail, which included an envelope with a hidden message inside. The envelope, which was shown onscreen, was addressed to "Mr. Bruce Wayne, 1918 Hill Road, Los Angeles, Calif." When exactly did Bruce Wayne move from Gotham City to the West Coast? Actually, this was a clear blooper as there were several references to Gotham City earlier in the serial.

## C. Accidents During Filming

A third kind of blooper occurred during filming when something unexpected happened. The mistake then remained in the final film, either because the problem was not noticed or if noticed, the producer did not want to go to the cost of re-shooting the scene.

A well-known example of this type of blooper occurred in the first chapter of *The Masked Marvel* (1943). The title character was pushed off a high fuel storage tank and fell toward the ground. Instead of a stunt man, a dummy of the real actor was used. As the dummy hit a girder on the side of the tank, the arm caught on a girder and the entire arm was ripped out of the body. However, in the resolution, and for the rest of the serial, the Masked Marvel had two arms. The film makers obviously did not have the time to create a new dummy and then redo the entire scene.

*Flash Gordon's Trip to Mars* (1938) had at least one such mistake. One of Azura's magical powers was to use the white sapphire to allow her to disappear in a cloud of smoke. In Chapter Seven, however, just as the smoke appeared, the viewer could see Azura start to run to her right. Then she disappeared from the screen. There would be no reason for Azura to run, after touching the white sapphire, unless Azura did not actually have the power to disappear. On the other hand, maybe it was only a special effect after all.

Another example occurred in Chapter Three of *Winners of the West* (1940). The heroine, Claire Hartford, played by Anne Nagle, was wearing a hat while riding on a buckboard. She was chased by Indians and at the side of a hill, the wagon fell over, dropping Nagle down the steep hillside. As she was rolling down the hill, her hat came off, revealing that some man was actually wearing her clothes and impersonating her. He was also a little stockier than Anne Nagle. It must be some clever trick on the part of the hero, Jeff Ramsey, to trap the villain, King Carter. But no, that was not right, because in the close-up at the bottom of the hill, it was Anne Nagle once again. As obvious as this mistake was, the director did not take the time to re-shoot the scene.

In Chapter Nine of *Superman* (1948), Lois Lane traveled to the airport to meet a Dr. Graham. The scenes with Lois at the airport waiting for Dr. Graham and then meeting a false Dr. Graham and his assistant were shot in front of a picture of the airport on a process screen. In the first shots of Lois alone, her shadow could be seen on the process screen when she turned. After Lois met the false Dr. Graham, when that actor turned to leave, his shadow could also be seen on the process screen.

In Chapter Seven of *Flying G-Men* (1939), a henchman named Steve was tied up by the G-Men. He then escaped and got into a fight, at which time his toupee started coming off, barely hanging onto the left side of his head. Later in the chapter, it happened again. In fact, there was even a continuity error, where the toupee was coming off his head in one shot but was miraculously back on his head in a shot from a slightly different angle.

In Chapter Six of *Batman* (1943), as the Caped Crusader was about to jump down from a fire escape, a number of cigarettes fell out of his cape, followed by the box. What message did this convey to the youth of America? Hopefully, Robin did not smoke also.

This next one is very hard to spot, but in Chapter 11 of *The Adventures of Captain Marvel* (1941), the Captain was using his super strength to remove a large tree that was blocking the road. In the background, on the left side of the screen, a figure stepped out from behind a rock and then immediately retreated behind the rock. It was probably one of the members of the crew who did not realize that filming was taking place. Probably no one noticed this mistake until it was too late to re-shoot the scene.

A crew member was probably also responsible for this last blooper. In Chapter Five of *Who's Guilty?* (1945), policeman Bob Stewart was questioning one of the suspects, Ruth Allen. He said to her, "Your motives may be above suspicion but your actions certainly aren't." At that point, two distinct coughs could be heard, emitted by someone off screen, probably a member of the crew.

## III. INSIDE JOKES

In Chapter Nine of *Spy Smasher* (1942) the villains had a secret roadway up a mountain blocked by a fence with a billboard on it. In fact, the fence was really a gate, which opened to provide access to the secret road. On the gate was a poster for *Dick Tracy vs. Crime, Inc.* (1941), the prior serial release from Republic.

In Chapter Seven of *The Black Widow* (1947), the heroine walked down the street past a fence which had two signs on it. One was for the Red Cross and the other was for *Jesse James Rides Again* (1947), Republic's most recent serial.

There was another one in the same chapter of the same serial. Steve Colt was interviewing all of the mediums and psychics in the city, believing one of them to be the evil Sombra. In one scene, he had a list on a piece of paper of all of the psychics to be interviewed. One was "Mme. Lydecker, 40 Thompson St." That was clearly a reference to Howard and Theodore Lydecker, Republic's special effects experts.

*The Black Widow* (1947). As Virginia Lindley walks down the street, Republic sneaks in some publicity for its most recent serial western, *Jesse James Rides Again*, with Clayton Moore.

*Zorro's Black Whip* (1944). Barbara Meredith, the Black Whip (Linda Stirling), is explaining her plan to capture the villains who are terrorizing the Idaho territory. Listening is federal agent Vic Gordon, played by George J. Lewis. Are the names Meredith and Gordon an inside joke?

In Chapter Three of *Daughter of Don Q* (1946), Dolores Quantero was shown a prison photograph of Donovan, the main henchmen. Around his neck he was wearing his prisoner number: 39013. Of course, that was a reference to *Daredevils of the Red Circle* (1939), whose main villain was Harry Crowell, an escaped convict. He preferred to be called by his prison number, 39013.

The following may only be coincidences but it is fun to assume that they were inside jokes. In *Zorro's Black Whip* (1944), the heroine and hero were named Barbara Meredith and Vic Gordon. In the *Jungle Girl* (1941), Nyoka's last name was Meredith and in *Perils of Nyoka* (1942), Nyoka's last name was Gordon.

In *SOS Coast Guard* (1937), starring Bela Lugosi, much of the action revolved around a freighter which sank. The freighter was named "Carfax," which brought memories of Carfax Abbey, where Dracula hid his coffin in London in the book, *Dracula*, and in the original movie starring Bela Lugosi.

That could be an inside joke. On the other hand, in *The Adventures of Captain Marvel* (1941), there was another ship that sank. It was also named "Carfax" so maybe that was just a popular name at Republic, unrelated to Bela Lugosi. Then perhaps the inside joke in *SOS Coast Guard* was the name of Lugosi's character, Boroff. Was that a contraction of the name of Lugosi's horror film rival, *Bor*is Karl*off*?

Universal Studios was also not above inserting an inside joke into one of its serials, either. In the introduction to Chapter Ten of *The Adventures of Smilin' Jack* (1943), the Territorial Division of the Department of Internal Affairs was having a meeting about the Japanese sneak attack on Pearl Harbor, which took place just the day before. One member was announcing the names of the casualties at Pearl Harbor and got through three names before he was interrupted. The third name was William Sickner, who was the director of photography on that serial and on many other Universal serials.

# Chapter 8
# Serial Sequels and Series

**Much like other types** of motion pictures, certain popular serials spawned sequels or started series. This occurred at each of the major serial studios. Upon occasion, some serials that seemed to be sequels, based on their titles, turned out not to be sequels at all. A summary of serial sequels and series is contained in Appendix B.

## I. SEQUELS AND SERIES

### Tailspin Tommy (Universal)

The first serial based upon a comic strip, *Tailspin Tommy* (1934) also spawned the first sound serial sequel, *Tailspin Tommy in the Great Air Mystery* (1935). The two serials were closely related with much of the action of the first serial set in the town of Littleville, where Tommy Tompkins, his friend, "Skeeter" Milligan, and Tommy's girlfriend-to-be, flying ace, Betty Lou Barnes, were introduced to each other. Indeed, it was Betty Lou who gave Tommy the nickname, "Tailspin Tommy." This was a change from the comic strip, where Tommy received that nickname at a young age, because he was so interested in planes. Tommy eventually earned his pilot's license and helped defeat the sabotage occurring at Three Point Airlines.

The sequel picked up where the first one left off, with the first chapter set partly in Littleville before Tailspin, Skeeter and Betty Lou became involved in evil doings in a Central American island known as Nazil. Airplane stunts and cliffhangers abounded in each serial. Although the three main characters came back in the second serial, only Noah Berry, Jr. reprised his role as Skeeter Milligan. Clark Williams replaced Maurice Murphy as Tommy and serial favorite, Jean Rogers, replaced Patricia Farr as Betty Lou.

## Flash Gordon (Universal)

The most famous serial series began with *Flash Gordon* (1936), and was followed by two sequels, *Flash Gordon's Trip to Mars* (1938) and *Flash Gordon Conquers the Universe* (1940). The unifying feature of each of these serials was Flash Gordon's battle on other planets against Emperor Ming of Mongo, who was intent on destroying the Earth. In the first serial, Ming sent the Planet Mongo hurtling to the Earth causing destruction across the globe, in the second serial Ming depleted nitron from the Earth's atmosphere causing hurricanes, tornadoes and the like, and in the third serial, Ming sent a plague known as the Purple Death to Earth, causing many deaths. Ming truly was merciless.

Flash set out to thwart Ming's evil plans, by travel twice to the Planet Mongo and once to Mars. Flash was accompanied on each of his journeys into space by Dr, Zarkov and Dale Arden. In the second serial, Happy Hapgood, a newspaper reporter, managed to sneak on board Zarkov's rocket ship for the trip to Mars.

*Flash Gordon's Trip to Mars* (1938). Flash Gordon and company are in the land of the Clay People, with the Clay King, played by C. Montague Shaw, seated in the center. The rest of the cast, pictured from left to right are Donald Kerr, Jean Rogers, Buster Crabbe, Frank Shannon and a particularly hefty-looking Richard Alexander.

Between the first and second serial, the cast remained incredibly consistent. Buster Crabbe played Flash Gordon, Jean Rogers was Dale Arden, Frank Shannon portrayed Dr. Zarkov, Richard Alexander was Prince Barin and Charles Middleton embodied Ming, the Merciless. While Crabbe, Shannon and Middleton reprised their roles for the third serial, there were a number of cast changes in that chapter play. Carol Hughes took over the role of Dale Arden, Roland Drew became Prince Barin, and Shirley Deane appeared as Ming's daughter, Princess Aura, who was not in the second serial. In the first serial, the role was portrayed by Priscilla Lawson.

There was an interesting continuity issue between the ending of the original serial and *Trip to Mars*. At the end of the original serial, Flash and the others were about to land safely on the Earth. At the beginning of the second serial, they were back in the rocket ship, about to land again. Dale had inexplicably changed from a blond to a brunette.

### Dick Tracy (Republic)

This was the longest series in serial history, comprised of four serials, each fifteen chapters in length. The serials were *Dick Tracy* (1937), *Dick Tracy Returns* (1938), *Dick Tracy's G-Men* (1939) and *Dick Tracy vs. Crime, Inc.* (1941). The sixty chapters ran a total of approximately eighteen hours.

In these serials, Dick Tracy was not the plainclothes detective from the comic strips but rather, was an FBI agent. Each serial was independent of the others, with Dick Tracy going up against a new villain in each. While the villains were not the strange characters from the comic strip, they were every bit as challenging, whether being the Lame One, Pa Stark, Zarnoff or the Ghost.

In the first serial, some series regulars were introduced, such as Gwen Andrews, the lab technician and female interest, Mike McGurk, who had some involvement with the FBI, Steve Lockwood, another FBI agent, and Junior, an orphan that Dick seemed to adopt. These characters continued over into the second installment, albeit portrayed by different actors. Also, Gwen appeared to have been demoted to a mere secretary. Steve and Gwen carried over into the third serial, again, with a new duo of actors. Gwen's role was even smaller than in the previous serial. At the end of *G-Men*, Dick Tracy was promoted to Assistant Director of the FBI. These three serials all used the same theme music beneath the credits.

In the fourth serial, all of the other regulars were gone. Dick Tracy, as portrayed by Ralph Byrd, was the only character to return. Indeed, the one unifying feature in all of these serials was Ralph Byrd's portrayal of Dick Tracy. Square-jawed himself, Byrd somewhat resembled the drawing of Dick Tracy and the role was remarkably well-suited to Byrd. Byrd went on to play the role in two feature films and a short-lived television show on ABC in 1950-1951.

## The Spider (Columbia)

The first serial sequel produced by Columbia involved the pulp character, the Spider, who appeared in two serials, *The Spider's Web* (1938) and *The Spider Returns* (1941). The Spider was a masked crime fighter whose real identity was Richard Wentworth, a noted criminologist. Wentworth apparently assisted the police, represented by Commissioner Kirk, whenever the police were overwhelmed by a particularly diabolical masked villain. Much like the Green Hornet, the police believed that the Spider was a criminal and thus the Spider was required to do battle with both good guys and bad guys.

*The Spider Returns* (1941). While Warren Hull, on the right, continued to play the Spider in this sequel, Dave O'Brien assumed the role of Jackson and Mary Ainslee assumed the role of Nita Van Sloan.

In the first serial, the Spider fought the ruthless criminal master-mind, the Octopus. The Spider was played by Warren Hull, who was later to portray the Green Hornet for Universal. The credits indicated that Hull also played the Spider and one of his aliases, small time hood, Blinky McQuaide. The serial was directed by James Horne and Ray Taylor.

The sequel, *The Spider Returns* (1941), came three years later. War-ren Hull was back in the lead and his Hindu assistant, Ram Singh, was once again played by Kenneth Duncan. The characters Commissioner Kirk (Joe Girard replacing Forbes Murray), girl friend Nita Van Sloan (Mary Ainslee replacing Iris Meredith), war time buddy Jackson (Dave O'Brien replacing Richard Fiske) and butler Jenkins (Alden Chase re-placing Donald Douglas) all returned in the new serial. The villain in this film was the mysterious and masked Gargoyle.

The second serial was solely directed by James Horne and that was, perhaps, why there was more silliness in this serial than in the original. Horne often seemed more interested in the henchmen than the main villain. The theme music for the second serial was also different from the first. Generally speaking, however, the two serials were similar, with Blinky McQuaide once again showing up in the second serial as an alias for Wentworth.

### The Lone Ranger (Republic)

At least in the beginning, *The Lone Ranger* (1938) followed the general plot of the radio show, with the masked rider of the plains fight-ing injustice in the early west. Also, the viewer did not know the true identity of the Lone Ranger or what he actually looked like. As the serial ended, however, the Lone Ranger unmasked, something unheard of in either the radio or television program.

In the sequel, *The Lone Ranger Rides Again* (1939), the Lone Ranger again had a secret identity, but this time it was known to the viewers. It was a different character than in the original. These serials really had little in common, except that Chief Thunder Cloud played Tonto in both and the Lone Ranger still had a horse named Silver. The neat thing about the sequel was its title. Rather than being called *The Lone Ranger Returns* or *The Lone Ranger and Tonto*, the filmmakers used the last line from the radio introduction: "The Lone Ranger Rides Again."

In some ways, there was a third mini-serial and that was the first

*The Lone Ranger* (1938). The Man of Mystery is talking to Father McKim (William Farnum), an ally in the fight against the evil Captain Smith.

three episodes of the television series which began in 1949. The first episode ended in a true cliffhanger, with a boulder about to be thrown on the Lone Ranger, in an attempt to knock him off a high hill. The second episode ended with a mild cliffhanger, with viewers puzzled concerning the Lone Ranger's secret plan to thwart Butch Cavendish.

These first three episodes were filled with serial regulars. In addition to Clayton Moore, Tristam Coffin played the Lone Ranger's brother, George J. Lewis played the traitorous Collins, Glenn Strange played head villain Butch Cavendish and George Chesboro played Doc Drummond. At the beginning of each episode of the television series, the Lone Ranger rode to a distinctive rock on his mount, Silver. This rock, known forever as "Lone Ranger Rock" can be seen for several seconds in Chapter Four of *Zorro Rides Again* (1937), for even longer in Chapters 12 and 13 of *Deadwood Dick* (1942) and in Chapter Nine of *Perils of Nyoka* (1942), although, unfortunately, in that last serial, Clayton Moore, one of the stars, did not ride by the rock.

**The Green Hornet (Universal)**

With the melody from Rimsky-Korsakov's "The Flight of the Bumble Bee" playing in the background, Universal introduced serial audiences to both *The Green Hornet* (1939) and its sequel, *The Green Hornet Strikes Again* (1940). These serials were true to their radio origin, with the Green Hornet, a masked crime fighter by night, actually being Britt Reid, a newspaper publisher, by day. The Hornet was assisted by Kato, his chauffeur, who was Reid's valet. His high speed car was the Black Beauty, although it was seldom referred to by that name in the serials.

Gordon Jones played the dual role of Reid/Hornet in the first serial. This was Jones' only serial role. He is probably best known to television audiences for playing Mike, the cop, on *The Abbott and Costello Show*. Jones was replaced in the sequel by Warren Hull, who was very familiar to serial fans, having played the title role in *The Spider Web* (1938) and its sequel and the title role in *Mandrake the Magician* (1939), both for Columbia. Other than that important change, there was much consistency between the two serials. Reid's secretary, Lenore Case, was played by Anne Nagel. Michael Axford, Reid's bodyguard and investigator, was played by Wade Boteler, although he also appeared to be more of a newspaper reporter in the sequel. Kato, the Oriental assistant, was played by Keye Luke.

The serials were also true to the subject of the radio show. In the first serial, the Hornet fought racketeers dabbling in fraudulent construction of public improvements, insurance fraud, auto theft, and the sabotaging of truck companies and bus lines. In the sequel, racketeers were still a problem, with schemes concerning an attempt to gain control of the aluminum industry with a fake heir, illegal lotteries and once again, truck hijacking and insurance fraud. Throughout it all, the Hornet was required to run from the police while chasing the real criminals.

**King of the Royal Mounted (Universal)**

This 1940 serial, and its sequel, *King of the Mounties* (1942), explored the wartime heroics of Sergeant Dave King, of the Royal Canadian Mounted Police. These two serials were part western and part modern serial, as King fought foreign agents in the Canadian countryside. In the first serial, the enemy was after Compound X, which could be used to fuel a mine that could destroy the British fleet. Because this was a serial, the substance could also be used to cure infantile paralysis. This led to the usual serial skirmishes between the good guys and bad guys.

The sequel involved enemy attempts to obtain a new type of plane detector, which had been developed by an American to prevent enemy attacks. Once again, Sergeant King tousled with enemy agents in Canada.

Sergeant King was played by Allan Lane in both serials. None of the other characters from the first serial carried over into the second one. In terms of setting, costume and theme, the serials were very similar.

## Don Winslow (Universal)

*Don Winslow of the Navy* (1942) and *Don Winslow of the Coast Guard* (1943) were both inspired by the comic strip adventures of Don Winslow, from Navy Intelligence. In addition to the hero carrying over into both serials, the villain was the same. The Scorpion, a character from the comic strips, survived the first serial but was apparently killed at the end of the second serial.

In the first serial, the Scorpion was hijacking ships, stealing Navy secrets and sabotaging important facilities, all for the purpose of handicapping the American war effort. In the sequel, the Scorpion was back to his bad ways, planning an invasion of the United States on the West Coast.

Don Terry played Don Winslow in both serials and his sidekick, Red Pennington, was played twice by Walter Sande. Don's Navy girlfriend, Mercedes Colby, appeared in both serials, played once by Claire Dodd and the second time by Elyse Knox. The Scorpion was also played by different actors in the two serials.

## Rex Bennett (Republic)

Republic released two Rex Bennett serials within about six months of each other. The first was *G-Men vs. the Black Dragon* (1943). In this tale, Bennett was fighting Japanese spies known as the Black Dragon Society, led by the evil Haruchi. The sequel was *Secret Service in Darkest Africa* (1943) sometimes known as *Manhunt in the African Jungle*. In that adventure, Bennett was fighting Nazis operating in Africa who were attempting to convince the African Arabs to support the cause of the Germans.

The only link between the serials was Rod Cameron, who played Bennett in both serials. This was a rare serial series, in that the Bennett character was original to the movies and not based on a character from another media or upon a character from real life.

## Batman (Columbia)

*Batman* set the record for longest time period between a serial and its sequel. The original serial was released in 1943 and the sequel, *Batman and Robin*, did not appear until 1949. The sequel was clearly produced in response to the success of *Superman* (1948).

Given the lapse of time between serials, it was not unexpected that the cast of the sequel would be entirely new. Lewis Wilson was replaced by Robert Lowery (Batman), Douglas Croft was replaced by John Duncan (Robin), and William Austin was replaced by Eric Wilton, uncredited (Alfred). Also, there was one great shot of stately Wayne Manor at the beginning of the original, which showed a large estate owned by Bruce Wayne. In the sequel, Bruce Wayne had apparently fallen on hard times and now lived in a rather modest home on a quiet street. For some reason, Commissioner Gordon was missing from the original but finally appeared in the sequel.

The one element that appeared in both serials was the Bat Cave, called the Bat's Cave in the original serial. Indeed, the Bat Cave was introduced in the first serial before it made its way to the newspaper

*Batman and Robin* (1949). The masked crime fighters are conducting a crime investigation in their laboratory in the Bat Cave. Pictured are John Duncan as Robin and Robert Lowery as Batman.

strip and the comic books. In both serials, there were actual bats flying around in the cave, creating an eerie effect. The Bat Cave seemed larger and had more scientific devices in the sequel than in the original. However, in both serials, the entrance from Wayne Manor into the cave was through a grandfather clock, a concept which was also used in the comic books.

There was little continuity between the two serials. The villain in the first was Nipponese spy, Dr. Daka, who was trying to help Japan conquer America during World War II. In the sequel, the Caped Crusaders were doing battle with the Wizard, a master criminal who was masked throughout the serial.

However, the serials did keep up with some changes in the comic book story over time. In the comics, during the war years, Batman dated nurse and socialite, Linda Page. That character was the female interest in the first serial, although she was no longer a nurse. By the time the sequel came around, the comic books had introduced Vicki Vale, a photo-journalist and friend of Bruce Wayne who was attempting to discover Batman's secret identity. Vicki was the female lead and an important character in *Batman and Robin*.

### Jesse James (Republic)

With *Jesse James Rides Again* (1947), Republic started the third longest serial series. At a total of 38 chapters, it was longer than any other series, with the exception of the *Dick Tracy* and *Flash Gordon* series. The unifying theme of the three serials was that Jesse James, and later his brother Frank, had a reputation for being villainous outlaws when, in fact, they were good guys who were simply misunderstood.

In the first serial, Jesse was chased out of Missouri and ended up in Happy Valley, Tennessee where, under the pseudonym, John C. Howard, he saved the ranchers of the area who were being chased off their land by a band of Black Raiders, who were interested in the oil under the ranchers' land. By the end of the serial, Jesse successfully helped the ranchers secure their land and the oil revenue. Sheriff Mark Tobin from Kentucky, who had been chasing Jesse, witnessed Jesse's good deeds and did not arrest him, claiming that his eyesight was now too poor to recognize him.

The second serial in the series was *Adventures of Frank and Jesse James* (1948). Clayton Moore reprised his role as Jesse James and Steve Darrell played Frank James, who was introduced to the series in this serial. At the beginning, Jesse recalled his encounter at the end of the prior serial with Sheriff Tobin, although, for some reason, Jesse forgot the end of the last serial and stated that the sheriff did not arrest him because the sheriff claimed that Jesse was outside his jurisdiction. In this serial, the James brothers were good guys who were unfairly accused of committing crimes throughout the west. They decided to help open a mine and use much of the proceeds from the mine to pay their alleged victims, thus clearing their names. However, to hide their identities, they had to use assumed names. Jesse was back using the alias, John Howard and Frank used Bob Carroll.

The final serial in the series was *The James Brothers of Missouri* (1949). Clayton Moore was now involved with *The Lone Ranger* television show, so he was replaced by Keith Richards as Jesse James. Robert Bice now played Frank James. Noel Neill, who was the female lead in the previous serial, was back, although in a different role. The Howard and Carroll aliases reappeared. The serial involved trouble between competing stagecoach lines.

Fred C. Brannon was the director on all three movies, although he was assisted by Thomas Carr on the first one and Yakima Canutt on the second one. The same theme music was used in the three serials. The plots of the three serials were independent of each other; they were clearly not based on the actual lives of the James brothers.

## Superman (Columbia)

*Superman* (1948) and its sequel, *Atom Man vs. Superman* (1950) were probably the most integrated serials in movie history. The four stars of the original serial continued into the sequel. Kirk Alyn was Superman, Noel Neill was Lois Lane, Tommy Bond was Jimmy Olsen and Pierre Watkin played Perry White. Not since *Flash Gordon's Trip to Mars* (1938) had all of the primary actors from one serial carried over into the sequel.

Spencer Bennet directed both serials, although Thomas Carr assisted him in the first one. The theme music behind the credits was identical in each serial. The flying sequences were done by cartoon in both, although the latter movie did have some film close-ups of Kirk Alyn when he was supposedly in the air. In Chapter Seven of the sequel, some footage from the first chapter of the original was shown, as Lex Luthor explained the origin of Superman to one of his henchmen.

*Atom Man vs. Superman* (1950). Atom Man, who may well be Lex Luthor (Lyle Talbot), is pictured with Lois Lane (Noel Neill) and one of Atom Man's men (Don Harvey).

## II. PRETENDERS

Sometimes, serials with similar names or similar characters appeared to be part of a series or to be a sequel, when, in actuality, they were not. Here are the relevant serials.

### Secret Agent X-9 (Universal)

There were two Universal serials titled *Secret Agent X-9*, one released in 1937 and one in 1945. Given that they had the same title, they cannot be deemed to be a series. Nor was the later one a remake of the earlier one, as they had distinct plots.

In the 1937 version, X-9 was a member of the FBI. In the 1945 version, he was a true spy, working for "Special Department Washington." In the earlier serial, X-9's real name was Dexter, based on a line from the early days of the comic strip, when X-9 told a client, "Call me Dexter. It's not my name but it will do." In the later serial, X-9 went by

*Secret Agent X-9* (1937). In this publicity photo the mysterious Blackstone, played by Henry Brandon, who could be Brenda, the lead villain, chokes Secret Agent X-9, played by Scott Kolk.

the name, Phil Corrigan, which was the real name of X-9 in the strips from the 1940s.

There were no carryover characters between the serials. Other than the hero being called Secret Agent X-9, the two serials really had nothing to do with each other. For that matter, they did not have much to do with the comic strip on which they were allegedly based. These serials were independent of each other and were not part of a serial series.

### Zorro (Republic)

The five Zorro serials made by Republic were independent works, even though the credits all referred to characters created by Johnston McCulley. The second one produced, *Zorro's Fighting Legion* (1939), was chronologically the first. It was the only serial to actually feature the character, Zorro. The setting was 1824, in the newly-created country of Mexico. Zorro was fighting a robot-like figure, Don Del Oro, who was trying to undermine the new country. When he was not wearing his

*Son of Zorro* (1947). Peggy Stewart, town post mistress and serial heroine, is holding an envelope with the proceeds of some gold sales. Unfortunately, the envelope may be at risk as bad guy Ken Terrell is looking on.

mask, Zorro was actually Don Diego, who pretended to be a coward. Zorro's identity was known only by his friend, Ramon.

*Son of Zorro* (1947) featured an offspring of Zorro but it was not his son. Zorro was actually Jeff Stewart, a cavalry officer returning to his hometown after the Civil War. Thus, the timing could have made Stewart the son of Zorro. However, Pancho, the family's Mexican servant, advised Stewart that he was a descendant of Zorro on his mother's side (presumably to explain his lack of Hispanic features). When there were bandits to be dealt with, Stewart put on the Zorro outfit to combat the forces of evil. He even used Zorro's original horse, El Rey.

The grandson of Zorro appeared in *Ghost of Zorro* (1949). He was Tom Mason, a survey engineer. When crooks attempted to sabotage the extension of telegraph lines across the west, Mason, with the assistance of Moccasin, his faithful companion, donned the Zorro garb and rode as the Ghost of Zorro, to defeat the criminals.

In these last two serials, the sword and bullwhip of Zorro were not incorporated into the story. Once those were gone, Zorro was simply just another masked cowboy hero, such as the Eagle in *The Vigilantes Are Coming* (1936). In fact, the Eagle made good use of a bull whip in that serial and even had a sword fight, so he was actually more like Zorro than the masked characters in the later Republic serials.

*Zorro Rides Again* (1937) was set in modern times, mainly in the west, but with several chapters in the city, including a cliffhanger fall off a high skyscraper. In this serial, Zorro was Don Manuel Vega. He was an offspring of the original Zorro, usually referred to as his great-grandson. Vega was assisted by Renaldo, a family retainer. He even rode El Rey, a descendant of the original Zorro's horse. Here, Zorro was fighting criminals who were trying to gain control of a railroad. The signature sword and bullwhip were prominent in this serial.

The final Zorro serial was *Zorro's Black Whip* (1944). Although the female lead dressed in an outfit similar to the Zorro clothes, when she fought crime as the Black Whip, and she had Zorro-like skills in the use of a bullwhip, she had no connection with Zorro. The Zorro name was not even mentioned in the serial. There was no contention that Barbara Meredith was an offspring of Zorro, on either her mother's or her father's side.

## Junior G-Men (Universal)

Despite the similarity in names, and the starring roles for the Dead End Kids, *Junior G-Men* (1940) and *Junior G-Men of the Air* (1942) had little in common. The first serial involved a gang of juvenile delinquents, led by Billy Barton, who were trying to locate Billy's father, Colonel Barton. Colonel Barton was being held by the order of the Flaming Torch, a group who was kidnapping prominent members of the military-industrial complex. The boys referred to the organization as "The Torchies."

FBI agent Jim Bradford was on the case. His nephew, Harry Trent, a goody two shoes if there ever was one, was a Junior G-Men. It was not really clear what that meant except that Trent seemed to be assisting his uncle in investigating crimes, rather than attending school. Harry attempted to convince Billy and his gang to join the Junior G-Men. At first, the gang was suspicious but by the end of the serial, with the Torchies captured, Billy and the gang became official Junior G-Men, whatever that meant.

*Junior G-Men of the Air* was also about a gang of juvenile delinquents who assisted the state bureau of investigation ("SBI"), calling into question whether there were any G-Men at all in this serial. This gang was led by Ace Holden, also played by Billy Halop. The characters of Jim Bradford and Harry Trent were missing, being replaced by Don Ames of the state bureau and Jerry Markham of the Junior G-Men, whatever that meant. Markham was played by Frank Albertson, who was 31 years old at the time of the serial. He should therefore have been out seeking gainful employment in the serial, rather than playing at policeman.

*Sea Raiders* (1941) is often grouped with the other two serials. Once again, it involved a gang of juvenile delinquents, played by the Dead End Kids, with the leader being portrayed by Billy Halop. However, the G-Men were not involved. The gang, despite their suspect backgrounds, successfully battled a gang of foreign saboteurs. The actors who appeared in the three serials who were also in *Dead End* (1937) were Billy Halop, Huntz Hall, Gabriel Dell and Bernard Punsley.

These were the only three serials where the Dead End Kids appeared as a large group. However, in *Sky Raiders* (1941), Billy Halop had a significant role as Tim Bryant, a young student who was a member of the Air Youth of America and who wanted to build airplanes when he grew up. He assisted Captain Bob Dayton of Sky Raiders, Inc. in fighting foreign agents.

Bobby Jordan, a Dead End Kids alumnus who was not in the other serials, played Jinx Roberts, one of the four flying cadets, in *Adventures of the Flying Cadets* (1943). Billy Benedict, who was not one of the Dead End Kids but did appear later in the Bowery Boys series as Whitey, played another one of the cadets. Benedict also had roles in several other serials, including a cameo appearance as Whitey in Chapter 11 of *Junior G-Men of the Air*.

## Jungle Girl (Republic)

*Jungle Girl*, the 1941 serial starring Frances Gifford, is often linked with *The Perils of Nyoka*, the 1942 serial starring Kay Aldridge. The latter is also known as *Nyoka and the Tiger Men*. The linkage is not justified. It is true that each serial was supposedly based on a work or characters created by Edgar Rice Burroughs. In fact, however, the serial plots were unrelated to any Burroughs work. In both serials, the lead heroine had the unusual first name of Nyoka, but there the similarity ended.

*Jungle Girl* (1941). Frances Gifford and Eddie Acuff are shown in a scene with child actor Tommy Cook.

In *Jungle Girl*, the heroine was Nyoka Meredith. She was a Tarzan-like individual, with sway over the jungle animals. The story took place in an African jungle. Nyoka's true father was killed early on in the serial. At the end of the serial, Nyoka left her jungle home to go off with the hero, Jack Stanton.

*Perils of Nyoka* told the story of Nyoka Gordon, who was searching for her father who was very much alive. The action took place in the Middle East. Nyoka was no longer a jungle girl. There were no characters in common with the prior serial; indeed, there were no ties at all between the two. These were two very good serials, but completely independent of each other.

### Rocket Men (Republic)

There were three late Republic serials which were often grouped together, not because they had overlapping characters and not because they had similar plots. Rather, the three serials made use of a similar device, the rocket suit. The rocket suit consisted of a jacket with rockets

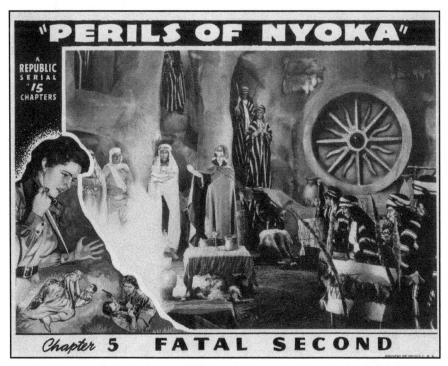

*Perils of Nyoka* (1942). While this lobby card does show Nyoka (Kay Aldridge) on the left, the emphasis is on Vultura (Lorna Gray), as she impersonates the Sun Goddess, tricking the Tauregs into believing that she is their rightful ruler.

on the back, a control device with switches marked on, off, up, down, fast and slow and a helmet to disguise the actor actually in the suit and to allow the same flying sequences to be used over and over again in subsequent productions.

The first of the group was *King of the Rocket Men* (1949), in which the flying suit was introduced. The suit was invented by Professor Millard, who permitted Jeff King to use it to fight the evil Dr. Vulcan, who had previously attempted to kill Professor Millard. Vulcan was intent on destroying the Earth, and was at least partially successful, causing great damage to New York City at the end of the chapter play. Despite the title, there was only one rocket man in the serial.

The sequel was *Radar Men from the Moon* (1952). Here, a few individuals from the Moon, who were not radar men, whatever that meant, were attempting to take over the Earth. They were challenged by Commando Cody, who had inexplicably obtained possession of Jeff King's

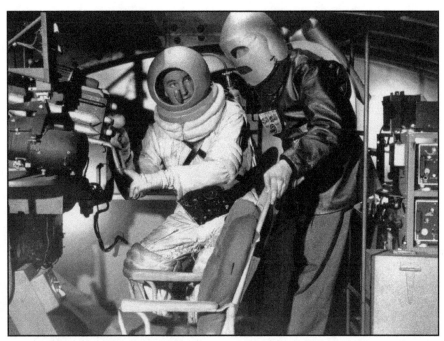

*Radar Men from the Moon* (1952). Commando Cody (George Wallace) is masquerading as a moon man on the left while Ted (William Blakewell) is in the flying suit.

flying suit. Professor Millard's invention was better than anyone could have imagined, as it even worked in the Moon's thin atmosphere. Needless to say, the invaders were defeated, in no small part as a result of the use of the flying suit.

The third serial in the group was *Zombies of the Stratosphere* (1952), which was released only six months after *Radar Men*. Proving that one size fit all, the rocket suit was now in the hands of Larry Martin, who used it to fight Martians who wanted to explode a hydrogen bomb on Earth, which would move Earth out of its orbit and allow Mars to take its place. Apparently, Mars was in need of a more temperate climate. It was likely that Mars was also in need of better scientists, as the plot strained credulity.

For the sake of completeness, mention must be made of a twelve chapter television series entitled *Commando Cody, Sky Marshall of the Universe* (1953). It involved Commando Cody from the second serial and the lead actor and actress (Judd Holdren and Aline Towne) from the third serial. There were no cliffhanger endings in the chapters and each half hour episode was a complete story. Because it was released in theaters before being shown on television, it is sometimes considered to be a serial. Because the flying suit did make an appearance, the "serial" is included in this discussion of the flying suit serials. However, *Commando Cody* is not included in the list of 231 Hollywood sound serials.

# Chapter 9
# Before and After They Were Stars

## I.  BEFORE THEY WERE MOVIE STARS

### John Wayne

Extensive research has failed to disclose any serial starring Greta Garbo, Katherine Hepburn, Cary Grant or Humphrey Bogart. One star, however, who was just as famous as those great stars, did appear in serials and that was John Wayne.

John Wayne started his movie career as an extra in silent films. His first starring role in the movies was in the sound western, *The Big Trail* (1930), directed by Raoul Walsh. This was a major production, being shot in a new 70 mm widescreen format. However, since few theater owners went to the expense of purchasing the new equipment necessary to show the movie in that format, the film was a failure.

After the lack of success of *The Big Trail*, Wayne was relegated to appearing in B-movies. Throughout the 1930s, he appeared in many B-westerns, often for Mascot and then Republic Studios, including performing in the *Three Mesquiters* series as Stoney Brooke. In 1939, he was tapped by John Ford to play the lead role of the Ringo Kid in *Stagecoach*, and after the success of that movie, there were no more B-pictures for John Wayne.

John Wayne had starring roles in three serials in the early 1930s, all for Mascot Pictures. Surprisingly, none of John Wayne's serials were westerns even though Mascot made a number of western serials. *The Three Musketeers* (1933), shot in the Arabian Desert, did have elements of the western, however, as horseback riding was the main mode of transportation for both the heroes and the villains.

Wayne's first serial was *The Shadow of the Eagle* (1932), wherein he played stunt flyer Craig McCoy, who was assisting the owner of a carni-

*The Three Musketeers* (1933). This was John Wayne's last of three serials. Also pictured from left to right are Rodney Hildebrand, Gordon De Main, Edward Piel and Ruth Hall. This is a publicity photograph as Hildebrand, playing Colonel DeMoyne, comes to save John Wayne in this scene, not to get the drop on him.

val against attacks from a group of businessmen and a villain known only as the Eagle. In the process, Wayne survived an attack from a low flying plane and a fall from a Ferris wheel. In the end, Wayne unmasked the Eagle, successfully starting his serial career.

Wayne's next serial was *The Hurricane Express* (1932). Here he starred as Larry Baker, a pilot, whose father, a railroad engineer, was killed by the Wrecker, a man who had some kind of vendetta against the railroad. Baker vowed to avenge his father's death and capture the Wrecker, which he did, after twelve exciting chapters. In the process, Baker avoided a number of perils, such as being knocked unconscious on railroad tracks as a train rolled over him and being crushed to death by a locomotive, which was dropped on him from a train hoist.

Wayne's final serial was *The Three Musketeers* (1933), in which he played Tom Wayne, an American, who was fighting a gun-runner in the Sahara

Desert known as El Shaitan. He was assisted by three soldiers from the French Foreign Legion who called themselves The Three Musketeers. Through the course of the serial, Wayne fought a charge of murder and escaped from deadly cliffhangers such as execution by a firing squad. At the end, he unmasked El Shaitan and got the girl. Although Wayne was clearly the star of the serial, he only received fourth billing behind the Musketeers.

Wayne's commanding screen presence did not come through in these serials. Perhaps it was because of his age, as he was only in his midtwenties at the time of these productions. The more likely reason, however, was that the Mascot product emphasized action and setting over acting, giving Wayne little chance to stand out in these serials. Also, closeups were at a minimum in the Mascot serial product, making it difficult for any actor to make a strong impact.

**Jennifer Jones**

Studios sometimes used the role of the female lead of a serial as an opportunity to provide work to a young actress, who presumably had some star potential. If there was a sequel to the original serial, the female

*Dick Tracy's G-Men* (1939). Here is Phyllis Isley, portraying Gwen Andrews, secretary to Ralph Byrd, playing Dick Tracy. Isley later changed her name to Jennifer Jones and became a star.

lead would often go to a different young actress so as to provide someone else with the same opportunity. Thus, the role of Tailspin Tommy's girl-friend, Betty Lou Barnes, was played by different actresses, Patricia Farr and Jean Rogers, in the two *Tailspin* serials. Nita Van Sloan, the fiancé of The Spider, was also played by two different actresses, Iris Meredith and Mary Ainslee, in the two *Spider* serials.

Similarly, in each of the first three *Dick Tracy* serials, there was a character named Gwen Andrews, who was Dick Tracy's secretary and in the first serial, she was also a lab technician. That part was played by Kay Hughes in *Dick Tracy* (1937), Lynn Roberts in *Dick Tracy Returns* (1938) and Phyllis Isley in *Dick Tracy's G-Men* (1939). By the time of that last serial, the part was so small that Gwen, who was significantly involved in the plot of the original serial, was a mere secretary with probably less than twenty speaking lines in the entire serial. She was not involved in any important story arcs or cliffhangers. Many times, her main function was to nod her head when someone spoke to her. It was no wonder that the role was eliminated in the fourth serial in the series.

Although Phyllis Isley did receive fourth billing in *Dick Tracy's G-Men* (1939) with her name on the main title card along with the three leading male stars and ahead of other actors with more significant parts, the serial was unlikely to rocket Isley to stardom and it did not. Indeed, after the completion of this serial, Isley asked to be released from her contract with Republic Pictures, so she could go back to theater work in New York, with her then husband, Robert Walker.

A few years later, she auditioned for a movie role with the Holly-wood producer, David O. Selznick. Selznick liked Isley but not her name, which he eventually changed to Jennifer Jones. Under that name, she starred in many famous motion pictures, including *Since You Went Away* (1944), *Duel in the Sun* (1946) and *Love Is a Many Splendored Thing* (1955). She was a rare serial performer in that she won an Academy Award, as best actress, for her performance in *The Song of Bernadette* (1943). As Jennifer Jones, Isley came a long way, very fast, from the nothing role of Gwen Andrews in *Dick Tracy's G-Men*.

## Boris Karloff

Much like many of the stars of the 1930s, Boris Karloff started his career in silent films, with some of his first roles as early as 1919. He had fairly steady work during the 1920s, but never became a featured player or a star. With the advent of sound films, Karloff continued to work steadily, including having an important role in Howard Hawks' *The Criminal Code* (1931), where Karloff repeated his stage role as a prisoner who became a killer. Later that same year, Karloff was chosen for the role of the monster in *Frankenstein* (1931) and his career as a star in horror films began.

Karloff appeared in a number of silent serials. He then appeared in the first ever sound serial, *King of the Kongo*, which was produced by Mascot in 1929. This serial was released as both a silent film and a part talking film. Karloff had a significant role as the apparent villain, Scarface Macklin, who was after a buried treasure.

Karloff's next serial appearance was in *King of the Wild* (1931), also released by Mascot. Karloff played Mustapha, an Arab villain. This was an important part in the serial and Karloff received a high billing.

In Karloff's final serial role, in *The Vanishing Legion* (1931), Karloff did not appear at all. Instead, he provided the voice of the villain in the serial, aptly named "The Voice," when the villain communicated over electronic devices to either his henchmen or other characters. Karloff was not seen in the serial and the villain was played by another actor when the villain's true identity was revealed in the last chapter of the serial.

## Gene Autry

When Gene Autry came to the movies in the mid-1930s, he was already an established radio and singing star. Discovered by Will Rogers, Autry began appearing on the radio in 1929 in Oklahoma. As he became more popular, he started to perform on *The National Barn Dance*, which was broadcast nationally from Chicago. In 1932, he had his first big record hit with "That Silver Haired Daddy of Mine."

After a small part in a feature western, *In Old Santa Fe* (1934) and then one in a serial, *Mystery Mountain* (1934), Autry received his first starring role in the movies. Radio's Singing Cowboy, as the credits stated, played a character named Gene Autry in the 1935 Mascot serial, *The Phantom Empire*. In this part western serial, Autry had a radio show in which Autry was the featured performer, generally singing western songs. This made Autry one of the first singing cowboys of the cinema. One of his pals in the movie was played by Smiley Burnette, who appeared with Autry in many of his later films. Thus, almost Autry's entire later screen persona was established in this serial.

Autry's career skyrocketed after the release of *The Phantom Empire*. Autry starred in over 90 feature films, almost all of which were westerns. From 1940 to 1956, he had a nationally broadcast radio show over CBS, entitled *Melody Ranch*. He wrote and recorded songs, selling over 100 million copies. He even conquered the new medium of television, appearing in *The Gene Autry Show* which ran on CBS from 1950 to 1956. Essentially, the television episodes were just a continuation of his B-movie career, as Autry, as usual, played a character named Gene Autry, he had his horse named Champion, and he had a sidekick, who in that case was played by Pat Buttram.

It is interesting that after *The Phantom Empire*, Autry never returned to serial work, even though he was employed at Republic, which made many serials. Autry's B-western career was so profitable, Republic probably did not want to waste his screen power in another serial. In the early 1940s, Autry was one of the highest grossing film stars in Hollywood, becoming the first cowboy star to appear in the list of motion pictures' Top Ten Moneymakers.

## George Brent

George Brent was a major star at Warner Brothers from 1932 into the 1940s. He is best remembered for those movie roles in which he played the romantic lead opposite a major female star of the 1930s and 1940s such as Jean Arthur, Greta Garbo, Barbara Stanwyck, Claudette Colbert and Bette Davis. Indeed, the twelve films in which he played opposite Bette Davis, such as *Jezebel* (1938) and *Dark Victory* (1939) are among his most famous movies.

Brent's first major motion picture was *42ⁿᵈ Street*, the famous Busby Berkley musical, which he made at Warner Brothers in 1933. Just two years before, Brent was featured in his only serial, *The Lightning Warrior* (1931). Here, Brent again played opposite one of the biggest Hollywood stars of the time, but in this case it was canine star, Rin-Tin-Tin. Despite portraying the hero, Brent was billed below Rin-Tin-Tin. While that was understandable, Brent was so unknown at the time that he was also billed below 14 year old child star, Frankie Darro, and also below an actor whose character was killed in the first chapter.

At the time of *The Lightning Warrior*, Brent was generally appearing in B-movies. After his contract with Warner Brothers ended in 1942, his career started on a downward spiral. By the 1950s, he was back to B-movies and appearing in television shows. He retired from the movies in 1953.

## Jon Hall

Jon Hall was a legitimate star in Hollywood, at least for a few years. He started his film career in 1935, receiving small parts in several films. His breakthrough movie was *The Hurricane* (1937), directed by John Ford. Hall, who starred opposite a young Dorothy Lamour, played Terengi, a native who was unjustly imprisoned on a South Seas island. When he escaped from prison, he was caught in a hurricane, making this one of the first disaster movies. The film was noted for its truly awesome special effects.

*The Hurricane* was a great success and Hall received starring roles in a number of movies. In particular, he made six color films at Universal during the early 1940s. These films co-starred Maria Montez and were generally set in exotic locales. Once interest in that type of film petered out, Hall was relegated to a career in B-movies and television.

Prior to becoming a star, Hall appeared in one serial, under his given name, Charles Locher. That serial was *The Amazing Exploits of the Clutching Hand*, an independent production from 1936. Hall played Frank Hobart, one of the minor villains in the piece. While Hall had no other serial roles, footage from *White Savage* (1943), one of his movies with Maria Montez, appeared in *Lost City of the Jungle* (1946).

## Lon Chaney, Jr.

Lon Chaney, Jr.'s career in serials was unusual in that he had the starring hero's role in his first and last serial, but then generally played henchmen in the serials in between. Creighton Chaney, as Lon Chaney, Jr. was then billed, starred in RKO's 1932 serial, *The Last Frontier*, as Tom Kirby, a newspaper publisher who also disguised himself as The Black Ghost, a Zorro-style figure, to fight injustice in the Old West. This was Chaney's first major role in the movies and did not immediately lead to any more starring roles.

Thereafter, Chaney generally played small roles in the movies until a breakout opportunity on stage, in the role of Lenny in John Steinbeck's *Of Mice and Men*. Chaney received good reviews for his stage performance and he was chosen to reprise the role of Lenny in the film version, which was released in 1939. Chaney also received good reviews for his film performance of the role of Lenny, but his career still stalled. Chaney therefore moved to Universal for the second Hollywood cycle of horror films which began around 1940. While at Universal, he played the Wolf Man, Dracula, Frankenstein and the Mummy, among other horror figures.

*Ace Drummond* (1936). Lon Chaney, Jr., with his hands up, is still playing henchmen at this stage of his career. Pictured on the left are John Trent, as Ace Drummond, and Jean Rogers as Peggy Trainor.

Although the 1941 release of *The Wolf Man* made Chaney a horror film star, he appeared in one more serial, *Overland Mail* (1942). There he returned to a hero's role, playing Jim Lane, trying to thwart troubles with the United States mail. It was Chaney's last serial role.

In between his first and last serials, Chaney's other serial roles were generally as a henchman, in *Undersea Kingdom* (1936), *Ace Drummond* (1936), *Secret Agent X-9* (1937) and *Riders of Death Valley* (1941). His only other serial role was as Armand Corday who was forced to work for the villainous El Shaitan, in *The Three Musketeers* (1933). It was a good part for Chaney, particularly since he did not play a henchman, but his character was killed off early in the film.

### Mickey Rooney

Mickey Rooney, famous child and teenage star, who was in movies and television for over seventy years, had an early serial role in the Clyde Beatty serial, *The Lost Jungle* (1934), as a boy at the circus in Chapter One. Although the part was uncredited, Rooney, who surprisingly is the tallest of the three companions at the circus, had several lines. At the time of the serial, Rooney was just a year away from his first major movie role, as Puck in *Midsummer Night's Dream* (1935). He was also just a few years away from his first Andy Hardy movie, a series for which he is most associated, along with the teenage musicals he did with Judy Garland at MGM, such as *Babes in Arms* (1939).

## Alan Ladd

Although Alan Ladd started in the movies in 1932, his major break in Hollywood did not occur until 1942, when he played the psychotic killer, Raven, in *This Gun for Hire* (1942). After that, he had a number of starring or featured roles in Hollywood movies, culminating with his most famous role as the title character in the western classic, *Shane* (1953). Ladd continued making movies until his death in 1964.

Prior to *This Gun for Hire*, Ladd had a number of small parts in movies, including an uncredited bit as a reporter at the end of *Citizen Kane* (1941). One of Ladd's other bit parts was as Gilpin, a student pilot, in Chapters Three and Four of *The Green Hornet* (1939). Although Ladd had a number of lines in the serial, including an argument with the Green Hornet who then knocked Gilpin out in order to prevent the young pilot from flying a sabotaged plane, Ladd did not receive screen credit. Also, Ladd had no close-ups in the film and although there were some medium shots of him, he is not easy to recognize in the serial.

## II. BEFORE THEY WERE FEATURED PERFORMERS

## Misha Auer

Misha Auer had a significant role as Carlo in *My Man Godfrey* (1936), for which he received an Academy Award nomination for Best Supporting Actor. From then on, he was regularly cast in zany comedy roles, such as the ballet instructor, Kolenkov, in *You Can't Take It With You* (1938). He also had featured roles in such films as *Destry Rides Again* (1939) and *And Then There Were None* (1945). With his Russian ancestry and accent, Auer tended to play foreigners in films.

Until his success in *Our Man Godfrey*, Auer worked in uncredited or small roles in B-movies. He made four serial appearances. The first was in *King of the Wild* (1931) where he played Prince Dakka, the second was in

*The Last of the Mohicans* (1932), where he played General Montcalm, and the third was in *Tarzan the Fearless* (1933) where he played Eltar, the high priest of Zar. His final serial appearance was as Tanaga, in *The Adventures of Rex and Rinty* (1935). In that serial, Auer played the ruler of small country of Sujan, whose people worshipped a black Arabian horse as a god. Although at the time Auer was just a year away from his breakout role in *My Man Godfrey*, the part of Tananga was a small part, with Auer only having significant screen time in the first and ending chapters of the serial.

## Lola Lane

Lola Lane is best known for the series of movies she made with her sisters, Rosemary and Priscilla, for Warner Brothers starting in the late 1930s. The first film was *Four Daughters*, released in 1938. Although there was a fourth Lane sister in real life, named Leota, the part of the fourth sister in the movie went to Gale Page. The film was a great success and led to several more joint appearances by the sisters, in *Daughters Courageous* (1939), *Four Wives* (1939) and *Four Mothers* (1941). Thereafter, Priscilla's career soared, with solo appearances in many films, while her sisters' careers faded.

Of the three sisters, only Lola appeared in a serial. It was a significant role, as the female lead, Marjorie Temple, in *Burn 'Em Up Barnes* (1934). Unknown to Marjorie Temple, she had inherited land which contained substantial oil deposits. Lyman Warren was attempting, by the usual nefarious means, to destroy Temple's vehicle transportation business, thus causing her to transfer the lands to Warren to raise money. Luckily, auto racing champion Barnes was on Marjorie's side and together they thwarted the evildoers.

Other than the movies she made with her sisters, Lola Lane usually appeared in B-movies which are long forgotten today. She retired from picture-making in 1946.

## Charles Bickford

Charles Bickford made only one serial appearance but it was an important role, as the main henchman, Wolf Reade, in *Riders of Death Valley* (1941). Wolfe was the leader of the henchmen who was not always subservient to the main villains or very respectful to his own henchmen.

Bickford never became a star in Hollywood, but he had constant work as a featured performer. He received three Academy Award nominations for Best Supporting Actor. The first was for the role of Father Peyramale in *The Song of Bernadette* (1943), which starred Jennifer Jones, who also only made one serial appearance. The second was for the part of Joseph Clancy, in *The Farmer's Daughter* (1947). The third was in the following year as the title character's father in *Johnny Belinda*.

## Lee J. Cobb

Lee J. Cobb was a well-known actor in both movies and television. Some of his most famous movie roles were as the waterfront boss, Johnny Friendly, in *On the Waterfront* (1954) and as one of the jurors in *12 Angry Men* (1957). He received two Academy Award nominations for Best Supporting Actor, one for *On the Waterfront* (1954) and the other for *The Brothers Karamazov* (1958).

Cobb is also well-remembered for his performance as Willy Loman in the television production of *Death of a Salesman* in 1966, a role he had originated on Broadway. He made many other appearances on television, including playing the role of Judge Garth, an owner of the Shiloh Ranch, on the long-running television western, *The Virginian*. Although the series ran for nine seasons on NBC, Cobb was only on the show during the first four seasons, from 1962 to 1966. *The Virginian* was the first 90 minute western series on television.

Cobb's first movie role was in *The Vanishing Shadow*, a 1934 serial from Universal. He had an unbilled part as a construction foreman on a road crew in Chapters Three and Four. That same footage was reused at the end of Chapter 11 of *The Phantom Creeps* (1939) as it set up a cliffhanger concerning an explosion on a road. Although Cobb did have a few lines of dialogue, his part was very small and very forgettable.

## Ruth Roman

Ruth Roman's first major screen appearance was as Lothel, the mystery queen of the jungle, in Universal's 1945 serial titled *Jungle Queen*. Although she received only fifth billing, it was a significant role as Roman stood out as the beautiful Lothel, in her white gown.

The role did not lead to any other serial appearances or to any significant roles in full length features. It was not until the late 1940s that she received important supporting roles in features, such as *Belle Starr's Daughter* (1948) and *The Champion* (1949). Then, in the 1950s, Roman played the female lead in several major motion pictures, such as

*Strangers on a Train* (1951), *Tomorrow is Another Day* (1951) and *The Far Country* (1955). When those roles dried up, she made many guest appearances on television programs, including a continuing role for one season on *Knots Landing*, in the middle 1980s.

## George Montgomery

George Montgomery Letz had one of the most significant roles in serial history. He played one of the five rangers who could be the title character in Republic's 1938 serial, *The Lone Ranger*. In that serial and in his other films of the era, where he received a credit, he was billed as George Letz. During this time period, Letz was a contract player at Republic, where he did bit parts and supporting roles in about thirty films, most of which were B-westerns. He also appeared in an uncredited bit part in *Hawk of the Wilderness* (1938) and may have been an extra in *Dick Tracy* (1937).

In 1938, Letz moved to 20th Century Fox and shortened his name to George Montgomery. There he starred in several major Hollywood productions such as *Orchestra Wives* (1942) with Glenn Miller, *Ten Gentlemen from West Point* (1942) with Maureen O'Hara, *China Girl* (1942) with Gene Tierney, *Roxie Hart* (1942) with Ginger Rogers, and *Coney Island* (1943) with Betty Grable. In the 1950s, Montgomery returned to his cinema roots, appearing in many western films. He passed away in 2000.

## Herman Brix/Bruce Bennett

Much like Johnny Weissmuller and Buster Crabbe, Herman Brix was an Olympic star before he became a movie Tarzan. Weissmuller won five gold medals for swimming in the 1924 and 1928 Olympic Games, Buster Crabbe won a bronze and gold medal for swimming in the 1928 and 1932 Olympic Games, respectively, and Brix won a silver medal for the shot put in the 1928 games. When MGM was auditioning for an actor to play Tarzan for *Tarzan, the Ape Man* (1932), Brix was the favorite to obtain the role, until he separated his shoulder while filming the football movie, *Touchdown* (1931). The role of Tarzan went to Weissmuller and the rest, as they say, is cinema history.

However, when Edgar Rice Burroughs was casting the role of Tarzan for a jungle serial Burroughs intended to produce, Burroughs chose Brix for the role. Brix starred in *The New Adventures of Tarzan* (1935), a 12

*Fighting Devil Dogs* (1938). Herman Brix in the center, who eventually changed his acting name to Bruce Bennett, has the secondary hero's role in this serial, supporting Lee Powell (right). Here, the two, along with Montagu Love, may be about to obtain a clue which will help them capture the evil Lightning.

chapter serial which was also released as two feature films. Brix then appeared in a number of serials, including *Shadow of Chinatown* (1936) as the hero, *The Lone Ranger* (1938), as one of the individuals who could be the masked rider and *The Fighting Devil Dogs* (1938) and *Daredevils of the Red Circle* (1939), as one of the leads. His best serial role was the title role in *Hawk of the Wilderness* (1938), where he played Kioga, a westerner raised in the jungle, much like Tarzan.

Around this time, Brix was disappointed with the roles he was receiving and the films in which he was appearing. He took two steps. One was to take acting lessons. The other was to change his name to Bruce Bennett. He then signed with Columbia Pictures but still appeared in small parts or in minor movies, with a few exceptions. His next major career move was signing with Warner Brothers in 1945. There, Bennett had important roles in important films and these are the roles for which he is most famous today. For example, he appeared as Joan Crawford's ex-husband in *Mildred Pierce* (1945), and as the fourth prospector who was killed in *Treasure of the Sierra Madre* (1948). He is also well-remembered for his role as an aging baseball player in *Angels in the Outfield* (1951), the latter being produced by MGM.

Thereafter, most of Bennett's performances were as a guest star on television programs. He never returned to serials after he became a well-known supporting player. He only appeared in serials under his given name, Herman Brix, and never under his film name, Bruce Bennett.

### Harry Carey

Harry Carey can be hard to characterize in terms of the timing of his serial work within his film career. Carey was a major star in silent films, starting with D.W. Griffith films and then continuing in a number of westerns, including many directed by John Ford. By the end of the silent era, he was one of the top western stars in Hollywood. He continued working into the talking era, being a lead in one of the most famous adventure films of the time, *Trader Horn*, made in 1931 by MGM.

Carey then moved to Mascot Pictures where he appeared in his only three serials. Despite the fact that Carey was already in his 50s, he had the lead hero's role in the western-oriented serials, *The Vanishing Legion* (1931), *The Last of the Mohicans* (1932) and *The Devil Horse* (1932).

After the serials, Carey continued to work steadily in Hollywood, often starring in B-westerns, and playing supporting roles in major films such as *The Angel and the Badman* (1947) and *Red River* (1948). However, Carey is best known to modern audiences for his portrayal of the President of the Senate, who allows the filibuster of Jefferson Smith (James Stewart) to continue, in *Mr. Smith Goes to Washington* (1939). For that role, Carey was nominated for an Oscar for Best Supporting Actor.

### J. Carrol Naish

J. Carrol Naish was of Irish descent yet it is believed he never played an Irishman in films. Instead, he often played Japanese, Italians, Arabs, Mexicans and other characters of obvious foreign origin. Today, Naish is best-remembered for playing supporting roles in B-movie mysteries, such as two *Bulldog Drummond* movies in the late 1930s and in horror films, such as his role as the hunchback, Daniel, in *House of Frankenstein* (1944). Yet, Naish did have significant supporting roles in A-Movies, and indeed, was nominated twice for an Academy Award in the Best Supporting Actor category.

Naish's first nomination was for Warner Brothers' 1943 film entitled *Sahara*, which starred Humphrey Bogart. Naish played an Italian prisoner of an American tank crew. His second nomination was for *A Medal for Benny*, a 1945 film from Paramount starring Dorothy Lamour. In that movie, Naish played the indigent Mexican father of a deceased war hero. Other major motion pictures in which Naish appeared were *The Fugitive* (1947) and *Rio Grande* (1950), both directed by John Ford.

Naish's first serial role was in *The Mystery Squadron* (1933) wherein he had a small role playing a foreman named Collins. However, for serial fans, Naish will always be best known for his portrayal of Dr. Daka, the lead villain in *Batman* (1943). Here, Naish gave one of the greatest portrayals of a villain in all of serials, as he played a Japanese spy in America during World War II who was attempting to undermine the American war effort. In the serial, Naish was as comfortable turning men into zombies as he was in feeding his killer alligators.

## Gabby Hayes

Gabby Hayes was the consummate supporting player in Hollywood westerns. Known for his whiskers, Hayes did appear clean-shaven in some early roles in the 1930s. However, when he became a regular supporting player to western heroes, he always had the beard. His first extended supporting role was as Windy Halliday, in 18 movies supporting Hopalong Cassidy from 1936 to 1939. Then Hayes moved to Republic Pictures, where he became a sidekick to Roy Rogers in 41 films. He also supported Wild Bill Elliott in eight films during the early 1940s.

Before he found his calling as a western supporting performer, Hayes appeared in two serials. The first was a tiny role in *The Lost Jungle* (1934), as a passenger on a dirigible. Hayes can be seen as a doctor talking to Sharkey during Chapter One of the serial before a storm causes the aircraft to crash. Hayes is better known for his role as Butterfield, the operator of a trading post who was not above dealing in slaves, in *The Lost City* (1935). It was a good, early role for Hayes as he had significant screen time over many chapters.

## Carole Landis

For a short time, Carole Landis received important roles in Hollywood and her future looked bright. Landis' breakout role was as Loana in *One Million B.C.* (1940), a role Raquel Welch had in the 1966 remake. She impressed audiences with her beauty (helped by her skimpy outfit) in this story set in prehistoric times. From that point, she received a number of good roles in films, such as *Topper Returns* (1941), *The Powers Girl* (1943) and the film noir classic, *I Wake Up Screaming* (1941). However, Landis never seemed to receive the lead female role; she often had the second most important female role in a movie. By the middle 1940s, her career was faltering and her personal life was in a shambles. She committed suicide in 1948 at the age of 29.

Prior to *One Million, B.C.*, Landis usually had small roles in the movies. Her most significant role during that time period was in the famous Witney/English serial, *Daredevils of the Red Circle* (1939). Landis played Blanche Granville, the granddaughter of Horace Granville, who had been taken prisoner by the escaped convict, 39013. Then the criminal impersonated the older Granville by use of a perfect life mask. Blanche was a small but important role in the serial, and she was involved in a surprise revelation at the end of the serial.

## III. BEFORE THEY WERE TELEVISION STARS

While television was a significant cause of the demise of the movie serial, it also provided much needed work for performers who were associated with serials. Many performed as guest stars on television shows in the 1950s and this work continued into the next two decades. Other serial regulars obtained starring or recurring roles in television shows. Here are some examples.

### Clayton Moore

Who was that masked man? The answer to that question was almost always "Clayton Moore," at least for viewers of *The Lone Ranger* television program, which had its original run on ABC television from 1949 to 1957. Moore also appeared in two original Lone Ranger movies, titled *The Lone Ranger* (1956) and *The Lone Ranger and the Lost City of Gold* (1958). After the show ended its original run and moved to syndication, Moore seldom appeared in public without his mask (or for a time, as a result of legal proceedings, without dark glasses), whether at personal appearances or in television commercials. Thus, many people have never actually seen Clayton Moore's face uncovered.

Before *The Lone Ranger* television program began, Moore appeared in a number of serials, usually without a mask. All of these early serials were made by Republic Pictures. Moore's first serial role was a very small, uncredited part in *Zorro's Fighting Legion* (1939), although no one has been able to actually locate him in the serial. His first significant serial role was as the male hero in *Perils of Nyoka* (1942). There he played Dr. Larry Grayson, who assisted Nyoka Gordon in her search for her father and a cure for cancer which was engraved on the Golden Tablets of Hippocrates.

His next serial role was as Ashe, the main henchman for the title villain in *The Crimson Ghost* (1946). It is somewhat disconcerting to see the virtuous Lone Ranger in an evil role, but Moore was convincing as he carried out the nefarious plans of the evil villain.

Moore returned to the hero's role as the title character in *Jesse James Rides Again,* a 1947 serial. In some ways, this part foreshadowed the Lone Ranger role because, while Jesse was a hero in this serial, most people

*Jesse James Rides Again* (1947). This was the first of three western serials in which Clayton Moore appeared at Republic, leading into his most famous role as the title character in the television show, *The Lone Ranger*. Also pictured is John Compton, playing Jesse James' sidekick, Steve Lane.

believed he was a criminal. In the serial, Moore showed off his horse riding and sharp shooting skills. Unlike the Lone Ranger, however, Jesse was not above shooting to kill, dispatching the main henchman with a flurry of bullets near the end of the serial.

Moore reprised the role of Jesse James in *Adventures of Frank and Jesses James*, a 1948 serial, in which Jesse and his brother assisted Judy Parker to thwart evildoers with designs on a gold mine. Many of the outdoor scenes in both serials were shot at the Iverson Ranch, familiar to viewers of *The Lone Ranger*.

Sandwiched in between the two Jesse James serials was an appearance as the hero in *G-Men Never Forget*, another 1948 serial. Moore played O'Hara, a federal agent on the trail of Murkland, a master criminal who, through the use of plastic surgery, was posing as the police commissioner. Murkland was played by Roy Barcroft, the chief henchman in *Jesse James Rides Again*.

In early 1949, Moore appeared as the grandson of the legendary hero Zorro, in *Ghost of Zorro*. In the film, Moore donned a mask for the first time, but only when he masqueraded as Zorro. As contrasted with later *The Lone Ranger* television show, Moore's face was uncovered when he portrayed his true identity, Ken Mason. This part can be seen as a tryout for the upcoming television show.

At that point, Moore received his now signature role in *The Lone Ranger*, which first aired on television in 1949. Thus, he did not reprise the role of Jesse James in the third serial in the series, *The James Brothers of Missouri* (1949). However, that was not the end of Moore's serial appearances.

During the third season of *The Lone Ranger*, from 1952-1953, Moore got into a salary or some other dispute with the producer of the series and he was replaced for the season by John Hart, who also appeared in serials, as discussed below. While on leave from the television series, Moore returned to his acting roots at Republic Pictures, playing the henchman for invaders from the moon, in *Radar Men from the Moon* (1952). Once again, Moore portrayed a bad guy, not in the tradition of the Lone Ranger.

Moore then left Republic Studios to appear in his first Columbia serial, *Son of Geronimo* (1952), a western, with Moore comfortably playing the hero, albeit without a mask. Moore's next serial role was for Republic, in *Jungle Drums of Africa* (1953), where he again played the hero, in a jungle setting. Moore then appeared in one more serial, *Gunfighters of the Northwest*, a 1954 cliffhanger from Columbia. Although he played a Mountie, Moore did not have top billing in the serial, and his part was much smaller than that of the main hero played by Jock Mahoney. His female co-star in those last two serials was Phyllis Coates, also probably best known for a television role, as Lois Lane, in the early episodes of *Superman*.

Prior to the release of *Gunfighters*, Moore patched up his differences with the producers of *The Lone Ranger* television program and returned to play the role with which he is most associated. While Moore had other movie roles and television appearances without his mask, the best place to see him, without the mask, is in his serial appearances for Republic Pictures, prior to becoming a star in television. Either as hero or villain, the distinctive Moore voice tells you that the actor is, in reality, that fabulous individual, the Lone Ranger.

Other actors associated with *The Lone Ranger* also made appearances in serials. Jay Silverheels, who played Tonto during the entire run of the television series, except for some episodes he missed when he had a mild heart attack, had an undistinguished film career before he appeared in *The Lone Ranger*. It is always surprising to see him appear in a small part as John Osceola in *Key Largo*, the 1948 film starring Humphrey Bogart and Edward G. Robinson. Also, just before being hired for *The Lone Ranger* television series, Silverheels appeared in the 1949 Gene Autry western, *The Cowboy and the Indians*, in which Clayton Moore also had a part. Silverheels was billed ahead of Moore in the credits. The two had several scenes together although there was no dialogue between them.

Silverheels had a number of uncredited bit parts in serials, usually playing a jungle native. For example, he can be seen as a lion man guard in several chapters of *Jungle Girl* (1941) such as at the end of Chapter Two when he was knocked out by Stanton, as a native warrior (the one on the right) who escorted the Phantom to the fire ceremony in Chapters Nine and Ten of *The Phantom* (1943), and as the second native killed at a shootout at a shack in Chapter Seven of *The Tiger Woman* (1944). Interestingly, in 1954, still during the run of *The Lone Ranger* television show, Silverheels had a good part in the western, *The Black Dakotas*, in which Clayton Moore also appeared.

As noted above, actor John Hart replaced Clayton Moore as the Lone Ranger during the 1952-1953 television season. During that time period, Hart starred in a total of 52 episodes of the television series.

*Adventures of Captain Africa* (1955). John Hart, who played the masked Lone Ranger for one season on television, plays the masked Captain Africa in this Columbia serial.

Interestingly, Hart had previously appeared in two other episodes of the series in other roles. Hart is truly the forgotten Lone Ranger. When the show moved into syndication, the Moore shows were repeated more than the Hart episodes and many people forgot that there had been another Lone Ranger. Hart also starred as Hawkeye in *Last of the Mohicans*, a 1957 television series which played for one season in syndication. His co-star, playing a Native American, was Lon Chaney, Jr., himself a serial veteran.

In terms of serials, Hart is best-known for playing the title character in *Jack Armstrong* (1947). Although Jack Armstrong was known as the All-American boy, Hart was 30 years old at the time he played the role. His other major role in serials was as the title character in one of Columbia's last serials, *Adventures of Captain Africa* (1955).

Hart also appeared in several other serials, in small parts which were often uncredited. For example, at the end of Chapter One of *Gunfighters of the Northwest*, three new Mounties appeared on the scene. One was Bram Nevin, who would go on to be one of the important leads in the serial. Another was Dan Wells, who would be killed almost immediately. Nevin was played by Clayton Moore and Wells was played by John Hart. Thus, for a very brief time, the two actors who played the Lone Ranger on television appeared alongside each other in a serial, and rode together to lead the fight for law and order in the Canadian west. Also, in 1973, Hart appeared in the western feature, *Santee*, in which Jay Silverheels had a good role.

### Duncan Renaldo

In the early 1950s, there were many half hour westerns on television which seemed to be offshoots of serials and B-movies. Often, serial stars and directors were involved in the productions. These shows included *The Lone Ranger*, *The Gene Autry Show*, *The Adventures of Kit Carson*, and *The Cisco Kid*. Duncan Renaldo, who was the star of *The Cisco Kid*, made many appearances in movie serials.

*The Cisco Kid* debuted on television in September, 1950, about one year after *The Lone Ranger*. It was similar to *The Lone Ranger* in that the Kid, along with his sidekick, Pancho (who had some trouble with the English language) traveled the Old West, fighting crime and injustice wherever they found it. The character itself, however, was created by the author O'Henry in a 1907 short story titled "The Caballero Way," and the Kid was the subject of numerous films before the television series was developed.

Indeed, Duncan Renaldo played the Cisco Kid a number of times in the movies. Monogram Studios produced a series of Cisco Kid movies in the 1940s. Duncan Renaldo was the original Cisco Kid in the series, taking the lead role in *The Cisco Kid Returns* (1945). He was in the next two features, before the role was taken over by Gilbert Roland.

United Artists started a new series in 1948 and brought Renaldo back to star as the Kid in *The Valiant Hombre* (1948) and four subsequent features. In all of these movies, his sidekick, Pancho, was played by Leo Carrillo.

When ZIV television decided to produce a television series of *The Cisco Kid*, it was natural to choose Renaldo and Leo Carrillo to reprise their roles of the Kid and Pancho from the United Artists movie series. It was a good choice as the series ran for six seasons in syndication, from 1950 to 1956, with 156 half-hour episodes produced. The series has historical significance, as it was the first television series to have its episodes shot in color.

Duncan Renaldo's career started in silent films and in the early years of sound movies he had small parts in many films and slightly larger roles in several serials. His first serial role came in *The Painted Stallion* (1937), where he played the important role of the henchman, Zamorro. He then had a small role in *The Jungle Menace* (1937). Next came one of his best-remembered serial appearances, as Renaldo, the faithful servant to Zorro, in *Zorro Rides Again* (1937). Since the Cisco Kid and Zorro have much in common, it was an interesting foreshadowing of Renaldo's later movie and serial career.

Thereafter, Renaldo's career continued in B-movies and serials. In *The Lone Ranger Rides Again* (1939), Renaldo played Juan Vasquez, who assisted the Lone Ranger and Tonto in their fight for law and order. In *King of the Texas Rangers* (1941), Renaldo played Pedro Garcia, a Mexican policeman, who assisted Tom King in breaking up a band of Fifth Columnists. Each of these serials had significant roles for Renaldo.

After a smaller henchman's role in *King of the Mounties* (1942), Renaldo played the role of Pierre LaSalle, a Free French officer during World War II, who assisted Rex Bennett in his fight against the Nazis in *Secret Service in Darkest Africa* (1943). Renaldo's final serial appearance was in *The Tiger Woman* (1944) as Jose Delgado, who assisted hero Allen Saunders in his quest to protect the jungle domain of the Tiger Woman.

Leo Carrillo was no stranger to serials, either, as he played one of the riders in *Riders of Death Valley* (1941). Actually, Carrillo played the same type of role in that serial as he played in *The Cisco Kid* television series as his character's name in the serial was Pancho, he was in the serial for comic relief, and he mangled the English language on many occasions.

## Noel Neill

Noel Neill and Clayton Moore were probably the only two television stars who could tie their important later roles on television to earlier serial appearances. Clearly, Moore's Republic serial appearances in westerns in the late 1940s led to his consideration for the Lone Ranger role on television. Neill's serial appearances contained a more direct link.

In 1948, Neill was chosen for the role of Lois Lane in the Columbia serial, *Superman*. This was a significant part for Neill, because other than Kirk Alyn in the dual role of Superman/Cark Kent, Neill was the star of the serial. The Lois Lane role was written in the classic manner, with Lane an ambitious reporter, always trying to scoop Clark Kent on a story.

Superman was one of the most successful serials of all time, leading to a sequel, *Atom Man vs. Superman* (1950). This is often deemed to be the last

*Superman* (1948). Noel Neill in her most famous role as Lois Lane, which she played in two serials and on the long-running television program. Also pictured is Kirk Alyn, as Clark Kent.

great serial. Neill reprised her role as Lois Lane, once more playing the woman reporter with gusto. There was a modern touch, as at one point, Lane left her job at the *Daily Planet* to become a television personality. However, in actuality, she was only working undercover, trying to trap arch-villain, Lex Luthor.

Even though the popularity of the serials led to interest in creating a television show, when casting began for the television series, *Adventures of Superman*, none of the actors from the serials were chosen to repeat their parts. George Reeves became Superman and Phyllis Coates played Lois Lane. However, after one season, Coates left the show. At that point, it was natural to offer the role to Neill, who gladly accepted the part. The television show ran for six seasons in syndication, from 1952 to 1958. Neill played Lois Lane for the last five seasons.

Prior to receiving her first serial role as Lois Lane, Neill played in uncredited parts and in B-movies. She also appeared in a series of movies in the mid-1940s at Monogram, known as "The Teenagers," in which she played teenager Betty Rogers. She also had an uncredited part as a native girl in *Brick Bradford* (1947). After *Superman*, she appeared in two serials for Republic, as the female lead in their Jesse James series. The serials were *Adventures of Frank and Jesse James* (1948), where Neill played Judy Powell, and *The James Brothers of Missouri* (1949), where she played Peg Royer. The parts were unrelated. In the first of those two serials, her co-star was Clayton Moore.

Neill was not the only star associated with *Adventures of Superman* who had a background in serials. Phyllis Coates and George Reeves also appeared in serials, as discussed below. In addition, John Hamilton played Perry White in the television series. Hamilton's career in Hollywood started in the early 1930s. He was in over 200 movies, usually in small, uncredited parts. He had a number of small roles in serials, including playing the father of Noel Neill's character in *The James Brothers of Missouri* (1949). Hamilton's character was killed off in the first chapter. However, his best-remembered serial role was as Professor Gordon, the father of Flash Gordon, in *Flash Gordon Conquers the Universe* (1940).

Robert Shayne, who played Inspector Henderson on the *Superman* television show, also performed in serials, although in his case, it was during the run of the television show. He played Major Conroy in *Trader Tom of the China Seas* (1954) and Jess Carter in *King of the Carnival* (1955). That means that of the five principal actors on *Adventures of Superman*, only Jack Larson, who played Jimmy Olson, did not appear in a movie serial.

## George Reeves

Superman himself, George Reeves, also made an appearance in serials. Reeves starred in the 1949 Columbia serial, *The Adventures of Sir Galahad*, playing the lead part of Sir Galahad. This was a true Knights of the Round Table adventure, with Sir Galahad in a full length serial quest to recover the magical sword Excalibur. That was Reeves' only serial appearance.

Reeves professed to be embarrassed by his role in *Sir Galahad*, as well as his most famous role as Superman in the 1950s television series. Of course, other stars of the television show, Noel Neill, John Hamilton, Robert Shayne and Phyllis Coates, as well as many of the guest stars on the show, appeared in serials, so there was no reason for Reeves to be ashamed of that role. Prior to the roles in the serial and the television show, Reeves had mostly small parts in movies, most famously as one of the Tarleton twins in *Gone with the Wind* (1939). Indeed, Reeves is remembered today almost solely for the serial and television roles of which he complained so much.

## Milburn Stone

Milburn Stone was actually one of the stars of a television western series for longer than Clayton Moore and Duncan Renaldo combined. Stone played Doc Adams on *Gunsmoke* which ran on CBS for 20 years, from 1955 to 1975. Stone eventually won an Emmy for the role. Doc Adams always seemed old, irascible and crusty on the show, even in the early years. Thus, it is surprising for many to discover that Stone was a leading man in some B-movies in the 1940s and had several serial roles before he became a star on television.

His first serial role was for Mascot Pictures, in *The Fighting Marines* (1935). He played a minor henchman in the serial and did not receive screen credit, although he appeared in several chapters. His next serial-related role was as Skeeter Milligan, in four *Tailspin Tommy* features made for Monogram Studios in 1939. Tailspin Tommy was the subject of two prior serials for Universal.

Stone's first starring role in serials was as the lead in *The Great Alaskan Mystery*, a 1944 serial for Universal Pictures. Stone played the hero, Jim Hudson, who fought Nazi spies in Alaska over a death weapon called the Peragron. This was followed by *The Master Key*, in 1945, where Stone played the hero, Tom Brant, a government agent fighting the Nazis for

*The Master Key* (1945). For those fans of the television series *Gunsmoke* who are only familiar with Milburn Stone for playing crusty old Doc Adams for 20 years, they may be surprised to learn that Stone was a leading man in several B-movies, including this serial. Pictured from left to right are Alfred LaRue, Jan Wiley, Dennis Moore and Milburn Stone, who plays federal agent Tom Brent.

control of the Orotron machine, a device which could turn seawater into gold. Stone also had an important villain's role in *The Royal Mounted Rides Again* (1945), and was the narrator for *The Scarlet Horseman* (1946).

With the defeat of the Nazis in World War II, Stone's serial roles dried up. Thereafter, he continued to play parts, large and small, generally in B-movies or television, until receiving his signature role as Doc Adams in *Gunsmoke* in 1955.

Interestingly, other actors on *Gunsmoke* had a serial background. When Dennis Weaver, who played the limping deputy Chester, decided to leave the show in 1964, a new character was written into the show. The character was Deputy Festus Hagen, played by Ken Curtis. Festus was more of a comic figure than Chester, as the character was written as a scruffy, hillbilly type. Curtis played the role for eleven years, until the end of the series in 1975.

Curtis played the hero in one serial, *Don Daredevil Rides Again* (1951). This role was the opposite of the Festus character, with Don Daredevil being a masked hero, much like Zorro or the Lone Ranger, who protected ranchers against invalid claims against their lands. Curtis, who married director John Ford's daughter, was also known for his roles in about a dozen John Ford westerns from the 1950s and 1960s, generally performing in small parts. Before landing his role in *Gunsmoke*, Curtis starred in the syndicated television series, *Ripcord*, about a sky diving business, which ran for 76 episodes from 1961 to 1962.

Other serial regulars who were also regulars on *Gunsmoke* were Glenn Strange (*The Hurricane Express* (1932), *Riders of Death Valley* (1941), and many others), who played Sam, the Bartender, from 1961 to 1973, Roy Barcroft (*Radar Men from the Moon* (1952), *G-Men Never Forget* (1948), and many others), who played a townsperson on the show for a number of episodes in the mid-1960s, and Tom Brown (*The Adventures of Smilin' Jack* (1943)) who played a rancher on the show in the late 1960s.

## Walter Brennan

Walter Brennan may be somewhat forgotten today but he was an important featured performer in Hollywood for many years. He won three Academy Awards for Best Supporting Actor (*Come and Get It* (1936), *Kentucky* (1938) and *The Westerner* (1940)) and was nominated for that award for *Sergeant York* (1941). Other notable supporting roles of Brennan were in *Meet John Doe* (1941), *The Pride of the Yankees* (1942) and *To Have and Have Not* (1944). Brennan was always busy in Hollywood, playing in quality movies into the 1950s. With the advent of television, Brennan also began guesting on television shows. That led to one of his best-remembered roles, as Grandpa Amos McCoy, on *The Real McCoys*.

The show concerned a mountain family from West Virginia who moved to a ranch in Southern California where they became farmers. The family consisted of Luke (Richard Crenna), his new bride, Kate (Kathleen Nolan); Luke's teenage sister, Hassie, and Luke's 11-year-old brother, Little Luke. Another popular cast member was Pepino, the family's loyal farm hand. However, at the center of the show, and the undisputed star of the show, was Grandpa, played by Walter Brennan. Grandpa was a cantankerous old geezer who liked to meddle in everyone's affairs. As the theme song said, he "roars like a lion but he's gentle as a lamb."

*The Real McCoys* debuted on ABC in 1957 and ran for 224 episodes, into 1963. In 1962, the show moved to CBS. *The Real McCoys* started the trend toward rural comedy shows, and was a forerunner of shows such as *The Beverly Hillbillies* and *The Andy Griffith Show*.

Brennan also starred for two seasons, from 1967 to 1969, in a half hour western, *The Guns of Will Sonnett,* on ABC. The show told the adventures of Will Sonnett, (Walter Brennan) a retired army scout, and his grandson Jeff, (Dack Rambo) as they traveled throughout the West in search of the Jeff's father, James, a gunslinger on the run who abandoned his family twenty years before. Brennan's other television series was *The Tycoon*, which only lasted for one season, in 1964-65.

Brennan's career in films started in the silent era, when he received work as an extra. These uncredited roles continued into the sound era, including a bit part in *The Bride of Frankenstein* (1935). At the same time, Brennan was starting to receive some credited supporting roles.

During this era, Brennan appeared in three serials. The first was *The Airmail Mystery*, a 1932 serial from Universal, in which Brennan received a screen credit for the role of Holly. The following year, Brennan received a credit for the role of Skid in another Universal serial, *The Phantom of the Air*. Brennan's final serial appearance was an uncredited bit part in the Universal serial, *Tailspin Tommy* (1934). In Chapter Eight, Brennan played a hospital orderly who was punched by Skeeter Milligan.

**Marjorie Lord**

*Make Room for Daddy* was one of the most popular comedy shows of the 1950s. It began on ABC television in 1953, switched to CBS in 1957 and was continuously on the air until 1964, a total of twelve seasons. It starred Danny Thomas as a night club singer, and the comedy situations involved his job and his family. After the first four seasons, the show was known as *The Danny Thomas Show*.

Danny Thomas' first wife, Margaret, was played by Jean Hagen, a legitimate movie personality, best known for her role as silent film star, Lina Lamont, in *Singing in the Rain* (1952). When Hagen decided to leave the television series in 1956, the Margaret character was written out as having died. Danny Thomas became a widower.

Shortly after Margaret's death, son Rusty contracted measles. Williams employed a registered nurse, Kathy O'Hara, to help with Rusty. Williams and the nurse fell in love and married a year later. The show then focused on the new family: Danny Williams, with his son Rusty, and Kathy Williams, with her daughter, Linda. Danny's oldest daughter was soon written out of the show. Kathy Williams was played by Marjorie Lord.

Marjorie Lord's career in movies began in 1937, and was pretty much uninspired, although she did appear in a number of B-movies for Universal in the 1940s. One of her earliest screen appearances was in the role of Janet Thompson, in the Universal serial, *The Adventures of Smilin' Jack* (1942). This was a nothing part as she played the friend of the hero, with little to do other than accidentally give secrets to the villainess, Fraulein von Teufel. In terms of the female roles in the serial, Lord was overshadowed by Rose Hobart playing the evil German. There was no comedy associated with Lord's role so it is unlikely that this serial was any factor in Lord winning the role of Danny William's second wife in the long running television program.

## Lloyd Bridges

Lloyd Bridges was famous for both movie and television roles. In movies, he was a featured performer in several well-remembered films, such as *High Noon* (1952), playing Gary Cooper's unfaithful deputy, and *Airplane* (1980), playing McCroskey, an air traffic controller. Bridges is better known for his television roles, and in particular, *Sea Hunt*, a popular show which ran in syndication for four seasons, starting in 1958. Bridges played Mike Nelson, a professional scuba diver who had many undersea adventures. He chased criminals and conducted salvage and rescue operations, all related in some way to the sea. Bridges also starred in *The Lloyd Bridges Show*, an anthology series, which ran for one season beginning in 1962.

Lloyd Bridges made only one appearance in serials, but it was an important one. He starred as Phil Corrigan in *Secret Agent X-9*, a serial released by Universal in 1945. This is one of the best spy serials ever produced and Bridges was excellent as the heroic secret agent. This serial was made toward the end of Universal's serial production and perhaps that is why Bridges never made any more serials.

## Leonard Nimoy

Leonard Nimoy is best known for his role as Mr. Spock in the original *Star Trek* television series, which ran on NBC from 1966 through 1969, and thereafter non-stop in syndication. He also appeared in that same role in six *Star Trek* movies. His other notable television role was as Paris, for two seasons (1969-1971) on *Mission: Impossible*.

Nimoy's first science fiction adventure was the twelve chapter Republic serial, *Zombies of the Stratosphere*, released in 1952. It seemed that some evil Martians wanted to blast the planet Earth out of its orbit and replace it with Mars. Nimoy played Narab, one of those invading Martians. Hero Larry Martin was called in and he was able to thwart the plan of the invaders, without the help of Captain Kirk or Mr. Spock.

Nimoy was purportedly paid only $500 for his performance in this serial. For some reason, this serial did not turn Leonard Nimoy into a star. His work after that was mainly as a guest star in television programs, until he found his success many years later in *Star Trek*.

## Noah Berry, Jr.

Noah Berry, Jr., son of silent and sound movie supporting actor, Noah Berry, Sr. was best known to television audiences for his role as Joseph "Rocky" Rockford, the father of Jim Rockford on *The Rockford Files*, a detective show which ran on NBC for six seasons beginning in 1974. Jim Rockford was different from the usual private detective of mystery fiction. He had an answering machine instead of a secretary, seldom used a gun, and avoided fights whenever he could. Rockford, as played by James Garner, was a very human detective, with a sense of humor.

*Riders of Death Valley* (1941). In the trailer, each of the stars is identified with the characteristic he brought to the serial. The best they could come up with for Noah Berry, Jr. is "Youthful Recklessness."

There were a number of regulars on the show during its run, but the most endearing one was Rockford's father, Rocky Rockford. He was a former truck driver who was not always happy with his son's detective career. Their spats were a source of humor for the show but also fostered the human element of the younger detective. In some ways, Berry was playing Gardner's amiable sidekick, used in the stories partially for humor and partially for support.

Berry was a natural for the role, since he had been playing hero's sidekicks for years, especially in his serial work. Thus, in *Tailspin Tommy* (1934), Berry played Skeeter Milligan, the sidekick for the title hero. Berry was so good in that role that he was the only principal to return in the sequel, *Tailspin Tommy in the Great Air Mystery* (1935). Other serial sidekick roles for Berry occurred in *Ace Drummond* (1936), *Riders of Death Valley* (1941) and *Overland Mail* (1942).

Surprisingly, Berry had two early serial appearances as the hero of the story. In *Heroes of the West* (1932), he played the young lead of the serial, helping to build a transcontinental railroad. In *The Call of the Savage* (1935), Berry played Jan, a jungle boy, involved in a search for a secret formula in the jungle. In all, Berry appeared in ten serials.

Another interesting serial connection for Berry was that he married the daughter of Buck Jones, the famous cowboy star who appeared in six serials. Berry and Jones appeared together in *Riders of Death Valley* (1941).

## Others

The king of the serials, Buster Crabbe, starred in *Captain Gallant of the Foreign Legion*, which ran on NBC from 1955 to 1957. The show was about an officer in the French Foreign Legion whose forces battled bandit tribes in Northern Africa. In addition, the Captain's son, Cuffy, lived with Gallant at the Legion fort. Cuffy was played by Crabbe's real-life son, Cullen. Fuzzy Knight, who had supporting roles in *The Oregon Trail* (1939) and *The Great Alaskan Mystery* (1944), played Private Fuzzy Knight in the television show.

Reed Hadley, who had some small roles in serials, such as a henchman's role in *Sky Raiders* (1941), is best known in serials for portraying the title character in *Zorro's Fighting Legion* (1939). There he played the dual role of the masked hero and his true identity of Don Diego Vega. In the 1950s, Hadley starred in two television series. The better known was *Racket Squad*, which ran for three seasons on CBS beginning in 1951. Much like *Dragnet*, the show was a police procedural based on actual case files related to the confidence racket. Hadley played Captain John Braddock, who was both the narrator and star of the show. When that show was canceled, Hadley starred in *The Public Defender*, a short-lived series which ran on CBS starting in 1954.

The Disney-produced television series *Zorro* ran on the ABC television network from 1957 to 1959, with four hour episodes shown in later years on *Walt Disney Presents*. The part of Zorro's father, Don Alejandro la Vega, was played by veteran serial actor George J. Lewis. For most of the series, Alejandro was not aware that his son, Don Diego de la Vega, was secretly Zorro, and Diego's apparent cowardice caused friction within the family. Interestingly, among Lewis' many serial roles was the part of Moccasin, Zorro's assistant in *Ghost of Zorro* (1949), and the part of government agent Vic Gordon, who aided the Black Whip in *Zorro's Black Whip* (1944). In *Ghost of Zorro* (and even in *Zorro's Black Whip* although the heroine was not named Zorro), Lewis donned the black garb in order to protect the masked hero, meaning that Lewis actually played Zorro in the movies before appearing as Zorro's father in the television series.

Smiley Burnette provided the comic relief in a number of serials, such as *The Undersea Kingdom* (1935) and *Dick Tracy* (1937). On television, he was a regular, although in a minor part, on *Petticoat Junction*, which ran on CBS from 1963 to 1970. An important element of the show was the Hooterville Cannonball, a steam train that ran from Sam Drucker's store in Hooterville to the Shady Rest Hotel, which was operated by Kate Bradley and her three pretty daughters. The Cannonball was run by engineers Floyd Smoot and Charlie Pratt. Pratt was played by Smiley Burnette from the beginning of the series until his death in 1967.

Rin-Tin-Tin, the star of many movie serials in the early 1930s, also had a long running television series, which was titled *The Adventures of Rin-Tin-Tin*. The series ran from 1954 to 1959 on ABC. In the first episode, a United States Cavalry troop discovered the remains of a wagon train attacked by Apache Indians. The only survivors were Rusty (Lee Aaker) and his German shepherd dog. The two were taken to Fort Apache by Lt. Rip Masters (James L. Brown) where Rusty was raised by soldiers at a cavalry post. The show was about the western adventures of Rusty and his dog, Rin-Tin-Tin, as they helped to establish law and order in old Arizona. Three German Shepherds played Rinty. Two of them were descendants of the original movie canine.

Ralph Byrd, who played Dick Tracy, among other serial heroes, starred in the television show, *Dick Tracy*, which ran on ABC starting in 1950. Although Tracy did battle with some of the famous comic strip villains, such as The Mole and Pruneface, this was apparently a low budget show with more talk than action. The show only lasted for one season on the network. Byrd continued to make shows for syndication until his death in 1952.

An interesting career twist involved William Tracy, who played young Terry Lee in the 1940 serial, *Terry and the Pirates*. Tracy was 23 years old at the time. In 1953, there was an 18 episode syndicated television show of the comic strip, in which Tracy played Hotshot Charlie, the friend of Terry Lee. Both were grown-ups in the series.

The half hour show, *Circus Boy*, ran on NBC for two seasons from 1956 to 1958. A ten year old boy, Corky Wallace, whose parents died in a high wire act, was adopted by the circus' owner, Big Tim Champion. The weekly show was about the travails of the circus and Corky's involvement with them. Mickey Braddock, who played Corky on the show, used his real name, Micky Dolenz, when he became a part of the singing group, the Monkees, who had their own television series in the 1960s. Other cast members of *Circus Boy* included Uncle Joey, a clown, and Pete, another circus employee. Big Tim Champion was played by Robert Lowery, best known to serial fans for playing Batman in *Batman and Robin* (1949). Lowery also starred in *Mystery of the River Boat* (1944) and *The Monster and the Ape* (1945). Pete was played by Guinn Williams, usually billed in movies as Guinn "Big Boy" Williams. He appeared in three serials, *The Mystery Squadron* (1933), *The Vigilantes Are Coming* (1936) and *Riders of Death Valley* (1941). Uncle Joey was played by Noah Berry, Jr., whose serial and television careers were discussed earlier in this chapter.

George Cleveland, who had small roles in many serials, such as *Robinson Crusoe of Clipper Island* (1936), *Flash Gordon* (1936), *The Lone Ranger* (1938) and *Drums of Fu Manchu* (1940), is best known to television viewers for his role as Gramps, on the original *Lassie* television show, known in syndication as *Jeff's Collie*. Cleveland appeared on the show from 1954 until his sudden death in 1957.

Stanley Andrews, who had small roles in a number of serials, but who also played the lead villain in *The Lone Ranger* serial (1938), hosted the western anthology show, *Death Valley Days*, playing the Old Ranger, from 1952 to 1964. The series was supposedly based on true stories which occurred in the desolation of Death Valley, California. The show, which ran in syndication for many more years after Andrews left the show, was subsequently hosted for two years by Ronald Reagan, just before he became governor of California.

Character actor William Fawcett had a number of serial roles in cliffhangers such as Merlin in *The Adventures of Sir Galahad* (1939) and the High Priest in *King of the Congo* (1952). However, he is probably best known to serial watchers for his portrayal of Professor Hammill, who may or may not have been the Wizard, in *Batman and Robin* (1949). Fawcett made many guest appearances on television shows in the 1950s. He was also a regular on *Fury*, the story of a horse and the boy who loved him, which ran on NBC on Saturday mornings for five years starting in 1955. The show was about an orphan, Joey (Bobby Diamond), who was adopted by a recently widowed rancher, Jim (Peter Graves), and the wild stallion that Jim had captured. Fawcett played Pete Wilkey, the ranch foreman, throughout the run of the series.

Keye Luke, who was a featured performer in five serials at Universal in the 1940s, was a regular on *Kung Fu*, the television series which ran on CBS for three seasons, from 1972 to 1975. The show related the story of Kwai Chang Caine, the orphaned son of a Chinese woman and an American man. Caine was raised by monks and trained to be a Shaolin master, an expert in Kung Fu. However, after an incident where he killed the Emperor's nephew, Caine fled China and arrived in the American west in the late 1800s. There he discovered he had a half-brother, Danny. While searching for his brother, Caine was chased by Chinese assassins and American bounty hunters and became involved in other western disputes. At those times of trouble, Caine thought back to his training at the monastery by his teachers, one of whom was the blind Master Po, played by Keye Luke in flashbacks.

Gordon Jones, who played the title character in *The Green Hornet* (1939) but not in the sequel, played Mike the cop on *The Abbott and Costello Show*, which ran for two seasons, in syndication, from 1952 to 1953. Richard Simmons, who had the title role in *Man with the Steel Whip* (1954), is best-remembered as playing the title role in *Sergeant Preston of the Yukon*, which ran on CBS for 78 episodes from 1955 to 1958. Preston was a member of the Royal Northwest Mounted Police who was assisted by his dog, Yukon King and his black horse, Rex. Jock Mahoney, who starred in three serial westerns for Columbia in the 1950s, starred in the syndicated western series, *The Range Rider*, from 1951 to 1953, playing the hero.

Gabriel Dell, one of the Dead End Kids, and therefore a performer in three serials at Universal, was a regular on Steve Allen's television shows in the late 1950s. Dell was best known for his impersonations of Count Dracula. Kenneth MacDonald, a villain in such serials as *The Phantom* (1943), switched to the side of law and order to portray a judge in many episodes of the *Perry Mason* television series in the 1950s and 1960s. Allan "Rocky" Lane, who had starring roles in several series, including the role of Jeff King in *King of the Royal Mounted* (1940) and *King of the Mounties* (1942), provided the voice for Mr. Ed, the talking horse, in the television series, *Mr. Ed*, which ran on CBS from 1961 to 1965.

In the early 1950s, Warren Hull, who once played the Green Hornet, the Spider and Mandrake the Magician, hosted a game show called *Strike It Rich* where contestants down on their luck would tell their sad story (such as a house fire, a terminal disease or the like) in the hopes that a local merchant would call in and donate a needed item to the pathetic contestant, which always seemed to occur. Jimmie Dodd, who performed on stage in *Mystery of the River Boat* (1944), was the adult leader of the Mouseketeers in *The Mickey Mouse Club*, which ran on ABC television on weekday afternoons for several seasons in the mid-1950s. Lyle Talbot, a serial regular, who among many roles played Lex Luthor in *Atom Man vs. Superman* (1950) played neighbor Joe Randolph for over ten years on *The Adventures of Ozzie and* Harriet, beginning in 1956. Virginia Christine, who was the main villain in *The Scarlet Horseman* (1946) and a henchwoman in *Raiders of Ghost City* (1944), was best known to television viewers for her role as Mrs. Olsen in a long running series of television commercials for Folger's Coffee in the 1960s and 1970s.

## IV. BEFORE AND AFTER THEY WERE FOOTBALL STARS

It was not unusual for "real people" to star in serials. Harry Houdini, the famous magician, starred in a fifteen chapter silent serial titled *The Master Mystery* (1920). Famous animal trainer Clyde Beatty appeared in *The Lost Jungle* (1934) and *Darkest Africa* (1936). Animal collector and zookeeper Frank Buck starred in *Jungle Menace* (1934).

Additionally, there were several serial stars, including Herman Brix and Johnny Mack Brown, who were football stars in college. There were only three, however, who were bona fide football stars in both college and the professional ranks.

## Red Grange

*The Galloping Ghost* (1931) brought famous football player Harold "Red" Grange to the screen in his only serial. Grange had previously appeared in some silent films. In the serial, Grange played a college football star, coincidentally with the name "Red Grange," who was first accused of gambling on football games and then of murder. By the end of the serial, Grange managed to clear his name in time to lead his school, Clay College, to an important victory over the rival Trojans.

Grange, whose nickname in real life was "The Galloping Ghost," thus providing the title for this serial, was a halfback for the University of Illinois where he played for three seasons from 1923 to 1925. In his very first college game, Grange scored three touchdowns. He only played 20 games in college but had 31 touchdowns and ran for a total 3,362 yards.

Grange signed with the Chicago Bears right out of college and played most of his professional career with that team. He was best at running the ball, but he was also great at passing, kicking, and defense. He was the biggest drawing card of the NFL in the early days of the league. Red Grange was still a professional football player for the Chicago Bears when *The Galloping Ghost* was made. He did not retire from professional football until 1934.

Grange became a charter member of both the College and Pro Football Halls of Fame. At Super Bowl XII in the Louisiana Superdome in 1978 (Dallas 27, Denver 10), Grange was given the honor of conducting the opening coin toss. He died in 1991 at the age of 87.

## Ernie Nevers

With the success of Red Grange in *The Galloping Ghost* (1931), it was natural for another studio to employ another famous football player as one of the leads in a serial. In this case it was Ernie Nevers, a star in both college and professional football.

Nevers played his college football at Stanford University, where he was an All-American. He was the hero of the 1925 Rose Bowl, where, although his team lost to Notre Dame, Nevers rushed for 114 yards on sore ankles that had been broken earlier in the season.

After he finished his Stanford career, Nevers signed professional basketball and baseball contracts. However, Nevers made his true name in professional sports in football. In 1926, Nevers turned pro with the NFL's Duluth Eskimos, with whom he played for two seasons. He sat out the 1928 season because of injuries and then returned to professional football with the Chicago Cardinals, where he played for three seasons, from 1929-1931. In the latter two seasons he was the player-coach. On November 28, 1929, Nevers set a league record by scoring all of his team's points, with six touchdowns and four extra point conversions as his team walloped the Chicago Bears, 40-6.

Nevers became a charter member of both the College Football Hall of Fame (1951) and the Pro Football Hall of Fame (1963). After his professional football career ended, Nevers starred in *The Lost Special* (1932) playing one of the heroes. He had a few other bit parts in movies but no other serial appearances.

### Slingin' Sammy Baugh

With *King of the Texas Rangers* (1941), "Slingin' Sammy" Baugh joined Red Grange and Ernie Nevers as a serial star who eventually became a charter member of both the College and Professional Football Halls of Fame. Baugh attended Texas Christian University on a baseball scholarship, but he also played football and basketball at the university. He was an All-American quarterback, leading TCU to bowl victories in his final two seasons.

In 1937, Baugh signed with the Washington Redskins, becoming the highest paid football player in the National Football League up until that time. He made $8,000 in his first season. Over time he was a quarterback, defensive back and one of the best punters ever. He is still the only player to lead the league in passing, punting and interceptions in the same season.

Because of his celebrity status in football, Republic approached him about appearing in *King of the Texas Rangers* and Baugh agreed. Filming took place for six weeks during the summer of 1941, so as not to interfere with his football season. Baugh was an accomplished horseback rider and did his own riding in the serial, except for the dangerous stunts. Although offered more roles by Republic, Baugh declined and so *King of the Texas Rangers* was his only film role, except for a small bit along with other professional football players in the feature *Triple Threat* (1948).

Baugh retired from professional football in 1952 after 16 seasons with the Washington Redskins. He was inducted into the Professional Football Hall of Fame as one of 17 charter members when it was established in 1963. He was also elected to the College Football Hall of Fame in 1951.

## IV. AFTER THEY WERE TELEVISION STARS

By the time most television stars might have been ready to return to serial work, serials were no longer being made in Hollywood. There were two exceptions: Clayton Moore and Phyllis Coates.

As noted above, Moore had a dispute with the producers of *The Lone Ranger* television show and he left the series in 1952. Moore was never a top movie star and he had few alternatives to continue working. He appeared in some other television shows, some B-movies and also returned to serials. His first serial at that time was *Radar Men from the Moon* (1952) for Republic Pictures. Moore was not even the star of that chapter play; he performed the role of the main henchmen. Moore then appeared in three other serials before returning to *The Lone Ranger* television series.

Phyllis Coates played Lois Lane during the first season (1952-53) of *Adventures of Superman*. She left the series at the end of the first season, either for personal reasons or to take the starring role in a proposed new

*Jungle Drums of Africa* (1953). This Republic serial stars two former television stars, Phyllis Coates, from *Adventures of Superman*, and Clayton Moore, from *The Lone Ranger*. By the time this serial was released, Moore was back on his television show. Pictured on the far right is Johnny Spencer.

series, which never made it to the air. Much like Moore, without a regular television series, Coates was relegated to other television guest appearances, B-movies and serials.

Her most famous serial role was the part of Jean Evans, *The Panther Girl of the Kongo*, in the 1955 serial from Republic Pictures. There she played a beautiful woman, raised in the jungle, who was also a documentary filmmaker. Her other serial roles were the female leads in *Jungle Drums of Africa* (1953) and *Gunfighters of the Northwest* (1954) both with Clayton Moore. In the latter serial, despite a high billing, Coates had a particularly small role.

## VI. AFTER THEY WERE MOVIE STARS

Generally, when a serial performer made it big in the movies, the actor or actress never returned to serials. Even George Brent, who turned to B-movies when his career faltered in the late 1940s, and Gene Autry, who only made B-movies, never made another serial once each became a star. Boris Karloff, even though he generally made only horror films and B-movies throughout his career, never returned to serials after his success in *Frankenstein* (1931).

As noted above, Misha Auer, Ruth Roman, Lola Lane and George Montgomery never quite became movie stars after their serial appearances. Although they did have significant film roles, they were generally no more than featured performers in the movies. However, none of them returned to the serial genre after achieving some success in Hollywood.

There were, however, some exceptions to the rule. For example, as noted above, Lon Chaney, Jr. made *Overland Mail* (1942) after his success in *The Wolf Man* (1941). The following are some of the other exceptions.

### Bela Lugosi

Orson Welles once said, commenting on his first film, *Citizen Kane* (1941), and his inability to top that film during his later film career, "I started at the top and worked down." The same, unfortunately, can be said for Bela Lugosi. His first major screen appearance was as the title character in *Dracula* (1931). The film made him an instant star. He then made some terrible career choices, such as turning down the role of the monster in

*Frankenstein* (1931) and then appearing in minor horror films or in supporting roles in other types of films. Indeed, in Lugosi's second major horror film, *Murders in the Rue Morgue* (1931), Lugosi received second billing to the unknown female lead, Sydney Fox. Feeling monetary constraints, Lugosi then started appearing in serials, and not even ones produced by Universal, the studio that had made him a star.

The first serial for Lugosi was *The Whispering Shadow*, released by Mascot Pictures in 1933, just two years after the release of *Dracula*. Lugosi played the role of Professor Anton Strang, the operator of a wax museum, who could be a master criminal. Lugosi followed that serial with one of the best-remembered roles that Lugosi ever had, as the title character in *The Return of Chandu*, a 1934 serial released by Principal Pictures.

Here, Lugosi, who was a romantic lead on the Hungarian stage, had his only opportunity in his long career to portray the romantic hero in a film. Chandu, of course, was not your normal romantic hero. Chandu was a master hypnotist and with the help of his yogi, he could perform feats of real

*The Return of Chandu* (1934). This was Bela Lugosi's only hero's role in his long screen career. Pictured in the main part of the card is Murdoch McQuarrie as the leader of the Ubasti, who is explaining to Maria Alba (Princess Nadji) that the Ubasti intend to kill Nadji and transfer her soul to the prone Princess Ossana, bringing Ossana back to life.

magic. All of these powers were needed as Chandu fought the ancient Ubasti who were after the soul of Princess Nadji, who was Chandu's girl friend. All went well, Chandu triumphed in the end and Lugosi even got the girl.

Lugosi's career was then revived somewhat at Universal and he appeared in three horror films with Boris Karloff. Toward the end of that horror cycle, Lugosi appeared in his third serial, *Shadow of Chinatown*, released by Victory Pictures in 1936. Here, Lugosi returned to a life of crime, as the evil Victor Poten, trying to destroy the Oriental trade in America.

Lugosi's next serial, *SOS Coast Guard* (1937), from Republic Pictures, was the best serial in which he ever appeared. He played the main criminal, Boroff, who was a mad scientist who had invented a disintegration gas which he was trying to sell to a foreign power. Hot on his trail was Terry Kent of the Coast Guard, played by Ralph Byrd.

Lugosi's final serial role was in *The Phantom Creeps*. It was released in 1939 and was the only serial Lugosi made for Universal, even though Lugosi had been one of the studio's biggest stars and Universal made many serials during the 1930s and 1940s. This serial was unusual in that it spent more time with the villain than with the hero. Lugosi therefore had one of his largest film roles, playing Dr. Alex Zorka, another mad scientist with a vendetta against society.

There was a horror film revival in 1939 and Lugosi had some good roles in the horror movies over the next decade, such as in *Son of Frankenstein* (1939), *Ghost of Frankenstein* (1942), *Return of the Vampire* (1944), and *Abbott and Costello Meet Frankenstein* (1948). However, most of Lugosi's roles during this time period until his death in 1956 were in B-movies or worse. Nevertheless, he never returned to the serial genre, which gave him some of his best roles, after he was no longer a star.

### Lionel Atwill

Lionel Atwill's career paralleled Lugosi's career somewhat, although Atwill's fall from stardom was not quite so precipitous. After appearing in a few silent films, Atwill starred in a number of films in the early 1930s, including two of Warner Brothers' most famous horror films, *Doctor X* (1932) and *Mystery of the Wax Museum* (1933). Throughout the 1930s, Atwill had good roles in important pictures with important stars such as *The Song of Songs* (1933) (Marlene Dietrich), *Stamboul Quest* (1934) (Myrna Loy), *The Age of Innocence* (1934) (Irene Dunne) and *Captain Blood* (1935) (Errol Flynn).

*Captain America* (1944). Even in this tame shot, Lionel Atwill exudes evil, playing the villainous Dr. Maldor, who is also the Scarab. *Captain America* was one of the four serials in which Atwill appeared, always as the main villain.

By the end of the 1930s, Atwill tended to be relegated to less important films, such as horror films and B-movie mysteries. These are, however, some of the roles he is best-remembered for today. They included *Son of Frankenstein* (1939), as Inspector Krogh with his false arm, *Man Made Monster* (1941) as mad scientist Paul Rigas who decided to perform electrical experiments on "Dynamo Dan" McCormick (Lon Chaney, Jr.) and *Sherlock Holmes and the Secret Weapon* (1943), as Professor Moriarty. Around Christmas, 1940, Atwill became involved in a sex scandal which occurred at his home, finishing any possibility that Atwill had of returning to stardom in A-Movies.

Shortly thereafter, Atwill made his first of four appearances in serials, always as the villain. Atwill's first cliffhanger was *Junior G-men of the Air* (1942) where Atwill played a Japanese spy chief named the "Baron." Despite being the main villain's role, it was a relatively small part.

In 1944, Atwill moved to Republic for what was Atwill's best serial role, playing respectable Dr. Maldor in *Captain America*. Maldor was in reality the particularly villainous "Scarab," out to steal devious devices such as a thermodynamic vibrator which could disintegrate all known materials.

Atwill then appeared in *Raiders of Ghost City* (1944), playing the villainous Alex Morel, a Prussian spy, who was stealing gold so that his country could purchase Alaska from the Russians. This was an excellent role for Atwill even though this was an atypical western for him. Luckily, Atwill never wore cowboy clothes or rode a horse, and thus he was able to remain convincing, as he always was, playing the main villain.

Atwill's final serial role could have been his best. He played Sir Eric Hazarias in *Lost City of the Jungle* (1946). Hazarias was a villain who was after the only antidote for the atomic bomb. Unfortunately, Atwill died during filming and a number of his best lines were then given to a different character. In addition, a double and stock footage had to be used in place of Atwill in other scenes in the serial.

**Tom Mix**

Tom Mix was the greatest cowboy star of the silent cinema, and with all respect to John Wayne, Gene Autry and Roy Rogers, perhaps of all time. He started in silent films as early as 1909, making shorts of from ten to twenty minutes in length. As his popularity grew, he began appearing in feature films, of about one hour in length. He performed in over 300 silent films. By the end of his silent movie career in 1929, Mix was 49 years old.

While many stars of silent films continued their movie careers into talking pictures, others had trouble making the cut, and if they continued to make films at all, ended their careers in B-movies and serials. This was obviously a step down for those actors as serials did not have the prestige of major silent films or, for that matter, the westerns of the silent era.

In the early days of sound movies, Mix did not make films, as he had a successful career headlining the Sells-Floto-Circus, which was a Wild West show. Mix had been a champion rodeo rider in his younger days. In 1932, Universal Studios enticed him back to the picture business and gave him relatively large budgets for a series of westerns. After making nine films for Universal, Mix decided to retire from the cinema.

Mix was then coaxed back to the big screen for one more performance by Nat Levine, who wanted Mix for one of Mascot Pictures' last serials, *The Miracle Rider* (1935). Mix readily agreed to appear, as he was paid $40,000 for four weeks of work. Even at the age of 55, Mix was still a true star of the cinema, lending his considerable screen presence to this modern western, complete with cars, a rocket and even text messaging and cell phones. This was the last screen appearance of Mix, who ended his career performing in Wild West shows in a circus he owned. Mix died in a car crash in 1940.

## Jackie Cooper

Jackie Cooper, who was born in 1922, began appearing in the *Our Gang* comedies in 1929, working in many of the short films over the next two years. Paramount Pictures then signed Cooper to the title role in the film, *Skippy* (1931), which earned him an Oscar nomination at the age of nine. Recognizing his star potential, MGM then signed Cooper to a contract. Over the next several years, he made five pictures with Wallace Berry, such as *The Champ* (1931), *The Bowery* (1933) and *Treasure Island* (1934).

By 1939, Cooper was 17 years old and no longer the child star with the winsome, pouty look. That probably explains his appearance in *Scouts to the Rescue*, a Universal serial from 1939, about a troop of Boy Scouts who battled Indians and counterfeiters. Cooper had the lead role as one of the Boy Scouts. Cooper still had enough star quality that he was billed above the title.

After *Scouts*, Cooper continued to appear in minor films until his career was interrupted by World War II. Thereafter, Cooper did substantial television work, both as a guest star and as a regular on *The People's Choice* (1955-1958), where he played a politician with a dog named Cleo whose thoughts could be heard by the audience and *Hennesey* (1959-1962), where he played an onshore navy doctor. Thereafter, Cooper directed a number of television shows. In 1978, Cooper received the acting role for which he is best known today, playing Perry White in the Christopher Reeves *Superman* series.

## Mae Clarke

Mae Clarke was never a major star in Hollywood although she did have some starring roles in films during the early 1930s, such as the female lead in James Whale's *Waterloo Bridge* (1931). Clarke is better-remembered for some of the smaller roles she had in films. Probably her most famous movie scene was in *Public Enemy* (1931), when Jimmy Cagney pushed a grapefruit into her face. As famous as the role was, Clarke did not receive a screen credit in the film. Her other famous role was as Elizabeth, the fiancée of Dr. Frankenstein in *Frankenstein* (1931). In that movie, her most famous scene was when she had the misfortune of being surprised by the monster on her wedding day.

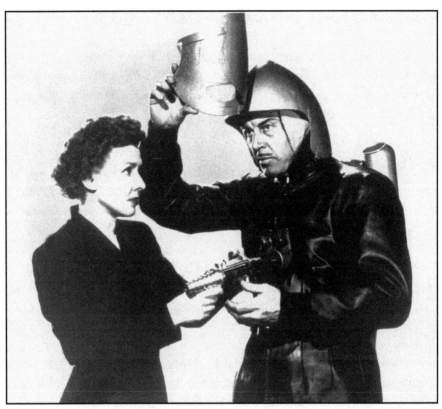

*King of the Rocket Men* (1949). Pictured are Mae Clarke, in her only serial role and Tristam Coffin, a serial regular, but in an unusual hero's role as Jeff King, the Rocket Man.

By the 1940s, Clarke was receiving only sporadic, small roles in movies. Her only memorable role during the decade was as the female lead in the Republic serial, *King of the Rocket Men* (1949), assisting Jeff King in his fight against the evil Dr. Vulcan. At the time of the release of that serial, Clarke was 39 years of age, which was much older than most female leads in serials. For example, Jean Rogers was only 22 years old when she made her last serial, Linda Stirling was only 26, and Noel Neill was only 30.

In this serial, because of the number of years that had gone by and her change from blond to dark hair, Clarke was virtually unrecognizable from her early film roles. After that one serial appearance, many of Clarke's later roles were as a guest star on television programs. She died in 1992.

## VII. OSCAR, TONY AND EMMY AWARD WINNERS

Although serials were low prestige work for performers, a number went on to win Hollywood's highest award, the Academy Award. John Wayne, who appeared in three serials for Mascot in the early 1930s, won the Academy Award for Best Actor for *True Grit* in 1969.

As noted above, Jennifer Jones, who had a small role in *Dick Tracy's G-Men* (1939) under her real name, Phyllis Isley, won the Academy Award for Best Actress for *Song of Bernadette* (1943). Walter Brennan, who had small roles in three serials in the early 1930s, won the Academy Award for Best Supporting Actor on three occasions. The films were: *Come and Get it* (1936), *Kentucky* (1938) and *The Westerner* (1940).

Franz Waxman never officially composed the score for a serial but his scores for *The Bride of Frankenstein* (1935) and other Universal Pictures were used in Universal serials. For example, parts of the score for *The Bride of Frankenstein* appeared in *Flash Gordon's Trip to Mars* (1938). Waxman won the Academy Award for Best Score in 1950 for *Sunset Boulevard* and in 1951 for *A Place in the Sun*.

Yakima Canutt, who appeared in numerous serials as an actor or a stunt man, and also co-directed a number of serials, received an Honorary Oscar in 1966. The award was for his achievements as a stunt man and for developing safety devices to protect stunt men everywhere.

Robert Boyle, who was the art director on *Don Winslow of the Navy* (1942), was awarded an Honorary Academy Award in 2008. The award was in recognition for one of the great film careers in art direction.

Mickey Rooney, who had a bit role in *The Lost Jungle* (1934), received a special Academy Award in 1938, along with Deanna Durbin, for their significant contribution in bringing to the screen the spirit and personification of youth, and as juvenile players setting a high standard of ability and achievement. Rooney also received an Honorary Oscar in 1983 for 50 years of versatility in a variety of memorable film performances.

Cy Feuer won the Tony Award, which is the Broadway equivalent of the Academy Award, for best producer of a musical in 1962, for *How to Succeed in Business without Really Trying*, That musical won the award for Best Musical as did another Broadway musical produced by Feuer, *Guys and Dolls*, in 1951. Feuer was nominated for a Tony Award several other times and in 2003 he received a Special Lifetime Achievement Award.

After graduating from Juilliard and working in the Roxy and Radio City Music Hall orchestras, Feuer came to Republic in the late 1930s, where he served as head of its music department until 1947, with a break during World War II. While at Republic, he composed the music for a number of serials, including *Drums of Fu Manchu* (1940), *Adventures of Red Ryder* (1940) and *King of the Royal Mounted* (1940).

In terms of Emmys, considered the highest award in television, there were several nominations over the years for former serial performers but only one award for performances in a regular series. That went to Milburn Stone, for Outstanding Performance for an Actor in a Supporting Role, in a Drama, for his portrayal of Doc Adams, in *Gunsmoke*, in 1968. Mickey Rooney also won an Emmy for outstanding acting in 1982 for the special, *Bill*, which was a television movie.

Child actor Jackie Cooper, who starred in *Scouts to the Rescue* (1939), made regular guest appearances on television and also starred in two television series, *The People's Choice* and *Hennesey*. Cooper never won an Emmy for those acting appearances, although he was nominated twice for *Hennesey*. He did, however, win Emmys for Best Director, for *M\*A\*S\*H* (1974) and *The White Shadow* (1979).

# Chapter 10
## Prolific Contributors To Serials

**The faces** of the serial were the performers who played the heroes on numerous occasions, such as Buster Crabbe, Tom Tyler and Kane Richmond or those who often played the heroine, such as Jean Rogers, Linda Stirling and Lucile Browne, or even those who played the villains on numerous occasions, such as Charles Middleton, Roy Barcroft or Walter Miller. There were, however, numerous individuals who made prolific contributions to serials, as producers, directors and character actors, who are not all that well-known to serial fans. This is a look at some of those unsung, yet important contributors to the sound movie serial.

## I. INFLUENTIAL PRODUCERS OF SERIALS

While a substantial number of serials were produced by a limited number of individuals, three of them, Nat Levine from Mascot, Henry MacRae from Universal and Sam Katzman from Columbia, stand out as the most influential producers of serials. Their collective influence extended from the beginning of the sound era to the end of serial production in the 1950s.

### Nat Levine
Nat Levine was born in New York City in 1899. When he dropped out of high school at the age of 14, Levine began working in the Loews theater chain, where he learned as much as he could about filmmaking. He worked his way up from work in the accounting department to becoming the personal secretary of the owner. In 1926, Levine, using the knowledge he had obtained over the years, produced a silent serial, *The Silent Flyer*, which was released by Universal Pictures. Levine made a quick $5000.00 for his efforts.

Recognizing the profitability of serials, Levine formed Mascot Pictures, a small studio which specialized in serials. The studio produced six silent serials and 24 sound serials, along with a few feature films. During the early sound era, it was Nat Levine at Mascot and Henry MacRae at Universal who kept the serial genre alive as none of the major studios produced serials and the other independent studios only produced a handful.

Levine can take credit for a number of important innovations or developments in the serial form. He pioneered the early use of sound, in the partially-talking serial, *King of the Kongo* (1929) and in some of the first all-talking serials, *The Lone Defender* (1930) and *Phantom of the West* (1930). In addition to giving John Wayne and Gene Autry some of their earliest screen appearances, he convinced Tom Mix to make one final screen appearance in Mascot's only 15 chapter serial, *The Miracle Rider* (1935). He also brought "real" people to the serials, such as Red Grange in *The Galloping Ghost* (1931) and Clyde Beatty in *The Lost Jungle* (1934). When Warner Brothers dropped Rin-Tin-Tin from its star line-up, Levine was quick to bring the famous canine to Mascot, where he starred in two serials.

*The Fighting Marines* (1935). In this last serial produced by Nat Levine for Mascot, Corporal Lawrence and Sergeant McGowan have captured Buchanan, who they believe is the villainous Tiger Shark. Pictured from left to right are Grant Withers, Frank Glendon and Adrian Morris.

In 1936, Mascot merged with other studios to form Republic Pictures. Levine's interest in the studio was soon bought out by Herbert Yates of CFI and although Levine thereafter worked for MGM for a short period of time, he was out of the motion picture business by the mid-1940s. However, the production team he organized at Mascot continued on at Republic, with actors, directors and technical staff originally from Mascot greatly influencing the Republic serial product over many years. In some ways, that may be his greatest legacy in the serial field. Nat Levine died in 1989 at the age of 90.

## Henry MacRae

Henry MacRae directed both silent and sound serials at Universal. He is better known today, though, as a producer of serials at Universal. MacRae was listed as the producer or associate producer on just about every serial released by Universal from 1930 until *Mystery of the River Boat* (1944), which was just about the entire sound serial product of Universal. In fact, MacRae died of a heart attack shortly before the completion of *Mystery of the River Boat* or he probably would have produced all of the remaining serials of Universal.

Henry MacRae was born in 1876 in Toronto, Canada. He came to Universal Studios around 1910 and by 1913 was the director general of production, approving projects brought to the studio by individual producers. MacRae was an innovator, being the first to use artificially lighted interiors, first to shoot outdoors at night and the first to use a wind machine in a movie. While it was Nat Levine who first used sound in serials at Mascot, MacRae produced the first very popular sound serial, *The Indians Are Coming* (1930). Universal gave the serial full promotional support and it made almost a million dollars in profit. Will Hays, the Postmaster General and soon to be censor of the movies, congratulated MacRae on bringing children back to the cinema. MacRae therefore ensured that serials would continue into the sound era.

In the mid-1930s, as serials were starting to lose their popularity, MacRae came up with the idea of basing serials on comic strip characters, who already had a built-in following. The first was *Tailspin Tommy* (1934) and then because of that chapter play's success, others such as *Ace Drummond* (1936) and *Radio Patrol* (1937) followed. MacRae also pushed the studio to adapt *Flash Gordon* for the screen and was able to convince the studio to invest in a large budget for the serial. The result was one of the most successful and entertaining serials of all time. As a result of MacRae's ideas, the serial form not only survived in the early sound era, it flourished.

MacRae continued to produce serials into the 1940s, emphasizing plot over cliffhangers. He was the producer or associate producer on over 50 serials, more than any other person. By the end of his life, he was the oldest living active movie producer. He died in 1944. There is a further discussion of Henry MacRae's life and work in serials in the next section of this chapter which concerns influential directors of serials.

### Sam Katzman

If Nat Levine and Henry MacRae kept the serial form going in the early 1930s, Sam Katzman must be credited with keeping the genre moving in the late 1940s and early 1950s. Katzman was born in 1901 in New York City. At the age of 13, he started as a prop boy in the movie industry at Fox Film Corporation. He worked his way up the film industry ladder and by 1933 created his first feature film as an independent producer. Katzman eventually moved to Monogram Pictures, where he produced low budget films such as the *Dead End Kids* and *Little Tough Guys* series and some minor comedies. That brought him to the attention of Columbia Pictures which hired him to supervise its production of serials. Katzman had previously produced some independent serials in the 1930s.

While the serials of Columbia of this era were far from high budget, Katzman did bring a new energy to Columbia's production, He lured veteran serial direct Spencer Gordon Bennet from Republic and employed veteran serial writer George Plympton from Universal, which was then out of serial production. He brought former Universal serial star Buster Crabbe back to the field in three Columbia cliffhangers and employed Clayton Moore and Kirk Alyn in serials for Columbia, both of whom were better known for their serial work at Republic.

Under Katzman's reign, Columbia continued to base serials on comic book characters, such as Superman, Batman, Blackhawk, Tex Granger, Hop Harrigan and the like. At the same time, Republic was only working with original characters so as to save the cost of paying fees for the use of these well-known heroes. Unlike Republic, Columbia also used a wide variety of serial subjects, such as whodunits, pirate adventures, knights of the roundtable, and space adventures, along with the requisite westerns and crime stories.

*The Sea Hound* (1947). This chapter play was produced by Sam Katzman and marked a return to serials for Buster Crabbe, after a seven year absence from the genre. Note the use of the sub-name, *Daredevil Adventures of Captain Silver*, a common practice at Columbia at that time. Also pictured is Ralph Hodges.

Sam Katzman promoted his serials in interesting ways. Most of them had a sub-name, which were sometimes part of the title, such as *Captain Video, Master of the Stratosphere* (1951), or sometimes just used in the advertising, such as *The Sea Hound, Daredevil Adventures of Captain Silver* (1947) He called his 1950s serials, "Super Serials," presumably because of their 15 chapter length and long serial chapters (at least as contrasted with those of the era produced by Republic), rather than the quality of the serials. These ideas must have worked, as Columbia outlasted all of the other studios in serial production. (A list of the Columbia serials which had sub-names is set forth in Appendix C.)

Serial production came to an end in the 1950s but not the career of Sam Katzman. He continued to produce low budget features, including science-fiction stories, teenage musicals, biker movies and even Elvis Presley movies for MGM. Indeed, Katzman produced

*Blackhawk* (1952). Kirk Alyn is pictured as the title character. This is the last of six serials in which Alyn starred. Producer Sam Katzman at Columbia was still basing serials on comic book characters at this time, a practice that had been long since abandoned by Republic.

movies at a rapid pace throughout the 1960s. Katzman died in 1973 at the age of 72.

## II. PROLIFIC DIRECTORS OF SERIALS

Many different individuals either directed or co-directed sound movie serials, which is not surprising since many of those serials had more than one director. What is surprising is how many of the serials were directed by a very small group of directors. For example, three individuals, either alone or with others, directed a total of 100 different serials, which is slightly less than half of all sound serials. Those directors were Ray Taylor, Spencer Gordon Bennet and Ford Beebe.

In addition, over 175 serials were directed by only ten different directors (although they may have had other co-directors), comprising a substantial portion of the 231 serials produced in Hollywood in the sound era. A list of the 12 most prolific serial directors and their serials is set forth on Appendix D. That list includes only those directors who directed or co-directed at least six serials during the sound era. The following is a short summary of the careers of those prolific serial directors.

### Ray Taylor and Lewis D. Collins

Ray Taylor directed or co-directed more sound movie serials than any other individual. In all, he directed 45 sound serials, of which 38 were for Universal. He also co-directed four serials at Republic, including *Dick Tracy* (1937), and two serials with James W. Horne at Columbia, namely *The Spider's Web* (1938) and *Flying G-Men* (1939). Also, Taylor directed one serial at an independent studio named Principal Pictures. The serial was *The Return of Chandu* (1934) with Bela Lugosi.

Ray Taylor was born in 1888 in Perham, Minnesota. After his military service in World War I, Taylor got his start in the film industry, eventually moving to Universal in the 1920s. Taylor's directing career started in silent films. His work included silent serials, such as *Fighting with Buffalo Bill* (1926) and *Whispering Smith Rides* (1927), both of which were re-made, to some degree, by Universal during the early sound era. He also directed the last all-silent Tarzan serial, *Tarzan the Mighty* (1928). However, Taylor is best-remembered for his sound serials for Universal.

Beginning with *Ace of Scotland Yard* (1929) and continuing through the mid-1930s, Taylor directed, on his own, 16 serials for Universal. The serials from this period are not that well-known, probably because they are so old, but included *Pirate Treasure* and *Perils of Pauline*, both from 1934. From 1938 onward, beginning with *Flaming Frontiers*, Taylor always had a co-director on his films, which was the usual practice during that era. This may also have been caused by Taylor's significant drinking problem. During this period, Taylor co-directed many well-known serials, such as *Flash Gordon Conquers the Universe* (1940), with Ford Beebe, and *Gang Busters* (1942), with Noel Smith.

*The Great Alaskan Mystery* (1944). This is a later Universal chapter play, directed by Ray Taylor and Lewis D. Collins, who directed almost all of the Universal serials of the time. Pictured in this lobby card from bottom left to the top are Fuzzy Knight, Marjorie Weaver, Milburn Stone and Ralph Morgan.

Beginning in 1943, Taylor co-directed 13 of the last 14 serials released by Universal, always with Lewis D. Collins as his co-director. Collins was born in 1899 in Baltimore, Maryland. He also started his directing career in silent films and continued directing numerous sound westerns, both before and after his work in serials. Some of the serials Taylor and Collins co-directed during the 1940s included *The Adventures of Smilin' Jack* (1943) and *Secret Agent X-9* (1945). For some reason, Taylor was not tapped to direct Universal's last serial, *The Mysterious Mr. M* (1946). That serial was co-directed by Lewis D. Collins, this time with Vernon Keays. In all, Collins directed 14 serials, all for Universal.

After Universal stopped its serial production, Ray Taylor continued directing westerns, including the Lash LaRue series at independent studios. Taylor died in 1952. Lewis D. Collins also continued directing westerns up until his death in 1954, generally at minor studios such as Monogram.

## Spencer Gordon Bennet

Spencer Gordon Bennet, also sometimes credited as Spencer G. Bennet and Spencer Bennet, was born on January 5, 1893. He began work in the movie industry in 1912, first as a stunt man and later as an actor for the Edison stock company. He then moved to Pathé in 1914, where he also did stunt work and minor acting jobs. Soon he was doing second unit directing work on two serials produced by George Seitz. By 1925, Bennet directed his first serial, entitled *Play Ball*. He directed several other silent serials, including *The Green Archer* (1925), which was remade in the sound era by Columbia, and *The House without a Key* (1925), a Charlie Chan serial.

In the sound era, Bennet's first serial was *The Last Frontier* (1932), which was RKO's only serial. Although he then made a few serials for Columbia, Bennet's sound serial directing career began in earnest in 1943 at Republic. There he directed or co-directed 13 serials, including such well known chapter plays as *The Masked Marvel* (1943), *The Tiger Woman* (1944) and *Zorro's Black Whip* (1944).

*The Black Widow* (1947) was directed by two prolific serial directors, Spencer Gordon Bennet and Fred C. Brannon. Sombra (Carol Forman) is about to put on a disguise as Anthony Warde and I. Stanford Jolley look on.

Bennet moved to Columbia in 1947, where he directed or co-directed all but one of Columbia's serials through the end of the serial era in 1956. The serials of that era are not as well respected as those from his Republic days, as budgets were cut sharply and the use of stock footage increased substantially. His serials from this era included the two *Superman* serials and other serials based on comic books such as *Batman and Robin* (1949) and *Blackhawk* (1952). Bennet has the distinction of directing two serials in 1956, the last year that chapter plays were made in Hollywood. Those serials were *Perils of the Wilderness* and *Blazing the Overland Trail*.

In all, Bennet directed 38 sound serials, including 24 at Columbia. He also directed approximately 15 silent serials and 54 feature films, most of which were westerns or other melodramas. Spencer Bennet died in 1987.

### Forde Beebe

Ford Beebe was born in 1888 in Grand Rapids, Michigan. Like Taylor and Bennet, Beebe's career also started in silent films, directing many features beginning in the early 1920s. Beebe also had a number of writing credits on silent films and this writing career was a helpful intro-

*Winners of the West* (1940). In this Universal serial directed by Ford Beebe and Ray Taylor, the female star is Anne Nagel, playing Claire Hartford.

duction into serials in the sound era. On *Tarzan the Tiger* (1929), a sound serial with no spoken dialogue, Beebe wrote the titles, something he had done for silent films. For *The Indians Are Coming* (1930), Universal's first all-talking serial, Beebe received one of the writing credits. He also contributed to the scripts of a number of serials at Mascot, including *The Galloping Ghost* (1931) and *The Vanishing Legion* (1931).

It was at Mascot studios where Beebe directed his first serials, directing four serials including *The Last of the Mohicans* (1932) and *The Adventures of Rex and Rinty* (1935). Three of those serials were co-directed with serial veteran, B. Reeves Eason. It was at Universal, however, where Beebe received his greatest serial fame, directing 21 serials there from 1936 to 1942. These included some of the best remembered serials of all time, including the last two *Flash Gordon* serials, *Buck Rogers* (1939), the two *Green Hornet* serials and *Riders of Death Valley* (1941). Six of those serials were co-directed by Ray Taylor. Ford Beebe died in 1978.

## William Witney and John English

William Witney and John English are the most famous directing duo in serial history. Together, from 1937 through 1941, they directed 17 serials at Republic. These serials included some of the greatest chapter plays of all time, such as the final three *Dick Tracy* serials, the first two *Zorro* serials and both *Lone Ranger* serials. They also directed *Daredevils of the Red Circle* (1939) and *Drums of Fu Manchu* (1940). Generally, Witney directed the action sequences and English directed the dialogue and dramatic scenes. This division of the labor allowed them to create many great serials within a short period of time.

Witney, who was born in 1915 in Oklahoma, began work in the film industry as a messenger at Mascot in the early 1930s. He gradually worked his way up through the editing department to become a script supervisor. He then co-directed two serials at Republic, before he first teamed with John English for *Zorro Rides Again* in 1937. In addition to the serials with English, Witney directed seven other serials at Republic, either on his own or with co-directors such as Alan James and Fred Brannon. Witney's solo efforts included *Spy Smasher* (1942) and *Perils of Nyoka* (1942), also two of the best-loved serials of all time. In all, Witney directed or co-directed 24 serials. He also directed many western features and worked in television, in shows such as *Alfred Hitchcock Presents* and *Bonanza*. He passed away in 2002.

*Adventures of Captain Marvel* (1941). This is Tom Tyler, in one of his most famous
serial roles. This chapter play was directed by the most famous serial team of all
time, William Witney and John English.

John English, who was born in 1903 in Cumberland, England,
directed only two serials without Witney. They were *Daredevils of the
West* (1943), a solo effort, and *Captain America* (1944), with Elmer Clifton.
English directed or co-directed a total of 19 serials. He also directed a
number of westerns for Republic and later Columbia, featuring their
most popular cowboy stars such as Gene Autry and Roy Rogers. During
the 1950s and 1960s, much like Witney, English worked in television,
once again directing many westerns. English died in 1969.

## Fred C. Brannon

Fred C. Brannon, also credited as Fred Brannon, presided over the decline and fall of the Republic serial empire. Brannon was born in 1901 in Louisiana. Brannon's directing career, which started in 1945 with *The Purple Monster Strikes*, was almost entirely limited to serials. At the beginning of that career, he had some of the best co-directors of serials, including Spencer Gordon Bennet and William Witney. After co-directing 11 serials at Republic, Brannon was on his own, being the sole director on 13 straight serials for Republic.

These serials, with their low budgets and increased use of stock footage, included some of the least respected serials at Republic. The only highpoint of this era was probably the three rocket suit serials directed by Brannon and even those were nothing special. Brannon would most likely have directed all of Republic's remaining serials had he not died suddenly in 1953 at the age of 51. At that point, Franklin Adreon, who had been producing the Brannon-directed serials, became the producer-director on the last five serials released by Republic, through *King of the Carnival* (1955). In all, Brannon directed 24 serials.

## B. Reeves Eason

B. Reeves Eason, sometimes billed as Breezy Eason, was born in 1886 in New York City. He was another sound serial director who started directing movies during the silent era. He also appeared as an actor in a number of silent films. With the advent of sound, Eason directed films starring famous cowboy stars such as Hoot Gibson, Ken Maynard and Dick Foran. He also did significant work at Mascot in serials, directing or co-directing eight of them, before moving on to Republic after the merger to direct three more. His nickname, Breezy, came from his ability to breeze through the shooting of his action sequences in record time.

Eason co-directed two of the best-known serials that Mascot produced, namely, *The Phantom Empire* and *The Miracle Rider*, both from 1935. After the three serials at Republic, Eason's serial career appeared to be over, although he continued to work steadily in films, directing B-movies and short films. When James Horne, Columbia's primary serial director, suddenly died in 1942, Columbia brought Eason to its studios to direct two serials, *The Phantom* (1943) and *The Desert Hawk* (1944).

Eason did little directing after those last two serials at Columbia. In all, Eason directed or co-directed 13 serials. He died in 1956.

## James W. Horne

James W. Horne was born in 1880 in San Francisco, California. He also began his career in silent films, and much like B. Reaves Eason, he worked both as an actor and a director. He even directed silent serials, such as *Bull's Eye* (1918) and *The Midnight Man* (1919). Horne is best known today for directing Laurel and Hardy and Charley Chase short comedies for Hal Roach. Indeed, he directed some of Laurel and Hardy's best known short subjects, such as *Big Business* (1929), where the comedy duo portrayed Christmas tree salesmen. He also directed one of their best full length features, *Way Out West* (1937), which included a famous soft shoe dance by the comedians.

In 1938, Columbia tapped Horne as its prime director for its serials. After co-directing two serials with Ray Taylor, including *The Spider's Web* (1938) which is often on serial fans' lists of great serials, Horne directed ten serials on his own, including *Deadwood Dick* (1940) and *The Spider Returns* (1941). Horne's serials are known for their humor,

*The Spider Returns* (1941) is one of the silliest serials directed by James W. Horne. Pictured from left to right are Richard Wentworth (Warren Hull), Ram Singh (Kenneth Duncan), Nita Van Sloan (Mary Ainslee), Jackson (Dave O'Brien) and Jenkins (Alden Chase).

often revolving around the antics of the henchmen and their relationship with the main villain. Horne died suddenly in 1942 from a cerebral hemorrhage, right when he was at the prime of his serial directing career.

### Henry MacRae

As described earlier in this chapter, Henry MacRae was perhaps the most famous producer of sound movie serials. However, MacRae also made significant contributions to the sound serial genre by directing six serials for Universal during the early days of talking pictures.

Henry MacRae began his directing career in silent films, co-directing his first serial in 1916 (*Liberty, A Daughter of the U.S.A.*). He then directed many other serials for Universal during the silent era, including *Elmo the Mighty* (1919) starring Elmo Lincoln, the first screen Tarzan and *The Dragon's Net* (1920), Universal's first 12 chapter serial. In the sound era, MacRae directed six serials at Universal from 1929 to 1932, including *Tarzan the Tiger* (1929), Universal's first serial with sound and *The Indians Are Coming* (1930), Universal's first all talking serial. After directing *The Lost Special* (1932), MacRae discontinued directing serials, focusing instead on producing serials almost to the exclusion of any other type of film.

### Armand Schaefer

Armand Schaefer was born in Canada in 1898. He entered the motion picture industry as a property man for Mack Sennet in 1924. He became an assistant director of westerns and serials for Action Pictures and then directed westerns for other companies. Schaefer was one of the most prolific directors of Mascot serials, directing eight of them from 1931 to 1935. His work included two of John Wayne's three serials and *The Miracle Rider* (1935) in which that other cowboy star, Tom Mix, appeared.

Much like Henry MacRae, Schaefer left directing for producing in the middle 1930s, although his producing work was generally not in the serial field. Indeed, Schaefer went into a partnership with Gene Autry in the 1940s and thereafter produced many of Autry's movies and television shows. Schaefer died in 1967.

### The Others

Wallace Grissell worked at the studios of both Republic and Columbia, co-directing a total of eight serials. On seven of them, Spencer Bennet was a co-director. Grissell was noted for co-directing Linda Stirling in two of her best serials, *The Tiger Woman* (1944) and *Zorro's Black Whip* (1944). Grissell's directing career was short-lived and other than his serials, Grissell only directed a few films, most of which were B-westerns.

Alan James co-directed six serials at both Universal and Republic in 1937 and 1938. His co-directors were Ray Taylor, Ford Beebe and William Witney. His best serial may be *SOS Coast Guard*, directed with William Witney in 1937. James was better known for directing westerns rather than serials, and particularly his westerns starring Ken Maynard.

## III. PROLIFIC SERIAL ACTORS

It is difficult to determine which actor made the most appearances in sound serials. Numerous character actors had prominent roles in one serial, uncredited roles in a different serial and then parts that were so small in other serials that if the viewer blinked, the actor's entire appearance would be missed. Other actors, who were also stuntmen, such as Yakima Canutt, Tom Steele, Eddie Parker, Ken Terrell, Duke Taylor and Dale Van Sickel, made numerous appearances in serials but often only as stunt men. Indeed, it has been stated that Steele appeared in around 80 serials and Parker in about 65 serials. However, since not all of those appearances were as actors, those performers are not included herein.

The first name on a list of most prolific serial performers is probably the least well known. Frank Ellis appeared in well over 400 sound films, of which 75% or more were westerns. Ellis also made approximately 25 films during the silent era. With regard to serials in the sound era, Ellis received work immediately, appearing in *The Indians Are Coming* (1930). His last serial role was in *The Great Adventures of Captain Kidd* (1953), so Ellis' serial career stretched over the entire sound serial era. In all, he appeared in about 45 serials. The heavy set actor (at least by the 1940s) seldom had a significant role in those serials, but rather, played minor henchmen, policemen or a townsperson. Ellis died in 1969.

Compared to the other prolific serial performers, Jack Ingram started late, making his first appearance in films in the mid-1930s. He rapidly began making numerous serial appearances starting with *Undersea Kingdom* (1936) and ending with *Riding with Buffalo Bill* (1954). In all, he made more than 45 serial appearances, including the henchman who masqueraded as the title character in *The Green Archer* (1940), as one of the

Stark boys in *Dick Tracy's Returns* (1938) and as the main henchman in *Superman* (1948). Indeed, almost all of Ingram's serial roles were as a henchman, with rare exceptions such as playing a policeman in *Who's Guilty?* (1945). Ingram is reputed to have appeared in slightly less than 300 sound films, with many of them being westerns. When his serial career ended, Ingram made guest appearances on television. Ingram died in 1969.

Tom London also started in silent films, beginning his screen career in 1915. His first serial credit was in *The Lion's Claw*, a Universal production from 1918. He continued working regularly in silent films and then appeared in early sound serials beginning with *Spell of the Circus* (1931). He is reputed to have appeared in more films (silent and sound) than any other actor. Some sources have him appearing in 2000 films, which does not seem possible. More likely, he appeared in around 500 sound films, with more than half being westerns. His final serial appearance was in *Gunfighters of the Northwest* (1954), one of the last serials ever made. In all, London appeared in around 50 sound serials. He is best-remembered

*Fighting Devil Dogs* (1938). Prolific serial performer Edmund Cobb is the next-to-the-last person on the right side of the table. Cobb plays a minor henchman in this chapter play. Here he is about to reveal the true identity of the Lightning, which does not speak positively for the longevity of his character. At the center of the table is Montagu Love, holding a radio-controlled gyroscope, to his right is Frank Baker and on either side of Cobb are Lee Powell and Herman Brix.

for playing henchmen in several of those serials, but he sometimes had a significant role, such as the hero's sidekick, Doc Laramie, in *Cody of the Pony Express* (1950). London died in 1963.

Edmund Cobb appears to be the actor who appeared in the most sound serials. Cobb started in the movies during silent films and moved easily into sound films. He is reputed to have been in over 450 sound films, including approximately 60 serials. His first sound serial role was in *The Indians Are Coming* (1930), one of the first sound serials ever made. His last serial appearance was in *Man with the Steel Whip* (1954), toward the end of Hollywood's serial production. That means that Cobb appeared in sound serials for almost 25 years. Some of his better-remembered roles were as a villain and potential candidate for Don Del Oro in *Zorro's Fighting Legion* (1939), as the almost silent Kuva in *The Sign of the Wolf* (1931) and as a villain being constantly chased by Rex and Rinty in *Law of the Wild* (1934). Cobb died in 1974.

Many serials had appearances by more than one of these actors. For example, all four appeared in *Zorro Rides Again* (1937) and in *The Lone Ranger* (1938), with each in relatively small roles. All four also appeared ten years later in *Superman* (1948) although in that serial, Ingram had an important henchman's role.

In terms of longevity, Al Ferguson played the villain Albert Werper in *Tarzan the Tiger* (1929), which was one of the earliest sound serials, although it was not a talking serial. He also had a smaller role as Fergie in the last Hollywood serial produced, *Blazing the Overland Trail* (1956). In all Ferguson appeared in over 40 serials.

Dennis Moore was far from a prolific serial performer, appearing in approximately ten serials. Moore, though, has a different record. Moore appeared in *The Mysterious Mr. M* (1946), which was Universal's last serial, playing one of the heroes. About ten years later, he appeared in *Blazing the Overland Trail* (1956), which was Columbia's last serial, playing one of the heroes. Thus, Moore appeared in the last serial for two of the three studios which produced serials in the 1940s and 1950s.

# Chapter 11
# Three Appreciations

*[Author's Note: For these three serials, I am writing in the first person, because these are not technically reviews but, rather, are remembrances of three serials which are special to me. I am too young to have seen serials in movie theaters. I have a vague recollection of watching serials on television in the 1950s but I cannot even remember which ones. However, in my twenties, I did get to see these three serials on television, one chapter a week, and I loved them. They started me on my serial viewing hobby. Even though I have now seen a number of other serials which I consider to be excellent and even though there may be better serials to watch, these three will always remain special to me.]*

## I. THE PHANTOM EMPIRE (1935)

It is amazing that Mascot Pictures made *The Phantom Empire*. Mascot was a B-movie studio which, frankly, made, B-movie serials. That is not to say that Mascot did not make several very enjoyable serials. I, like many serial fans, enjoy *The Miracle Rider* (1935) and *The Vanishing Legion* (1931). I also like *The Three Musketeers* (1933) and some others, although that view is surely not embraced by everyone. As good as many of the Mascot serials were, however, they were still very typical serials, with standard plots and standard cliffhangers. The good ones simply turned out better than other Mascot or independent serials of the era.

There is almost nothing typical about *The Phantom Empire*. It is a science fiction serial, when there had been no science fiction movies made up until that time. Sure, there were the mad scientist movies, such as *Frankenstein* (1931) and *The Invisible Man* (1933). There were mov-

*The Phantom Empire* (1935). In a scene on the surface world, cowboy star Gene Autry captures one of Professor Beetson's henchmen, who has just been double-crossed and shot by the evil Professor Beetson.

ies which involved visits to prehistoric areas, such as *The Lost World* (1925) and *King Kong* (1933). But there had been no movies which involved earthmen traveling to different civilizations or strange visitors from other planets coming to Earth. This serial involves both.

But, this is not just a science fiction serial. It is also a western, although set in the 1930s when there were also radios and cars. It is a musical, since it stars Radio's Singing Cowboy, Gene Autry. *The Phantom Empire* was therefore the first (and last) combination science fiction/western/musical ever made.

This serial has multiple plots, many of which are unusual. Oddly, the core plot is a very standard serial plot. Professor Beetson and his henchmen have arrived out west to dig for radium, which they believe is buried beneath the Earth's surface. Unfortunately for them, when they arrive to begin their explorations, they discover that Radio Ranch is in operation right in the area in which they want to dig. Radio Ranch appears to be a dude ranch and people want to stay there because it is the site of a daily radio show starring Gene Autry. Beetson decides that he needs to rid the west of Gene Autry, which will lead to the demise of Radio Ranch, affording Beetson the chance to search for the radium in private.

Of course, during his lifetime, Gene Autry became a shrewd businessman and a multi-millionaire. But, in 1935, that attribute was not evident. Apparently, Autry signed a contract with the radio network that provided that if Autry missed his 2:00 P.M. radio broadcast, even one time and even if he had a good excuse, he would lose the radio contract and Radio Ranch. This unusual situation gives Beetson just the opportunity he needs. If he can somehow prevent Autry from appearing for one of the radio broadcasts, Autry will lose his contract and everyone will leave Radio Ranch. Accordingly, Beetson sets out to do this, first framing Autry for a murder and later trying to kill him.

The other main plot involves the scientific city of Murania, which is located just a 25,000 foot elevator ride down from the Earth's surface. Murania is an advanced society where robots do all of the difficult work, leaving the inhabitants with time to think. It is led by Queen Tika, who despises the surface world, even though she likes to watch it on her flat screen, circular television. Queen Tika's goal is to ensure that the surface people do not discover Murania and somehow infect the lower world with whatever disease the surface people have. Therefore, from time to time, she also wants to kill Gene Autry, thus preventing his radio broadcast, so as to rid the area of Radio Ranch.

This creates an important subplot for the serial, i.e., Autry's daily rush to return to the ranch for his 2:00 P.M. broadcast. I am an attorney, and for me, this plot point has always raised a serious problem. Just about every contract I draft has a force majeure clause which generally states that if either party is prevented or delayed in completing his obligations due to war, casualty, labor strikes, terrorism or other causes reasonably beyond that party's control, the delay is excused. Why isn't there such a provision in Autry's contract? If he actually loses Radio Ranch, some frontier lawyer is going to have a major malpractice case on his hands.

After watching *The Phantom Empire*, whenever I draft a contract, I always want to revise the standard force majeure clause, to provide that if either party is prevented or delayed in completing performance due to war, casualty, labor strikes, being stuck 25,000 feet below the Earth's surface, or terrorism, the delay is excused. Luckily, I have always avoided the temptation.

*The Phantom Empire* (1935). There is an unusual battle going on in the underground city of Murania, featuring surface people, robots and Muranians. From left to right, the surface people are Frankie Darro, William Moore and Smiley Burnette.

Another important plot in the serial is the disloyalty of the Queen Tika's right hand man, Lord Argo. He and some other soldiers are plotting to overthrow the Queen and take over the City. The reasons for their disaffection are not clear. While the Queen does not have the greatest personality, she does not seem all that bad, particularly compared to her contemporaries, Emperor Ming and Unga Kahn. It could also be that Argo and his men are frustrated because there do not appear to be any women in Murania other than the Queen.

The dissidents' actual complaint seems to be the Queen's viciousness when a soldier makes a mistake. One unlucky fellow fails to capture Gene Autry twice and as a result, he is sentenced to death. As they say in Murania, "Two strikes and you're out." We then find out that the Queen has already put 37 soldiers to death that year, and it is apparently early in the year. I wonder what happens if someone commits a serious crime in Murania.

Another plot involves the Thunder Riders, the Queen's surface army. They ride on horseback, wearing gas masks because the Earth's atmosphere is a problem for them. Their horses' hoof beats make such loud noise that when the Thunder Riders all ride together, it sounds like thunder.

Frankie and Betsy Baxter, children of one of the owners of Radio Ranch, spot the Thunder Riders one day and decide to create a Junior Thunder Riders Club, emulating the helmeted riders. There are about ten kids in the club, which means the club includes all of the children within a hundred mile radius of Radio Ranch, since the area seems sparsely populated. To emulate the real Thunder Rider's helmets and masks, the Junior Thunder Riders wear a bucket with an inverted hook on the top and capes on their backs. All of their mothers must have been pretty upset the day when all of their buckets suddenly disappeared and they could no longer do the wash. But, then, much like Murania, there do not seem to be any women in the surface world either.

The acting in the serial is up and down. Frank Glendon, who portrays Professor Beetson, is convincing in his villainous role, sometimes pretending to be just another honest scientist. It is helpful that he and the other members of his gang are not portrayed by the usual serial regulars but rather, are fresh faces as serials go. However, after the first half of the serial, Beetson disappears for long sections of the story.

Frankie Darro, already a serial veteran at age 18, plays Frankie Baxter, son of one of the owners of Radio Ranch. Darro's enthusiasm in his role is contagious, as he leads the Junior Thunder Riders to the rescue of Gene Autry time and time again. Betsy King Ross, playing Betsy Baxter, does a nice job in one of her few movie roles. She is never grating, as other child actors can be. If her line reading is not always convincing, at least she seems very natural in the western setting. This may be because, in real life, Betsy is apparently the "World Champion Trick Rider," as it states in her billing. It is not clear where she won that title but she does no fancy riding in this serial. Nevertheless, she is another fresh face who adds to the uniqueness of the serial.

Acting honors go to Wheeler Oakman, playing Lord Argo, at once subservient to Queen Tika but ready to lead the revolution in an instant if his duplicity is ever discovered. Oakman always played villains convincingly and he surely seems very comfortable once he takes the reins of power in Murania, happily dispatching former associates of the Queen to their death.

Unfortunately, the acting of the two leads is disappointing. Dorothy Christie, who plays Queen Tika, has some unusual lines to deliver in this serial and she is not always convincing. Gene Autry, in his first major film role, is likable when he is singing and performing on the radio, but when he

*The Phantom Empire* (1935). Pictured are the Baxter siblings, hiding from the villains. Frankie Darro, prolific child actor in serials in the 1930s is on the left and Betsy King Ross, World's Champion Trick Rider, is on the right.

has to deliver any significant lines in the serial, he is not up to the task. In the last chapter, when Autry is trying to convince Queen Tika to leave Murania, the ensemble acting between the two is some of the worst in serial history.

With the many plots and musical interludes, it is hard to believe that there is time for comic relief, yet somehow, that is also squeezed into the story. Here, it is provided by Smiley Burnette and William Moore, who play two ranch hands who are radio performers on Autry's daily radio show. As usual, much of the comic relief is humorless and seems to be more filler than story. However, I have to say, once Burnette and Moore are trapped in Murania in two of the later chapters, I laughed out loud several times at some of their antics. First, they dress as some of the mechanical men and in that disguise, hit some of the unsuspecting Muranian guards on the head with sledge hammers. Later, as they are pulling switches in the palace, they cause several of the mechanical men to dance. Let the news go out to all serial fans. Smiley Burnette was actually funny in a serial.

...

As I look at what I've written above, even I wonder why I love this serial so much. After all, there are several ridiculous plots and the overall acting is just fair at best. I haven't even mentioned the lack of music during the chapters, the generally weak cliffhangers and some primitive special effects.

And yet, this serial is wonderful. It proves that old adage that the whole can sometimes be better than the sum of its parts. While it may be hard to express in words why this serial is so wonderful, perhaps the reason is really obvious. The serial is simply fun to watch.

One of the reasons is the scientific city of Murania, which itself is one of the stars of the serial. Indeed, it has its own title card during the credits. The miniatures of the city, generally shown in long shot, are excellent. The city seems more futuristic than those shown in bigger budget films of the era such as *Metropolis* (1927) or *Things to Come* (1936). Through the use of matte shots and process screens, the action appears to actually take place in the futuristic city.

Unlike many Mascot serials, Murania is well-populated, with many people and even robots walking through the town when Gene is trying to escape. We meet a number of important characters there, such as Lord Argo, the Lord High Chancellor, Mal, the Queen's top assistant, Rab, the crazy scientist who has invented a disintegrator ray and Thunder Rider Captain Orn who is sent to death by the Queen in Chapter Three and stoically accepts his fate. Murania comes alive in this serial, as Atlantis never did in *The Undersea Kingdom* (1936). When the surface people finally make it to Murania, their jeopardy seems very real since Murania seems very real.

One of the joys of watching serials today is the too tempting opportunity to make fun of the story and of course, if it is a science fiction serial, to make fun of the science. I suspect audiences may even have done this back in 1935. So, here it goes.

Why are Frankie and Betsy not terribly upset when their father is killed? They seem to forget him almost immediately. Why, in the first chapter, if Gene Autry is the star of a radio show, does he stage a stage coach robbery out on the plains leading to Radio Ranch? Why, in the radio drama performed during the episode, do they act out the entire story instead of just reading the script into the microphones? Autry's radio audience cannot see it and there are really not that many people at the ranch who can watch the show either.

Turning to Murania, if the Muranians need to wear a mask in the Earth's atmosphere so that they can safely breathe, why can Autry and the other surface people exist in Murania without a mask? At what point in the rapid 25,000 foot elevator ride down to Murania do the passengers' ears pop and how much does it hurt? How does Lord Argo know that when surface people are brought back from the dead, they can only speak the language of the dead? Autry was the first surface person ever to visit Murania, much less be brought back to life in the radium revival chamber.

There are obviously many more questions or inconsistencies about the serial. When they are pointed out, they simply add to the fun.

However, I believe the real secret of this serial is its audacity. The filmmakers attempted to juggle many plots and types of stories in the air and they succeeded. The City of Murania and the Queen's aversion to the surface world would have been a sufficient plot point for any serial. Here, however, the revolution in the underground city was added. Autry's attempts to defeat the villainy of Professor Beetson in the surface world could alone have been the basis for an entire serial plot but there the Junior Thunder Riders were added. Throw in some music and comedy and practically every type of movie story is present in this serial. If one of the stories gets boring, just switch to one of the other ones.

Even at the end, Murania is destroyed by the middle of the last chapter and the rest of the story appears to a standard western plot, in which Beetson is finally brought to justice for his crimes. However, just when the serial seems to return to the mundane, it turns out that Frankie Baxter has invented television and television that works over a long distance, apparently without a camera. Add a repeat of the opening song, "Uncle Noah's Ark," and the serial comes to a satisfying close.

No matter how many times I view *The Phantom Empire*, I always think at some point: did I really just hear that? Did I really just see that? No matter how old I am when I re-watch it, I always view *The Phantom Empire* with a sense of wonder.

CREDITS: Producer: Nat Levine; Director: Otto Brower and Breezy Eason; Story: Wallace McDonald, Gerald Geraghty and H. Freedman; Continuity: John Rathmell and Armand Shaeffer; Photography: Ernest Miller and William Nobles. Mascot (1935), 12 Chapters.

CAST: Gene Autry (Gene Autry); Frankie Darro (Frankie Baxter); Betsy King Ross (Betsy Baxter); Dorothy Christie (Queen Tika); Wheeler Oakman (Argo); Charles K. French (Mal); Warner Richmond (Rab); Frank Glendon (Professor Beetson); Lester "Smiley" Burnette (Oscar); William Moore (Pete); Edward Piel, Sr. (Dr. Cooper); Jack Carlyle (Saunders). Featuring the scientific City of Murania.

## II. FLASH GORDON (1936)

*Flash Gordon* has the best first chapter in serial history. Titled "The Planet of Peril," it starts with two scientists at a planetarium, one of whom is Professor Gordon, the father of Flash Gordon. The two scientists conclude that the Earth is doomed because a rogue planet is on course to crash into the Earth. In fact, people all over the planet are worried, a fact which is confirmed by stock footage of civilizations as far

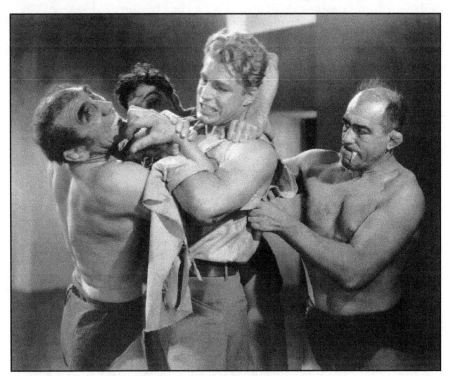

*Flash Gordon* (1936). In this publicity photo for the first chapter of the serial, it is hard to believe that an ex-polo player will be able to defeat these three strange wrestlers from Mongo but that is what happens.

away as India and Arabia. The situation is so serious that Flash Gordon has agreed to give up his polo game in Europe to return to America to be with his father at the end.

On the intercontinental plane from Europe to America, Flash meets Dale Arden, who is very upset by the bumpy plane ride amid a meteor storm. When the passengers are required to bail out of the plane, the two do it together. When they land on the ground, they immediately meet Dr. Zarkov, who has a rocket ship ready to go to Mongo, the onrushing planet. Zarkov has a plan to save the Earth. With very little persuading, Flash and Dale agree to go with Zarkov on his space adventure, even though the three of them barely know each other.

After a short rocket trip, they arrive on a desolate portion of Mongo where they first come upon three dinosaur-like inhabitants of the planet. While that danger is avoided, the three earthlings are then captured by Emperor Ming's men and taken to the palace. Ming immediately dispatches Zarkov to the laboratory, with the dubious expectation that Zarkov will help him conquer the Earth. Once that is out of the way, Ming quickly becomes interested in Dale and her obvious beauty. A protective Flash then roughs up Ming, who punishes Flash by sending him to the arena, to wrestle three unusual fellows in a handicap match.

Ming's daughter, Princess Aura, tells Ming that if Flash survives the fight, "He is mine." The odds are against Flash but in an exciting display of wrestling ability by a former polo player, Flash defeats all three grapplers. Ming, however, is not impressed and decides to drop Flash into a bottomless pit. By an unusual set of circumstances, Aura and Flash drop into the pit together. The chapter ends.

All of this takes place in just 20 minutes. There is more action in those 20 minutes than in entire serials of the era produced by some of the independent studios. To top the chapter off, it ends with the exciting wrestling match and a great cliffhanger.

That is not all that is special about this chapter. There is much intentional and unintentional humor. In addition to the reference to the polo match, when Zarkov tells Flash he wants to travel to the other planet to alter its course and save the Earth, Flash says," Well, it's worth trying." As they start out, Flash asks Zarkov if he thinks the rocket ship will work. Zarkov responds that he has experimented with models. Flash then asks, "They ever come back?" Zarkov, not willing to be topped by his new crew member, replies, "They weren't supposed to."

On board the rocket ship, there is only one seat and Flash and Dale have to ride standing up, holding onto the side like subway passengers. Zarkov forgets to turn on the oxygen and Dale almost suffocates. A last minute pull on the counter-magnets prevents the rocket ship from crashing into the surface of the Planet Mongo. With material like this, who needs Happy Hapgood for comic relief?

By the second chapter, Ming has decided to stop the Planet Mongo from destroying the Earth, so the rest of the serial concerns keeping Dale out of the clutches of Ming and somehow bringing the space soldiers back to Earth safely. In the ensuing chapters, Flash and the gang visit various parts of Mongo, such as the undersea world of Kala, the Shark King, and the above-world city of King Vultan and his hawk men. Flash also meets other people of the planet, such as Thun, leader of the Lion Men, and Prince Barin, the legitimate ruler of Mongo.

One of the greatest assets of the serial is the acting. *Flash Gordon* boasts three of the greatest performances in serial history. One is by a relatively minor player, John Lipson, who essays the role of King Vultan. Vultan is a stocky character, with two wings on his back. He has one of

*Flash Gordon* (1936). This is a publicity photo of four of the main characters from the serial, who, from left to right, are Dr. Zarkov (Frank Shannon), Prince Barin (Richard Alexander), Princess Aura (Priscilla Lawson), and Flash Gordon (Buster Crabbe).

the jolliest laughs on the planet, particularly when he is doing evil, such as sending Flash to the furnace rooms or sending his bear-like creature, Urso, to scare Dale. He is a glutton, as he guzzles wine, tears off bread from the loaf and eats meat right off the bone. He even tries to entertain Dale by creating shadow animals on the wall. Vultan, as played by Lipson, is one of the most memorable villains in serial history.

However, the most memorable villain in serial history is Emperor Ming, often referred to as Ming the Merciless. The first close-up of Charles Middleton, as Ming, conveys much. With his bald head, long eyebrows, Fu Manchu mustache and beard, wearing a robe with a high back and pointed collar, Ming is the epitome of villainy, before he ever speaks a word. Middleton is always convincing in his role, attempting to send Flash to his death, forcing a marriage on Dale or double crossing his daughter. He punctuates his nasty edicts with a "Heh, Heh," as he delights in his own villainy. Middleton delivers lines like, "Capture them at once; prepare the execution chamber," as though he really means it.

Much of the credit for the success of the serial must go to Buster Crabbe, for his performance as Flash Gordon. The former Olympic athlete was always in good shape and he is therefore believable fighting the monsters of Mongo or eluding Ming's forces. As silly as some of the dialogue may be, there is an earnestness about Crabbe's performance that allows the serial to maintain its credibility. Even his oft-repeated line, "Steady, Dale," makes sense when spoken by Crabbe.

Chocolate/Vanilla. Coke/Pepsi. Princess Aura/Dale Arden. Sometimes when good things come in pairs, it can be hard to determine which the better one is. I have always leaned toward Jean Rogers as Dale Arden. Her eyes, her hair, her skin; ah, she is beautiful. Those are not my words. Those are Ming's words when he first spots Dale, and this is before she appears in the sexy attire that the women of Mongo apparently wear on a daily basis. It is true that Dale's main contributions to the serial are her very wide eyes when Flash is in trouble, her loud screams and her penchant for fainting when the going gets tough. But, to paraphrase an old Bob Hope joke, Dale is what the space soldiers are fighting for.

Others prefer Priscilla Lawson, as Princess Aura. While not as pretty as Dale Arden, she is quite attractive, particularly in her form fitting long dresses, with bare midriff, which amply show off her full figure. More importantly, unlike Dale, Aura does not just stand around and scream. In fact, she rescues Flash on a number of occasions, such as from the

Octosac in Kala's underground world, from the deadly static machine in Vultan's city in the sky and from the deadly orangopoid in the arena in the city in the sky. On the other hand, there is a true mean streak in her, as Aura deliberately destroys Kala's undersea world, lies to either Flash or Dale to break the two up and even kidnaps Flash, on one occasion, to take him to a far away land. Of course, it must be disconcerting to Aura that every time she rescues Flash, Flash's first question is always about Dale. But, if you like your women bad and beautiful, Aura is for you.

This is the only serial soap opera. Let me see if I can keep up with this. Ming likes Dale. Dale likes Flash. Aura likes Flash. Flash likes Dale. Prince Barin likes Aura. Vultan likes Dale. Poor Dr. Zarkov. No one seems interested in him. Beauty always wins out over brains, even on Mongo.

The soap opera highlights the sexual element of the serial. The sexual element starts in the first chapter, as Ming appraises the blonde-haired Dale's beauty with obvious lechery. When Princess Aura appears, she and Dale look each other up and down, realizing they may have a rivalry on their hands. In Chapter Two, when Aura and Flash are running from Ming's men, and they are close together, Aura starts to rub Flash's arm while she looks at him with lust.

There is sexual tension throughout the movie between Ming, Dale, Flash and Princess Aura. Even King Vultan gets in the act, and like Ming, wants to marry Dale. Vultan's unique approach to court-ship involves scaring her with the bear-like beast, Urso, and then trapping her against a wall, hoping to grab her trembling body. While these may not be the best methods for winning the heart of Dale, there is a true erotic aspect to those scenes. No other serial has this element to it.

Indeed, there is a moment in the middle of the serial, Chapter Ten, when Flash and Dale kiss. Is there any other sound serial where the principals kiss in the middle of the tale? Probably not. It is this sexual element that, even in our day, makes this serial interesting to adults as well as young-sters.

Jean Rogers was one of the queens of the serials, appearing in six serials in the 1930s, most notably in *Flash Gordon* and its sequel. Here she is pictured on a cigarette card from the 1930s.

There is often criticism of the special effects in the serial. Of course, they seem primitive by today's standards. Vultan's planet hanging in the air and Kala's undersea kingdom are clearly models, and not great ones at that. In order to land, rocket ships have to turn in slow circles until they eventually reach the surface of Mongo. However modern computer-generated effects can become tiresome very quickly. Here, I like the rocket ships, even though they sometimes waver in the air and land in that circular motion. The dinosaur-like monsters seem realistic to me, and I believe this is the only serial that spent the time and money to create those types of creatures, except for Mascot's *King of the Kongo* (1929), which had one such awkward creature stumbling along. With Flash becoming invisible at one point and the flying hawk men falling from the sky, the effects really are quite special in this serial.

The filmmakers have created an incredible world of fantasy on Mongo, capturing Alex Raymond's comic strip vision to perfection. Unlike *The Phantom Empire* (1935), this is a pure science fiction serial and not a combination western and musical. But, the serial also has elements of a gladiator picture, with Flash periodically being sent to the arena to fight the three strange grapplers, the masked swordsman of Mongo and the orangapoid. It also has elements of movies such as *King Kong* (1933), with trips to prehistoric areas, as Flash is constantly encountering strange monsters of Mongo such as the large lizards, the orangapoid and the Fire Monster.

The serial is a travelogue, exploring many of the strange civilizations of Mongo, whether on the surface, below the surface or in the sky. The serial is like an expedition, with Flash meeting many of the unusual rulers of Mongo, such as Thun, Kala and Vultan. The serial is a love story; the serial is a satire. Best of all, the serial is a science fiction adventure, with a great hero and an evil villain. It has survived the test of time and remains, not just for me, one of the most popular serials of all time.

CREDITS: Producer: Henry MacRae; Director: Frederick Stephani; Screenplay: Frederick Stephani, George Plympton, Basil Dickey and Ella O'Neill; Photography: Jerry Ash and Richard Fryer; Electrical Effects: Norman Dewes; Special Properties: Elmer A. Johnson. Based on the newspaper feature entitled "Flash Gordon" owned and copyrighted by King Features Syndicate. Universal (1936) 13 chapters.

CAST: Buster Crabbe (Flash Gordon); Jean Rogers (Dale Arden), Charles Middleton (Emperor Ming); Priscilla Lawson (Princess Aura); Frank Shannon (Doctor Zarkov); Richard Alexander (Prince Barin), John Lipson (Vultan), Theodore Lorch (High Priest), Richard Tucker (Professor Gordon), George Cleveland (Professor Hensley), James Pierce (King Thun), Duke York, Jr. (King Kala), Muriel Goodspeed (Zona), Earl Askam (Torch), House Peters, Jr. (Shark Man)

## III. ZORRO'S BLACK WHIP (1944)

Even with over 200 serials produced in Hollywood in the talking era, *The Phantom Empire* (1935) and *Flash Gordon* (1936) are special, with their foundation in science fiction, trips to other worlds, and scientific devices such as ray guns, rockets, radium tubes and the like. The only other serials that have some or many of these elements are the *Flash Gordon* sequels, *Buck Rogers* (1939) and maybe *Brick Bradford* (1947) Sure, there is a trip to the moon in *Radar Men from the Moon* (1952), but the moon in that serial is desolate and, frankly, somewhat backward. It is therefore easy to see why *The Phantom Empire* and *Flash Gordon* are special to me.

My third appreciation is about *Zorro's Black Whip*, a Republic serial from 1944. On its face, this is a good but fairly standard serial product from Republic. It was produced at the time when Republic was starting to make shorter serials and relying more on its cliffhanger formula than bringing innovation to its product. Yet *Zorro's Black Whip* always seems fresh to me, even after watching many other serials and, for that matter, many other westerns.

I believe the serial's freshness comes from having a woman in the serial lead. When I first saw *Zorro's Black Whip*, with many less serials under my belt, I dubbed it the first feminist serial. I now know there are several others, such as *The Tiger Woman* (1944) and *Jungle Girl* (1941). The use of a female lead in those serials also brings freshness to them. But *Zorro's Black Whip* is set in the Old West where, at least in the movies, only men were the heroes. With the exception of, perhaps, Annie Oakley or maybe Calamity Jane in *Deadwood Dick* (1940) and *Custer's Last Stand* (1936), the women of westerns were usually school marms, daughters of ranchers, people attacked on stagecoaches, victims of villainy or window dressing without significant parts.

*Zorro's Black Whip* (1944). Linda Stirling is shown in her true identity, as Barbara Meredith, before she becomes the Black Whip. Tom London, who is about to die, is on the left and George J. Lewis is in the center.

*Zorro's Black Whip* provides a true western heroine, in the person of Barbara Meredith. She is up against terrible odds, as Hammond, a businessman and town elder, is the secret leader of a gang of criminals who are not above using murder, robbery and sabotage to prevent a vote on statehood for Idaho in 1889, just so they can continue their criminal activities without federal interference. When her brother, the original Black Whip, is killed in the first chapter, Meredith takes on his crusade in favor of statehood.  Meredith becomes The Black Whip, donning her brother's costume, using his whip and riding his horse, and doing such a good job that no one knows the original Black Whip has died. She also takes over as the publisher of the town newspaper, in and of itself a big assignment for a western female.

It also helps that Barbara Meredith is played by Linda Stirling, the 1940s queen of the serials. While others have criticized her sometimes wooden performances in her serials, she does well in the heroic roles of the Black Whip or as the title character in *The Tiger Woman* (1944). She is quite attractive as Barbara Meredith, with her long hair, cowboy hat, fringed vest, western skirt and cowboy boots. She is even more attractive as the Black Whip, dressed all in black. Of course, many of her scenes as the Black Whip are performed by a stunt double, so there are not that many chances to view Stirling as the masked heroine.

What makes Republic serials so special? For one thing, it is the fights. There is generally one per chapter in most Republic serials and while *Zorro's Black Whip* does not have quite so many, there are still plenty of fights to satisfy the avid serial fan. Most of the fisticuffs involve Vic Gordon fighting one or two of Hammond's henchmen. In the first chapter, the newspaper office is destroyed in a fight. In the second chapter it is Hammond's office. In each chapter, the fight moves around and across the rooms, on top of desks and over railings. Everything that is breakable breaks. Anything that can be thrown is thrown. By the end of the fight, there is not much left in good condition in the room.

The contrast with the fights in the serials of other studios is stark. Often, in other productions, there are just arms flailing and people being punched, with no story being told. In the Columbias, it is not unusual for Jack Holt or the Spider or Deadwood Dick to fight four or five henchmen at a time, and win! The Republic fights, on the other hand, are believable, at least in context, and are always exciting.

The chase scenes in Republic serials, as exemplified by *Zorro's Black Whip*, are particularly impressive. Here, rather than the usual one on one chase, there is often a one on one on one chase, with the Black Whip chasing the henchmen who are chasing Vic Gordon. Or, it is a henchman chasing the Black Whip who is racing to town to save Gordon from being lynched, once again allowing for cuts between three scenes rather than the usual two in a standard chase. Camera angles are fresh, with shots bordered by trees and boulders or the use of interesting angles, such as the one in Chapter One of the heads of the horses, as they are rapidly pulling a wagon. And, doesn't the Iverson Movie Ranch look particularly scenic and beautiful in this serial, as the chase sequences wind around large portions of the ranch?

Republic always took care with its cliffhangers and again, *Zorro's Black Whip* is no exception. Often, the cliffhangers are spectacular. If you're like me, a good avalanche or explosion is always exciting. In Chapter Nine, the villains blow up a mountain to send large boulders down on a cabin in which the Black Whip and Vic Gordon are trapped. Here the rocks are huge and devastate the structure. The Lydecker special effects make the avalanche seem realistic. Even the standard wagon-over-the-cliff at the end of Chapter One is thrilling. The cliff is high and the fall over the cliff is shot from below, making it seem that the wagon is flying through the air.

The serial also tries different variations on standard cliffhangers. [*Here I do have to warn about upcoming spoilers.*] In Chapter Seven, "Wolf Pack," the Black Whip is fighting henchmen on top of a high rock. She knocks one of them off a cliff and he falls a long way down, landing on the ground. The fight continues and a villain hits the Black Whip with a barrel, which knocks her over the cliff. As the chapter ends, the Black Whip is clearly falling off the high cliff.

In the next chapter, she is saved when she falls through a canvas on a wagon in a wagon train that is passing by below. The canvas breaks the fall. The Black Whip would obviously rather be lucky than good. Nevertheless, it is a clever resolution to the cliffover. It is set up well as the wagon train played a prominent role at the end of the prior episode.

*Zorro's Black Whip* also manages to let the heroine escape from an

*Zorro's Black Whip* (1944). In this publicity photo, the unmasked Black Whip, played by Linda Stirling, is showing her skills with a bullwhip and a gun, attributes that come in handy during the serial.

explosion without a time expansion cheat. In Chapter Six, henchmen are on top of a cliff, with dynamite, looking down on a tent of a miner. The Black Whip arrives and unaware of the terror from above, enters the tent to look around. The henchmen drop the dynamite on the tent and it explodes, with the Black Whip apparently inside. The whole scene is shot from above, from the perspective of the henchmen.

In the next chapter, more of the events are shown from the Black Whip's perspective. She walks into the tent, sees nothing, and continues through the back of the tent into a cave. The explosion does no harm. There is no time expansion cheat but just an event shown from a different angle. The Black Whip does not mystically realize there is trouble and rush out the back of the tent, but naturally continues her explorations into the cave before the explosion. The resolution is logical and not a cheat. Also, we get to see another great explosion.

Even the "small" cliffhangers are fun. In Chapter Five, the cliffhanger involves the villains forcing The Black Whip to remove her mask and finally reveal her true identity. In Chapter Ten, a henchman delivers a blow with a pitchfork to the Whip's prone body. Each of these is resolved without a cheat.

Sure, the same footage of the Black Whip entering and leaving her hideout behind the waterfall is shown in each chapter, which becomes irritating when watching the serial at home on successive days. That was probably not such a big problem in 1944, when the serial was seen once a week at a movie theater.

Sure, there is the standard economy chapter which interrupts the flow of the serial at just the wrong time. Sure, the Black Whip gets into fights with two very large henchmen, played by Hal Taliaferro and John Merton, and she holds her own, even though she is substantially smaller and is a woman. Sure the serial ends abruptly in the last chapter, with Hammond discovered and the chapter play quickly coming to an end.

Yet, somehow it all comes together. *Zorro's Black Whip* reminds me of *The Crimson Ghost* (1946), another Republic serial from the same era, with its standard Republic serial plot mixed with great stunts, fights, special effects and cliffhangers. Both serials transcend the limitations of the form, becoming, in their own way, as much fun as *The Phantom Empire* (1935).

Most serial fans would choose *Spy Smasher* (1942), *Zorro's Fighting Legion* (1939), or, perhaps, *The Adventures of Captain Marvel* (1941) as the best of the Republic serials. I like them all. But, the television shows, movies and serials that we saw when we were younger always remain more special than those we see when we are older. Perhaps that is one of the reasons why this serial will always be special to me. Thus, *Zorro's Black Whip* remains, with *The Phantom Empire* and *Flash Gordon*, one of the serials I appreciate the most.

CREDITS: Associate Producer: Ronald Davidson; Director: Spencer Bennet and Wallace Grissell; Second Unit Director: Yakima Canutt; Photography: Bud Thackery; Writer: Basil Dickey, Jesse Duffy, Grant Nelson and Joseph Poland; Musical Director: Richard Cherwin; Special Effects: Theodore Lydecker. "Zorro" character created by Johnston McCulley. Republic (1944) 12 Chapters.

CAST: George J. Lewis (Vic Gordon), Linda Stirling (Barbara Meredith), Lucien Littlefield (Tenpoint Jackson), Francis McDonald (Hammond), Hal Taliaferro (Henchman Baxter), John Merton (Henchman Ed Harris), John Hamilton (Banker), Tom Chatterton (Merchant), Tom London (Commissioner Bradley), Jack Kirk (Marshall), Jay Kirby (Randolph Meredith), Si Jenks (Zeke Haydon), Stanley Price (Hedges), Tom Steele (Hull and others), Duke Green (Evans and others), Dale Van Sickel (Danley and others), Forrest Taylor (Becker).

# Appendix A
# Serial Sources

## I. COMIC STRIPS

| | | |
|---|---|---|
| Tailspin Tommy | 1934 | Universal |
| Tailspin Tommy in the Great Air Mystery | 1935 | Universal |
| Flash Gordon | 1936 | Universal |
| Ace Drummond | 1936 | Universal |
| Secret Agent X-9 | 1937 | Universal |
| Radio Patrol | 1937 | Universal |
| Jungle Jim | 1937 | Universal |
| Tim Tyler's Luck | 1937 | Universal |
| Flash Gordon's Trip to Mars | 1938 | Universal |
| Red Barry | 1938 | Universal |
| Buck Rogers | 1939 | Universal |
| Flash Gordon Conquers the Universe | 1940 | Universal |
| Don Winslow of the Navy | 1942 | Universal |
| Don Winslow of the Coast Guard | 1943 | Universal |
| The Adventures of Smilin' Jack | 1943 | Universal |
| Secret Agent X-9 | 1945 | Universal |
| | | |
| Dick Tracy | 1937 | Republic |
| Dick Tracy Returns | 1938 | Republic |
| Dick Tracy's G-Men | 1939 | Republic |
| King of the Royal Mounted | 1940 | Republic |
| Adventures of Red Ryder | 1940 | Republic |
| Dick Tracy vs. Crime, Inc. | 1941 | Republic |
| King of the Mounties | 1942 | Republic |

| Mandrake the Magician | 1939 | Columbia |
|---|---|---|
| Terry and the Pirates | 1940 | Columbia |
| The Phantom | 1943 | Columbia |
| Brenda Starr, Reporter | 1945 | Columbia |
| Brick Bradford | 1947 | Columbia |
| Bruce Gentry | 1949 | Columbia |

## II. COMIC BOOKS

| Captain Marvel | 1941 | Republic |
|---|---|---|
| Spy Smasher | 1942 | Republic |
| Captain America | 1944 | Republic |

| Batman | 1943 | Columbia |
|---|---|---|
| Hop Harrigan | 1946 | Columbia |
| The Vigilante | 1947 | Columbia |
| Tex Granger | 1948 | Columbia |
| Superman<br>*Also from the Radio* | 1948 | Columbia |
| Congo Bill | 1948 | Columbia |
| Batman and Robin | 1949 | Columbia |
| Atom Man vs. Superman<br>*Also from the Radio* | 1950 | Columbia |
| King of the Congo | 1952 | Columbia |
| Blackhawk | 1952 | Columbia |

## III. PULP MAGAZINES AND OTHER PERIODICALS

| Tarzan the Fearless<br>*Also from Novels* | 1933 | Principal |
|---|---|---|
| The New Adventures of Tarzan<br>*Also from Novels* | 1935 | Burroughs |
| The Call of the Savage<br>*Also from Novels* | 1935 | Universal |
| The Adventures of Frank Merriwell | 1936 | Universal |

| | | |
|---|---|---|
| Zorro Rides Again | 1937 | Republic |
| *Also from Novels* | | |
| Zorro's Fighting Legion | 1939 | Republic |
| *Also from Novels* | | |
| Drums of Fu Manchu | 1940 | Republic |
| *Also from Novels* | | |
| Zorro's Black Whip | 1944 | Republic |
| *Also from Novels* | | |
| Son of Zorro | 1947 | Republic |
| *Also from Novels* | | |
| Ghost of Zorro | 1949 | Republic |
| *Also from Novels* | | |
| | | |
| The Spider's Web | 1938 | Columbia |
| The Shadow | 1940 | Columbia |
| The Spider Returns | 1941 | Columbia |

## IV. RADIO SERIES

| | | |
|---|---|---|
| The Return of Chandu | 1934 | Principal |
| | | |
| The Green Hornet | 1939 | Universal |
| The Green Hornet Strikes Again | 1940 | Universal |
| Gangbusters | 1942 | Universal |
| | | |
| The Lone Ranger | 1938 | Republic |
| The Lone Ranger Rides Again | 1939 | Republic |
| | | |
| Captain Midnight | 1942 | Columbia |
| Chick Carter, Detective | 1946 | Columbia |
| Jack Armstrong | 1947 | Columbia |
| The Sea Hound | 1947 | Columbia |

## V. NOVELS AND OTHER LONGER WORKS

The Clutching Hand           1936    Stage and Screen

The Last Frontier             1932    RKO

The Last of the Mohicans      1932    Mascot
The Three Musketeers         1933    Mascot

Tarzan the Tiger             1929    Universal
    *Also from Periodicals*
The Lightning Express         1930    Universal
The Indians Are Coming       1930    Universal
Battling With Buffalo Bill      1931    Universal
The Jungle Mystery          1932    Universal
The Red Rider               1934    Universal
Wild West Days            1937    Universal

Hawk of the Wilderness       1938    Republic
    *Also from Periodicals*

| | | |
|---|---|---|
| Jungle Girl | 1941 | Republic |
| Perils of Nyoka | 1942 | Republic |
| Haunted Harbor | 1944 | Republic |
| | | |
| The Mysterious Pilot | 1937 | Columbia |
| The Green Archer | 1940 | Columbia |
| Mysterious Island | 1951 | Columbia |

## VI. SHORT STORIES

| | | |
|---|---|---|
| The Jade Box | 1930 | Universal |
| The Lost Special | 1932 | Universal |
| Heroes of the West | 1932 | Universal |
| Gordon of Ghost City | 1933 | Universal |
| The Roaring West | 1935 | Universal |
| Flaming Frontiers | 1938 | Universal |
| Scouts to the Rescue | 1939 | Universal |
| Overland Mail | 1942 | Universal |
| | | |
| The Great Adventures of Wild Bill Hickok | 1938 | Columbia |

## VII. MISCELLANEOUS SOURCES

| | | |
|---|---|---|
| Clancy of the Mounted<br>*Poem* | 1933 | Universal |
| | | |
| Adventures of Sir Galahad<br>*Epic Poems & Others* | 1949 | Columbia |
| Captain Video<br>*Television* | 1951 | Columbia |

# Appendix B
# Serial Sequels and Series

## I. SEQUELS AND SERIES

| | | |
|---|---|---|
| Tailspin Tommy<br>  12 Chapters | 1934 | Universal |
| Tailspin Tommy in the Great Air Mystery<br>  12 Chapters | 1935 | Universal |
| Flash Gordon<br>  13 Chapters | 1936 | Universal |
| Flash Gordon's Trip to Mars<br>  15 Chapters | 1938 | Universal |
| Flash Gordon Conquers the Universe<br>  12 Chapters | 1940 | Universal |
| Dick Tracy<br>  15 Chapters | 1937 | Republic |
| Dick Tracy Returns<br>  15 Chapters | 1938 | Republic |
| Dick Tracy's G-Men<br>  15 Chapters | 1939 | Republic |
| Dick Tracy vs. Crime, Inc.<br>  15 Chapters | 1941 | Republic |
| The Spider's Web<br>  15 Chapters | 1938 | Columbia |
| The Spider Returns<br>  15 Chapters | 1941 | Columbia |

| | | |
|---|---|---|
| The Lone Ranger<br>　15 Chapters | 1938 | Republic |
| The Lone Ranger Rides Again<br>　15 Chapters | 1939 | Republic |
| The Green Hornet<br>　13 Chapters | 1939 | Universal |
| The Green Hornet Strikes Again<br>　13 Chapters | 1940 | Universal |
| King of the Royal Mounted<br>　12 Chapters | 1940 | Republic |
| King of the Mounties<br>　12 Chapters | 1942 | Republic |
| Don Winslow of the Navy<br>　12 Chapters | 1942 | Universal |
| Don Winslow of the Coast Guard<br>　13 Chapters | 1943 | Universal |
| G-Men vs. the Black Dragon<br>　15 Chapters | 1943 | Republic |
| Secret Service in Darkest Africa<br>　15 Chapters | 1943 | Republic |
| Batman<br>　15 Chapters | 1943 | Columbia |
| Batman and Robin<br>　15 Chapters | 1949 | Columbia |
| Jesse James Rides Again<br>　12 Chapters | 1947 | Republic |
| Adventures of Frank and Jesse James<br>　13 Chapters | 1948 | Republic |
| The James Brothers of Missouri<br>　12 Chapters | 1949 | Republic |

| | | |
|---|---|---|
| Superman | 1948 | Columbia |
| 15 Chapters | | |
| Atom Man vs. Superman | 1950 | Columbia |
| 15 Chapters | | |

## II. PRETENDERS

| | | |
|---|---|---|
| Secret Agent X-9 | 1937 | Universal |
| 12 Chapters | | |
| Secret Agent X-9 | 1945 | Universal |
| 13 Chapters | | |
| | | |
| Zorro Rides Again | 1937 | Republic |
| 12 Chapters | | |
| Zorro's Fighting Legion | 1939 | Republic |
| 12 Chapters | | |
| Zorro's Black Whip | 1944 | Republic |
| 12 Chapters | | |
| Son of Zorro | 1947 | Republic |
| 13 Chapters | | |
| Ghost of Zorro | 1949 | Republic |
| 12 Chapters | | |
| | | |
| Junior G-Men | 1940 | Universal |
| 12 Chapters | | |
| Junior G-Men of the Air | 1942 | Universal |
| 12 Chapters | | |
| | | |
| Jungle Girl | 1941 | Republic |
| 15 Chapters | | |
| The Perils of Nyoka | 1942 | Republic |
| 15 Chapters | | |
| | | |
| King of the Rocket Men | 1949 | Republic |
| 12 Chapters | | |
| Radar Men from the Moon | 1952 | Republic |
| 12 Chapters | | |
| Zombies of the Stratosphere | 1952 | Republic |
| 12 Chapters | | |

# Appendix C

# Serials With Sub-Names

**Columbia** had a practice, in some of its later serials, with adding a sub-name to the serial, explaining the name of the serial character or describing the serial in more depth. Sometimes the sub-name became an official part of the title, such as *Tex Granger, Midnight Rider of the Plains*. On other occasions, the sub-names were just used in the advertising, lobby cards and posters for the serials. Here is a list of those Columbia serials, with commas inserted to distinguish between the main name and the sub-name, although sometimes colons were used and sometimes no punctuation was used.

*Deadwood Dick, Most Colorful Character of the Old West!* (1940)
*Hop Harrigan, America's Ace of the Airways* (1946)
*Chick Carter, Detective, Master Mystery-Smasher* (1946)
*Son of the Guardsman, Gallant Fighter of the Greenwood* (1946)
*Jack Armstrong, The All-American Boy* (1947)
*The Sea Hound, Daredevil Adventures of Captain Silver* (1947)
*Brick Bradford, Amazing Soldier of Fortune* (1947)
*The Vigilante, Fighting Hero of the West* (1947)
*Tex Granger, Midnight Rider of the Plains* (1948)
*Congo Bill, King of the Jungle* (1948)
*Bruce Gentry, Daredevil of the Skies* (1949)
*The Adventures of Sir Galahad, Boldest Knight of the Round Table* (1949)
*Cody of the Pony Express, Far-Famed Fighting Frontiersman* (1950)
*Pirates of the High Seas, Phantom Raiders of the Deep* (1950)
*Roar of the Iron Horse, Rail-Blazer of the Apache Trail* (1951)
*Mysterious Island, Captain Harding's Fabulous Adventures* (1951)
*Captain Video, Master of the Stratosphere* (1951)

*King of the Congo, The Mighty "Thunda"* (1952)
*Blackhawk, Fearless Champion of Freedom* (1952)
*Son of Geronimo, Apache Avenger* (1952)
*The Lost Planet, Conqueror of Space* (1953)
*The Great Adventures of Captain Kidd, King of Pirates* (1953)
*Riding With Buffalo Bill, Champion of the Roaring West!* (1954)
*Gunfighters of the Northwest, Last of the White Horse Rebels!* (1954)
*Adventures of Captain Africa, Mighty Jungle Avenger!* (1955)
*Perils of the Wilderness, Gun Emperor of the Northwest!* (1956)
*Blazing the Overland Trail, Heroes of the Pony Express!* (1956)

Republic also did this once, although it was with the non-serial television show, which appeared in theaters as a serial: *Commando Cody, Sky Marshall of the Universe* (1953).

# Appendix D
## Prolific Serial Directors
### (Six Serials or More)

## I. RAY TAYLOR (45)

| | | |
|---|---|---|
| The Ace of Scotland Yard | 1929 | Universal |
| The Jade Box | 1930 | Universal |
| Finger Prints | 1931 | Universal |
| Danger Island | 1931 | Universal |
| Battling with Buffalo Bill | 1931 | Universal |
| The Airmail Mystery | 1932 | Universal |
| Heroes of the West | 1932 | Universal |
| The Jungle Mystery | 1932 | Universal |
| Gordon of Ghost City | 1933 | Universal |
| Clancy of the Mounted | 1933 | Universal |
| The Phantom of the Air | 1933 | Universal |
| The Perils of Pauline | 1934 | Universal |
| Pirate Treasure | 1934 | Universal |
| The Roaring West | 1935 | Universal |
| Tailspin Tommy in the Great Air Mystery | 1935 | Universal |
| The Phantom Rider | 1936 | Universal |
| Flaming Frontiers<br>  with Alan James | 1938 | Universal |
| The Green Hornet<br>  with Ford Beebe | 1939 | Universal |
| Scouts to the Rescue<br>  with Alan James | 1939 | Universal |
| Flash Gordon Conquers the Universe<br>  with Ford Beebe | 1940 | Universal |
| Winners of the West<br>  with Ford Beebe | 1940 | Universal |

| | | |
|---|---|---|
| Riders of Death Valley<br>  with Ford Beebe | 1941 | Universal |
| Sky Raiders<br>  with Ford Beebe | 1941 | Universal |
| Don Winslow of the Navy<br>  with Ford Beebe | 1942 | Universal |
| Gang Busters<br>  with Noel Smith | 1942 | Universal |
| Junior G-Men of the Air<br>  with Lewis D, Collins | 1942 | Universal |
| The Adventures of Smilin' Jack<br>  with Lewis D, Collins | 1943 | Universal |
| Don Winslow of the Coast Guard<br>  with Lewis D. Collins | 1943 | Universal |
| Adventures of the Flying Cadets<br>  with Lewis D. Collins | 1943 | Universal |
| The Great Alaskan Mystery<br>  with Lewis D. Collins | 1944 | Universal |
| Raiders of Ghost City<br>  with Lewis D. Collins | 1944 | Universal |
| Mystery of the River Boat<br>  with Lewis D. Collins | 1944 | Universal |
| Secret Agent X-9<br>  with Lewis D. Collins | 1945 | Universal |
| Jungle Queen<br>  with Lewis D. Collins | 1945 | Universal |
| The Master Key<br>  with Lewis D. Collins | 1945 | Universal |
| Royal Mounted Rides Again<br>  with Lewis D. Collins | 1945 | Universal |
| The Scarlet Horseman<br>  with Lewis D. Collins | 1946 | Universal |
| Lost City of the Jungle<br>  with Lewis D. Collins | 1946 | Universal |
| | | |
| The Return of Chandu | 1934 | Principal |

| | | |
|---|---|---|
| The Vigilantes Are Coming<br>   with Mack V. Wright | 1936 | Republic |
| Robinson Crusoe of Clipper Island<br>   with Mack V. Wright | 1936 | Republic |
| Dick Tracy<br>   with Alan James | 1937 | Republic |
| The Painted Stallion<br>   with Alan James and William Witney | 1937 | Republic |
| The Spider's Web<br>   with James W. Horne | 1938 | Columbia |
| Flying G-Men<br>   with James W. Horne | 1939 | Columbia |

## II. SPENCER GORDON BENNET (38)

| | | |
|---|---|---|
| The Last Frontier<br>   with Thomas Storey | 1932 | RKO |
| Young Eagles<br>   Chapter One only | 1934 | First Division |
| Secret Service in Darkest Africa | 1943 | Republic |
| The Masked Marvel | 1943 | Republic |
| The Tiger Woman<br>   with Wallace Grissell | 1944 | Republic |
| Haunted Harbor<br>   with Wallace Grissell | 1944 | Republic |
| Zorro's Black Whip<br>   with Wallace Grissell | 1944 | Republic |
| Manhunt of Mystery Island<br>   with Wallace Grissell, Yakima Canutt | 1945 | Republic |
| Federal Operator 99<br>   with Wallace Grissell, Yakima Canutt | 1945 | Republic |
| The Purple Monster Strikes<br>   with Fred C. Brannon | 1945 | Republic |
| The Phantom Rider<br>   with Fred C. Brannon | 1946 | Republic |

| | | |
|---|---|---|
| King of the Forest Rangers<br>    with Fred C. Brannon | 1946 | Republic |
| Daughter of Don Q<br>    with Fred C. Brannon | 1946 | Republic |
| Son of Zorro<br>    with Fred C. Brannon | 1947 | Republic |
| The Black Widow<br>    with Fred C. Brannon | 1947 | Republic |
| | | |
| The Mysterious Pilot | 1937 | Columbia |
| The Secret Code | 1942 | Columbia |

| | | |
|---|---|---|
| The Valley of the Vanishing Men | 1942 | Columbia |
| Brick Bradford | 1947 | Columbia |
| Superman<br>    with Thomas Carr | 1948 | Columbia |
| Congo Bill<br>    with Thomas Carr | 1948 | Columbia |
| Batman and Robin | 1949 | Columbia |
| Bruce Gentry—Daredevil of the Skies<br>    with Thomas Carr | 1949 | Columbia |
| Adventures of Sir Galahad | 1949 | Columbia |
| Atom Man v, Superman | 1950 | Columbia |
| Cody of the Pony Express | 1950 | Columbia |
| Pirates of the High Seas<br>    with Thomas Carr | 1950 | Columbia |
| Roar of the Iron Horse<br>    with Thomas Carr | 1951 | Columbia |
| Mysterious Island | 1951 | Columbia |
| Captain Video<br>    with Wallace Grissell | 1951 | Columbia |
| King of the Congo<br>    with Wallace Grissell | 1952 | Columbia |
| Blackhawk<br>    with Fred F. Sears | 1952 | Columbia |
| Son of Geronimo | 1952 | Columbia |
| The Lost Planet | 1953 | Columbia |
| Gunfighters of the Northwest<br>    with Charles S. Gould | 1954 | Columbia |
| Riding with Buffalo Bill | 1954 | Columbia |
| Adventures of Captain Africa | 1955 | Columbia |
| Perils of the Wilderness | 1956 | Columbia |
| Blazing the Overland Trail | 1956 | Columbia |

## III. FORD BEEBE (25)

| | | |
|---|---|---|
| The Vanishing Legion<br>    with B. Reeves Eason | 1931 | Mascot |
| The Shadow of the Eagle | 1932 | Mascot |

| | | |
|---|---|---|
| The Last of the Mohicans<br>    with B. Reeves Eason | 1932 | Mascot |
| The Adventures of Rex and Rinty<br>    with B. Reeves Eason | 1935 | Mascot |
| Ace Drummond<br>    with Cliff Smith | 1936 | Universal |
| Jungle Jim<br>    with Cliff Smith | 1937 | Universal |
| Secret Agent X-9<br>    with Cliff Smith | 1937 | Universal |
| Wild West Days<br>    with Cliff Smith | 1937 | Universal |
| Radio Patrol<br>    with Cliff Smith | 1937 | Universal |
| Tim Tyler's Luck<br>    with Wyndham Gittens | 1937 | Universal |
| Flash Gordon's Trip to Mars<br>    with Robert Hill | 1938 | Universal |
| Red Barry<br>    with Alan James | 1938 | Universal |
| The Green Hornet<br>    with Ray Taylor | 1939 | Universal |
| Buck Rogers<br>    with Saul Goodkind | 1939 | Universal |
| The Phantom Creeps<br>    with Saul Goodkind | 1939 | Universal |
| The Oregon Trail<br>    with Saul Goodkind | 1939 | Universal |
| Flash Gordon Conquers the Universe<br>    with Ray Taylor | 1940 | Universal |
| Winners of the West<br>    with Ray Taylor | 1940 | Universal |
| Junior G-Men<br>    with John Rawlins | 1940 | Universal |
| The Green Hornet Strikes Again<br>    with John Rawlins | 1940 | Universal |
| Riders of Death Valley<br>    with Ray Taylor | 1941 | Universal |

| | | |
|---|---|---|
| Sea Raiders | 1941 | Universal |
| with John Rawlins | | |
| Sky Raiders | 1941 | Universal |
| with Ray Taylor | | |
| Don Winslow of the Navy | 1942 | Universal |
| with Ray Taylor | | |
| Overland Mail | 1942 | Universal |
| with John Rawlins | | |

## IV. WILLIAM WITNEY AND JOHN ENGLISH

### William Witney (7)

| | | |
|---|---|---|
| The Painted Stallion | 1937 | Republic |
| with A James & R. Taylor | | |
| SOS Coast Guard | 1937 | Republic |
| with Alan James | | |
| Spy Smasher | 1942 | Republic |
| Perils of Nyoka | 1942 | Republic |
| King of the Mounties | 1942 | Republic |
| G-Men vs. the Black Dragon | 1943 | Republic |
| The Crimson Ghost | 1946 | Republic |
| with Fred C. Brannon | | |

### John English (2)

| | | |
|---|---|---|
| Daredevils of the West | 1943 | Republic |
| Captain America | 1944 | Republic |
| with Elmer Clifton | | |

### Witney and English (17)

| | | |
|---|---|---|
| Zorro Rides Again | 1937 | Republic |
| The Lone Ranger | 1938 | Republic |
| The Fighting Devil Dogs | 1938 | Republic |
| Dick Tracy Returns | 1938 | Republic |

| | | |
|---|---|---|
| Hawk of the Wilderness | 1938 | Republic |
| The Lone Ranger Rides Again | 1939 | Republic |
| Daredevils of the Red Circle | 1939 | Republic |
| Dick Tracy's G-Men | 1939 | Republic |
| Zorro's Fighting Legion | 1939 | Republic |
| Drums of Fu Manchu | 1940 | Republic |
| Adventures of Red Ryder | 1940 | Republic |
| King of the Royal Mounted | 1940 | Republic |
| Mysterious Dr. Satan | 1940 | Republic |
| Adventures of Captain Marvel | 1941 | Republic |
| Jungle Girl | 1941 | Republic |
| King of the Texas Rangers | 1941 | Republic |
| Dick Tracy vs. Crime, Inc. | 1941 | Republic |

## V. FRED C. BRANNON (24)

| | | |
|---|---|---|
| The Purple Monster Strikes<br>with Spencer Bennet | 1945 | Republic |
| The Phantom Rider<br>with Spencer Bennet | 1946 | Republic |
| King of the Forest Rangers<br>with Spencer Bennet | 1946 | Republic |
| Daughter of Don Q<br>with Spencer Bennet | 1946 | Republic |
| The Crimson Ghost<br>with William Witney | 1946 | Republic |
| Son of Zorro<br>with Spencer Bennet | 1947 | Republic |
| Jesse James Rides Again<br>with Thomas Carr | 1947 | Republic |
| The Black Widow<br>with Spencer Bennet | 1947 | Republic |
| G-Men Never Forget<br>with Yakima Canutt | 1948 | Republic |
| Dangers of the Canadian Mounted<br>with Yakima Canutt | 1948 | Republic |
| Adventures of Frank and Jesse James<br>with Yakima Canutt | 1948 | Republic |

| | | |
|---|---|---|
| Federal Agents vs. Underworld, Inc. | 1949 | Republic |
| Ghost of Zorro | 1949 | Republic |
| King of the Rocket Men | 1949 | Republic |
| The James Brothers of Missouri | 1949 | Republic |
| Radar Patrol vs. Spy King | 1949 | Republic |
| The Invisible Monster | 1950 | Republic |
| Desperadoes of the West | 1950 | Republic |
| Flying Disc Man from Mars | 1950 | Republic |
| Don Daredevil Rides Again | 1951 | Republic |
| Government Agents vs. Phantom Legion | 1951 | Republic |
| Radar Men from the Moon | 1952 | Republic |
| Zombies of the Stratosphere | 1952 | Republic |
| Jungle Drums of Africa | 1953 | Republic |

## VI. LEWIS D. COLLINS (14)

| | | |
|---|---|---|
| Junior G-Men of the Air<br>  with Ray Taylor | 1942 | Universal |
| The Adventures of Smilin' Jack<br>  with Ray Taylor | 1943 | Universal |

| | | |
|---|---|---|
| Don Winslow of the Coast Guard<br>  with Ray Taylor | 1943 | Universal |
| Adventures of the Flying Cadets<br>  with Ray Taylor | 1943 | Universal |
| The Great Alaskan Mystery<br>  with Ray Taylor | 1944 | Universal |
| Raiders of Ghost City<br>  with Ray Taylor | 1944 | Universal |
| Mystery of the River Boat<br>  with Ray Taylor | 1944 | Universal |
| Secret Agent X-9<br>  with Ray Taylor | 1945 | Universal |

| | | |
|---|---|---|
| Jungle Queen | 1945 | Universal |
| with Ray Taylor | | |
| The Master Key | 1945 | Universal |
| with Ray Taylor | | |
| Royal Mounted Rides Again | 1945 | Universal |
| with Ray Taylor | | |
| The Scarlet Horseman | 1946 | Universal |
| with Ray Taylor | | |
| Lost City of the Jungle | 1946 | Universal |
| with Ray Taylor | | |
| The Mysterious Mr. M | 1946 | Universal |
| with Vernon Keays | | |

## VII. B. REEVES EASON (13)

| | | |
|---|---|---|
| The Vanishing Legion | 1931 | Mascot |
| with Ford Beebe | | |
| Galloping Ghost | 1931 | Mascot |
| The Last of the Mohicans | 1932 | Mascot |
| with Ford Beebe | | |
| Law of the Wild | 1934 | Mascot |
| with A Schaefer | | |
| Mystery Mountain | 1934 | Mascot |
| with Otto Brower | | |
| The Phantom Empire | 1935 | Mascot |
| with Otto Brower | | |
| The Miracle Rider | 1935 | Mascot |
| with A Schaefer | | |
| The Adventures of Rex and Rinty | 1935 | Mascot |
| with Ford Beebe | | |
| | | |
| The Fighting Marines | 1935 | Republic |
| with Joseph Kane | | |
| Darkest Africa | 1936 | Republic |
| with Joseph Kane | | |
| Undersea Kingdom | 1936 | Republic |
| with Joseph Kane | | |
| | | |
| The Phantom | 1943 | Columbia |
| The Desert Hawk | 1944 | Columbia |

## VIII. JAMES W. HORNE (12)

| | | |
|---|---|---|
| The Spider's Web<br>  with Ray Taylor | 1938 | Columbia |
| Flying G-Men<br>  with Ray Taylor | 1939 | Columbia |
| The Shadow | 1940 | Columbia |
| Terry and the Pirates | 1940 | Columbia |
| Deadwood Dick | 1940 | Columbia |
| The Green Archer | 1940 | Columbia |
| White Eagle | 1941 | Columbia |
| The Spider Returns | 1941 | Columbia |
| The Iron Claw | 1941 | Columbia |
| Holt of the Secret Service | 1941 | Columbia |
| Captain Midnight | 1942 | Columbia |
| Perils of the Royal Mounted | 1942 | Columbia |

## IX. ARMAND SCHAEFER (8)

| | | |
|---|---|---|
| The Lightning Warrior<br>  with Ben Kline | 1931 | Mascot |
| The Hurricane Express<br>  with J.P. McGowan | 1932 | Mascot |
| The Three Musketeers<br>  with Colbert Clark | 1933 | Mascot |
| Fighting with Kit Carson<br>  with Colbert Clark | 1933 | Mascot |
| The Lost Jungle<br>  with David Howard | 1934 | Mascot |
| Burn 'Em Up Barnes<br>  with Colbert Clark | 1934 | Mascot |
| Law of the Wild<br>  with B. Reeves Eason | 1934 | Mascot |
| The Miracle Rider<br>  with B. Reeves Eason | 1935 | Mascot |

## X. WALLACE GRISSELL (8)

| | | |
|---|---|---|
| The Tiger Woman<br>    with Spencer Bennet | 1944 | Republic |
| Haunted Harbor<br>    with Spencer Bennet | 1944 | Republic |
| Zorro's Black Whip<br>    with Spencer Bennet | 1944 | Republic |
| Manhunt of Mystery Island<br>    with Spencer Bennet, Yakima Canutt | 1945 | Republic |
| Federal Operator 99<br>    with Spencer Bennet, Yakima Canutt | 1945 | Republic |
| Who's Guilty?<br>    with Howard Bretherton | 1945 | Columbia |
| Captain Video<br>    with Spencer Bennet | 1951 | Columbia |
| King of the Congo<br>    with Spencer Bennet | 1952 | Columbia |

## XI. HENRY MACRAE (6)

| | | |
|---|---|---|
| Tarzan the Tiger | 1929 | Universal |
| The Lightning Express | 1930 | Universal |
| Terry of the Times | 1930 | Universal |
| The Indians Are Coming | 1930 | Universal |
| Detective Lloyd | 1932 | Universal |
| The Lost Special | 1932 | Universal |

## XII. ALAN JAMES (6)

| | | |
|---|---|---|
| Flaming Frontiers<br>  with Ray Taylor | 1938 | Universal |
| Scouts to the Rescue<br>  with Ray Taylor | 1939 | Universal |
| Red Barry<br>  with Ford Beebe | 1938 | Universal |
| Dick Tracy<br>  with Ray Taylor | 1937 | Republic |
| The Painted Stallion<br>  with Ray Taylor and<br>  William Witney | 1937 | Republic |
| SOS Coast Guard<br>  with William Witney | 1937 | Republic |

# Bibliography

**BOOKS:**

Barbour, Alan G. *Days of Thrills and Adventures.* New York, NY. The MacMillan Company, 1970.

Brooks, Tim and Marsh, Earle. *Complete Directory to Prime Time Network TV Shows 1946-Present (Revised Edition), The.* New York, NY: Ballantine Books, 1981.

Cline, William C. *In the Nick of Time: Motion Picture Serials.* Jefferson, NC and London: McFarland & Co. Inc, 1990.

Cox, J. Randolph. *The Dime Novel Companion: A Source Book.* Westport, CT: Greenwald Press, 2000.

DeAndrea, William. *Encyclopedia Mysteriosa.* New York, NY: MacMillan, 1994.

Dixon, Wheeler W. *The "B" Directors A Biographical Directory.* Metuchen, N.J. and London: The Scarecrow Press, Inc., 1983.

Dunning, John. *On the Air: The Encyclopedia of Old Time Radio.* New York, NY. Oxford University Press, 1998.

Goulart, Ron. *Comic Book Encyclopedia.* New York, NY: HarperEntertainment, 2004.

Goulart, Ron. *Encyclopedia of American Comic Books, The.* Oxford, England: Maple-Vail Book Manufacturing Group, 1990.

Halliwell, Leslie. *Halliwell's Filmgoer's Companion* (8th Ed.). New York, NY: Charles Scribner's Sons, 1985.

Harmon, Jim and Glut, Donald F. *Great Movie Serials, Their Sound and Fury, The.* Garden City, NY. Double Day & Company, Inc., 1972.

Kinnard, Roy. *Science Fiction Serials.* Jefferson, NC: McFarland & Company, Inc., 1998.

Kohl, Leonard J. *Sinister Serials of Boris Karloff, Bela Lugosi and Lon Chaney, Jr.* Baltimore, Maryland: Midnight Marquee Press, Inc., 2000.

Lackman, Ron. *Encyclopedia of American Radio, The.* New York, NY: Checkmark Books, 2000.

Mank, Gregory William. *Hollywood's Maddest Doctors, A Biography of Lionel Atwill, Colin Clive and George Zucco.* Baltimore, Maryland: Midnight Marquee Press, Inc., 1998.

Mast, Gerald. *A Short History of the Movies.* Indianapolis, In. The Bobbs-Merrill Company, Inc., 1971.

Rainey, Buck, *Sweethearts of the Sage.* Jefferson, NC: McFarland & Company, Inc., 1992.

Stedman, Raymond W. *The Serials: Suspense and Drama by Installment.* Norman, Ok. University of Oklahoma Press, 1971/1977.

Steinbrenner, Chris and Penzler, Otto. *Encyclopedia of Mystery and Detection.* New York, NY: McGraw-Hill, Inc., 1976.

Truffaut, Francois. *Hitchcock by François Truffaut.* New York, NY: Simon and Schuster, 1966

Tuska, Jon. *Encyclopedia of Frontier and Western Fiction.* New York, NY: McGraw-Hill, Inc, 1983.

Weiss, Ken. *To Be Continued: American Sound Serials 1929-1956* (3rd Ed). New Rochelle, NY: Love's Labor Press, 2002.

Wiley, Mason and Bona, Damien. *Inside Oscar.* New York, NY: Ballantine Books, 1968.

Witney, William. *In a Door, into a Fight, out a Door, into a Chase: Moviemaking Remembered by the Guy at the Door,* Jefferson, NC and London, McFarland & Co., Inc., 1996.


**MAGAZINES:**

Culp, Lisa-Anne, "Clayton Moore." *Filmfax,* (Dec. /Jan. 1992): 45-49, 66.

Everson, William K. "Serials with Sound." *Films in Review,* (June, 1953): 269-276.

Geltzer, George, "40 Years of Cliffhanging." *Films in Review* (February, 1958): 60-67.

Jackson, Charles Lee, II. "The Man Who Would Be Serial King." *Filmfax* (May, 1990). 76-79, 87.

Schultz, Wayne. "Literature of the Lost Serials." *Serial Report* 58 (July/ Sept. 2006): 2-6, many other articles from the magazine.


**WEBSITES:**

Anderson, Chuck. *The Old Corral.* http://www.b-westerns.com.

Cole, Neil A. *Superman Super Site,* http://www.supermansupersite.com.

Gay, Bob, The Bookshelf- The Insidious Fu Manchu, (Sept, 2002) at
*The Nostalgia League*, http://thenostalgialeague.com, and other
writings on the website.

Markstein, Don. *Don Markstein's Toonopedia*.
http://www.toonopedia.com.

Severson, Aaron, *Golden Age of Batman Chronology, The*
http://ourworld.cs.com/argentprime/batman.htm.

*Bill & Sue-On Hillman's ERBzine*,
http://greenbriarpictureshows.blogspot.com.

*Files of Jerry Blake, The.* http://filesofjerryblake.netfirms.com.

*Greenbriar Picture Shows*, http://greenbriarpictureshows.blogspot.com.

*In the Balcony.* http://www.inthebalcony.com.

*Lambiek Comiclopedia.* http://lambiek.net/artists.

*Serial Squadron, Academy of Cliffhanger Arts and Sciences, The.*
http://www.serialsquadron.com/index.html.

# Index